Business Intelligence and Agile Methodologies for Knowledge-Based Organizations:

Cross-Disciplinary Applications

Asim Abdel Rahman El Sheikh
The Arab Academy for Banking and Financial Sciences, Jordan

Mouhib Alnoukari
Arab International University, Syria

A volume in the Advances in Business
Information Systems and Analytics
(ABISA) Book Series

Senior Editorial Director:	Kristin Klinger
Director of Book Publications:	Julia Mosemann
Editorial Director:	Lindsay Johnston
Acquisitions Editor:	Erika Carter
Development Editor:	Myla Harty
Production Editor:	Sean Woznicki
Typesetters:	Christen Croley, Adrienne Freeland
Print Coordinator:	Jamie Snavely
Cover Design:	Nick Newcomer

Published in the United States of America by
Business Science Reference (an imprint of IGI Global)
701 E. Chocolate Avenue
Hershey PA 17033
Tel: 717-533-8845
Fax: 717-533-8661
E-mail: cust@igi-global.com
Web site: http://www.igi-global.com

Library of Congress Cataloging-in-Publication Data

Business intelligence and agile methodologies for knowledge-based
organizations: cross-disciplinary applications / Asim Abdel Rahman El Sheikh and Mouhib Alnoukari, editors.
    p. cm.
  Includes bibliographical references and index.
  Summary: "This book highlights the marriage between business intelligence and knowledge management through the use of agile methodologies, offering perspectives on the integration between process modeling, agile methodologies, business intelligence, knowledge management, and strategic management"--Provided by publisher.
  ISBN 978-1-61350-050-7 (hardcover) -- ISBN 978-1-61350-051-4 (ebook) -- ISBN 978-1-61350-052-1 (print & perpetual access) 1. Business intelligence. 2. Knowledge management. I. El Sheikh, Asim Abdel Rahman. II. Alnoukari, Mouhib, 1965-
  HD38.7.B8715 2012
  658.4'72--dc23
                        2011023040

This book is published in the IGI Global book series Advances in Business Information Systems and Analytics (ABISA) Book Series (ISSN: 2327-3275; eISSN: 2327-3283)

British Cataloguing in Publication Data
A Cataloguing in Publication record for this book is available from the British Library.

All work contributed to this book is new, previously-unpublished material. The views expressed in this book are those of the authors, but not necessarily of the publisher.

Advances in Business Information Systems and Analytics (ABISA) Book Series

Madjid Tavana
La Salle University, USA

ISSN: 2327-3275
EISSN: 2327-3283

MISSION

The successful development and management of information systems and business analytics is crucial to the success of an organization. New technological developments and methods for data analysis have allowed organizations to not only improve their processes and allow for greater productivity, but have also provided businesses with a venue through which to cut costs, plan for the future, and maintain competitive advantage in the information age.

The **Advances in Business Information Systems and Analytics (ABISA) Book Series** aims to present diverse and timely research in the development, deployment, and management of business information systems and business analytics for continued organizational development and improved business value.

COVERAGE

- Big Data
- Business Decision Making
- Business Information Security
- Business Process Management
- Business Systems Engineering
- Data Analytics
- Data Management
- Decision Support Systems
- Management Information Systems
- Performance Metrics

IGI Global is currently accepting manuscripts for publication within this series. To submit a proposal for a volume in this series, please contact our Acquisition Editors at Acquisitions@igi-global.com or visit: http://www.igi-global.com/publish/.

Titles in this Series

For a list of additional titles in this series, please visit: www.igi-global.com

Information Systems and Technology for Organizations in a Networked Society
Tomayess Issa (Curtin University, Australia) Pedro Isaías (Universidade Aberta, Portugal) and Piet Kommers (University of Twente, The Netherlands)
Business Science Reference • copyright 2013 • 432pp • H/C (ISBN: 9781466640627) • US $185.00 (our price)

Cases on Enterprise Information Systems and Implementation Stages Learning from the Gulf Region
Fayez Albadri (ADMO-OPCO, UAE)
Information Science Reference • copyright 2013 • 370pp • H/C (ISBN: 9781466622203) • US $185.00 (our price)

Business Intelligence and Agile Methodologies for Knowledge-Based Organizations Cross-Disciplinary Applications
Asim Abdel Rahman El Sheikh (The Arab Academy for Banking and Financial Sciences, Jordan) and Mouhib Alnoukari (Arab International University, Syria)
Business Science Reference • copyright 2012 • 370pp • H/C (ISBN: 9781613500507) • US $185.00 (our price)

Business Intelligence Applications and the Web Models, Systems and Technologies
Marta E. Zorrilla (University of Cantabria, Spain) Jose-Norberto Mazón (University of Alicante, Spain) Óscar Ferrández (University of Alicante, Spain) Irene Garrigós (University of Alicante, Spain) Florian Daniel (University of Trento, Italy) and Juan Trujillo (University of Alicante, Spain)
Business Science Reference • copyright 2012 • 374pp • H/C (ISBN: 9781613500385) • US $185.00 (our price)

Electronic Supply Network Coordination in Intelligent and Dynamic Environments Modeling and Implementation
Iraj Mahdavi (Mazandaran University of Science and Technology, Iran) Shima Mohebbi (University of Tehran, Iran) and Namjae Cho (Hanyang University, Korea)
Business Science Reference • copyright 2011 • 434pp • H/C (ISBN: 9781605668086) • US $180.00 (our price)

Enterprise Information Systems Design, Implementation and Management Organizational Applications
Maria Manuela Cruz-Cunha (Polytechnic Institute of Cavado and Ave, Portugal) and Joao Varajao (University of Tras-os-Montes e Alto Duoro, Portugal)
Information Science Reference • copyright 2011 • 622pp • H/C (ISBN: 9781616920203) • US $180.00 (our price)

Pervasive Computing for Business Trends and Applications
Varuna Godara (CEO of Sydney College of Management, Australia)
Information Science Reference • copyright 2010 • 336pp • H/C (ISBN: 9781605669960) • US $180.00 (our price)

DISSEMINATOR of KNOWLEDGE

www.igi-global.com

701 E. Chocolate Ave., Hershey, PA 17033
Order online at www.igi-global.com or call 717-533-8845 x100
To place a standing order for titles released in this series, contact: cust@igi-global.com
Mon-Fri 8:00 am - 5:00 pm (est) or fax 24 hours a day 717-533-8661

Table of Contents

Foreword

Business intelligence is made possible by the existence of Information Technology. Business intelligence aims to support better business decision-making. To use agile methodologies and to develop Information Technology faster and cheaper is to put an icing on the cake. I doubt that Hans Peter Luhn was aware of the consequences of Business intelligence when he coined the term in 1958. Today, 50 years later, "Business Intelligence and Agile Methodologies for Knowledge-Based Organizations: Cross-Disciplinary Applications" is coming out.

The book is comprised of fifteen chapters and is a collaboration work of 29 scholars from 8 different countries and 11 different research organizations. The end product is made possible by the use of the impossible ideas dreamt by visionaries, where the first two chapters discuss the body of knowledge of both business intelligence & agile software, followed by chapter 3 and 4, which discuss knowledge management and discovery in relation to agility essence. Subsequently, Business intelligence agile methodologies, agile modeling, agile approach, and governance are discussed in chapters 5, 6, 7, and 8. Business intelligence & adaptive software development are covered in chapter 9, followed by chapter 10, which covers *yahoo* experience in brand lifting. Throughout the next three chapters, the authors tackle issues like: risk management in business intelligence and agile methodology, business intelligence governance in e-government system, and business intelligence in higher education. Ultimately, the last chapter discusses Web engineering and business intelligence.

The 1st chapter, *Business Intelligence: Body of Knowledge,* attempts to define Business Intelligence body of knowledge. The chapter starts with a historical overview of Business Intelligence stating its different stages and progressions. Then, the authors present an overview of what Business Intelligence is, architecture, goals, and main components including: data mining, data warehousing, and data marts. Finally, the Business Intelligence 'marriage' with knowledge management is discussed in details.

The 2nd chapter entitled: *Agile Software: Body of Knowledge.* The chapter explains agile methodologies, its general characteristics, and quick description of the famous agile methods known in the industry and research.

The 3rd chapter with the topic: *Knowledge Management in Agile Methods Context: What Type of Knowledge is Used by Agilests?* Provides an overview on the knowledge management techniques used in different software development processes with focus on agile methods. Then tests the claim of more informal knowledge sharing, and see the mechanisms used to exchange and document knowledge.

The 4th chapter: *Knowledge Discovery Process Models: From Traditional to Agile Modeling*, provides a detailed discussion on the Knowledge Discovery (KD) process models that have innovative life cycle steps. The chapter proposes a categorization of the existing KD models. Furthermore, the chapter deeply analyzes the strengths and weaknesses of the leading KD process models, with the supported commercial systems and reported applications, and their matrix characteristics.

The 5th chapter *Agile Methodologies for Business Intelligence* explores the application of agile methodologies and principles to business intelligence delivery. The practice of business intelligence delivery with an Agile methodology has yet to be proved to the point of maturity and stability; the chapter outlined Agile principles and practices that have emerged as best practices and formulate a framework to outline how an Agile methodology could be applied to business intelligence delivery.

Likewise, the 6th chapter has the title of: *BORM: Agile Modeling for Business Intelligence*, whereby BORM (Business and Object Relation Modeling) method is described and presented through an application example created in Craft a CASE analysis and modeling tool. The chapter begins by introducing fundamental principles of BORM method. Then the chapter goes on to highlights most important concepts of BORM. In order to further enhance the understanding of BROM, the chapter applies BROM on a simple, descriptive example. .

The 7th chapter entitled: *Agile Approach to Business Intelligence as a Way to Success* presents an overview of several methodological approaches used in Business Intelligence (BI) projects, as well as Data Warehouse projects. In this chapter, the authors show that there is a strong relationship between the so-called Critical Success Factors of BI projects and the Agile Principles. As such, with basis on sound analysis, the authors conclude that successful BI methodologies must follow an agile approach.

In this context, the 8th chapter, with the title: *Enhancing BI Systems Application through the Integration of IT Governance and Knowledge Capabilities of the Organization*, cites a study reports the results of an empirical examination of the effect of IT governance framework based on COBIT and Organizational Knowledge Pillars in enhancing the IT Governance framework (Business / IT Strategic alignment, Business value delivery, risk management, Resource management, performance measurement) to improve the Business Intelligence Application and Usability within the organization. Quantitative method is adopted for answering the research questions.

The 9th chapter: *ASD-BI: A Knowledge Discovery Process Modeling Based on Adaptive Software Development Agile Methodology* proposes a new knowledge discovery process model named "ASD-BI" that is based on Adaptive Software Development (ASD) agile methodology. ASD-BI process model was proposed to enhance the way of building Business Intelligence and Data Mining applications.

While the 10th chapter: *Measurement of Brand Lift from a Display Advertising Campaign*, describes an Advanced Business Intelligence System have been built at *Yahoo!* to measure the lift in brand awareness driven from the display advertising campaigns on Yahoo network. It helped us to show to the advertisers that display advertising is working in lifting awareness and brand affinity.

Whereas, the 11th chapter entitled: *Suggested Model for Business Intelligence in Higher Education*, describes a data mining approach as one of the business intelligence methodologies for possible use in higher education. The importance of this model arises from the fact that it starts from a system approach to the university management, looking at the university as input, processing, output, and feedback, and then applies different business intelligence tools and methods to every part of the system in order to enhance the business decision making process.

The 12th chapter: *Business Intelligence and Agile Methodology for Risk Management in Knowledge-Based Organizations*, discusses and explores the role of Business Intelligence and Agile methodology in managing risk effectively and efficiently. It explores the risk management traditional tools that are commonly used, the role of Business Intelligence in risk management, and the role of agile methodology in risk management.

The 13th chapter: *Towards a Business Intelligence Governance Framework within E-Government System*, will take E-Government project in Syria as case study to explore, empirically, the main barriers of E-Government project in developing countries; how to take benefits from business intelligence (BI) to build a framework, which could be adopted by developing countries in their E-Government projects.

In the same context, the 14th chapter: *Business Intelligence in Higher Education – an Ontological Approach*, presents an ontology-based knowledge management system developed for a Romanian university. The starting point for the development knowledge management system is the classic Information Management System (IMS), which is used for the education & training and research portfolio management. .

In conclusion, the last chapter entitled *Web Engineering and Business Intelligence: Agile Web Engineering Development and Practice* highlights the main issues related to Web engineering practices and how they support business intelligence projects, the need for Web engineering, and the development methods used in Web engineering. Web Engineering is a response to the early, chaotic development of Web sites and applications as well as recognition of the deference between web developers and conventional software developers. Viewed broadly, Web Engineering is both a conscious and pro-active approach and a growing collection of theoretical and empirical researches.

Evon M. O. Abu-Taieh
International Journal of Aviation Technology, Engineering and Management (IJATEM)

Evon M. O. Abu-Taieh *currently manages the SDI/GIS World Bank project in Jordan and lectures in AIU, after serving for 3 years as Economic Commissioner for Air Transport in the Civil Aviation Regulatory Commission-Jordan. She has a PhD in simulation and is a USA graduate for both her Master of Science and Bachelor's degrees with a total experience of 21 years. Dr. Abu-Taieh is an author of many renowned research papers in the airline, IT, PM, KM, GIS, AI, simulation, security, and ciphering.* She is the editor/author of Utilizing Information Technology Systems across Disciplines: Advancements in the Application of Computer Science, Handbook of Research on Discrete Event Simulation Environments: Technologies and Applications, and Simulation and Modeling: Current Technologies and Applications. She is Editor-in-Chief of the International Journal of Aviation Technology, *and Engineering and Management and has been a guest editor for the* Journal of Information Technology Research. *Dr. Abu-Taieh holds positions on the editorial board of the* International Journal of E-Services and Mobile Applications, International Journal of Information Technology Project Management, *and* International Journal of Information Systems and Social Change. *In her capacity as head of IT department in the ministry of transport for 10 years, she developed systems such as ministry of transport databank, auditing system for airline reservation systems, and maritime databank, among others. Furthermore, she has worked in the Arab Academy as an Assistant Professor, a Dean's Assistant, and London School of Economics (LSE) Program Director in AABFS. She has been appointed many times as track chair and reviewer in many international conferences:* IRMA, CISTA, WMSCI, *and Chaired* AITEM2010.

Preface

More than 2300 years ago Aristotle said that:" *All men by nature desire knowledge* ". No doubt Aristotle was right because until now with all advanced sciences that we have today in the 21st century human beings are still looking for knowledge.

Business Intelligence and Agile Methodologies for Knowledge-Based Organizations: Cross-Disciplinary Applications is one of the first essays that highlight the "marriage" between business intelligence and knowledge management through the use of agile methodologies.

In 1996, the Chinese Organization for Economic Cooperation and Development (OECD) redefined "knowledge-based economies" as: *economies which are directly based on the production, distribution and use of knowledge and information.* According to the definition, data mining and knowledge management, and more generally Business Intelligence (BI), should be the foundations for building the knowledge economy.

Business Intelligence applications are of vital importance for many organizations and can make the difference in any organization. You can collect, clean and integrate all your data, you can also, analyze, mine and dig more into your data, and you can make right decision, at the right time by using BI dashboards, alerts and reports.

Business Intelligence can also help organizations managing, developing and communicating their intangible assets such as information and knowledge. Thus, it can be considered as an imperative framework in the current knowledge-based economy arena. Organizations such as Continental Airlines have invested in Business Intelligence generate increases in revenue and cost saving equivalent to 1000% return on investment (ROI).

Business Intelligence can be also considered as a strategic framework, as it is becoming increasingly important in strategic management, and in supporting business strategies. IT-enabled strategic management addresses the business intelligence role in strategy formulation and implementation processes. Drucker, the pioneer of "management by objectives", was one of the first who recognized the dramatic changes IT brought to management.

However, Business Intelligence applications still face failures in determining the process model adopted. As the world becomes increasingly dynamic, the traditional static modeling may not be able to deal with it. Traditional process modeling requires a lot of documentation and reports. This makes traditional methodology unable to fulfill dynamic requirement changes in our rapidly changing environment.

One solution is to use agile modeling that is characterized by flexibility and adaptability. On the other hand, Business Intelligence applications require greater diversity of technology, business skills, and knowledge than the typical applications, which means it may benefit a lot from features of agile software development.

To successfully implement Business Intelligence applications in our agile era, different areas should be examined in addition to considering the transition into knowledge-based economy. The areas to be examined in this book are: methodologies, architecture, components, technologies, agility, adaptability, tools, strategies, applications, knowledge and history.

In *Business Intelligence and Agile Methodologies for Knowledge-Based Organizations: Cross-Disciplinary Applications,* Business Intelligence is discussed from a new point of view, as it will tackle, and for the first time, the agility character of Business Intelligence applications. This book highlights, through its fifteen chapters, the integration between: process modeling, agile methodologies, business intelligence, knowledge management, and strategic management.

Now, the main question is: why our book will create added value in the field? Our response is:

- Most organizations are using business intelligence and data mining applications to enhance strategic decision making and knowledge creation and sharing.
- Data mining is at the core of business intelligence and knowledge discovery.
- Most of current business intelligence applications are unable to fulfill the dynamic requirement changes in our complex environment.
- Finally, knowledge is the result of intelligence and agility…

Though, the overall objectives of this book are: to provide a comprehensive view of business intelligence and agile methodologies, to provide cutting edge research on applying agile methodologies on business intelligence applications by leading scholars and practitioners in the field, to provide a deep analysis for the relationship between business intelligence, agile methodologies and knowledge management, and to demonstrate the previous objectives through both theory and practice.

The book caters the needs of scholars, PhD candidates, researchers, as well as graduate level students of computer science, Information Science, Information Technology, operations research, business and economics disciplines. The target audience of this book is academic libraries throughout the world that are interested in cutting edge research on business intelligence, agile methodologies, and knowledge management. Another important market is Master of Business Administration (MBA), Master of Executive Business Administration (EMBA), and Master of E-Business programs which have Information Systems components as part of their curriculum.

The book encompasses 15 chapters. On the whole, the chapters of this book fall into six categories, while crossing paths with different disciplines. The 1st category, *business intelligence*, concentrates on business intelligence theories, tools, architecture, and applications. The 2nd category, *agile methodologies*, concentrates on agile theories, methods, and characteristics, while the 3rd concentrates on *knowledge management in agile methods context*, whereas the 4th concentrates on knowledge discovery and business intelligence *process modeling*, surveying all the used processes used from traditional till agile methodologies, The 5th category tackle the main focus of this book, the use of *agile methodologies for business intelligence*. This category was highlighted by more than six chapters. The last and 6th category discusses the *application of agile methodologies and business intelligence* in different areas including: higher education, e-government, public regional management systems, risk management, e-marketing, IT governance, and web engineering.

Chapter 1, *Business Intelligence: Body of Knowledge,* provides an overview of the business intelligence history, definitions, architecture, goals, and components including: data mining, data warehousing, and data marts. It also highlights the close relationship between business intelligence and knowledge management.

Chapter 2, *Agile Software: Body of Knowledge,* provides an overview of the agile methodology history, principles, techniques, characteristics, and methods. The chapter explains in details the main agile methods including: eXtreme Programming (XP), Scrum, Crystal, Feature-Driven Development (FDD), Adaptive Software Development (ASD), and DSDM. For each agile method, the author explains its lifecycle, its principles and techniques, and its roles and responsibilities.

Chapter 3, *Knowledge Management in Agile Methods Context: What Type of Knowledge is Used by Agilests?* provides an overview on the knowledge management techniques used in different software development processes with focus on agile methods. In this chapter, the author has demonstrated the results of email-based panel of experts' survey. The survey was published in July 2008 on Scott Ambler's website www.ambysoft.com. More than 300 agile practitioners was asked about the mechanisms used to exchange and document knowledge and in which context every mechanism is applied

Chapter 4, *Knowledge Discovery Process Models: From Traditional to Agile Modeling,* provides a detailed discussion on the Knowledge Discovery (KD) process models that have innovative life cycle steps. It proposes a categorization of the existing KD models. The chapter deeply analyzes the strengths and weaknesses of the leading KD process models, with the supported commercial systems and reported applications, and their matrix characteristics.

Chapter 5, *Agile Methodologies for Business Intelligence,* explores the application of agile methodologies and principles to business intelligence delivery. The practice of business intelligence delivery with an agile methodology has yet to be proven to the point of maturity and stability; this chapter outlines agile principles and practices that have emerged as best practices and formulate a framework to outline how an agile methodology could be applied to business intelligence delivery.

Chapter 6, *BORM: Agile Modeling for Business Intelligence,* proposes a new business intelligence model based on agile modeling. The proposed model named BORM (Business and Object Relation Modeling) is described in details by explaining its fundamental principles and its most important concepts. The chapter will then explore the three areas of BORM modeling in Model-Driven Approach (MDA) perspective. The chapter will also describe the business model, scenarios, and diagram. Finally, the model validation will be explained using one of the recent BORM applications of organizational modeling and simulation. The aim of the project is the improvement of decision-making on the level of mayors and local administrations. It offers the possibility to model and simulate real life situations in small settlements.

Chapter 7, *Agile Approach to Business Intelligence as a Way to Success,* presents an overview of several methodological approaches used in business intelligence and data warehousing projects. In this chapter, the authors have presented and analyzed the Critical Success Factors of Business Intelligence projects. On the other side, the authors have collected all Agile Principles that guide Agile development methodologies. Finally they have analysed the relationships between these two sources, respectively BI success factors and agile principles, to evaluate how adequate may be to use an Agile Approach to manage Business Intelligence projects. As a result, the authors show a strong relationship between the so-called Critical Success Factors for BI projects and the Agile Principles. Hence, based on sound analysis, concluding that successful BI methodologies must follow an agile approach.

Chapter 8, *Enhancing BI Systems Application through the Integration of IT Governance and Knowledge Capabilities of the Organization,* reports the results of an empirical examination of the effect of IT governance framework based on COBIT and Organizational Knowledge Pillars in enhancing the IT

Governance framework (Business / IT Strategic alignment, Business value delivery, risk management, Resource management, performance measurement) to enhance the Business Intelligence Application and Usability within the organization. Quantitative method is adopted for answering the research questions. Using confirmatory factor analysis techniques, the effects of the combination between IT governance factors seen by ITGI and organizational knowledge pillars of the firm on BI Systems application in it were tested and confirmed and the models were verified.

Chapter 9, *ASD-BI: A Knowledge Discovery Process Modeling Based on Adaptive Software Development Agile Methodology,* proposes a new knowledge discovery process model named "ASD-BI" that is based on Adaptive Software Development (ASD) agile methodology. ASD-BI process model was proposed to enhance the way of building Business Intelligence and Data Mining applications. The main contribution of this chapter is the demonstration that ASD-BI is adaptive to environment changes, enhances knowledge capturing and sharing, and helps in implementing and achieving organization's strategy. ASD-BI process model will be validated by using a case study on higher education.

Chapter 10, *Measurement of Brand Lift from a Display Advertising Campaign*, describes an advanced Business Intelligence System; built at Yahoo to measure the lift in brand awareness driven from the display advertising campaigns on Yahoo network. The author describes the methodology to measure the lift in Brand Awareness from a Display Ad campaign and a system to compute this metric. This system is a great help to any sales team, when they are working with advertisers to show them the value of their marketing investments and want to get bigger return business.

Chapter 11, *Suggested Model for Business Intelligence in Higher Education*, describes a data mining approach as one of the business intelligence core components for possible use in higher education. The importance of the model arises from the reality that it starts from a system approach to university management, looking at the university as input, processing, output, and feedback, and then applies different business intelligence tools and methods to every part of the system in order to enhance the business decision making process. The suggested model was validated using a real case study at the Arab International University.

Chapter 12, *Business Intelligence and Agile Methodology for Risk Management in Knowledge-Based Organizations*, discusses and explores the role of Business Intelligence and Agile methodology to manage risks effectively and efficiently. The authors describe, highlight and investigate the different techniques and tools that are mostly used in Risk Management giving the focus for the Business Intelligence based on providing examples on some of the mostly used tools. The authors also shed lights on the role of agile in managing risk in this knowledge based economy.

Chapter 13, *Towards a Business Intelligence Governance Framework within E-Government System*, presents a BI governance framework within E-Government system derived from an empirical study with academics and experts from public and private sector. An analysis of the findings demonstrated that the business/IT alignment is very important to E-Government success and the important role of BI use in E-Government system.

Chapter 14, *Business Intelligence in Higher Education: An Ontological Approach*, presents an ontology-based knowledge management system developed for a Romanian university. The ontologies were implemented using Protege. The results are very encouraging and suggest several future developments.

Chapter 15, *Web Engineering and Business Intelligence: Agile Web Engineering Development and Practice*, highlights the main issues related to Web engineering practices and how they support business intelligence projects. It also explains the need for Web engineering, and the development methods used in Web engineering.

In conclusion, the book is one of the first attempts to highlight the importance of using agile methodologies for business intelligence applications. Although, the research direction is new, the book's chapters raise very important research results in different areas. The editors are proud of the book's research methodologies and the high level of work provided.

Asim Abdel Rahman El Sheikh
Arab Academy for Banking and Financial Sciences, Jordan

Mouhib Alnoukari
Arab International University, Syria

Acknowledgment

The editors would like to acknowledge the relentless support of the IGI team, for their significant help. Moreover, the authors would like to extend their gratitude to Mrs. Jan Travers, Director of Intellectual Property and Contracts at IGI Global. Likewise, the authors would like to extend their gratitude to the Development Division at IGI Global; namely Myla Harty, editorial assistant.

In this regard, the authors also express their recognition to their respective organizations and colleagues for their moral and continuous support. By the same token, the editors would like to thank the reviewers for their great work and their valuable notes and evaluations. Special thanks would be forwarded to Dr. Salah Dowaji, Dr. Zaidoun Alzoabi, and Dr. Ramez Hajislam for their hard work, and their constant demand for perfection.

Finally, the editors would like to thank Mrs. Sara Al-Ahmad for all the time she spent spell checking important parts of this book.

Asim Abdel Rahman El Sheikh
Arab Academy for Banking and Financial Sciences, Jordan

Mouhib Alnoukari
Arab International University, Syria

Chapter 1
Business Intelligence:
Body of Knowledge

Mouhib Alnoukari
Arab International University, Syria

Humam Alhammami Alhawasli
Arab Academy for Banking and Financial Sciences, Syria

Hatem Abd Alnafea
Arab Academy for Banking and Financial Sciences, Syria

Amjad Jalal Zamreek
Arab Academy for Banking and Financial Sciences, Syria

ABSTRACT

This chapter attempts to define the knowledge body of Business Intelligence. It provides an overview of the context we have been working in. The chapter starts with a historical overview of Business Intelligence stating its different stages and progressions. Then, the authors present an overview of what Business Intelligence is, its architecture and goals, and its main components including: data mining, data warehousing, and data marts. Finally, the Business Intelligence 'marriage' with knowledge management is discussed in details. The authors hope to contribute to the recent discussions about Business Intelligence goals, concepts, architecture, and components.

INTRODUCTION

Business Intelligence is becoming an important IT framework that can help organizations managing, developing and communicating their intangible assets such as information and knowledge. Thus, it can be considered as an imperative framework in the current knowledge-based economy era.

Business Intelligence applications are mainly characterized by flexibility and adaptability in which traditional applications are not able to deal with. Traditional process modeling requires a lot of documentation and reports and this makes traditional methodology unable to fulfill the dynamic requirements of changes of our high-speed, high-change environment (Gersten, Wirth, and Arndt, 2000).

DOI: 10.4018/978-1-61350-050-7.ch001

An important question raised by many researchers (Power, 2007; Shariat & Hightower, 2007) as to what was the main reason pushing company to search for BI solutions, and what differentiates BI from Decision Support System (DSS) systems? In fact, over the last decades, organizations developed a lot of Operational Information Systems (OIS), resulting in a huge amount of disparate data that are located in different geographic locations, on different storage platforms, with different forms. This situation prevents organization from building a common, integrated, correlated, and immediate access to information at its global level. DSS have been evolved during the 1970s, with the objective of providing organization's decision makers with the required data to support decision-making process. In the 1980s, Executive Information System (EIS) was evolved to provide executive officers with the information needed to support strategic decision-making process. in 1990s BI was created as data-driven DSS, sharing some of the objectives and tools of DSS and EIS systems.

BI architectures include data warehousing, business analytics, business performance management, and data mining. Most of BI solutions are dealing with structured data (Alnoukari, and Alhussan, 2008). However, many application domains require the use of unstructured data (or at least semi-structured data), e.g. customer e-mails, web pages, competitor information, sales reports, research paper repositories, and so on (Baars, and Kemper, 2007).

Any BI solution can be divided into the following three layers (Alnoukari, and Alhussan, 2008): data layer, which is responsible for storing structured and unstructured data for decision support purposes. Structured data is usually stored in Operational Data Stores (ODS), Data Warehouses (DW), and Data Marts (DM) while unstructured data are handled by using Content and Document Management Systems. Data are extracted from operational data sources, e.g. SCM, ERP, CRM, or from external data sources, e.g. market research data. Data extracted from data sources are then transformed and loaded into DW using ETL tools. The second layer is the analytical layer which provides functionality in order to analyze data and provide knowledge including OLAP and data mining. The third layer is the visualization layer which can be realized using some sort of software portals (BI portal).

Our main focus in this chapter is to provide an overview of Business Intelligence by focusing on its body of knowledge. The authors start by providing a historical overview of Business Intelligence explaining the evolution of its concepts, followed by a brief discussion about different definitions and concepts of this field. The authors will describe the different layers and components of Business Intelligence application. Finally, the core body of knowledge, and the marriage between Business Intelligence and Knowledge Management will be discussed in details.

HISTORICAL OVERVIEW

In his article "A Business Intelligence System." Which have been published in IBM Journal, Luhn had defined intelligence as: "the ability to apprehend the interrelationships of presented facts in such a way as to guide action towards a desired goal.", (Luhn, 1958).

Business Intelligence is considered as a result of Decision Support Systems progression (DSS). DSS was mainly evolved in the 1970s. Model-driven DSS was the first DSS models that use limited data and parameters to help decision makers analyzing a situation (Power, 2007).

Data-driven DSS was also introduced as a new DSS direction by the end of the 1970s. It focused more on using all available data (including historical data) to provide executives with more insights about their organization's current and future situation. Executive Information Systems (EIS) and Executive Decision Support (ESS) are examples of data-derived DSS (Power, 2007).

In the late of 1980s, the client/server era has helped BI concept to evolve specially when Business Process Reengineering became the main trend of the industry, and the implementations of relational technologies – especially SQL skills - were transported between systems (Biere, 2003). During this period, the new idea of information warehousing was raised. Although the concept itself was brilliant, the data was never converted into clear information, the idea was simply to leave the data as it was and where it was but to have an access to it from anywhere using the early Business Intelligence tools.

In the 1990s, after the information warehousing quickly vanished, the data warehousing era takeover. This era introduced a way to not only reorganize data but to transform it into a much cleaner and easier to follow form. Data Warehousing is actually a set of processes designed to extract, clean, and reorganize data, enabling users to get a clearer idea of exactly what kind of data they are dealing with and its relevance to the issue they are addressing.

In this era, DSS was pushed notably by the introduction of Data Warehousing (DW) and On-Line analytical Processing (OLAP) which provide a new category of data-driven DSS. OLAP tools provide users with the way to browse and summarize data in an efficient and dynamic way (Shariat, and Hightower, 2007). In other word, OLAP tools provide an aggregated approach to analyze large amount of data (Hofmann, 2003). Data Warehousing is mainly composed of two components, data repository, or data warehouse, and metadata. Data warehouse is a logical collection of integrated data gathered from various operational data sources. Metadata is a set of rules that guide all data preparation operations (Shariat, and Hightower, 2007).

In the year 1989, Howard Dresner, the member of the Gartner group, was the first who introduced the term "Business Intelligence"(BI) as an umbrella term that "describe a set of concepts and methods to improve business decision making by using fact-based support systems" (Power, 2007).

Taking common BI concepts with data warehouse technologies, well developed enterprise application tools and on line analytical processing (OLAP) assists in faster collection, analysis or data research (Flanglin, 2005). Hence, BI technology assists in extracting information from the available data and using them as knowledge in developing innovative business strategies. But the growing competition in market is forcing small to large organizations to adopt BI to understand economic trends and have an in depth knowledge about the operation of a business.

Those years has considered a new era for BI, where packaged Business Intelligence solutions are provided on demand. Golfarelli had described a new approach of BI called "Business Performance Management (BPM)" which "requires a reactive component capable of monitoring the time-critical operational processes to allow tactical and operational decision-makers to tune their actions according to the company strategy", (Golfarelli, Stefano, and Iuris, 2004).

Colin in her paper " The Next Generation of Business Intelligence: Operational BI" describes the term "Operational BI", that is used to react faster to business needs and to anticipate business problems in advance before they become major issues, (Colin, 2005).

Similarly, many researchers were talking about the term "Real-time Business Intelligence" which has a very close relationship with the Operational BI, and targeting to reach the almost real-time decision making and a much higher degrees of analytics involved within business intelligence (Azvine, Cui, and Nauck, 2005).

Many other concepts had appeared in many areas: Ad-hoc and Collaborative BI (Berthold, et al., 2010), BI networks, Portals and thinner clients (Biere, 2003).

BUSINESS INTELLIGENCE: CONCEPTS AND DEFINTIONS

Decision support is aimed at supporting managers taking the right decisions (Jermol, Lavrac, and Urbancic, 2003). It provides a wide selection of decision analysis, simulation and modeling techniques, which include decision trees and belief networks. Also, decision support involves software tools such as Decision Support Systems (DSS), Group Decision Support and Mediation Systems (GDSMS), Expert Systems (ES), and Business Intelligence (BI) (Negash, 2004).

Decision makers depend on accurate information when they have to make decisions. Business Intelligence can provide decision makers with such accurate information, and with the appropriate tools for data analysis (Jermol, Lavrac, and Urbancic, 2003; Negash, 2004). It is the process of transforming various types of business data into meaningful information that can help, decision makers at all levels, getting deeper insight of business (Power, 2007; Girija, and Srivatsa, 2006).

In 1996, the Organization for Economic Cooperation and Development (OECD) redefined "knowledge-based economies" as: "Economies which are directly based on the production, distribution and use of knowledge and information" (Weiss, Buckley, Kapoor, and Damgaard, 2003).

According to the definition, Data Mining and Knowledge Management, and more generally Business Intelligence (BI), should be the foundations for building the knowledge economy.

BI is becoming vital for many organizations, especially those have extremely large amount of data (Shariat, and Hightower, 2007). Organizations such as Continental Airlines have seen investment in Business Intelligence generate increases in revenue and cost saving equivalent to 1000% return on investment (ROI) (Watson, Wixom, Hoffer, Anderson-Lehman, and Reynolds, 2006).

Business Intelligence is becoming an important IT framework that can help organizations managing, developing and communicating their intangible assets such as information and knowledge. Thus it can be considered as an imperative framework in the current knowledge-based economy era.

BI is an umbrella term that combines architectures, tools, data bases, applications, practices, and methodologies (Turban, Aronson, Liang, and Sharda, 2007; Cody, Kreulen, Krishna, and Spangler, 2002).

Weiss defined BI as the: "Combination of data mining, data warehousing, knowledge management, and traditional decision support systems" (Weiss, Buckley, Kapoor, and Damgaard, 2003).

According to Stevan Dedijer (the father of BI), Knowledge management emerged in part from the thinking of the "intelligence approach" to business. Dedijer thinks that "Intelligence" is more descriptive than knowledge. "Knowledge is static, intelligence is dynamic" (Marren, 2004).

For the purpose of this dissertation the following definition of BI applies: "The use of all the organization's resources: data, applications, people and processes in order to increase its knowledge, implement and achieve its strategy, and adapt to the environment's dynamism" (Authors).

THE GOAL OF BUSINESS INTELLIGENCE

The goal for any BI solution is to access data from multiple sources, transform these data into information and then into knowledge. The main focus of any BI solution is to improve organization's decision making capabilities. This can be done using the knowledge discovered from the data mining phase for the purpose to support decision makers by explaining current behavior, or predicting future results (Kerdprasop, and Kerdprasop, 2007).

The main complex part in any BI system is in its intelligence ability. This is mainly found in the post data mining phase where the system has to interpret its data mining results using a visual environment. The measure of any business intelligence solution is its ability to derive knowledge from data. The challenge is to meet the ability of identifying patterns, trends, rules, and relationships from large amount of information which is too large to be processed by human analysis alone.

BUSINESS INTELLIGENCE ARCHITECTURE

Any Business Intelligence application can be divided into the following three layers (Azvine, Cui, and Nauck, 2005; Baars, and Kemper, 2007; Shariat, and Hightower, 2007):

1. Data layer: responsible for storing structured and unstructured data for decision support purposes. Structured data is usually stored in Operational Data Stores (ODS), Data Warehouses (DW), and Data Marts (DM). Unstructured data are handled by using Content and Document Management Systems. Data are extracted from operational data sources, e.g. SCM, ERP, CRM, or from external data sources, e.g. market research data. Data are extracted from data sources that are transformed and loaded into DW by ETL tools.
2. Analytics layer: provides functionality to analyze data and provide knowledge. This includes OLAP, data mining, aggregations, etc.
3. Visualization layer: realized by some sort of BI applications or portals.

Data Warehouse and Data Mart

During the last two decades, data warehouses have gained a great reputation as a part of any decision support systems. Data warehouse came as a result of the failure of the mainframe systems to support enterprise decision making, those systems clustered the business entities across many production databases, aiming to enhance the performance level, but due to nature of the complex quires, the load generated create the need to separate the operational data from the data required to generate the DSS reports.

Ralph Kimball has defined the data warehouse as "A copy of transaction data, specifically structured for query and analysis" (Kimball, 2002). Barry Devlin defined it as: "A data warehouse is a simple, complete and consistent store of data obtained from a variety of sources and made available to users in a way they can understand and use it in a business context" (Devlin, 1997). Bill Inmon (the father of the data warehouse) defined data warehouse as: "a collection of integrated, subject-oriented databases designed to support the DSS (Decision Support Systems) function, where each unit of data is relevant to some moment in time. The data warehouse contains atomic data and lightly summarized data…" (Inmon, 2005).

Data marts were viewed as limited alternatives to fully populated enterprise data warehouses. Today, data marts have surged in popularity. Frequently, they serve as more manageable, cost-effective stepping-stones to the data warehouse. A data mart is a collection of subject areas organized for decision support based on the needs of a given department. Inmon defines Data Mart as follows: "a departmentalized structure of data feeding from the data warehouse where data is de-normalised based on the department's need for information" (Inmon, 2005).

The union of business process data marts is not a data warehouse, as Ralph Kimball and his collaborators suggest because this union doesn't necessarily provide management decision support for departments, or for departmental interactions among themselves and with the external world. (Kimball, Reeves, Ross, and Thornthwaite, 1998).

Data warehousing, in practice, focuses on a single large server or mainframe that provides a consolidation point for enterprise data coming from diverse production systems. It protects data production sources and gathers data into a single unified data model, but does not necessarily focus on providing end-user with an access to that data. Conversely data mart ignores the practical difficulties of protecting production systems from the impact of extraction. Instead it focuses on the knowledge needed from one or more areas of the business.

Data Mining

It is noted that the number of databases keeps growing rapidly because of the availability of powerful and affordable database systems. Millions of databases have been used in business management, government administration, scientific and engineering data management, and many other applications. This explosive growth in data and databases has generated an urgent need for new techniques and tools that can intelligently and automatically transform the processed data into useful information and knowledge, which provide enterprises with a competitive advantage, working asset that delivers new revenue, and to enable them to better service and retain their customers (Stolba, and Tjoa, 2006).

Data mining is the search for relationships and distinct patterns that exist in datasets but they are "hidden" among the vast amount of data (Jermol, Lavrac, and Urbancic, 2003; Turban, Aronson, Liang, & Sharda, 2007). Data mining can be effectively applied to many areas (Alnoukari, and Alhussan, 2008; Watson, Wixom, Hoffer, Anderson-Lehman, and Reynolds, 2006) including: marketing (direct mail, cross-selling, customer acquisition and retention), fraud detection, financial services (Srivastava, and Cooley, 2003), inventory control, fault diagnosis, credit scoring (Shi, Peng, Kou, and Chen, 2005), network management, scheduling, medical diagnosis and prognosis. There are two main sets of tools used for data mining (Corbitt, 2003; Baars & Kemper, 2007): discovery tools (Wixom, 2004; Chung, Chen, and Nunamaker jr, 2005), and verification tools (Grigori, Casati, Castellanos, Dayal, Sayal,

and Shan, 2004). Discovery tools include data visualization, neural networks, cluster analysis and factor analysis. Verification tools include regression analysis, correlations, and predictions.

Data mining application are characterized by the ability to deal with the explosion of business data and accelerated market changes, these characteristics help providing powerful tools for decision makers, such tools can be used by business users (not only statisticians) for analyzing huge amount of data for patterns and trends. Consequently, data mining has become a research area with increasing importance and it involved in determining useful patterns from collected data or determining a model that fits best on the collected data (Fayyad, Piatetsky-Shapiro, and Smyth, 1996; Mannila, 1997; Okuhara, Ishii, and Uchida, 2005). Different classification schemes can be used to categorize data mining methods and systems based on the kinds of databases to be studied, the kinds of knowledge to be discovered, and the kinds of techniques to be utilized (Lange, 2006).

A data mining task includes pre-processing, the actual data mining process and post-processing. During the pre-processing stage, the data mining problem and all sources of data are identified, and a subset of data is generated from the accumulated data. To ensure quality the data set is processed to remove noise, handle missing information and transformed it to an appropriate format (Nayak, and Qiu, 2005). A data mining technique or a combination of techniques appropriate for the type of knowledge to be discovered is applied to the derived data set. The last stage is post-processing in which the discovered knowledge is evaluated and interpreted.

The most widely used methodology when applying data mining processes is named CRISP-DM. It was one of the first attempts towards standardizing data mining process modeling (Shearer, 2000). CRISP-DM has six main phases, starting by business understanding that can help in converting the knowledge about the project objectives and requirements into a data mining problem definition, followed by data understanding by performing different activities such as initial data collection, identifying data quality problems, and other preliminary activities that can help users be familiar with the data. The next and the most important step is data preparation by performing different activities to convert the initial raw data into data that can be fed into modeling phase. This phase includes tasks such as data cleansing and data transformation. Modeling is the core phase which can use a number of algorithmic techniques (decision trees, rule learning, neural networks, linear/logistic regression, association learning, instance-based/nearest-neighbor learning, unsupervised learning, and probabilistic learning, etc.) available for each data mining approach, with features that must be weighed against data characteristics and additional business requirements. The final two modules focus on the evaluation of module results, and the deployment of the models into production. Hence, users must decide on what and how they wish to disseminate/deploy results, and how they integrate data mining into their overall business strategy (Shearer, 2000).

THE KNOWLEDGE DIMENSION OF BUSINESS INTELLIGENCE

Knowledge was defined as "justified true belief" (Nonaka, 1994), which is subjective, difficult to codify, context-related, rooted in action, relational, and is about meaning. Knowledge differs from information as the later is objective and codified in any explicit forms such as documents, computer databases, and images.

Knowledge is usually identified to have two types: tacit and explicit (Nonaka, and Takeuchi, 1995). Tacit knowledge is personal, context-specific, and resides in human beings minds, and is therefore difficult to formalize, codify and communicate. It is personal knowledge that is embedded in individual experience and involves intangible factors such as personal belief, perspective, and value system. Tacit knowledge is difficult to communicate and share in the organization and must thus be converted into words or forms of explicit knowledge. On the other hand explicit knowledge is the knowledge that is transmittable in formal, systematic languages. It can be articulated in formal languages, including grammatical statements, mathematical expressions, specifications, manuals and so forth. It can be transmitted across individuals formally and easily.

Knapp defined Knowledge Management (KM) as "the process of making complete use of the value generated by the transfer of intellectual capital, where this value can be viewed as knowledge creation, acquisition, application and sharing", (Knapp, 1998).

Business Intelligence is a good environment in which 'marrying' business knowledge with data mining could provide better results (Anand, Bell, and Hughes, 1995; Cody, Kreulen, Krishna, and Spangler, 2002; Weiss, Buckley, Kapoor, and Damgaard, 2003; Graco, Semenova, and Dubossarsky, 2007). They all agree that knowledge can enrich data by making it "intelligent", thus more manageable by data mining. They consider expert knowledge as an asset that can provide data mining with the guidance to the discovery process. Thus, it says in a simple word, "data mining cannot work without knowledge". Weiss et al. clarifies the relationships between Business Intelligence, Data Mining, and Knowledge Management (Weiss, Buckley, Kapoor, and Damgaard, 2003).

McKnight has organized KM under BI. He suggests that this is a good way to think about the relationship between them (McKnight, 2002). He argues that KM is internal-facing BI, sharing the intelligence among employees about how effectively to perform the variety of functions required to make the organization go. Hence, knowledge is managed using many BI techniques.

Haimila also sees KM as the "helping hand of BI" (Haimila, 2001). He cites the use of BI by law enforcement agencies as being a way to maximize their use of collected data, enabling them to make faster and better-informed decisions because they can drill down into data to see trends, statistics and match characteristics of related crimes.

Cook and Cook noted that many people forget that the concepts of KM and BI are both rooted in pre-software business management theories and practices. They claim that technology has served to cloud the definitions. Defining the role of technology in KM and BI– rather than defining technology as KM and BI – is seen by Cook and Cook as a way to clarify their distinction (Cook, and Cook 2000).

Text mining, seen primarily as a KM technology, adds a valuable component to existing BI technology. Text mining, also known as intelligent text analysis, text data mining or knowledge-discovery in text (KDT), refers generally to the process of extracting interesting and non-trivial information and knowledge from unstructured text. Text mining is a young interdisciplinary field that draws on information retrieval, data mining, machine learning, statistics and computational linguistics. As most information (over 80 percent) is stored as text, text mining is believed to have a high commercial potential value.

Text mining would seem to be a logical extension to the capabilities of current BI products.

However, its seamless integration into BI software is not quite so obvious. Even with the perfection and widespread use of text mining capabilities, there are a number of issues that Cook and Cook contend that must be addressed before KM (text mining) and BI (data mining) capabilities truly merge into an effective combination. In particular, they claim it is dependent on whether the software vendors are interested in creating technology that supports the theories that define KM and providing tools that deliver complete strategic intelligence to decision-makers in companies. However, even if they do, Cook and Cook believe that it is unlikely that technology will ever fully replace the human analysis that

leads to stronger decision making in the upper echelons of the corporation.

The authors provide the following findings:

- BI focuses on explicit knowledge, but KM encompasses both tacit and explicit knowledge.
- Both concepts promote learning, decision making, and understanding. Yet, KM can influence the very nature of BI itself.
- Integration between BI and KM and makes it clear that BI should be viewed as a sub-set of KM.
- Fundamentally, Business Intelligence and Knowledge Management have the same objective - to focus on improving business performance. If we agree that Business Intelligence is comprised of Customer, Competitor and Market Intelligence and that the purpose of Business Intelligence is to support strategic decision-making, grow the business and monitor the organization's competitors,
- The business intelligence concern of DSS in company and deal with customers and competitors where as knowledge management concern about employees

CONCLUSION

There are people who think that BI encapsulates KM and they do believe so because they argue that BI is the mean to manage the different knowledge in any organization "Share the knowledge". actually it is a good way to see it, but if we are trying to look deeper into the different types of knowledge including tacit and explicit knowledge. Actually, KM can be seen as a boarder notation than BI because BI deals mainly with structured data, while KM deals with both structured and unstructured data.

Conceptually, it is easy to understand how knowledge can be thought of as an integral component of BI and hence decision making. This chapter argued that KM and BI, while differing, they need to be considered together as necessarily integrated and mutually critical components in the management of intellectual capital.

In this chapter, the authors provide a detailed overview of Business Intelligence including: definitions, concepts, goals, architecture, components, and mainly its body of knowledge.

REFERENCES

Albescu, F., Pugna, I., & Paraschiv, D. (2008). Business intelligence & knowledge management – Technological support for strategic management in the knowledge based economy. *Informatica Economica, 4*(48), 5–12.

Alnoukari, M., & Alhussan, W. (2008). Using data mining techniques for predicting future car market demand. *Proceedings of International Conference on Information & Communication Technologies* (pp. 929-930). Damascus, Syria: IEEE.

Anand, S. S., Bell, D. A., & Hughes, J. G. (1995). The role of domain knowledge in data mining. *Proceedings of the 4th International Conference on Information and Knowledge Management,* Baltimore, Maryland, USA (pp. 37-43). New York, NY: ACM.

Azvine, B., Cui, Z., & Nauck, D. D. (2005). Towards real-time business intelligence. *BT Technology Journal.*

Baars, H., & Kemper, H. G. (2007). Management support with structured and unstructured data-An integrated business intelligence framework. *Information Systems Management, 25,* 132–148. doi:10.1080/10580530801941058

Berthold, H., Rösch, P., Zöller, S., Wortmann, F., Carenini, A., & Campbell, S. …Zimanyi, E. (2010). An architecture for ad-hoc and collaborative business intelligence. In F. Daniel, L. Delcambre, F. Fotouhi, I. Garrigos, G. Guerrini, J.-N. Mazon,…E. Zimanyi (Eds.), *Proceedings of the 2010 EDBT/ICDT Workshops, Lausanne, Switzerland (ACM ICPS '10).* New York, NY: ACM.

Biere, M. (2003). *Planning for the Future—What's the Next Wave of Business Intelligence?* Chung, W., Chen, H., & Nunamaker Jr, J. F. (Spring 2005). A visual framework for knowledge discover on the Web: An empirical study of business intelligence exploration. *Journal of Management Information Systems, 21*(4), 57–84.

Cody, W., Kreulen, J., Krishna, V. & Spangler, W. (2002). The integration of business intelligence and knowledge management. *IBM Systems Journal.*

Colin, W. (2005). The Next Generation of Business Intelligence: Operational BI. *Information management magazine.*

Cook, C., & Cook, M. (2000). *The convergence of knowledge management and business intelligence.* New York, NY: Auerbach Publications.

Corbitt, T. (2003). Business intelligence and data mining. *Management services magazine,* 18-19.

Devlin, B. (1997). *Data Warehouse: From architecture to implementation.* Boston, MA: Addison-Wesley.

Fayyad, U., Piatetsky-Shapiro, G., & Smyth, P. (1996). From data mining to knowledge discovery in databases. *AI Magazine,* 37–54.

Flanglin, R. (2005). *Business intelligence 101.* Retrieved on June 01, 2010, from Power Home-Biz: http:// www.powerhomebiz.com/ 062005/ intelligence.htm.

Gersten, W., Wirth, R., & Arndt, D. (2000). Predictive modeling in automotive direct marketing: Tools, experiences and open issues. *The 6th ACM SIGKDD International Conference on Knowledge Discovery and Data Mining (KDD-2000)* (pp. 398-406). Boston, MA, USA: ACM.

Girija, N., & Srivatsa, S. K. (2006). A research study- Using data mining in knowledge base business strategies. *Information Technology Journal, 5*(3), 590–600. doi:10.3923/itj.2006.590.600

Golfarelli, M., Stefano, R., & Iuris, C. (2004). Beyond data warehousing: What's next in business intelligence? *7th ACM International Workshop on Data Warehousing and OLAP* (pp. 1-6). New York, NY: ACM.

Graco, W., Semenova, T., & Dubossarsky, E. (2007). Toward knowledge-driven data mining. *ACM SIGKDD Workshop on Domain Driven Data Mining (DDDM2007)* (pp. 49-54). San Jose, California, USA: ACM.

Grigori, D., Casati, F., Castellanos, M., Dayal, U., Sayal, M., & Shan, M.-C. (2004). Business process intelligence. *Computers in Industry, 53,* 321–343. doi:10.1016/j.compind.2003.10.007

Haimila, S. (2001). KM in practice: The helping hand of BI, *KMWorld, 10*(10).

Inmon, W. H. (1995). What is a Data Warehouse? *Prism Tech Topic, 1*(1).

Jermol, M., Lavrac, N., & Urbancic, T. (2003). Managing business intelligence in a virtual enterprise: A case study and knowledge management lessons learned. *Journal of Intelligent & Fuzzy Systems,* 121–136.

Kerdprasop, N., & Kerdprasop, K. (2007). Moving data mining tools toward a business intelligence system. *Transactions on engineering, computing and technology,* 19, 117-122.

Kimball, R. (1996). *The data warehouse toolkit.* New York, NY: John Wiley & Sons.

Kimball, R., Reeves, L., Ross, M., & Thornthwaite, W. (1998). *The data warehouse life cycle toolkit.* New York, NY: John Wiley & Sons.

Knapp, E. (1998). Knowledge management. *Business and Economic Review, 44*(4).

Lange, K. (2006). Differences between statistics and data mining. *DM Review, 16*(12), 32–33.

Luhn, H. P. (1958). *A business intelligence system.* IBM Journal.

Mannila, H. (1997). Methods and problems in data mining. In F. Afrati, & P. Kolaitis (Eds.), *International Conference on Database Theory.* Delphi, Greece: Springer-Verlag.

Marco, D. (2002). *The key to knowledge management.* Retrieved at http:// www.adtmag.com/article.asp?id=6525

Marren, P. (2004). The father of business intelligence. *The Journal of Business Strategy, 25*(6), 5–7.

Nayak, R., & Qiu, T. (2005). A data mining application: Analysis of problems occurring during a software project development process. *International Journal of Software Engineering and Knowledge Engineering, 15*(4), 647–663. doi:10.1142/S0218194005002476

Negash, S. (2004). Business intelligence. *Communications of the Association for Information Systems, 13,* 177–195.

Nemati, H., Steiger, D., Iyer, L., & Herschel, R. (2002). Knowledge warehouse: An architectural integration of knowledge management, decision support, artificial intelligence and data warehousing. *Decision Support Systems,* (Spring): 2002.

Nonaka, I. (1994). A dynamic theory of organizational knowledge creation. *Organization Science, 5*(1), 14–27. doi:10.1287/orsc.5.1.14

Nonaka, I., & Takeuchi, H. (1995). *The knowledge-creating company.* New York, NY: Oxford University Press, Inc.

Okuhara, K., Ishii, H., & Uchida, M. (2005). Support of decision making by data mining using neural system. *Systems and Computers in Japan, 36*(11), 102–110. doi:10.1002/scj.10577

Power, D. J. (2007). *A brief history of decision support systems, version 4.0.* Retrieved on July 23, 2010, from *DSSResources.com.*

Shariat, M., & Hightower, R. (2007). Conceptualizing business intelligence architecture. *The Marketing Management Journal, 17*(2), 40–46.

Shearer, C. (2000). The CRISP-DM Model: The new blueprint for data mining. *Journal of Data Warehousing, 5*(4), 13–22.

Shi, Y., Peng, Y., Kou, G., & Chen, Z. (2005). Classifying credit card accounts for business intelligence and decision making: A multiple-criteria quadratic programming approach. *International Journal of Information Technology & Decision Making,* 581–599.

Srivastava, J., & Cooley, R. (2003). Web business intelligence: Mining the Web for actionable knowledge. *INFORMS Journal on Computing, 15*(2), 191–207. doi:10.1287/ijoc.15.2.191.14447

Stolba, N., & Tjoa, A. M. (2006). The relevance of data warehousing and data mining in the field of evidence-based medicine to support healthcare decision making. *Enformatika, 11,* 12–17.

Thong, J. (1999). An integrated model of Information Systems adoption in small businesses. *Journal of Management Information Systems, 15*(4), 187–214.

Turban, E., Aronson, J. E., Liang, T. P., & Sharda, R. (2007). *Decision support and business intelligence systems* (8th ed.). Upper Saddle River, NJ: Pearson Prentice Hall.

Watson, H. J., Wixom, B. H., Hoffer, J. A., Anderson-Lehman, R., & Reynolds, A. M. (2006). Real-time business intelligence: Best practices at Continental Airlines. *Information Systems Management,* 7–18. doi:10.1201/1078.1058053 0/45769.23.1.20061201/91768.2

Weiss, S. M., Buckley, S. J., Kapoor, S., & Damgaard, S. (2003). Knowledge-based data mining. [Washington, DC, USA: ACM.]. *SIGKDD, 03,* 456–461.

Wikipedia. org (2010). *Data warehouse, Wikipedia the Free encyclopedia.* Retrieved on July 13, 2010, from www.wikipedia.org/ wiki/ Data_warehouse.

ADDITIONAL READING

Alnoukari, M., Alzoabi, Z., & Hanna, S. (2008). Applying adaptive software development (ASD) agile modeling on predictive data mining applications: ASD-DM methodology. *International Symposium on Information Technology* (pp. 1083-1087). Kuala Lumpur, Malaysia: IEEE.

Alnoukari, M., El Sheikh, A., & Alzoabi, Z. (2009). Applying ASD-DM methodology on business intelligence solutions: A case study on building customer care data mart. In A. P. Abraham (Ed.), *Data Mining 2009, IADIS Multi Conference On Computer Science And Information Systems (MCCMIS 2009),* (pp. 153-157). ALGARVE, PORTUGAL.

Anand, S. S., Bell, D. A., & Hughes, J. G. (1995). The role of domain knowledge in data mining. *Proceedings of the 4th International Conference on Information and Knowledge Management,* Baltimore, Maryland, United States (pp. 37-43). New York, NY: ACM.

Bauer, K. (2005). *Predictive analytics: Data mining with a twist.* DM Review Journal.

Berry, M. J., & Gordon, L. (1997). *Data mining techniques: For marketing, sales, and customer support*. New York, NY: Wiley.

Boddy, D., Boonstra, A., & Kennedy, G. (2005). *Managing Information Systems: An organisational perspective* (2nd ed.). Harlow: Pearson.

Brachman, R. J., & Anand, T. (1994). The process of knowledge discovery in databases: *A first sketch. Workshop on knowledge discovery in databases* (pp. 1-11). AAAI.

Buchner, A. G., Mulvenna, M. D., Anand, S. S., & Hughes, J. G. (1999). An Internet-enabled knowledge discovery process. *Proceedings of the 9th International Database Conference*, Hong Kong (pp. 13-27).

Cabena, P., Hadjinian, P., Stadler, R., Verhees, J., & Zanasi, A. (1998). *Discovering data mining: From concept to implementation*. Upper Saddle River, New Jersey: Prentice Hall.

Caprace, J.-D., Losseau, N., Archambeau, D., Bair, F., & Philippe, R. (2007). *A data mining analysis applied to a straightening process database. Computer Applications and Information Technology in the Maritime Industries-COMPIT'07* (pp. 186–196). Italy: Cortona.

Castellano, M., Mastronardi, G., Aprile, A., Minardi, M., Catalano, P., & Dicensi, V. (2007). A decision support system base line flexible architecture to intrusion detection. *Journal of Software*, *2*(6), 30–41. doi:10.4304/jsw.2.6.30-41

Chung, W., Chen, H., & Nunamaker, J. F. Jr. (2005, Spring). A visual framework for knowledge discover on the Web: An empirical study of business intelligence exploration. *Journal of Management Information Systems*, *21*(4), 57–84.

Cios, K., Teresinska, A., Konieczna, S., Potocka, J., & Sharma, S. (2000). Diagnosing myocardial perfusion from PECT bull's-eye maps—A knowledge discovery approach. *IEEE Engineering in Medicine and Biology Magazine. Special Issue on Medical Data Mining and Knowledge Discovery*, *19*(4), 17–25.

Cios, K. J., Pedrycz, W., Swiniarski, R. W., & Kurgan, L. A. (2007). The knowledge discovery process. In *Data mining: A knowledge discovery process* (p. 606). Berlin-Heidelberg, Germany: Springer.

Collier, K., Carey, B., Grusy, E., Marjaniemi, C., & Sautter, D. (1998). *A perspective on data mining. Northern Arizona University*. USA: Centre for Data Insight.

Diko, F., Alzoabi, Z., & Alnoukari, M. (2008). *Enhancing education quality assurance using data mining, case study: Arab International University Systems*. Budapest, Hungary: Third European Quality Assurance Forum.

Edelstein, H. (1998). Data mining: let's get practical. *DB2 Magazine, 3*(2), 38-40.

Euler, T. (2005). Publishing operational models of data mining case studies. *International Conference on Data Mining: Workshop on Data Mining Case Studies*, Houston, Texas, USA (pp. 99-106). New York, NY: IEEE.

Gessner, G. H., & Volonino, L. (Spring 2005). Quick response improves returns on business intelligence investments. *Journal of Information Systems Management*, 66-74.

Herring, J. P. (1988, May/June). Building a business intelligence systems. *The Journal of Business Strategy*, 4–9. doi:10.1108/eb039219

Inmon, W. H. (2005). *Building the data warehouse*. John Wiley and Sons.

Jermol, M., Lavrac, N., & Urbancic, T. (2003). Managing business intelligence in a virtual enterprise: A case study and knowledge management lessons learned. *Journal of Intelligent & Fuzzy Systems*, 121–136.

Jourdan, Z., Rainer, R. K., & Marshall, T. E. (2007). Business intelligence: An analysis of the literature. In T. &. Group (Ed.), *Information Systems Management, 25*, 121-131.

Michalewicz, Z., Schmidt, M., Mich, M., & Chiriac, C. (2006). *Adaptive business intelligence*. Berlin-Heidelberg, Germany: Springer.

Paladino, B., & William, N. (2008). Moving strategy forward: Merging the balanced scorecard and business intelligence. *Business Performance Management*, 12-17.

Pant, P. (2009, August 4). Essential components of a successful BI strategy. *Information Management Special Reports*.

Rennolls, K., & AL-Shawabkeh, A. (2008). Formal structures for data mining, knowledge discovery and communication in a knowledge management environment. *Intelligent Data Analysis, 12*, 147–163.

Rupnik, R., & Kukar, M. (2007). Decision support system to support decision processes with data mining. *Journal of Information and Organizational Sciences*, 217-232.

Sabherwal, R., & Chan, Y. E. (2001). Alignment between business and IS strategies: A study of prospectors, analyzers, and defenders. *Information Systems Research*, 11–33. doi:10.1287/isre.12.1.11.9714

Schreiber, G., Akkermans, H., Anjewierden, A., Hoog, R. D., & Shadbolt, N. ... Velde, W. V. (1999). *Knowledge engineering and management: The CommonKADS methodology*. Cambridge, MA: MIT-Press.

Wee, C. H., & Leow, M. L. (1994). Competitive business intelligence in Singapore. *Journal of Strategic Marketing, 1*, 112–139. doi:10.1080/09652549400000006

Wixom, B. H. (2004). Business intelligence software for the classroom: Microstrategy resources on the Teradata University network. *Communications of the Association for Information Systems, 14*, 234–246.

KEY TERMS AND DEFINITIONS

Body of Knowledge (BoK): The sum of body of all knowledge elements in a particular field.

Business Intelligence (BI): An umbrella term that combines architectures, tools, data bases, applications, practices, and methodologies. It is the process of transforming various types of business data into meaningful information that can help, decision makers at all levels, getting deeper insight of business.

Data Mining (DM): The process of discovering interesting information from the hidden data that can either be used for future prediction and/or intelligently summarizing the details of the data.

Data Warehouse (DW): A physical repository where relational data are specially organized to provide enterprise-wide, cleansed data in a standardized format.

Decision Support System (DSS): An approach (or methodology) for supporting making. It uses an interactive, flexible, adaptable computer-based information system especially developed for supporting the solution to a specific nonstructured management problem.

Knowledge: About meaning. It is subjective, difficult to codify, context-related, rooted in action, and relational.

Knowledge Management (KM): The acquisition, storage, retrieval, application, generation, and review of the knowledge assets of an organization in a controlled way.

Chapter 2
Agile Software:
Body of Knowledge

Zaidoun Alzoabi
Martin Luther University, Germany

ABSTRACT

The term Agile Method of software development was coined in the 2001. This approach is character-ized with creativity, flexibility, adaptability, responsiveness, and human-centricity. Researchers have suggested that the complex, uncertain, and ever-changing environment is pushing developers to adopt agile methods rather than traditional software development. Agile methodologist claim that their Agile methods is the answer for the software engineering chaotic situation, in which projects are exceeding their time and budget limits, requirements are not fulfilled, and consequently ending up with unsatisfied customers. In this chapter we will explain agile methodology, its general characteristics, and quick description of the famous agile methods known in the industry and research.

INTRODUCTION

The term Agile Method of software development was coined in the 2001 (Agile Manafesto). This approach is characterized with creativity, flex-ibility, adaptability, responsiveness, and human-centricity (Abrahamsson, et al. 2002). Researchers have suggested that the complex, uncertain, and ever-changing environment is pushing developers to adopt agile methods rather than traditional soft-ware development. That is because the uncertain environment is pushing for flexibility in changing requirements (Manninen & Berki 2004). More-over, the advancements made in developing users knowledge of computers and computer application made it possible for users to actively participate in the development process, a matter that is lack-ing in traditional software development processes (Monochristou and Vlachopoulou 2007).

DOI: 10.4018/978-1-61350-050-7.ch002

This agility, however, is challenged with some quality-related issues (Bass, 2006). That is, despite of the quality features in agile methods, there is some compromise on the amount of information and knowledge communicated to customers arising due to the lack of documentation that strongly characterizes agile methods (Ambler 2005, McBreen 2003, Berki 2006). This was due to the innate trend in agile methods to concentrate on human-based techniques in communicating knowledge such as on-site-customer, pair programming, and daily short meetings.

The human-centricity of Agile methods implies that the main focus of the software production process is to maximize the knowledge transferred and shared among various stakeholders of the software project. Hence, we will investigate the knowledge component in the main Agile method: extreme programming, despite the fact the other Agile methods show clear KM techniques.

Agile methods in fact came as response to the failure software projects were facing. Agile methods came after decades of applying traditional, process-based software development methodologies that are characterized with heavy documentation, strong emphasis on the process, and less communication with customers (Beck, 2000)

The rest of the chapter is organized as follows: first we will introduce agile methods history, explaining how agile methods emerged through last two decades. Then we will explain what are the major agile principles, concepts, and trends. After that we will move to discuss the most famous agile methods, namely: extreme programming, scrum, Feature Driven Development FDD, Adaptive Software Development, ASD, Crystal, Lean Software Development, and Agile Modeling. Finally we conclude our chapter by discussing agile methods pros and cons as found in the literature.

AGILE DEVELOPMENT HISTORY

On February 11-13, 2001, representatives from Extreme Programming, SCRUM, DSDM, Adaptive Software Development, Crystal, Feature-Driven Development, Pragmatic Programming, and others sympathetic to the need for an alternative to documentation driven, heavyweight software development processes, gathered at the Snowbird resort in Utah to form what is known now by the Agile Alliance.

However, this was just to coin the name Agile, not to say that agile methodologies were born at that time. Several agile methods had been by that time already born and applied in throughout the 1990's. Figure 1 shows the early history of Agile methods.

From the figure we can see the following observations from the history of agile methods development:

- Agile methods were already in practice for more than half a decade before forming the Agile Alliance.
- The first two agile methods were DSDM and Scrum.
- Rapid Application Development and object-oriented development could be considered the transitional method between traditional development methods and agile methods.
- Between 1998 and 2002 is the most productive period for agile methods as the Agile Alliance was formed and many agile methods came into existence.
- After 2002 agile methods use in the industry has grown exponentially (Begel and Nagappan 2007,) with XP and Scrum taking the lead.

Figure 1. History of agile development, adapted from Abrahamsson et al. (2003)

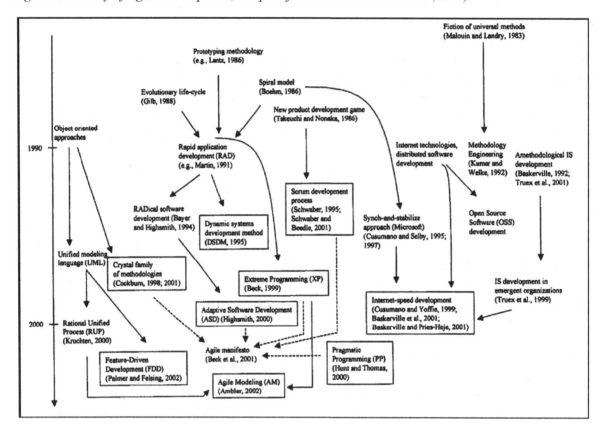

AGILE PRINCIPLES AND TECHNIQUES

Agile Principles

Agile software development is not a set of tools or a single methodology, but a philosophy in its own. Agile was a significant departure from the heavyweight document-driven software development methodologies such as waterfall and spiral methods that were popular since 1970 when Waterfall method was established by (Royce 1970)

While the publication of the "Manifesto for Agile Software Development" didn't start the move to agile methods, which had been going on for some time, it did signal industry acceptance of agile philosophy. The manifesto states the major principles of agile methods in the manifesto homepage as: "We are uncovering better ways

of developing software by doing it and helping others do it".

Through this work we have come to value:

- Individuals and interactions over processes and tools
- Working software over comprehensive documentation
- Customer collaboration over contract negotiation
- Responding to change over following a plan
- That is, while there is value in the items on the right,
- We value the items on the left more. (Agilemanifesto.org)

Agile main characteristics could be summarized as follows:

- **Iterative**: The word iterative means developing software through multiple repetitions. Agile methodologies attempt to solve a software problem by finding successively approaching a solution beginning from an initial minimal core set of requirements. This means that the agile team designs a core for the system and then changes the functionality of each subsystem with each new release as the requirements are updated for each attempt. That is, unlike traditional software development methods that try to devise a full-fledged solution at one shot, agile methodologists understand the difficulties face customers in expressing their requirements in the correct way and rather start with some core functions of the system and then change the system after getting deep understanding of the customers' needs and wants through extensive collaboration with all project stakeholders.

- **Incremental**: As a result to the iterative approach of the agile methods, each subsystem is developed in a manner that lets more requirements to be unveiled and used to develop other subsystems based on previous ones. The approach is to modularize the system into smaller subsystems according to the specified functionalities and add new functionalities with each new release. Each release has to be a fully testable and usable subsystem. As the development continues, new increments are added until the complete system is realized (Mnkandla and Dwolatzky 2007).

- **Simplicity**: The KISS principle is centric to the agile development methods. Simple code, design, tests, and documentation will help in doing things fast and adjusting things as required (Beck 2000).

- **Human-Centricity**: Agile methods realize that humans are the sponsors, users, and developers of the system, and that heavy communication with project stakeholders will allow for more stakeholders' satisfaction.

- **Interaction with Customers**: This principle is again central in agile methods as they focus on concepts like on-site customers to have an immediate feedback to the required functionalities as they come into existence allowing for more accuracy and customer satisfaction.

- **Self-Organizing**: This term introduces a radical approach to the management notation. Here agile methods assumes skilled highly qualified developers who should have the liberty to plan, organize, coordinate and control the software project without a real supervision (Beck 2000). In the agile development setup, the "self-organizing" concept gives the team autonomy to organize itself to best complete the work items. This means that how the system development is approached, technologies used, communication with users, etc. is left entirely to team to best find the solution. This approach is entirely different than traditional way were project managers had to control the progress of the work.

- **Flexibility**: This principle means that solution is devised based on certain situational conditions that are dealt with in high flexibility and that system is adapted on the spot without hesitation (Beck 2000).

- **Nimbleness**: In agile software development there quick delivery of the product to gain more interaction with the users is a must. This is usually done through frequent releases of usable subsystems within a period ranging from one week to four weeks. A release is " (a release) should be as small as possible, containing the most valuable business requirements" (Beck 2000). This gives good spin-offs as the customer will start using the system before it is completed.

- **Readiness for Motion**: In agile development, the general intention is to reduce all activities and material that may either slow the speed of development or increase bureaucracy.

- **Activity**: This involves doing the actual writing of code as opposed to all the planning that sometimes takes most of the time in software development. This is emphasized through self-documenting code as the main documentation activity.
- **Dexterity in motion**: This means that agile methodologists emphasize the need for highly skilled developers to develop the code. The skills referred to are the mental skills that will arm the developers for programming challenges and team dynamics.
- **Adjustability**: This means two things; firstly there must be some tolerance in changing the set of activities and technologies that constitute an agile development process. That is developers –applying the self organizing principle- have the liberty to modify the life-cycle, artifacts, processes, etc. according to situation. Secondly the requirements, code, and the design/architecture must be allowed to change to the advantage of the customer.
- **Lightweight**: This implies minimizing everything that is seen unnecessary in the development process such as excessive documentation, extensive planning, etc.) in order to increase the speed and efficiency in development. Instead, agile methods replace heavy documentation with more lively discussions with on-site customers (Beck 2000).
- **Efficient**: This means doing only that work that will deliver the desired product with as little overhead as practically possible.
- **Low-Risk**: This means relying on the practical lines and leaving the unknown until it is known. With small releases, developers will plan for shorter periods allowing the unknown to be uncovered gradually as the project progresses.

- **Predictable**: This implies that agile methodologies are based on what practitioners do all the time, in other words the world of ambiguity is reduced. This however does not mean that planning, designs, and architecture of software are predictable. It means that agility allows development of software in the most natural ways that trained developers can determine in advance based on special knowledge.
- **Scientific**: This means that the agile software development methodologies are based on sound and proven scientific principles.
- **Fun Way**: This is because developers are allowed to do what they like most (i.e., to spend most of their time writing good code that works). To the developers, agility provides a form of freedom to be creative and innovative without making the customer pay for it, instead the customer benefits from it. In principle developers like coding the most and hate other activities that are seen less creative, time consuming, and boring such as documentation.

Agile Techniques

In order to allow the aforementioned principles to find way in the development life, agile methods use several techniques that help in increasing flexibility, nimbleness, interaction with customers, and lightweight. In the following we discuss these techniques.

- **Refactoring**: This technique allows developers to reach the required functionality first and then look for a better "look" for the code. That is, after the functionality is gotten, small changes to code are introduced to the code so that behavior is not affected, Resulting code is of higher quality (Ambler, 2005).
- **Test-Driven Development**: This technique implies that automated tests are designed before coding commences. Design a test,

write the code, run the test, make changes until the test passes (Ambler, 2005).

- **Acceptance Testing**: A final test that is done on the finished system, usually involving the users, sponsors, customer, etc. (Huo, Verner, Zhu, & Babar, 2004).
- **Continuous Integration**: "Code is integrated and tested after a few hours—a day of development at most" (Beck 2000). This allows for early error-detection.
- **Pair Programming**: Two developers work together in turns on one PC, Bugs are identified as they occur, Hence the product is of a higher quality (Huo et al., 2004). The two work as a small team, one thinks strategically and the other thinks tactically. The two can exchange roles (Beck 1999).
- **Pair Swapping**: pairs change on an ad hoc manner allowing for more knowledge sharing and hence better quality resulting from exchange of ideas and better communication.
- **On-Site Customers**: A customer, who is a member of the development team, will be responsible for clarifying requirements and will give immediate feedback to the development team (Huo et al., 2004).

AGILE METHODS IN USE

In the following we discuss the well-known agile methods focusing on life cycle, practices and principles, and main roles and responsibilities.

Extreme Programming (XP)

eXtreme Programming as an identifiable methodology is distinguished by twelve main practices, along with a number of secondary practices (Beck, 2000), (Newkirk, 2002). These practices are similar to the activities or techniques of conventional methodologies, in that they are particular things that programmers actually do to produce software.

XP has four core values that are used to guide the practices that are employed. These values are:

- **Communication**: This includes communication between all team members, customers, programmers and managers.
- **Simplicity**: "What is the simplest thing that could possibly work?" The message is very clear. Given the requirements for today design and write your software. Do not try to anticipate the future, let the future unfold.
- **Feedback**: XP practices are designed to illicit feedback early and often. The practices such as short releases, continuous integration, testing provide very clear feedback.
- **Courage**: XP changes the position of software engineers from defense to offense. It takes courage to say I have done enough design for now and I'll let the future happen.

In order to realize these values XP put under one umbrella 12 practices that programmers have developed over decades, integrated them, and tried to make sure they are practiced well. These practices are discussed in the following paragraph.

XP Life Cycle

XP has a 5-phases life cycle consisting of exploration, planning, iterations to release, productionizing, and maintenance and death. Figure 2 shows these phases.

In the exploration phase, customers write their stories about features they want to see in the system and team members try different architectures and technologies to decide on the approach and applicability. The exploration phase takes around 1 to 2 weeks during which customers, users, and team members hold extensive workshop to decide on the best solution.

During planning phase, user stories are prioritized, releases are agreed upon, and estimation

Figure 2. XP lifecycle, adapted from Abrahamsson et al. (2002)

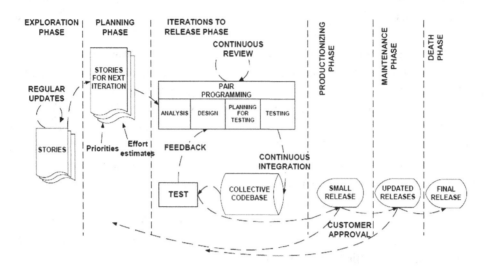

of the work needed is made. The planning phase does not take more than few days.

In the iterations to release phase, several iterations are made to reach one release. A release is a working software delivering one or more functionality.

The productionizing phase sees more testing to make sure the system has delivered what is supposed to do, and new changes –if required– are introduced.

In the maintenance to death phase, the system will be up and running while other parts of the system are being developed. Here customers are supported during their early use of the system, without discontinuing frequent discussions with them about the other stories under development. If no features are to be added, the system goes into the death phase, where attention is focused on other issues like reliability and performance.

XP Principles and Techniques

XP has twelve guiding principles and practices. These are

- **Planning**: Determine the scope of the next iteration by working with customers who provide business priorities and with programmers who provide technical estimates.

- **Small Releases**: Get the system into production quickly. This is a key factor in getting feedback on the actual software.

- **Metaphor**: Understand how the whole system works. This is important for both developers and customers

- **Simple Design**: One of the key values is simplicity. The system should be designed for the features that are implemented today, and add features gradually.

- **Testing**: Tests include unit tests, which programmers write and acceptance tests, which customers write. Tests are the indicator of completion.

- **Refactoring**: Programmers are responsible for improving the design of existing software without changing its behavior.

- **Pair Programming**: Working with a partner is a requirement when writing production code.

- **Collective Ownership**: Anyone on the team can change any part of the system.

- **Continuous Integration**: Programmers integrate and build the software many times a day.

- **40-Hour Week**: XP encourages working for 5days X 8 hours.
- **On-Site Customer**: The customer is on the team, available to answer questions full-time.
- **Coding Standards**: Communication is a key value. Adopting coding standards improves communication.

XP Roles and Responsibilities.

The main roles in XP are:

- **Programmers**: The programmer plays a central role in XP as he/she gathers requirements, analyzes them, designs the solution, devises the solution, and tests it. "Actually, if programmers could always make decisions that carefully balanced short-term and long-term priorities, there would be no need for any other technical people on the project besides programmers." (Beck 1999).
- **Customers**: the customer carries the responsibility to stay attached to the development team to keep relaying requirements and tests the system for functionality and usability.
- **Tester**: "Since a lot of testing responsibility lies on the shoulders of the programmers, the role of tester in an XP team is really focused on the customer" (Beck 1999). The tester is responsible for helping the customer to choose and write functional tests, and to help programmers do the test.
- **Tracker**: The tracker is the person who should go back to earlier estimates and give feedback on the project's status.
- **Coach**: The coach is responsible for the process as a whole. He/she has to be aware if people are deviating from the team's process and bring this to the team's attention. The overall mission of the coach is guidance and support not control.

Scrum

Scrum is an agile software methodology that has gained increasing importance both in research and academia. The term Scrum originally is borrowed from rugby, "getting an out of play ball back into the game" (Schwaber and Beedle 2002). (Nonaka and Takeuchi 1986) were the first ones to discuss Scrum methodology and its variants in product development with small teams.

Scrum does not specify any production technique; it rather relies on applying industrial process control on software development. The characteristics of Scrum methodology are (Schwaber and Beedle 2002):

- The only defined phases are the first and last (Planning and Closure), where all processes, inputs and outputs are well defined. The flow is linear, with some iterations in the planning phase.
- The Sprint phase is an empirical process. Many of the processes in the sprint phase are unidentified or uncontrolled. It is treated as a black box that requires external controls. Accordingly, controls, including risk management, are put on each iteration of the Sprint phase to avoid chaos while maximizing flexibility.
- Sprints are nonlinear and flexible. Where available, explicit process knowledge is used; otherwise tacit knowledge and trial and error is used to build process knowledge. Sprints are used to evolve the final product.
- The project is open to the environment until the Closure phase. The deliverable can be changed at any time during the Planning and Sprint phases of the project. The project remains open to environmental complexity, including competitive, time, quality, and financial pressures, throughout these phases.

Figure 3. Scrum lifecycle

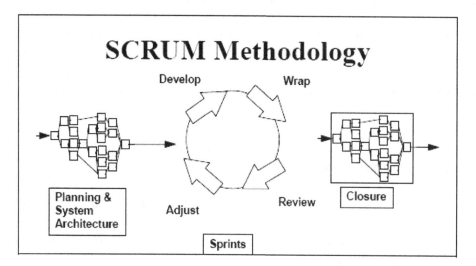

Scrum Lifecycle

Figure 3 shows Scrum lifecycle:

The lifecycle of Scrum has three groups of phases: pregame, game, postgame. In brief these phase groups could be explained as:

The pregame phase, which consists of:

- **Planning**: Definition of a new release based on currently known backlog (product functionality requirement) requirements, along with an estimate of its schedule and cost. How much conceptualization and analysis is made, depends on whether the system is new (deep analysis), or the system is being enhanced (small analysis)
- **Architecture**: Design how the backlog items will be implemented. This phase includes system architecture modification and high level design.

The game phase, which consists of:

- **Development Sprints (release)**: Development of new release functionality, with constant respect to the variables of time, requirements, quality, cost, and com-petition. Interaction with these variables defines the end of this phase. There are multiple, iterative development sprints, or cycles, that are used to evolve the system.

The postgame phase, which consists of:

- **Closure**: Preparation for release, including final documentation, pre-release staged testing, and release.

Scrum Principles and Techniques

In Scrum, the delivered product is flexible. Its content is bound by any project determinants i.e. time, cost, scope, and quality. "The deliverable determinants are market intelligence, customer contact, and the skill of developers" (Schwaber 2004). As flexibility is one of Scrum's values continuous changes to the deliverable content happen in response to environment. The deliverable can be determined anytime during the project. In order to fulfill the flexibility aim, Scrum follows the following principles:

- Small working teams.
- On-the-stand, short meetings.

- Process adaptable to both technical & business changes
- Process yields frequent SW increments
- Development work & people who perform it are partitioned "into clean, low coupling partitions (packets)"
- Constant testing & documentation is performed
- Scrum process provides the "ability to declare a product done whenever required"

Scrum uses the following controls to keep adjustments controllable:

- **Backlog**: Product functionality requirements that are not adequately addressed by the current product release. Bugs, defects, customer requested enhancements, etc. are backlog items.
- **Release/Enhancement**: backlog items that are to be called for at some point of time based on the environment variables.
- **Packets**: Product components or objects that must be changed to implement a backlog item into a new release.
- **Changes**: Changes that must occur to a packet to implement a backlog item.
- **Problems**: Technical problems that occur and must be solved to implement a change.
- **Risks**: risks that affect the success of the project are continuously assessed and responses planned.
- **Solutions**: responses to the risks, which often result in changes.
- **Issues**: Overall project and project issues that are not defined in terms of packets, changes and problems.

Scrum Roles and Responsibilities

Scrum identifies the following roles:

- **Product Owner**: The person who is responsible for creating and prioritizing the Product Backlog i.e. requirements. Based on perceived importance, the product owner chooses what is to be included in every iteration/Sprint, and reviews the system at the end of the Sprint for quality control.
- **Scrum Master**: He is an expert in Scrum and understands the one who knows and reinforces the product iteration and goals and the Scrum values and practices, conducts the daily meeting (the Scrum Meeting) and the iteration demonstration (the Sprint Review), listens to progress, removes impediments (blocks), and provides resources. The Scrum Master is also a Developer (see below) and participates in product development (is not just management).
- **Development Team**: The Scrum Team is committed to achieving a Sprint Goal and has full authority to do whatever it takes to achieve the goal. The size of a Scrum team is seven, plus or minus two.

Crystal

Similar to Scrum Crystal was developed to address the variability and unpredictability of the environment and the specific characteristics of the project (Cockburn 2001). Similar to the other agile methods, Crystal starts with a shallow plan based on existing knowledge about the project. Crystal author Alistair Cockburn feels that the base methodology should be "barely sufficient." He contends, "You need one less notch control than you expect, and less is better when it comes to delivering quickly"(Highsmith and Cockburn 2001).

Actually, Crystal is a family of methodologies depending on the size of the project. According to the team's size there are different "Crystals" ranging from clear to red passing through yellow and orange depending on the size if the project. The most agile version is Crystal Clear, followed by Crystal Yellow, Crystal Orange, and Crystal Red.

Figure 4. Crystal increment lifecycle

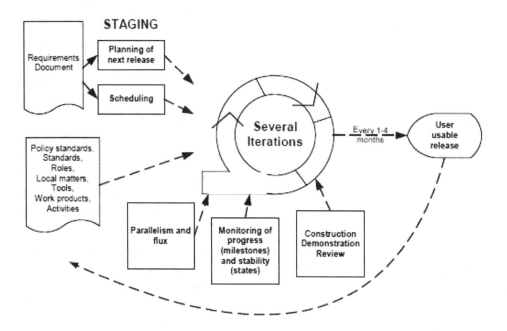

ONE INCREMENT

Crystal Lifecycle

Figure 4 shows Crystal one increment lifecycle.

As seen in the figure, one increment consists of one or more iterations. The process is characterized by: incremental delivery, releases are four months at max, automated testing, direct user involvement, two user reviews per release, and methodology-tuning retrospectives. Progress is tracked by software delivered or major decisions reached, not by documents completed (Williams 2007).

Crystal Principles and Techniques

Crystal methodology relies on several distinguishing features. These are:

- Customizable family of development methodologies for small to very large teams.

- Methodology dependent on size of team and criticality of project
- Emphasis of face-to-face communication
- Consider people, interaction, community, skills, talents, and communication as first-order effects.
- Start with minimal process and build up as absolutely necessary.

Also, there are two important rules methodology. First, incremental cycles must not exceed four months. Second, reflection workshops must be held after every delivery so that the methodology is self-adapting.

Cockburn states in his official website the general principles of the method: "Crystal is a family of human-powered, adaptive, ultralight, "stretch-to-fit" software development methodologies.

- "Human-powered" means that the focus is on achieving project success through enhancing the work of the people involved (other methodologies might be process-centric, or architecture-centric, or tool-centric, but Crystal is people-centric).

- "Ultralight" means that for whatever the project size and priorities, a Crystal-family methodology for the project will work to reduce the paperwork, overhead and bureaucracy to the least that is practical for the parameters of that project.
- "Stretch-to-fit" means that you start with something just smaller than you think you need, and grow it just enough to get it the right size for you (stretching is easier, safer and more efficient than cutting away)."

Crystal is non-jealous, meaning that a Crystal methodology permits substitution of similar elements from other methodologies. (Cockburn 2010)"

Crystal uses several techniques. These are:

- **Staging**: this activity involves panning for the next release, where the team, in collaboration with the customer identifies the requirements to be implemented in the next three to four months.
- **Review and Revision**: Each iteration (construction, demonstration, and review) is reviewed by the team to verify stability and productivity.
- **Monitoring**: Progress of the project is monitored against time, cost, scope, and quality. Milestones are evaluated to check fluctuation in productivity, and to reach stability through the remedying the fluctuation causes.
- **Parallelism and Flux**: Once stability is reached, teams can proceed with maximum parallelism to enhance productivity.
- **Holistic Diversity Strategy**: In Crystal orange, where larger teams exist, cross functional teams are built to diversify expertise in all teams to ensure maximum knowledge sharing.

- **Methodology Tuning Technique**: This technique is central in Crystal as it allows teams through interviews and workshops to identify the best approach towards the project in hand, as there is a different approach for every single case (project).
- **User Viewing**: Two user viewings per release are suggested in Crystal clear and three in Crystal orange.
- **Reflection Workshops**: Pre-increment and post increment reflection workshops are necessary with a recommended mid-increment workshop.

Crystal Roles and Responsibilities

Crystal family includes various roles. These are: project sponsor, business expert, usage expert, technical facilitator, business analyst, project manager, architect, design mentor, lead designer-programmer, designer-programmer, UI designer, reuse point, writer, and tester. These roles are grouped into various teams; these are: System planning Project monitoring, architecture, technology, functions, infrastructure, and external test.

Feature-Driven Development FDD

Feature Driven Development is an agile software development methodology by Jeff De Luca and Peter Code. This methodology got its recognizable name in 1997.

FDD uses small, client-valued functions referred to as features. These features are small building blocks for planning, reporting and progress tracking that lasts between two to three weeks.

The important step is to split the requirements as features, which are then implemented in an extremely iterative manner. The requirements are broken down into features. Features are explained in client-valued functions with a clear syntax.

Figure 5. FDD lifecycle, adapted from Palmer, & Felsing (2002)

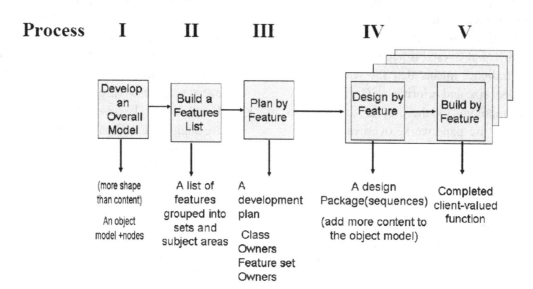

FDD Lifecycle

Figure 5 shows the lifecycle of FDD.

FDD begins with a domain object model that is built with the help of Domain Experts. The knowledge resulting from the modeling activity and other requirement activities, the developers create a features list. Then a tentative plan is built and responsibilities are assigned. Small groups of features are constructed.

In the first phase, domain experts and developers work together under the supervision of an experienced Object modeler known as a chief architect. Domain experts conduct a high-level walkthrough of the scope of the system and its context. Then they perform more detailed walkthroughs of each area of the problem domain. After each walkthrough, developers and domain experts work in small groups to produce object models for the domain area in hand. Each group creates its own model and presents its results for peer review and discussion. One of the proposed models or a mix of two or more models is selected by consensus, which becomes the model for that domain area.

In the second phase, a team headed by the chief Programmers from is formed to decompose the domain functionality. Then the team break the domain into a number of a major feature Sets on the basis of the domain partitioning that is suggested by the domain experts. Each area is then divided into a number of activities. Each step within an activity is identified as a feature resulting in a hierarchically categorized features list.

FDD Principles and Techniques

FDD has a number of practices that supports agility as well as control. The best practices used in FDD are:

- **Domain Object Modeling**: This means constructing class diagrams representing the most significant types of objects within the problem domain and the relationships between them. Here the problem is broken down into the significant objects involved. The design and implementation of each object or class identified in the model is a smaller problem to solve. When the completed classes are combined, they form the solution to the larger problem. "Modeling in Color" is the best technique for Domain Object Modeling. This technique depends on creating ordinary UML classes but it adds color definition to the classes. The colors are yellow (representing roles), blue (representing a catalogue-like description), green (representing places or things), and pink (representing a moment of time representing a process).

- **Developing by Feature**: Any function, whose implementation will take more than two weeks, is decomposed into smaller functions, so that the resulting function is implementable in two weeks. In a business system, a feature represents a step in some activity within a business process. A feature is a small, client valued function that can be implemented in two weeks. The feature naming template is: <action>the <result><by|for |of | to|><a(n)><object>

- **Class (Code) Ownership**: Class code ownership in a development process denotes who (person or role) is ultimately responsible for the contents of a class (piece of code). FDD uses individual ownership i.e. developers are assigned ownership of a set of classes from the domain object model.

- **Feature Team**: The implementation of a feature may involve more than one class, which means the need for more than one Class Owner. Thus the feature Owner is supposed to have a team lead job, in which he coordinates the efforts of multiple developers. Similar to the feature itself, the feature team is small in nature. This team owns all the code needed to change for that feature, there is no need to wait for other teams to change code, which in fact leads to collective ownership.

- **Inspections**: A design inspection with the feature team members and/or with other project members is held on regular basis to ensure quality. The decision to inspect within

the feature team or with other project team members is that of the Chief Programmer. On acceptance a to-do list is generated per affected class, and each team member adds their tasks to their calendar task list. The Chief Programmer must also merge changes from the shared Feature Team Area into the change control system.

- **Regular Build Schedule**: To ensure maximum integration, all the source code, along with the libraries and components on which it depends for the completed features, is taken at regular periods, and the complete system is build. This ensures that there is always a demonstrable system available.

- **Configuration Management**: This helps in identifying the latest versions of completed source code files and provides historical tracking of all information artifacts in the project.

- **Progress Reporting**: Throughout the project, the team performs frequent, appropriate, and accurate progress reporting at all levels, inside and outside the project, based on completed work is done, to ensure tracking and adherence to the plan.

FDD Roles and Responsibility

FDD identifies six key roles and implies a number of others.

- **Project Manager**: he/she is the administrative head of the project, who is responsible for reporting progress, managing budgets, HR management, and managing equipment, space, and resources, etc.

- **Chief Architect**: he/she has the responsibility for the overall design of the system. He/she is responsible for heading the workshop design sessions where the team collaborates in the design of the system. The work requires both excellent technical and modeling skills as well as good facilitation skills to run the workshops.

- **Development Manager**: He/she has the technical expertise to lead the day-to-day development activities. He/she is also responsible for resolving everyday conflicts for resources when the Chief Programmers cannot do it between themselves.
- **Chief Programmers**: These are experienced developers. They participate in the high-level requirements analysis and design activities of the project and are responsible for leading small teams of three to six developers through more detailed analysis, design and development of the new software's features.
- **Class Owners**: These are developers who work as members of small development teams lead by chief programmer to design, code, test, and document the features required by the new software system.
- **Domain Experts**: These are business people to whom the problem belong. These could be users, customers, business analysts, or any mix of these. They provide the knowledge needed by the developers to understand the system and develop it. Their knowledge and participation are extremely significant to the successful delivery of the system.

Along with these roles there are other supporting roles that could be summarized as follows:

- **Release Manager**: He/she is the one who is in contact with chief programmers tom make sure they report progress each week, and reports progress to the project manager.
- **Language Guru**: He/she is a person who is responsible for knowing a programming language or a specific technology inside out. In projects where a programming language or technology is used for the first time, then this role is special.

- **Build Engineer**: He/she is responsible for setting up, maintaining, and running the regular build process.
- **Tool-Smith**: He/she creates small development tools for the development team, test team, and data conversion team.
- **System Administrator**: He/she configures, manages, and troubleshoots any servers and network of workstations specific to the project team.
- **Tester**: He/she is responsible for independent verification of the system's functions to check whether requirements have been fulfilled correctly.
- **Deployers**: He/she converts existing data to the new formats required by the new system and work on the physical deployment of new releases of the system.
- **Technical Writer**: He/she writes and maintains user documentation.

Adaptive Software Development ASD

Adaptive Software Development (ASD) is an agile method developed by James A. Highsmith that offers an adaptive approach to dynamic and high-changing software projects (Highsmith 2002). Highsmith starts from the premises that it is not possible to plan successfully in a fast moving and unpredictable business environment. Hence, ASD replaces the static plan-design life cycle by a more adaptive, flexible, and dynamic speculate-collaborate-learn life cycle.

Due to the unpredictability of software projects, Highsmith sees planning as something hard to do in an adaptive environment. In contrast to traditional planning where things have to be done according to a rigid plan, adaptive environment sees deviations as a guide towards the correct solution.

ASD is results and quality oriented rather than process and activates. And to do so, ASD focuses on collaboration amongst project stakeholders to make up for the planning problems. Management

Figure 6. ASD lifecycle, adapted from Highsmith (2000)

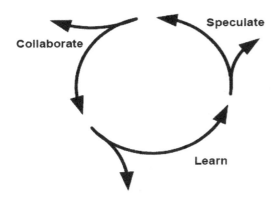

is about facilitating communication among people rather than directing people of what they should do.

ASD Lifecycle

ASD's lifecycle consists of three non-linear, overlapping phases as shown in figure 6.

During Speculate phase, the aim is to define the project mission and to clarify the unclear parts of the system. During the Collaborate phase, the importance of teamwork for developing high-change systems is highlighted. Finally, the Learn phase stresses the need to discover and react to mistakes, and that requirements may well change during development.

Figure 7 shows the detailed lifecycle of ASD.

ASD Principles and Techniques

ASD builds upon several principles and techniques; these are:

- **Mission Driven**: all activities in each iteration must be tailored to fit the overall mission of the project. The mission itself could be modified as the project proceeds.
- **Component-Based**: development activities do not focus on tasks but on results and hence on working software.
- **Iterative**: as the software development is characterized with turbulence, there will be no specific planning, but a series of iterations that result in a working software.
- **Time-Boxed**: Fixing deadlines will lead the developers to make the tradeoff decisions early in the project and will lead to more realistic approach in development.
- **Change-Tolerant**: Change is one constant characteristic of software development. This

Figure 7. ASD lifecycle, adapted from Highsmith (2000)

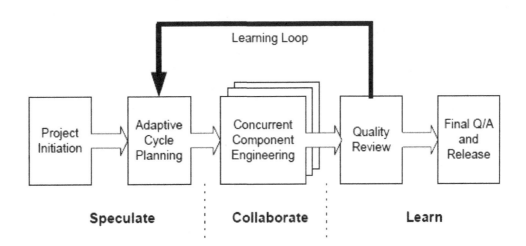

leads the developers to continuously evaluate the software, verify it against requirements, and do the adjustments accordingly.

- **Risk Driven**: Software development is characterized with risks, so risks are evaluated as early as possible and plans to mitigate them is developed.

ASD Roles and Responsibilities

ASD does not specify many roles as it opposes detailed planning that defines who does what. However, it specifies few roles; these are:

- **Executive Sponsor**: A person who claims the overall responsibility of the system.
- **Facilitator**: A person who is entitled to coordinate discussions sessions.
- **Developers**: The people who carries out development process.

DSDM

DSDM came into existence in 1994 and since then it has become the number one framework for rapid application development in the UK (Stapleton 1997). DSDM is a non-profit and nonproprietary framework for RAD development, maintained by the DSDM Consortium. The developers of the method maintain that in addition to serving as a method in the generally accepted sense DSDM also provides a framework of controls for RAD, supplemented with guidance on how to efficiently use those controls, which were borrowed from PRINCE2 management methodology. DSDM is recommended to be applied with PRINCE2 (DSDM consortium 2010).

Similar to ASD, DSDM uses time boxing concept, as it emphasizes fixing deadlines and resources and crafting the plan accordingly.

DSDM Lifecycle

DSDM has five phases shown in figure 8. These phases are: feasibility study, business study, functional model iteration, design and build iteration, and implementation The first two phases are sequential and done only once per project. The other three phases are iterative and incremental and they contain the real production of software. DSDM implements iterations through time-boxing the production process, where each time-box last usually for few weeks at max.

During feasibility study phase, stakeholders checks whether DSDM is applicable to the project in hand.

In the business study phase, features of the business and technology are analyzed. DSDM suggest holding workshops, where a sufficient number of the customer's experts are gathered to be able to consider all relevant facets of the system, and to be able to agree on development priorities.

In the functional model iteration phase, the contents and approach for the iteration are planned, the iteration gone through, and the results analyzed for further iterations. Both analysis and coding are done, prototypes are built, and the lessons learnt from them are used in improving the analysis models. The prototypes are not to be entirely removed, but improved gradually to get to the quality that is required in the final system.

In the design and build iteration phase, the real construction of the system occurs. The output of this phase is a Tested System that meets at least the minimum agreed set of requirements. Design and build are iterative, and the design and functional prototypes are reviewed by the users, and further development is based on the users' comments.

The final phase is the implementation phase where the system is deployed into its actual operational environment, where users are trained, and the system goes into real functioning.

Figure 8. DSDM lifecycle, adapted from Stapelton (1997)

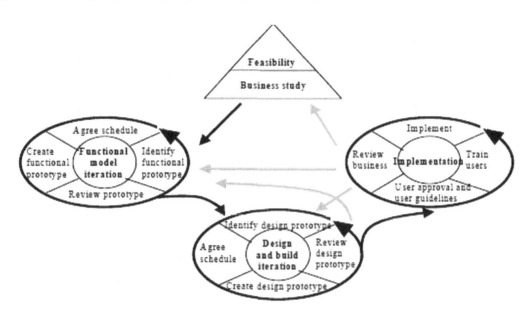

DSDM Principles and Techniques

DSDM official website defines several principles and techniques. These are:

- **Active user involvement is imperative**: A few experienced users have to be present throughout the development of the system to ensure timely and accurate feedback.
- **DSDM teams must be empowered to make decisions**: The users and developers must have the knowledge and experience make decisions.
- **The focus is on frequent delivery of products**: Similar to all other agile methods, the development process is incremental and the delivery cycle is short so that users can provide accurate feedback in a timely manner.
- **Fitness for business purpose is the essential criterion for acceptance of deliverables**: "Build the right product before you build it right". This is similar to XP's refac-

toring principle, where the focus is on effectiveness of the code and then efficiency.

- **Iterative and incremental development is necessary to converge on an accurate business solution**: In software engineering industry, system requirements usually change over the project life and hence, letting systems evolve through iterative, incremental process, errors can be detected and corrected early.
- **All changes during development are reversible**: In the course of development, a wrong path may easily be taken. By using short iterations and ensuring that previous states in development can be reverted to, the wrong path can safely be corrected.
- **Requirements are baselined at a high level**: Requirements should only be specified at a high level, so that detailed requirements are changed as needed. This ensures that essential requirements are captured at an early stage, and details are left until later stages so that changes are adopted in a straight forward manner.

- **Testing is integrated throughout the life-cycle**: Every system component should be tested by the developers and ambassador as soon as they are developed. The way development is incremental, so is testing. Regression testing is particularly emphasized because of the evolutionary development style.

A collaborative and cooperative approach shared by all stakeholders is essential: In order for the DSDM to succeed, all stakeholders must have high commitment to the project, and intensive collaboration must be there.

DSDM Roles and Responsibilities

DSDM defines several roles and responsibilities. These include the following:

- **Project Board**: The Project Board is not specifically required by DSDM, but it sits comfortably within the DSDM project framework. The Project Board consists of two roles: Executive and Senior User
- **The Project Manager**: He/she is responsible for the successful delivery of the agreed products, to the agreed standard of quality, on time and within budget, and capable of delivering the benefits stated in the PID. The Project Manager may come from IT or the user community, and reports to the Project Board.
- **Senior developers** are experienced developers who have technical and leadership expertise. These senior developers lead other developers in the project.
- **Technical coordinator**: He/she is the one who defines the system architecture and who holds responsibility for the technical quality of the system.
- **Ambassador user**: is an experienced user who stays with the project team while production. He/she has the responsibility for

conveying customers' knowledge to the developers and for having an eye of the overall quality of the system.
- **Visionary**: He/she is the user who has the most accurate perception of the business objectives of the system and the project. The Visionary is could be also the one who initiated the idea of the required system.
- **Executive Sponsor**: is the person from the user organization who has the related financial authority and responsibility. The Executive Sponsor therefore has ultimate power in making decisions
- **Team Manager**: This individual is responsible for ensuring that the development team meets its objectives by delivering the required system.
- **Project Support**: An organization may establish a Project support Office to provide administrative support to the Project Manager, either because of the volume of work or to assist in the use of particular tools in the project (for example project management or configuration management tools). This could include providing the scribe and facilitator roles required by DSDM projects.
- **Project Assurance**: In DSDM projects, the Project Assurance Team may be redundant because of the far closer relationship and involvement of the business and users and the increased visibility offered by frequent deliverables. DSDM projects are often carried out to a fixed budget and decisions are always based on the business benefit. The project assurance needs in DSDM projects can be effectively fulfilled by the Ambassador User and Technical Coordinator.

CONCLUSION

In this chapter we identified the main features of agile methods. The main features were flexibility, readiness for change, collaboration with customers, self-organizing, and nimbleness.

We also identified the most well known agile methods, specifying their practices, techniques, roles, and processes. We could figure out the most common features amongst these as:

- Customer collaboration is a must. The roles: ambassador users, on-site customers, and expert users appear almost in all methods.
- Integrated, ongoing testing.
- Lightweight documentation.
- Incremental and iterative development.

One notice we found, is that despite ample literature found on agile methods there is no agile body of knowledge, which can be very helpful for industrialists and researchers.

Another issue about agile methods and business intelligence is that there is few work on the integration of the two. That is, applying agile methods in business intelligence projects. An example of the two is the work of (Alnoukari, 2008) that could use ASD in data mining projects and identified some suitability of Agile methods in the context of business intelligence. These are:

- Agile methods focus on intensive communication with customers to get the "right" list of requirements, something that is really required by business intelligence projects.
- Business intelligence projects require the delivery of unstructured reports and queries, and this again is supplied by agile methods' principle of embracing change.

REFERENCES

Abrahamsson, P., Salo, O., Ronkainen, J., & Warsta, J. (2002). Agile software development methods: Review and analysis. *VVT Publications, 478*, 7–94.

Abrahamsson, P., Warsta, J., Siponen, T. M., & Ronkainen, J. (2003). New directions on Agile methods: A comparative analysis. In ICSE '03: *Proceedings of the 25th International Conference on Software Engineering*, Washington, DC., USA (pp. 244– 254). IEEE Computer Society.

Ambler, S. (2005). Quality in an agile world. *Software Quality Professional, 7*(4), 34–40.

Bass, L. (2006). Designing software architecture to achieve quality attribute requirements. In *Proceedings of the 3rd IFIP Summer School on Software Technology and Engineering,* South Africa (pp. 1-29).

Beck, K. (2000). *Extreme programming explained: Embrace change.* Boston, MA: Addison-Wesley.

Begel, A., & Nagappan, N. (2007). Usage and perceptions of Agile software development in an industrial context: An exploratory study. *Proceedings of the 1st International Symposium on Empirical Software Engineering and Measurement, ESEM 2007*, Madrid, Spain.

Berki, E. (2006). Examining the quality of evaluation frameworks and metamodeling paradigms of Information Systems development methodologies. In Duggan, E., & Reichgelt, H. (Eds.), *Measuring Information Systems delivery quality*. Hershey, PA: Idea Group Publishing. doi:10.4018/978-1-59140-857-4.ch012

Highsmith, J. (2002). *Agile software development ecosystems.* Boston, MA: Addison-Wesley.

Highsmith, J., & Cockburn, A. (2001). *The business of innovation.* IEEE Computer.

Huo, M. Verner, J. Zhu, L. & Babar, M. (2004). MA Computer Software and Applications Conference, 2004. COMPSAC 2004. *Proceedings of the 28th Annual International.*

Manninen, A., & Berki, E. (2004). Coordinating the quality of requirements change and organisational communication. An evaluation framework for requirements management tools. In Edgar-Neville, D. Ross, M. & Staples, G. (Eds), the *Proceedings of New Approaches to Software Quality. Software Quality Management XII*. University of KENT at Canterbury, British Computer Society.

McBreen, P. (2003). *Quality assurance and testing in agile projects*. McBreen Consulting. Retrieved on January 12, 2006, from http:// www.mcbreen. ab.ca/ talks/ CAMUG.pdf

Mnkandla, E., & Dwolatzky, B. (2004). Balancing the human and the engineering factors in software development. In the *Proceedings of the IEEE AFRICON 2004 Conference*. Gaborone, Bostwana (pp. 1207-1210).

Monochristou, V., & Vlachopoulou, M. (2007). Agile software development quality assurance, 4, 71-90. Hershey, PA: Idea Group.

Newkirk, J. (2002). *Introduction to Agile processes and extreme programming*. Reading, MA: Addison-Wesley.

Nonaka, I., & Takeuchi, H. (1995). *The knowledge-creating company*. New York, NY: Oxford University Press.

Royce, W. (1970). Managing the development of large software systems. In *The Proceedings of IEEE WESCON* (pp. 1-9).

Schwaber, K. (2004). *SCRUM development process*. Retrieved on January, 2004, from http:// jeffsutherland.com/ oopsla/ schwapub.pdf

Schwaber, K., & Beedle, M. (2001). *Agile software development with Scrum*. Upper Saddle River, NJ: Prentice Hall.

Stapleton, J. (1997). *DSDM-Dynamic systems development method*. Boston, MA: Addison Wesley.

Williams, L. (2007). *A survey of Agile development methodologies*. Retrieved from agile.csc.ncsu.edu/ SEMaterials/ AgileMethods.pdf.

KEY TERMS AND DEFINITIONS

Agile Software Development Methods: A set of software processes that are characterized by creativity, flexibility, adaptability, responsiveness, and human-centricity. It focuses on communication among the development team and with customers, less documentation, and embrace for change.

Acceptance Testing: A final test that is done on the finished system, usually involving the users, sponsors, customer, etc.

Continuous Integration: Code is integrated and tested after a few hours-a day of development at most. This allows for early error-detection.

On-Site Customers: A customer, who is a member of the development team, will be responsible for clarifying requirements and will give immediate feedback to the development team.

Pair Programming: Two developers work together in turns on one PC, Bugs are identified as they occur, Hence the product is of a higher quality. The two work as a small team, one thinks strategically and the other thinks tactically. The two can exchange roles.

Pair Swapping: Pairs change on an ad hoc manner allowing for more knowledge sharing and hence better quality resulting from exchange of ideas and better communication.

Refactoring: Allows developers to reach the required functionality first and then look for a better "look" for the code. That is, after the functionality is gotten, small changes to code are introduced to the code so that behavior is not affected, Resulting code is of higher quality.

Test-Driven Development: Implies that automated tests are designed before coding commences. Design a test, write the code, run the test, make changes until the test passes.

Chapter 3
Knowledge Management in Agile Methods Context:
What Type of Knowledge Is Used by Agilests?

Zaidoun Alzoabi
Martin Luther University, Germany

ABSTRACT

Agile methods are characterized with flexibility, reliance on tacit knowledge, and face to face communication in contrast to traditional methods that rely on explicit knowledge sharing mechanism, extensive documentation, and formal means of communication. In this chapter, the authors will have a look at the knowledge management techniques used in different software development processes with focus on agile methods. Then they will test the claim of more informal knowledge sharing and see the mechanisms used to exchange and document knowledge. The test is on the basis of a survey conducted by Scott Ambler in 2009, where he surveyed over 300 agile practitioners asking them about mechanisms used and in which context every mechanism is applied.

DOI: 10.4018/978-1-61350-050-7.ch003

INTRODUCTION

Knowledge management (KM) is often confused with business intelligence (BI). According to a survey by OTR consultancy, 60 percent of consultants did not understand the difference between the two (Herschel and Jones, 2005). Gartner consultancy clarifies this by explaining BI as set of all technologies that gather and analyze data to improve decision making. In BI, intelligence is often defined as the discovery and explanation of hidden, inherent and decision-relevant contexts in large amounts of business and economic data. On the other hand KM is described as a systematic process of finding, selecting, organizing, presenting and sharing knowledge in a way that improves organizations' comprehension in a specific area of interest. KM helps an organization to gain insight and understanding from its own experience. This means that BI in its own is one of the tools that help organizations in extracting and presenting more knowledge with the help of IT in order to enhance its competitive position in the market.

(Nonaka and Takeuchi 1995) define knowledge as "justified true belief" which is subjective, difficult to codify, context-related, rooted in action, relational, and is about meaning. This differs from information as the later is objective and codified in many explicit forms such as documents, computer databases, images and the like (Wiig 1997). Knowledge is usually identified to have two types: tacit and explicit [Nonaka and Takeuchi 1995]. Tacit knowledge is personal, context-specific, and resides in human beings minds, and is therefore difficult to formalize, codify and communicate. It is personal knowledge that is embedded in individual experience and involves intangible factors such as personal belief, perspective, and value system. Tacit knowledge is difficult to communicate and share in the organization and must thus be converted into words or forms of explicit knowledge. On the other hand, explicit knowledge is knowledge that is transmittable in formal, systematic languages. It can be articulated

in formal languages, including grammatical statements, mathematical expressions, specifications, manuals and so forth. It can be transmitted across individuals formally and easily.

Between these two types, four transitions might occur:

- Tacit to tacit (socialization): the process of sharing experiences and thereby creating new tacit knowledge, such as shared mental models and technical skills.
- Tacit to explicit (externalization): the process of articulating tacit knowledge into explicit concepts.
- Explicit to explicit (combination): the process of systematizing concepts into a knowledge system, i.e. combining different bodies of explicit knowledge.
- Explicit to tacit (internalization): the process that is closely related to "learning by doing" in which a person tries to incorporate others explicit knowledge and hence transforms it into own tacit knowledge without the need to relive the experience.

Figure 1 shows the four modes transitions of knowledge

In this chapter we will present the knowledge management methodologies used by agilests. We do not focus on the knowledge provided by the BI applications, but with the knowledge management techniques used by agilests in order to build BI applications. This is very important as building business intelligence applications depends on extracting as much knowledge as possible from owners, users, developers, and managers in order to achieve effectiveness and efficiency.

Agile methods have more focus on tacit knowledge rather than explicit. In this chapter we will test that empirically through a survey that was conducted on a sample of Agile software practitioners. The survey was conducted by Scott Ambler and the data is published on www.ambysoft.com. This survey was performed the last week of July

Figure 1. Four modes transitions of knowledge, adapted from Nonaka and Takeuchi (1995)

	Tacit Knowledge	**To**	Explicit knowledge
Tacit Knowledge	(Socialisation) Sympathized Knowledge		(Externalization) Conceptual Knowledge
From			
Explicit knowledge	(Internalization) Operational Knowledge		(Combination) Systemic Knowledge

2008 and there were 337 respondents. The survey was announced on the Extreme Programming (XP), Test-Driven Development (TDD), Scrum Development, Agile Modeling, and Agile Databases mailing lists. The goal was to find out what agile developers were actually doing to compare it with what's being talked about.

We have tried our own survey and distributed it to the same group of participants, but got a very low response rate, something that Scott Ambler himself suffered from. This low response rate is may be due to boredom of Agile community being surveyed quite frequently. This has led us to use the same questionnaire used by Scott Ambler who allows the use of his raw data (www. ambysoft.com).

This of course has led to difficulty in the process of operationalization of the theoretical framework. We will explain how we tackled these problems later in this chapter.

THE SURVEY DESIGN

(Stroh 2000) says that a questionnaire is used to explore a large number of people's views. Hence, we used this method to gain general picture of

factors relating to knowledge sharing techniques used by Agile methods adopters affecting the quality of software developed using agile methods in general. Statistically, it is believed that large sample size of questionnaires is designed for un-biased statistical results, which can be implied for the whole population (Miller et al., 2002). (Harris and Schaubroeck 1990) recommend a minimum sample size of 200 to guarantee robust structural equation modeling.

The data for this research was collected from different groups, all of which are listed on an agile-related group. These are Extreme Programming (XP), Test-Driven Development (TDD), Scrum Development, Agile Modeling, and Agile Databases. These groups have over 3000 members, making it an appealing population to test the hypotheses of the research.

The email-based questionnaire has several advantages. These are:

- High anonymity
- Email-based questionnaires can reach the respondents anywhere they are. This is of extreme importance to us as-according to the best of our knowledge- there are no Agile developers in the region.
- The respondent has ample time to respond and has even the ability to clarify some ambiguous concepts.
- There is high confidence in the data quality, as there is no need for a process of data entry.
- However, it has some disadvantages too:
- Response rate is low.
- Respondents cannot clarify questions.

A word of notification is very important, as the scale used in the survey is heterogeneous in the sense that some are 5-scale and others are 7-scale questions. Hence, we had to recompute some of the variables to unify the scale. The unified scale is Likert 5-points where responses were given the values 1 to 5 and 1 is the lowest and f is the highest, whether 5 means common or strongly agree. The " I don't know " response was given the value zero so that it does not affect results.

In the following sections, we will describe the theoretical framework, the process of operationalizing the framework of the hypotheses through the questionnaire, and then we conclude with the findings of the survey.

Hypothesis and Conceptual Model

It is obvious that a "good" software development method is the one that maximizes knowledge exchanged among all stakeholders, that software quality requires concentration on both tacit and explicit knowledge, and that the phase of the project and the type of the knowledge sharing stakeholders, imply the focus of the type of knowledge. That is, more explicit knowledge is needed when talking to customers especially during the requirements gathering phase. On the other hand more tacit knowledge sharing is required among developers especially during the production phase of the project.

Our hypotheses could be based on the following statements:

- Knowledge, both tacit and explicit, sharing enhances software quality.
- Explicit knowledge sharing enhances software quality
- Tacit knowledge sharing enhances software quality.
- The need for tacit and explicit knowledge sharing differs according to the knowledge recipient. That is, the knowledge recipient could be a development teammate or a business stakeholder, and every one of them requires different knowledge sharing technique.
- There is a difference in evaluating explicit knowledge among different types of stakeholders in software engineering projects developed using Agile methods.

- The size of the organization has an effect on the knowledge sharing techniques used.
- The experience of the developer has an effect on the knowledge sharing methods used.
- The experience in Agile development methodologies has an effect on the knowledge sharing techniques used.
- The type of media has an effect on the software quality.

These statements arise from the following questions:

- Does software quality rely on the amount of knowledge exchanged?
- Is there a need for different knowledge sharing techniques when communicating with customers and development teammates?
- Does the role played by the project stakeholder have any effect on the use of knowledge sharing techniques?
- Do we need more explicit knowledge in bigger organizations?
- Do less experienced developers use more tacit knowledge sharing techniques?
- Do less experienced Agile organizations use more tacit knowledge sharing techniques?
- Does type of media used in the knowledge sharing has an effect on the software quality?

The theoretical framework is show in Figure 2.

Variables Definitions

In the following we explain the variables used:

- Explicit knowledge sharing: the use of explicit type of knowledge, such as documents, charts and the like.

Figure 2. Common management practices

7. For each of the following management practices, please indicate how commonly they are practiced on your agile software development projects.	Very Common	Common	Sometimes	Not Common	Very Uncommon	Never	Don't Know	Response Count
Burndown Chart	41.8% (102)	17.2% (42)	14.8% (36)	4.9% (12)	5.7% (14)	12.3% (30)	3.3% (8)	244
Daily Scrum Meeting	63.5% (155)	16.4% (40)	9.4% (23)	4.5% (11)	2.5% (6)	3.3% (8)	0.4% (1)	244
High-Level Release Planning	29.5% (72)	31.6% (77)	26.2% (64)	7.0% (17)	2.0% (5)	2.9% (7)	0.8% (2)	244
Iteration/Sprint Planning	57.8% (141)	25.4% (62)	9.8% (24)	3.7% (9)	0.0% (0)	2.0% (5)	1.2% (3)	244
Prioritized Worklist	44.7% (109)	32.8% (80)	12.7% (31)	5.7% (14)	1.6% (4)	0.8% (2)	1.6% (4)	244
One Product Owner/Customer	27.0% (66)	25.8% (63)	24.2% (59)	10.2% (25)	8.6% (21)	1.6% (4)	2.5% (6)	244
Produce Potentially Shippable Software Each Iteration/Sprint	25.4% (62)	26.6% (65)	25.8% (63)	12.7% (31)	6.1% (15)	2.0% (5)	1.2% (3)	244
Retrospectives	36.5% (89)	24.6% (60)	16.4% (40)	8.6% (21)	8.2% (20)	3.7% (9)	2.0% (5)	244
Status Reports	21.3% (52)	26.2% (64)	23.8% (58)	13.9% (34)	3.7% (9)	5.7% (14)	5.3% (13)	244
Story Board with Task Breakdowns	29.5% (72)	18.4% (45)	20.5% (50)	13.5% (33)	8.6% (21)	8.2% (20)	1.2% (3)	244
							answered question	244
							skipped question	93

- Tacit knowledge sharing: the use of informal communication techniques to share knowledge, such as face –to-face communication
- Explicit knowledge sharing techniques with business stakeholder (BIZ.E): use of explicit knowledge sharing techniques with business stakeholders
- Tacit knowledge sharing techniques within teammates (TE.E): use of explicit knowledge sharing techniques with teammates.
- Tacit knowledge sharing techniques with business stakeholder BIZ.T: use of tacit knowledge sharing techniques with business stakeholders
- Tacit knowledge sharing techniques within teammates (TE.T): use of tacit knowledge sharing techniques with teammates.
- Explicit knowledge sharing: general use of explicit knowledge sharing techniques.
- Tacit knowledge sharing: general use of tacit knowledge sharing techniques.
- Software quality (SQ): the degree to which the software product satisfies customers' requirements and achieves technical excellence.

Our hypotheses are demonstrated as follows:

H10: There is no relation between software quality and the amount of tacit knowledge sharing used.

- ○ H11: There is a positive relation between software quality and the amount of tacit knowledge sharing used.
- H20: There is no relation between software quality and the amount of tacit knowledge sharing used within the team.
- ○ H21: There is a positive relation between software quality and the amount of tacit knowledge sharing used within the team.
- H30: There is no relation between software quality and the amount of explicit knowledge sharing used.
- ○ H31: There is a positive relation between software quality and the amount of explicit knowledge sharing used.
- H40: There is no relation between software quality and the amount of explicit knowledge sharing used within the team.
- ○ H41: There is a positive relation between software quality and the amount of explicit knowledge sharing used within the team.
- H50: There is no relation between software quality and the amount of explicit knowledge sharing used with business stakeholders.
- ○ H51: There is a positive relation between software quality and the amount of explicit knowledge sharing used with business stakeholders.
- H60: There is no relation between software quality and the amount of tacit knowledge sharing used with business stakeholders.
- ○ H61: There is a positive relation between software quality and the amount of tacit knowledge sharing used with business stakeholders.
- H70: The size of organizations has no effect on the relation between software quality and the application of different knowledge sharing techniques.

- ○ H71: The size of organizations has an effect on the relation between software quality and the application of different knowledge sharing techniques.
- H80: Agile experience of the organization has no effect on the relation between software quality and the application of different knowledge sharing techniques.
- ○ H81: Agile experience of the organization has an effect on the relation between software quality and the application of different knowledge sharing techniques.
- H90: IT experience of the team has no effect on the relation between software quality and the application of different knowledge sharing techniques.
- ○ H91: IT experience of the team has an effect on the relation between software quality and the application of different knowledge sharing techniques.
- H10 0: the stakeholder type has no effect on the relation between software quality and the application of different knowledge sharing techniques.
- ○ H10 1: the stakeholder type has an effect on the relation between software quality and the application of different knowledge sharing techniques.
- H11 0: the stakeholders' collocation has no effect on the relation between software quality and the application of different knowledge sharing techniques.
- ○ H11 1: the stakeholders' collocation has an effect on the relation between software quality and the application of different knowledge sharing techniques.

Operational Definitions

Operationalization of concepts is necessary to measure them. However, observing human behavior, attitude, and reactions could be time consuming and laborious. Hence, the best way could be by asking people to report about their behaviors, beliefs, thoughts, and attitudes. Operationalization could be done through questionnaires due to its effectiveness and efficiency. As we discussed earlier, the survey was conducted by Scott Ambler and contained over 65 questions testing all practices in Agile methods. However we included practices that are relevant to knowledge sharing and excluded those which we think are not. The following are the questions of the questionnaire we did include in the analysis:

1. Which best describes your current position- (this describes the position of the individual in the company he/she works for)?
2. How many years of experience in IT do you have?
3. What is the total number of people in your organization?
4. Where are you based?
5. Which sector is your organization primarily in?
6. How many years has your organization been doing agile?
7. How commonly do you use Burndown chart on your agile software development projects?
8. How commonly do you use Daily Scrum Meeting chart on your agile software development projects?
9. How commonly do you use High-level release planning on your agile software development projects?
10. How commonly do you use Iteration/Sprint planning on your agile software development projects?
11. How commonly do you use Prioritized worklist on your agile software development projects?

12. How commonly do you use Status report on your agile software development projects?
13. How commonly do you use Story board with Task breakdowns on your agile software development projects?
14. How commonly do you use Collective code ownership on your agile software development projects?
15. How commonly do you use Follow coding standards on your agile software development projects?
16. How commonly do you use Follow database standards on your agile software development projects?
17. How commonly do you use Follow User interface standards on your agile software development projects?
18. How commonly do you use Pair programming on your agile software development projects?
19. How commonly do you use Automated acceptance testing on your agile software development projects?
20. How commonly do you use Continuous Integration on your agile software development projects?
21. How commonly do you use active stakeholder participation on your agile software development projects?
22. How commonly do you use Documentation treated as a requirement on your agile software development projects?
23. How commonly do you use Executable specifications on your agile software development projects?
24. How commonly do you use Initial Architecture Envisioning on your agile software development projects?
25. How commonly do you use Initial Requirements Envisioning on your agile software development projects?
26. How commonly do you use JIT model storming on your agile software development projects?

27. Our highest priority is to satisfy the customer through early and continuous delivery of valuable software.

28. Our agile project teams welcome new or changing requirements, even "just before delivery".

29. Project stakeholders work closely with our agile teams and are readily available.

30. Our agile teams give continuous attention to technical excellence and good design.

31. We do some initial requirements modeling at the beginning of agile projects for scoping and planning purposes.

32. We do some initial architecture modeling at the beginning of agile projects to get going in the right technical direction.

33. At regular intervals our agile teams demonstrate potentially shippable software to their stakeholders.

34. At regular intervals the team reflects on how to become more effective in future iterations/sprints.

35. How much effective it is to use Face to Face (F2F) communication for conveying information within the team?

36. How much effective it is to use Face to Face (F2F) at a whiteboard for conveying information within the team?

37. How much effective it is to use detailed documentation for conveying information within the team?

38. How much effective it is to use overview documentation for conveying information within the team?

39. How much effective it is to use overview diagrams for conveying information within the team?

40. How much effective it is to use online chat for conveying information within the team?

41. How much effective it is to use teleconference calls for conveying information within the team?

42. How much effective it is to use videoconferencing for conveying information within the team?

43. How much effective it is to use face to face (F2F) communication for conveying information within our stakeholders?

44. How much effective it is to use face to face (F2F) whiteboard for conveying information within our stakeholders?

45. How much effective it is to use detailed documentation for conveying information within our stakeholders?

46. How much effective it is to use e-mail for conveying information within our stakeholders?

47. How much effective it is to use overview documentation for conveying information within our stakeholders?

48. How much effective it is to use overview diagrams for conveying information within our stakeholders?

49. How much effective it is to use online chat for conveying information within our stakeholders?

50. How much effective it is to use teleconference calls for conveying information within our stakeholders?

51. How much effective it is to use video conferencing for conveying information within our stakeholders?

We excluded from our analysis the questions we thought irrelevant to our discussions or have no real distinguishing between tacit and explicit knowledge. Table 1 shows these questions and the reason behind their exclusion:

Following Figure 2 we can see that the dependent variable is software quality. According to Juran -the quality legend-, quality is fitness for use, which means the following two things: first, quality consists of those product features that meet the needs of the customers and thereby provide product satisfaction. second Quality consists of freedom from deficiencies" (Juran and Gryna 1988). To measure software quality we follow the

Table 1. Excluded questions from the survey

Question	Exclusion reason
We build agile teams around motivated individuals.	No knowledge sharing is emphasized
Our agile teams are provided with the environment and support that they need to succeed.	No knowledge sharing is emphasized
Our agile teams are trusted to get the job done.	No knowledge sharing is emphasized
Our agile teams are self-organizing.	No knowledge sharing is emphasized
Our agile teams are allowed to work at a sustainable pace.	No knowledge sharing is emphasized
Simplicity, the art of maximizing the amount of work not done, works well in practice for our agile teams	No knowledge sharing is emphasized
Our agile teams identify what "done" means at the beginning of each iteration/sprint	No distinction between tacit or explicit form
Our agile teams only take credit for work that is actually "done" at the end of each iteration/sprint.	No knowledge sharing is emphasized
Our agile teams have an understanding of the correct balance of documentation or other artifacts for delivery	Is not a practice of knowledge sharing
The team actually adjusts its behavior in the next iteration/sprint by focusing on the highest priority item(s).	No knowledge sharing is emphasized

major trend in the software industry that quality is satisfaction of customers through fulfilling their needs and providing them with zero defect products.

The following questions measure this variable:

- Our highest priority is to satisfy the customer through early and continuous delivery of valuable software.
- Our agile project teams welcome new or changing requirements, even "just before delivery".
- Our agile teams give continuous attention to technical excellence and good design.
- At regular intervals our agile teams demonstrate potentially shippable software to their stakeholders.
- At regular intervals the team reflects on how to become more effective in future iterations/sprints.

We have distinguished two types of questions:

First, there are questions that have clear focus on the recipient of the knowledge i.e. teammate or business stakeholder. For example, a question like "How much effective it is to use face to face (F2F) communication for conveying information within our stakeholders?" has a clear focus on tacit knowledge sharing with business stakeholders. On the other hand, there are questions that speak of tacit or explicit knowledge without a focus on the knowledge recipient. For example the question: "How commonly do you use Documentation treated as a requirement on your agile software development projects?" speaks of explicit knowledge without the focus on the knowledge recipient.

Table 2 illustrates the concepts measured and the measurement method.

Also, we categorized the questions according to the knowledge sharing media. For example, question like: "How much effective it is to use e-mail for conveying information within our stakeholders?" is about using e-media as a means for explicit knowledge sharing with business stakeholders.

Descriptive Statistics

First let us look at the management practices.

Table 2. Operational definition

Variable Name	Operational definition	Measurement indicator
Importance of tacit knowledge sharing in software development	The extent to which the tacit knowledge sharing activities enhances the software quality	How commonly do you use Daily Scrum Meeting chart on your agile software development projects? How commonly do you use active stakeholder participation on your agile software development projects? How commonly do you use JIT model storming on your agile software development projects? Project stakeholders work closely with our agile teams and are readily available
Importance of explicit knowledge sharing in the software development.	The extent to which the explicit knowledge sharing activities enhances the software quality	How commonly do you use Burndown chart on your agile software development projects. How commonly do you use High-level release planning on your agile software development projects? How commonly do you use Iteration/Sprint planning on your agile software development projects? How commonly do you use Prioritized work list on your agile software development projects? How commonly do you use Status report on your agile software development projects? How commonly do you use Story board with Task breakdowns on your agile software development projects?
Importance of explicit knowledge sharing to communicate with teammates, in the software development.	The extent to which the explicit knowledge sharing activities with teammates enhance the software quality	How commonly do you use Follow coding standards on your agile software development projects? How commonly do you use Follow database standards on your agile software development projects? How commonly do you use Follow User interface standards on your agile software development projects? How commonly do you use Documentation treated as a requirement on your agile software development projects? How commonly do you use Executable specifications on your agile software development projects? How commonly do you use Initial Architecture Envisioning on your agile software development projects? How commonly do you use Initial Requirements Envisioning on your agile software development projects? How much effective it is to use detailed documentation for conveying information with our stakeholders?
Importance of tacit knowledge sharing to communicate with teammates, in the software development.	The extent to which the tacit knowledge sharing activities with teammates enhance the software quality.	How commonly do you use Collective code ownership on your agile software development projects? How commonly do you use Pair programming on your agile software development projects? How commonly do you use Continuous Integration on your agile software development projects? How much effective it is to use Face to Face (F2F) communication for conveying information within the team? How much effective it is to use Face to Face (F2F) at a whiteboard for conveying information within the team? How much effective it is to use online chat for conveying information within the team? How much effective it is to use teleconference calls for conveying information within the team? How much effective it is to use videoconferencing for conveying information within the team?

continued on following page

Table 2. Continued

Variable Name	Operational definition	Measurement indicator
Importance of tacit knowledge sharing to communicate with business stakeholders, in the software development.	The extent to which the tacit knowledge sharing activities with business stakeholders enhance the software quality.	How much effective it is to use face to face (F2F) communication for conveying information within our stakeholders? How much effective it is to use face to face (F2F) whiteboard for conveying information within our stakeholders? How much effective it is to use online chat for conveying information within our stakeholders? How much effective it is to use teleconference calls for conveying information within our stakeholders? How much effective it is to use video conferencing for conveying information within our stakeholders?
Importance of explicit knowledge sharing to communicate with business stakeholders, in the software development.	The extent to which the explicit knowledge sharing activities with business stakeholders enhance the software quality.	How commonly do you use Automated acceptance testing on your agile software development projects? How commonly do you use Initial Architecture Envisioning on your agile software development projects? How commonly do you use Initial Requirements Envisioning on your agile software development projects? We do some initial requirements modeling at the beginning of agile projects for scoping and planning purposes. We do some initial architecture modeling at the beginning of agile projects to get going in the right technical direction. How much effective it is to use detailed documentation for conveying information within our stakeholders? How much effective it is to use e-mail for conveying information within our stakeholders? How much effective it is to use overview documentation for conveying information within our stakeholders? How much effective it is to use overview diagrams for conveying information within our stakeholders?

From Figure 2 we can see that contrary to what the literature says, explicit knowledge sharing is very common in the reality practices of the Agile development community. For example we can see that around 60% of the respondents are using Burndown charts, more than 60% use high-level release planning, and more 83% are using iteration planning. However, the percentage of heavier formats of explicit knowledge is lesser than those who are using lighter formats. For example, only 47.5 use status report, and around 47% use story board with task breakdowns. This means that agile methods adopters do not really focus only on tacit knowledge sharing, but they like lighter formats of explicit knowledge sharing mechanisms.

Uses of tacit knowledge sharing mechanisms such as daily on-the-stand meetings is clearly dominant within the agile community with more than 80% using this method, allowing for more socialization i.e. tacit knowledge sharing

Second, we will look at the development practices (see Figure 3).

The surprise here is that a method used for tacit knowledge sharing, which has many advocators specially in the XP community, is not really emphasized, with only 18.5% using it commonly and 28.3% use it from time to time. On the other hand Collective Code Ownership, which has some features of tacit and explicit knowledge sharing, has more than 55% using it.

On the other side, following database, coding, and interface standards, which are of explicit nature is strongly supported within the community with coding standards supporters exceeding 65%.

Again we can see here that when it comes to development practices, Agilests are really using explicit knowledge sharing mechanisms as well as tacit knowledge sharing. That again contradicts what the literature says.

Figure 3. Common development practices

8. For each of the following development practices, please indicate how commonly they are practiced on your agile software development projects.	Very Common	Common	Sometimes	Not Common	Very Uncommon	Never	Don't Know	Response Count
Collective Code Ownership	34.4% (84)	23.8% (58)	20.5% (50)	11.5% (28)	3.7% (9)	2.9% (7)	3.3% (8)	244
Follow Coding Standards	27.0% (66)	37.3% (91)	22.5% (55)	5.3% (13)	4.1% (10)	1.2% (3)	2.5% (6)	244
Follow Database Standards	21.7% (53)	33.2% (81)	18.4% (45)	9.4% (23)	3.3% (8)	2.5% (6)	11.5% (28)	244
Follow User Interface Standards	17.6% (43)	32.8% (80)	29.9% (73)	9.4% (23)	2.9% (7)	2.5% (6)	4.9% (12)	244
Pair Programming	9.4% (23)	11.1% (27)	28.3% (69)	15.6% (38)	20.1% (49)	13.1% (32)	2.5% (6)	244
							answered question	244
							skipped question	93

Third, let us look at the documentation and modeling practices used by the community (see Figure 4).

From figure 4 we can see that practices involving socialization with business stakeholders, which means that tacit knowledge sharing is emphasized through active stakeholder participation. Moreover, use of documentation as the major explicit knowledge sharing mechanism is a common practice at least for more than 40% of the respondents. Also, and to our surprise, there seems a phase that is not really admitted by many Agilests, through which explicit knowledge sharing is heavily used by them, the requirement envisioning phase, or the analysis phase. For example, around 50% are frequently using initial architecture envisioning and initial requirements envisioning. This is supported by the answers of question 22, where more than 70% agreed that they do some initial requirements modeling, and through the answers of question 24, where more than 70% agreed that they do some initial architecture modeling at the beginning of the project. Also, more than 50% agree that before the iteration starts they identify what is "done" i.e. they identify the requirements mainly for each iteration.

Finally let us the questions directly related to knowledge sharing during the development process. Questions 32 and 33 are discussed in Figures 5 and 6, respectively.

Again we can see here that both types of knowledge are emphasized, but the emphasis clearly differs according to the knowledge recipient: business stakeholder or team members. For example, 26.5% use detailed documentation when it comes to communicate with business stakeholders, whereas 20.5% use it to communicate within the team. On the other hand, the use of overview documentation as a communication method within the development team becomes more effective. For example over 73% use overview diagrams to communicate within the devel-

Figure 4. Common modeling practices

10. For each of the following modeling and documentation practices, please indicate how commonly they are practiced on your agile software development projects.								
	Very Common	Common	Sometimes	Not Common	Very Uncommon	Never	Don't Know	Response Count
Active Stakeholder Participation	23.4% (57)	**34.0% (83)**	27.9% (68)	8.6% (21)	3.3% (8)	1.6% (4)	1.2% (3)	244
Documentation Treated as a Requirement	16.0% (39)	23.4% (57)	**27.5% (67)**	18.4% (45)	4.5% (11)	7.4% (18)	2.9% (7)	244
Executable Specifications	6.6% (16)	16.8% (41)	19.7% (48)	**21.7% (53)**	12.3% (30)	15.6% (38)	7.4% (18)	244
Initial Architecture Envisioning	13.1% (32)	**33.6% (82)**	29.1% (71)	13.1% (32)	2.5% (6)	2.9% (7)	5.7% (14)	244
Initial Requirements Envisioning	13.5% (33)	**38.5% (94)**	25.0% (61)	10.2% (25)	2.9% (7)	3.3% (8)	6.6% (16)	244
Just In Time (JIT) Model Storming	7.8% (19)	**18.9% (46)**	17.6% (43)	16.0% (39)	7.8% (19)	13.5% (33)	18.4% (45)	244
							answered question	244
							skipped question	93

Figure 5. Knowledge sharing practices within team

32. We find the following strategies for conveying information WITHIN THE TEAM to be:							
	Very Effective	Effective	Neutral	Ineffective	Very Ineffective	Don't Know	Response Count
Face-to-face (F2F) communication	**67.0% (148)**	29.0% (64)	3.2% (7)	0.5% (1)	0.0% (0)	0.5% (1)	221
F2F at a Whiteboard	**67.3% (148)**	25.9% (57)	4.5% (10)	0.0% (0)	0.5% (1)	1.8% (4)	220
Detailed documentation	1.4% (3)	19.1% (42)	**38.2% (84)**	29.1% (64)	9.5% (21)	2.7% (6)	220
Email	3.6% (8)	36.4% (80)	**41.4% (91)**	16.4% (36)	2.3% (5)	0.0% (0)	220
Overview documentation	7.3% (16)	**50.0% (110)**	25.5% (56)	9.1% (20)	2.3% (5)	5.9% (13)	220
Overview diagrams	11.4% (25)	**62.7% (138)**	16.8% (37)	3.2% (7)	1.8% (4)	4.1% (9)	220
Online Chat	12.3% (27)	**42.9% (94)**	23.7% (52)	6.8% (15)	1.8% (4)	12.3% (27)	219
Teleconference Calls	8.2% (18)	**36.8% (81)**	20.5% (45)	13.2% (29)	3.2% (7)	18.2% (40)	220
Videoconferencing	6.4% (14)	16.1% (35)	19.7% (43)	6.0% (13)	2.8% (6)	**49.1% (107)**	218
						answered question	221
						skipped question	116

Figure 6. Knowledge sharing practices with business stakeholder

33. We find the following strategies for conveying information WITH OUR STAKEHOLDERS to be:							
	Very Effective	Effective	Neutral	Ineffective	Very Ineffective	Don't Know	Response Count
Face-to-face (F2F) communication	60.5% (133)	30.9% (68)	3.6% (8)	1.8% (4)	0.0% (0)	3.2% (7)	220
F2F at a Whiteboard	43.8% (95)	31.3% (68)	11.1% (24)	2.8% (6)	0.9% (2)	10.1% (22)	217
Detailed documentation	4.1% (9)	22.4% (49)	29.7% (65)	27.4% (60)	10.0% (22)	6.4% (14)	219
Email	6.4% (14)	42.9% (94)	30.6% (67)	16.4% (36)	2.3% (5)	1.4% (3)	219
Overview documentation	10.0% (22)	43.4% (95)	22.8% (50)	10.0% (22)	1.8% (4)	11.9% (26)	219
Overview diagrams	12.3% (27)	42.5% (93)	20.5% (45)	10.5% (23)	2.3% (5)	11.9% (26)	219
Online Chat	2.7% (6)	16.9% (37)	25.1% (55)	17.4% (38)	5.5% (12)	32.4% (71)	219
Teleconference Calls	6.4% (14)	35.5% (78)	25.0% (55)	10.5% (23)	2.3% (5)	20.5% (45)	220
Videoconferencing	5.9% (13)	17.8% (39)	19.2% (42)	6.4% (14)	0.5% (1)	50.2% (110)	219
						answered question	221
						skipped question	116

opment team and 54.8% use it to communicate within business stakeholders, 57.3% use overview documentation to communicate within the development team and 53.4% use it to communicate within business stakeholders.

This explicit knowledge sharing becomes more effective in big organizations. Crosstabs between detailed documentation and size of the project reveal that the need for explicit knowledge sharing increases with organization's size.

Tacit knowledge sharing within development team and with stakeholders is emphasized through face-to-face communication, which is much more effective than electronic communication methods. Socialization through face-to-face communication is strongly emphasized. Over 90% find face-to-face communication is effective when communicating with business stakeholders, and 96% when communicating with other team members.

Inferential Statistics

Following our theoretical frame work we have conducted our analysis using SPSS. The variables were defined as follows:

- SQ: Software quality, in terms of fitness of the software to the customers' requirements.
- Tacit: general adoption of tacit knowledge techniques with customers or teammates.
- Explicit: general adoption of explicit knowledge techniques with customers or teammates.
- TE.E: The use of explicit knowledge sharing techniques within the development team. These techniques include but not limited to, use of overview documentation, detailed documentation, use of models, executable specification, white board discus-

Figure 7. Correlations of different knowledge sharing practices with software quality

Correlations

		SQ	Tacit	TE.E	TE.T	BIZ.T	BIZ.E	Explicit
SQ	Pearson Correlation	1	.623*	.366*	.558*	.334*	.381*	.495**
	Sig. (2-tailed)		.000	.000	.000	.000	.000	.000
	N	225	225	225	225	218	225	225
Tacit	Pearson Correlation	.623*	1	.288*	.386*	.318*	.313*	.563**
	Sig. (2-tailed)	.000		.000	.000	.000	.000	.000
	N	225	236	236	236	218	236	236
TE.E	Pearson Correlation	.366*	.288*	1	.593*	.274*	.550*	.336*
	Sig. (2-tailed)	.000	.000		.000	.000	.000	.000
	N	225	236	236	236	218	236	236
TE.T	Pearson Correlation	.558*	.386*	.593*	1	.457*	.372*	.352*
	Sig. (2-tailed)	.000	.000	.000		.000	.000	.000
	N	225	236	236	236	218	236	236
BIZ.T	Pearson Correlation	.334*	.318*	.274*	.457*	1	.299*	.154*
	Sig. (2-tailed)	.000	.000	.000	.000		.000	.023
	N	218	218	218	218	218	218	218
BIZ.E	Pearson Correlation	.381*	.313*	.550*	.372*	.299*	1	.313*
	Sig. (2-tailed)	.000	.000	.000	.000	.000		.000
	N	225	236	236	236	218	236	236
Explicit	Pearson Correlation	.495*	.563*	.336*	.352*	.154*	.313*	1
	Sig. (2-tailed)	.000	.000	.000	.000	.023	.000	
	N	225	236	236	236	218	236	236

**. Correlation is significant at the 0.01 level (2-tailed).

*. Correlation is significant at the 0.05 level (2-tailed).

sions, and even photos or emails. This variable checks the extent the software quality depends on the use of explicit knowledge to communicate with other teammates.

- TE.T: The use of tacit knowledge sharing techniques within the development team. These techniques include on-the-stand meetings, use of chat, telephone calls, pair programming etc.
- BIZ.E: The use of explicit knowledge sharing techniques with business stakeholders. These techniques include but not limited to, use of overview documentation, detailed documentation, use of models, executable specification, white board discussions, and even photos or emails.
- BIZ.T: The use of tacit knowledge sharing techniques with business stakehold-

ers. These techniques include on-the-stand meetings, use of chat, telephone calls, and on-site customers.

Figure 7 shows first the correlation matrix among the 7 variables:

As the matrix clearly shows, there is a strong relationship between knowledge sharing and software quality. The strongest relationship is among tacit knowledge sharing usage and software quality, although there is strong evidence that software quality relies on both tacit and explicit knowledge sharing. Figure 8 shows the strength of this relationship ordered from the highest to the lowest.

Figure 8 clearly shows that reliance on tacit knowledge sharing techniques is more than those of explicit. However, the respondents admit that

Figure 8. Correlation between software quality and other variables

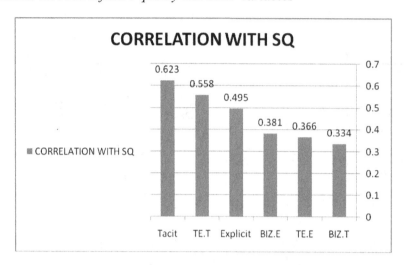

Figure 9. Multiple regression

Variables Entered/Removed[b]

Model	Variables Entered	Variables Removed	Method
1	Explicit, BIZ.T, BIZ. E, TE.T, Tacit, TE.E[a]	.	Enter

a. All requested variables entered.

b. Dependent Variable: SQ

successful software projects require both tacit and explicit knowledge. Moreover, and to our expectation, respondents do believe that communicating with business stakeholders is more reliant on explicit methods. This is understandable for two main reasons:

It is difficult to have on-site customers on full-time basis all the time of the project. Use of tacit knowledge sharing techniques requires strong mutual trust, something that is difficult to achieve due to the short time allowed to start the project.

A multiple regression was conducted to identify the main variables affecting the dependent variable. Figure 9 shows the results.

Looking at the model summery table in Figure 10 we can see that can see that 50% of the variance in software quality is explained by the aforementioned variables, which is something acceptable taking into consideration that software quality relies on other factors (see Figure 11).

On the other hand, the coefficients table shows that the most significant variables are: tacit, TE.T, and explicit and if a linear equation is to be built, it would be:

$$SQ = 0.365TACIT + 0.307TE.T + 0.144 EXPLICIT + 0.105 BIZ.E$$

This leads us to the following conclusion: software quality relies on tacit knowledge sharing especially among teammates, which means that H20 and H21a are substantiated. Also, it tells us that H11 and H11a are substantiated, which means that explicit knowledge sharing is required and especially with business stakeholders.

One should note that the weaker relationship is when we use tacit knowledge sharing techniques with business stakeholders, and explicit knowledge sharing techniques when talking to teammates.

In the following section we discuss the effect of the moderating variables on the model.

Figure 10. Model summary

Model Summary

Model	R	R Square	Adjusted R Square	Std. Error of the Estimate
1	.709[a]	.503	.489	.49850

a. Predictors: (Constant), Explicit, BIZ.T, BIZ.E, TE.T, Tacit, TE.E

Figure 11. Multiple regressions and model summary

Coefficients[a]

Model		Unstandardized Coefficients		Standardized Coefficients	t	Sig.
		B	Std. Error	Beta		
1	(Constant)	−.037	.312		−.117	.907
	Tacit	.352	.063	.365	5.607	.000
	TE.E	−.085	.083	−.070	−1.033	.303
	TE.T	.419	.093	.307	4.512	.000
	BIZ.T	.046	.061	.043	.766	.444
	BIZ.E	.141	.081	.105	1.733	.085
	Explicit	.145	.063	.144	2.313	.022

a. Dependent Variable: SQ

The Effect of Moderating Variables

The four moderating variables are:

- Organizational size.
- Experience of the respondent.
- Experience in Agile methods in the organization the respondent is working for.
- The knowledge sharing media.

Organizational Size

We expected that the larger the organization the more the need for explicit knowledge sharing, for both communicating with business stakeholders and teammates. Tables 3-8 show the results for different organizations sizes.

Figure 12 shows the trend in correlations according to the size of the organization for every variable:

The figure clearly shows less reliance on tacit knowledge sharing techniques when the size of organization becomes bigger.

Figure 13 shows that there is no difference in the use of explicit knowledge sharing techniques when the size is less than 1000 but there is clear evidence that this becomes obvious for organizations of more than 1000 employees.

Although, TE.E is not significant at 1 to 10 employees' organizations, there still an increase in the use of team explicit knowledge sharing for larger organizations. And despite that we did not hypothesize that, it seems that big organizations

Table 3. Correlations of different knowledge sharing practices with software quality: size 1-10 people

		SQ	Tacit	TE.E	TE.T	BIZ.T	BIZ.E	Explicit
SQ	Pearson Correlation	1	.673(**)	.318	.311	.639(**)	.233	.551(**)
	Sig. (2-tailed)		.000	.121	.131	.001	.261	.004
	N	25	25	25	25	24	25	25
Tacit	Pearson Correlation	.673(**)	1	.513(**)	.306	.374	.474(*)	.719(**)
	Sig. (2-tailed)	.000		.006	.121	.072	.013	.000
	N	25	27	27	27	24	27	27
TE.E	Pearson Correlation	.318	.513(**)	1	.480(*)	.512(*)	.604(**)	.432(*)
	Sig. (2-tailed)	.121	.006		.011	.010	.001	.024
	N	25	27	27	27	24	27	27
TE.T	Pearson Correlation	.311	.306	.480(*)	1	.402	.414(*)	.264
	Sig. (2-tailed)	.131	.121	.011		.051	.032	.183
	N	25	27	27	27	24	27	27
BIZ.T	Pearson Correlation	.639(**)	.374	.512(*)	.402	1	.436(*)	.289
	Sig. (2-tailed)	.001	.072	.010	.051		.033	.171
	N	24	24	24	24	24	24	24
BIZ.E	Pearson Correlation	.233	.474(*)	.604(**)	.414(*)	.436(*)	1	.426(*)
	Sig. (2-tailed)	.261	.013	.001	.032	.033		.027
	N	25	27	27	27	24	27	27
Explicit	Pearson Correlation	.551(**)	.719(**)	.432(*)	.264	.289	.426(*)	1
	Sig. (2-tailed)	.004	.000	.024	.183	.171	.027	
	N	25	27	27	27	24	27	27

Figure 12. Relationship between tacit knowledge sharing and software quality

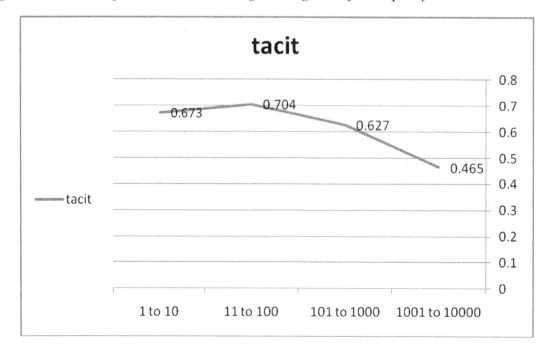

Table 4. Correlations of different knowledge sharing practices with software quality: size 11-100 people

		SQ	Tacit	TE.E	TE.T	BIZ.T	BIZ.E	Explicit
SQ	Pearson Correlation	1	.704(**)	.383(**)	.497(**)	.365(**)	.376(**)	.558(**)
	Sig. (2-tailed)		.000	.001	.000	.003	.002	.000
	N	67	67	67	67	66	67	67
Tacit	Pearson Correlation	.704(**)	1	.133	.243(*)	.403(**)	.223	.516(**)
	Sig. (2-tailed)	.000		.278	.046	.001	.068	.000
	N	67	68	68	68	66	68	68
TE.E	Pearson Correlation	.383(**)	.133	1	.710(**)	.268(*)	.608(**)	.264(*)
	Sig. (2-tailed)	.001	.278		.000	.029	.000	.030
	N	67	68	68	68	66	68	68
TE.T	Pearson Correlation	.497(**)	.243(*)	.710(**)	1	.398(**)	.416(**)	.250(*)
	Sig. (2-tailed)	.000	.046	.000		.001	.000	.040
	N	67	68	68	68	66	68	68
BIZ.T	Pearson Correlation	.365(**)	.403(**)	.268(*)	.398(**)	1	.382(**)	.206
	Sig. (2-tailed)	.003	.001	.029	.001		.002	.097
	N	66	66	66	66	66	66	66
BIZ.E	Pearson Correlation	.376(**)	.223	.608(**)	.416(**)	.382(**)	1	.319(**)
	Sig. (2-tailed)	.002	.068	.000	.000	.002		.008
	N	67	68	68	68	66	68	68
Explicit	Pearson Correlation	.558(**)	.516(**)	.264(*)	.250(*)	.206	.319(**)	1
	Sig. (2-tailed)	.000	.000	.030	.040	.097	.008	
	N	67	68	68	68	66	68	68

Figure 13. Relationship between explicit knowledge sharing and software quality

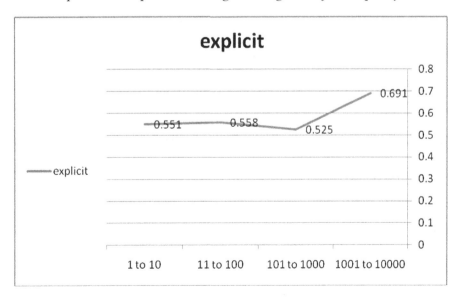

Table 5. Correlations of different knowledge sharing practices with software quality: size 101-1000 people

		SQ	Tacit	TE.E	TE.T	BIZ.T	BIZ.E	Explicit
SQ	Pearson Correlation	1	.627(**)	.367(**)	.509(**)	.174	.305(*)	.525(**)
	Sig. (2-tailed)		.000	.002	.000	.170	.012	.000
	N	67	67	67	67	64	67	67
Tacit	Pearson Correlation	.627(**)	1	.381(**)	.506(**)	.279(*)	.317(**)	.673(**)
	Sig. (2-tailed)	.000		.001	.000	.025	.007	.000
	N	67	71	71	71	64	71	71
TE.E	Pearson Correlation	.367(**)	.381(**)	1	.591(**)	.328(**)	.509(**)	.313(**)
	Sig. (2-tailed)	.002	.001		.000	.008	.000	.008
	N	67	71	71	71	64	71	71
TE.T	Pearson Correlation	.509(**)	.506(**)	.591(**)	1	.467(**)	.352(**)	.431(**)
	Sig. (2-tailed)	.000	.000	.000		.000	.003	.000
	N	67	71	71	71	64	71	71
BIZ.T	Pearson Correlation	.174	.279(*)	.328(**)	.467(**)	1	.295(*)	.107
	Sig. (2-tailed)	.170	.025	.008	.000		.018	.402
	N	64	64	64	64	64	64	64
BIZ.E	Pearson Correlation	.305(*)	.317(**)	.509(**)	.352(**)	.295(*)	1	.302(*)
	Sig. (2-tailed)	.012	.007	.000	.003	.018		.010
	N	67	71	71	71	64	71	71
Explicit	Pearson Correlation	.525(**)	.673(**)	.313(**)	.431(**)	.107	.302(*)	1
	Sig. (2-tailed)	.000	.000	.008	.000	.402	.010	
	N	67	71	71	71	64	71	71

Figure 14. Relationship between explicit knowledge sharing techniques within the team and software quality

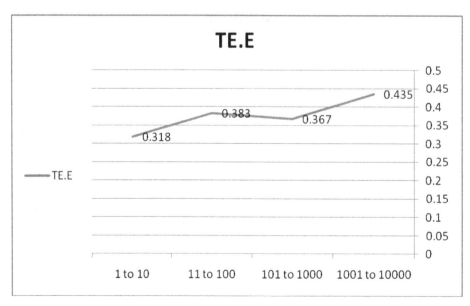

Table 6. Correlations of different knowledge sharing practices with software quality: size 1001-10000 people

		SQ	Tacit	TE.E	TE.T	BIZ.T	BIZ.E	Explicit
SQ	Pearson Correlation	1	.465(**)	.435(**)	.711(**)	.305	.505(**)	.691(**)
	Sig. (2-tailed)		.002	.005	.000	.062	.001	.000
	N	40	40	40	40	38	40	40
Tacit	Pearson Correlation	.465(**)	1	.239	.461(**)	.155	.316(*)	.545(**)
	Sig. (2-tailed)	.002		.123	.002	.354	.039	.000
	N	40	43	43	43	38	43	43
TE.E	Pearson Correlation	.435(**)	.239	1	.451(**)	.166	.505(**)	.352(*)
	Sig. (2-tailed)	.005	.123		.002	.318	.001	.021
	N	40	43	43	43	38	43	43
TE.T	Pearson Correlation	.711(**)	.461(**)	.451(**)	1	.505(**)	.295	.604(**)
	Sig. (2-tailed)	.000	.002	.002		.001	.055	.000
	N	40	43	43	43	38	43	43
BIZ.T	Pearson Correlation	.305	.155	.166	.505(**)	1	.013	.208
	Sig. (2-tailed)	.062	.354	.318	.001		.937	.210
	N	38	38	38	38	38	38	38
BIZ.E	Pearson Correlation	.505(**)	.316(*)	.505(**)	.295	.013	1	.368(*)
	Sig. (2-tailed)	.001	.039	.001	.055	.937		.015
	N	40	43	43	43	38	43	43
Explicit	Pearson Correlation	.691(**)	.545(**)	.352(*)	.604(**)	.208	.368(*)	1
	Sig. (2-tailed)	.000	.000	.021	.000	.210	.015	
	N	40	43	43	43	38	43	43

Figure 15. Relationship between tacit knowledge sharing techniques within the team and software quality

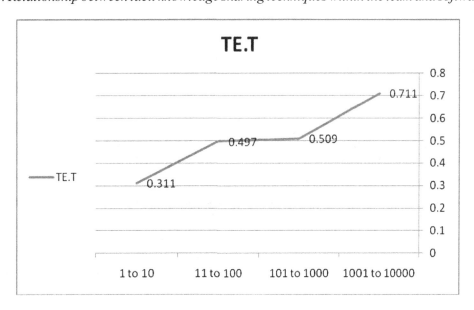

Table 7. Correlations of different knowledge sharing practices with software quality: size 10001-100000 people

		SQ	Tacit	TE.E	TE.T	BIZ.T	BIZ.E	Explicit
SQ	Pearson Correlation	1	.465(**)	.435(**)	.711(**)	.305	.505(**)	.691(**)
	Sig. (2-tailed)		.002	.005	.000	.062	.001	.000
	N	40	40	40	40	38	40	40
Tacit	Pearson Correlation	.465(**)	1	.239	.461(**)	.155	.316(*)	.545(**)
	Sig. (2-tailed)	.002		.123	.002	.354	.039	.000
	N	40	43	43	43	38	43	43
TE.E	Pearson Correlation	.435(**)	.239	1	.451(**)	.166	.505(**)	.352(*)
	Sig. (2-tailed)	.005	.123		.002	.318	.001	.021
	N	40	43	43	43	38	43	43
TE.T	Pearson Correlation	.711(**)	.461(**)	.451(**)	1	.505(**)	.295	.604(**)
	Sig. (2-tailed)	.000	.002	.002		.001	.055	.000
	N	40	43	43	43	38	43	43
BIZ.T	Pearson Correlation	.305	.155	.166	.505(**)	1	.013	.208
	Sig. (2-tailed)	.062	.354	.318	.001		.937	.210
	N	38	38	38	38	38	38	38
BIZ.E	Pearson Correlation	.505(**)	.316(*)	.505(**)	.295	.013	1	.368(*)
	Sig. (2-tailed)	.001	.039	.001	.055	.937		.015
	N	40	43	43	43	38	43	43
Explicit	Pearson Correlation	.691(**)	.545(**)	.352(*)	.604(**)	.208	.368(*)	1
	Sig. (2-tailed)	.000	.000	.021	.000	.210	.015	
	N	40	43	43	43	38	43	43

rely on explicit knowledge sharing techniques, even within teammates (see Figure 14).

Although not significant at 1 to 10 employees' organizations, there is a trend towards more tacit communications for larger organizations. Comparing this to Figure 15, we can say that bigger organizations rely more on all types of knowledge whether tacit or explicit, although the focus on tacit knowledge remains dominant.

Figure 16 shows that reliance on tacit knowledge sharing to communicate with business stakeholders has less effect on software quality especially for bigger organizations, taking into consideration that from 101 to 1000 is statistically insignificant.

Figure 17 again shows that more explicit knowledge sharing techniques is required in communicating with business stakeholders especially in bigger organizations, taking into consideration that from 101 to 1000 is supported only at 90% confidence level, contrary to the rest that are supported at 95% confidence level.

The Effect of the Experience of the Respondent

We expected that more experienced Agile methods adopters are more willing to use more knowledge sharing focusing more on explicit knowledge. That is, by adding more experience software developers become more mature and willing to use more

Table 8. Correlations of different knowledge sharing practices with software quality: size 100000+ people

		SQ	Tacit	TE.E	TE.T	BIZ.T	BIZ.E	Explicit
SQ	Pearson Correlation	1	.644(**)	.220	.593(*)	.439	.719(**)	-.009
	Sig. (2-tailed)		.005	.395	.012	.078	.001	.974
	N	17	17	17	17	17	17	17
Tacit	Pearson Correlation	.644(**)	1	.174	.520(*)	.268	.609(**)	.125
	Sig. (2-tailed)	.005		.504	.032	.299	.010	.632
	N	17	17	17	17	17	17	17
TE.E	Pearson Correlation	.220	.174	1	.673(**)	-.126	.441	.621(**)
	Sig. (2-tailed)	.395	.504		.003	.631	.076	.008
	N	17	17	17	17	17	17	17
TE.T	Pearson Correlation	.593(*)	.520(*)	.673(**)	1	.477	748(**)	.388
	Sig. (2-tailed)	.012	.032	.003		.053	.001	.124
	N	17	17	17	17	17	17	17
BIZ.T	Pearson Correlation	.439	.268	-.126	.477	1	.346	-.004
	Sig. (2-tailed)	.078	.299	.631	.053		.174	.989
	N	17	17	17	17	17	17	17
BIZ.E	Pearson Correlation	.719(**)	.609(**)	.441	.748(**)	.346	1	-.063
	Sig. (2-tailed)	.001	.010	.076	.001	.174		.810
	N	17	17	17	17	17	17	17
Explicit	Pearson Correlation	-.009	.125	.621(**)	.388	-.004	-.063	1
	Sig. (2-tailed)	.974	.632	.008	.124	.989	.810	
	N	17	17	17	17	17	17	17

Figure 16. Relationship between tacit knowledge sharing techniques with business stakeholders and software quality

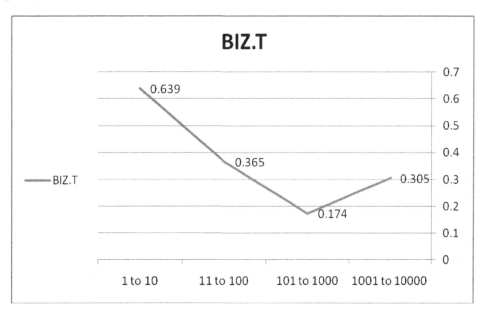

Figure 17. Relationship between explicit knowledge sharing techniques with business stakeholders and software quality

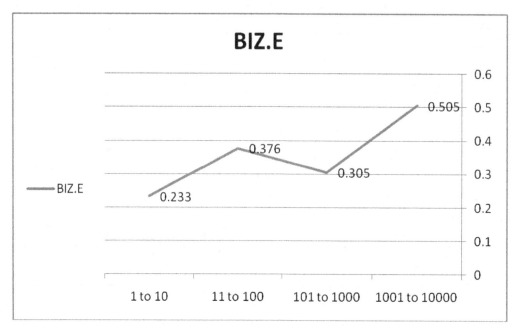

Figure 18. Relationship between tacit knowledge sharing techniques and software quality according to the experience of the developers

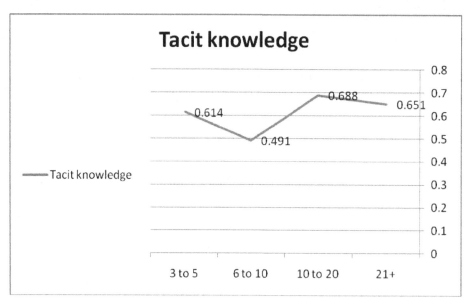

formal techniques such as documentation than inexperienced ones. Hence we tested that on our sample. Tables 9-12 show the results of correla-

tions among the different variables at different levels of experience of the developers.

We have excluded developers who are less than two years of experience as the number of

Table 9. Correlations of different knowledge sharing practices with software quality for people who have 3 to 5 years of experience

		SQ	Tacit	TE.E	TE.T	BIZ.T	BIZ.E	Explicit
SQ	Pearson Correlation	1	.614(**)	.615(**)	.857(**)	.261	.437	.267
	Sig. (2-tailed)		.007	.007	.000	.296	.070	.285
	N	18	18	18	18	18	18	18
Tacit	Pearson Correlation	.614(**)	1	.738(**)	.624(**)	.209	.590(**)	.427
	Sig. (2-tailed)	.007		.000	.003	.404	.006	.061
	N	18	20	20	20	18	20	20
TE.E	Pearson Correlation	.615(**)	.738(**)	1	.714(**)	.221	.710(**)	.512(*)
	Sig. (2-tailed)	.007	.000		.000	.377	.000	.021
	N	18	20	20	20	18	20	20
TE.T	Pearson Correlation	.857(**)	.624(**)	.714(**)	1	.530(*)	.535(*)	.479(*)
	Sig. (2-tailed)	.000	.003	.000		.024	.015	.033
	N	18	20	20	20	18	20	20
BIZ.T	Pearson Correlation	.261	.209	.221	.530(*)	1	.320	.315
	Sig. (2-tailed)	.296	.404	.377	.024		.195	.203
	N	18	18	18	18	18	18	18
BIZ.E	Pearson Correlation	.437	.590(**)	.710(**)	.535(*)	.320	1	.369
	Sig. (2-tailed)	.070	.006	.000	.015	.195		.109
	N	18	20	20	20	18	20	20
Explicit	Pearson Correlation	.267	.427	.512(*)	.479(*)	.315	.369	1
	Sig. (2-tailed)	.285	.061	.021	.033	.203	.109	
	N	18	20	20	20	18	20	20

respondents in this category is only 7, which may lead to wrong conclusions.

Figure 18 show the trend in correlations according to the level of experience of the respondents for every one of the 6 variables:

Although there is a decrease in the level of correlation between software quality and tacit knowledge sharing for people with 6 to 10 experience, there can be no inference that the focus of tacit knowledge for Agile adopters becomes of less intense after more experience is incurred.

Figure 19 shows the relationship between software quality and adoption of tacit knowledge sharing techniques within the development team.

To our expectation, less focus on tacit knowledge sharing techniques within the development team becomes clear for more experienced developers.

Figure 20 shows the relationship between software quality and adoption of explicit knowledge sharing techniques within the development team.

Not to our expectation, the Agile developers do not rely on using explicit knowledge sharing techniques after getting more experience in the field.

Figure 21 shows the relationship between software quality and adoption of tacit knowledge sharing techniques with business stakeholders.

Again, we cannot conclude that more experience results in less usage of tacit knowledge sharing techniques.

Table 10. Correlations of different knowledge sharing practices with software quality for people who have 6 to 10 years of experience

		SQ	Tacit	TE.E	TE.T	BIZ.T	BIZ.E	Explicit
SQ	Pearson Correlation	1	.491(**)	.394(**)	.584(**)	.458(**)	.385(**)	.462(**)
	Sig. (2-tailed)		.000	.003	.000	.001	.004	.000
	N	55	55	55	55	53	55	55
Tacit	Pearson Correlation	.491(**)	1	.301(*)	.479(**)	.421(**)	.291(*)	.741(**)
	Sig. (2-tailed)	.000		.021	.000	.002	.026	.000
	N	55	59	59	59	53	59	59
TE.E	Pearson Correlation	.394(**)	.301(*)	1	.707(**)	.345(*)	.614(**)	.363(**)
	Sig. (2-tailed)	.003	.021		.000	.011	.000	.005
	N	55	59	59	59	53	59	59
TE.T	Pearson Correlation	.584(**)	.479(**)	.707(**)	1	.576(**)	.532(**)	.523(**)
	Sig. (2-tailed)	.000	.000	.000		.000	.000	.000
	N	55	59	59	59	53	59	59
BIZ.T	Pearson Correlation	.458(**)	.421(**)	.345(*)	.576(**)	1	.314(*)	.215
	Sig. (2-tailed)	.001	.002	.011	.000		.022	.123
	N	53	53	53	53	53	53	53
BIZ.E	Pearson Correlation	.385(**)	.291(*)	.614(**)	.532(**)	.314(*)	1	.303(*)
	Sig. (2-tailed)	.004	.026	.000	.000	.022		.020
	N	55	59	59	59	53	59	59
Explicit	Pearson Correlation	.462(**)	.741(**)	.363(**)	.523(**)	.215	.303(*)	1
	Sig. (2-tailed)	.000	.000	.005	.000	.123	.020	
	N	55	59	59	59	53	59	59

Figure 19. Relationship between tacit knowledge sharing techniques within the development team and software quality according to the experience of the developers

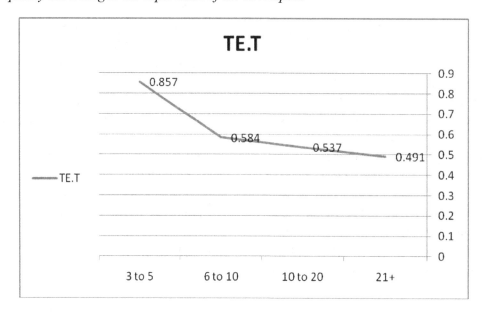

Table 11. Correlations of different knowledge sharing practices with software quality for people who have 11 to 20 years of experience

		SQ	Tacit	TE.E	TE.T	BIZ.T	BIZ.E	Explicit
SQ	Pearson Correlation	1	.688(**)	.349(**)	.537(**)	.297(**)	.332(**)	.486(**)
	Sig. (2-tailed)		.000	.000	.000	.004	.001	.000
	N	99	99	99	99	94	99	99
Tacit	Pearson Correlation	.688(**)	1	.159	.281(**)	.326(**)	.247(*)	.476(**)
	Sig. (2-tailed)	.000		.109	.004	.001	.012	.000
	N	99	103	103	103	94	103	103
TE.E	Pearson Correlation	.349(**)	.159	1	.518(**)	.188	.407(**)	.182
	Sig. (2-tailed)	.000	.109		.000	.070	.000	.065
	N	99	103	103	103	94	103	103
TE.T	Pearson Correlation	.537(**)	.281(**)	.518(**)	1	.380(**)	.263(**)	.152
	Sig. (2-tailed)	.000	.004	.000		.000	.007	.125
	N	99	103	103	103	94	103	103
BIZ.T	Pearson Correlation	.297(**)	.326(**)	.188	.380(**)	1	.262(*)	.044
	Sig. (2-tailed)	.004	.001	.070	.000		.011	.672
	N	94	94	94	94	94	94	94
BIZ.E	Pearson Correlation	.332(**)	.247(*)	.407(**)	.263(**)	.262(*)	1	.328(**)
	Sig. (2-tailed)	.001	.012	.000	.007	.011		.001
	N	99	103	103	103	94	103	103
Explicit	Pearson Correlation	.486(**)	.476(**)	.182	.152	.044	.328(**)	1
	Sig. (2-tailed)	.000	.000	.065	.125	.672	.001	
	N	99	103	103	103	94	103	103

Figure 20. Relationship between explicit knowledge sharing techniques with business stakeholders and software quality according to the experience of the developers

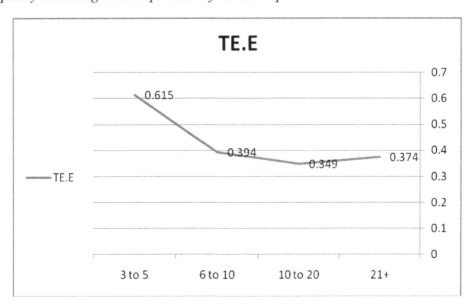

Table 12. Correlations of different knowledge sharing practices with software quality for people who have 21+ years of experience

		SQ	Tacit	TE.E	TE.T	BIZ.T	BIZ.E	Explicit
SQ	Pearson Correlation	1	.651(**)	.374(*)	.491(**)	.336(*)	.496(**)	.614(**)
	Sig. (2-tailed)		.000	.011	.001	.024	.001	.000
	N	45	45	45	45	45	45	45
Tacit	Pearson Correlation	.651(**)	1	.452(**)	.423(**)	.312(*)	.348(*)	.656(**)
	Sig. (2-tailed)	.000		.002	.003	.037	.018	.000
	N	45	46	46	46	45	46	46
TE.E	Pearson Correlation	.374(*)	.452(**)	1	.582(**)	.302(*)	.666(**)	.571(**)
	Sig. (2-tailed)	.011	.002		.000	.044	.000	.000
	N	45	46	46	46	45	46	46
TE.T	Pearson Correlation	.491(**)	.423(**)	.582(**)	1	.417(**)	.378(**)	.539(**)
	Sig. (2-tailed)	.001	.003	.000		.004	.010	.000
	N	45	46	46	46	45	46	46
BIZ.T	Pearson Correlation	.336(*)	.312(*)	.302(*)	.417(**)	1	.396(**)	.218
	Sig. (2-tailed)	.024	.037	.044	.004		.007	.150
	N	45	45	45	45	45	45	45
BIZ.E	Pearson Correlation	.496(**)	.348(*)	.666(**)	.378(**)	.396(**)	1	.287
	Sig. (2-tailed)	.001	.018	.000	.010	.007		.054
	N	45	46	46	46	45	46	46
Explicit	Pearson Correlation	.614(**)	.656(**)	.571(**)	.539(**)	.218	.287	1
	Sig. (2-tailed)	.000	.000	.000	.000	.150	.054	
	N	45	46	46	46	45	46	46

Figure 21. Relationship between tacit knowledge sharing techniques with business stakeholders and software quality according to the experience of the developers

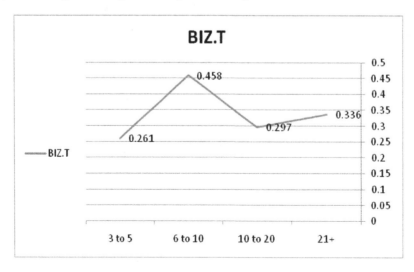

Figure 22 shows the relationship between software quality and adoption of explicit knowledge sharing techniques with business stakeholders.

Again here we can see that more experience does not yield more use of explicit knowledge techniques with business stakeholders.

Figure 23 shows the relationship between software quality and adoption of explicit knowledge sharing techniques in general.

To our expectation, adoption of general explicit knowledge sharing techniques increases as the experience of Agile methods adopters. This

Figure 22. Relationship between explicit knowledge sharing techniques with business stakeholders and software quality according to the experience of the developers

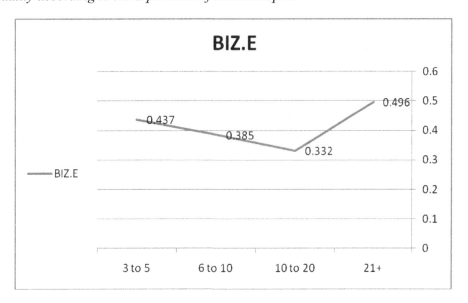

Figure 23. Relationship between explicit knowledge sharing techniques and software quality according to the experience of the developers

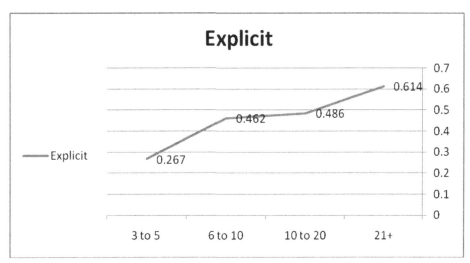

becomes of specific importance as all correlations are statistically significant at 99% confidence level.

The other factor i.e. type of respondents cannot be substantiated as most of the correlations are statistically insignificant except for developer stakeholder, so no comparisons can be made with statistically significant confidence.

The Effect of the Agile Experience of the Organization the Respondent Is Working for

Table 13-16 shows the results of the effect of Agile experience of the organization

As we can see, we cannot verify the effect of this moderating variable due to the insignificance

in the statistics due to the small sizes of the groups. This could be due to the imbalance in the years of experience categories.

Effect of Using E-Media (Collocation of Development Stakeholders)

The following table shows the results of using traditional methods Vs. electronic communication methods:

- Survey validity and reliability
- Sample size adequacy

The sample size used in this survey is 334 respondents. However, after the deletion of missing responses that skipped most of the answers the

Table 13. 1 to 2 years

		SQ	Tacit	TE.E	TE.T	BIZ.T	BIZ.E	Explicit
SQ	Pearson Correlation	1	.710(**)	.309(**)	.587(**)	.375(**)	.297(**)	.617(**)
	Sig. (2-tailed)		.000	.003	.000	.000	.004	.000
	N	91	91	91	91	88	91	91
Tacit	Pearson Correlation	.710(**)	1	.248(*)	.383(**)	.264(*)	.178	.588(**)
	Sig. (2-tailed)	.000		.014	.000	.013	.079	.000
	N	91	98	98	98	88	98	98
TE.E	Pearson Correlation	.309(**)	.248(*)	1	.607(**)	.241(*)	.617(**)	.317(**)
	Sig. (2-tailed)	.003	.014		.000	.024	.000	.001
	N	91	98	98	98	88	98	98
TE.T	Pearson Correlation	.587(**)	.383(**)	.607(**)	1	.416(**)	.462(**)	.463(**)
	Sig. (2-tailed)	.000	.000	.000		.000	.000	.000
	N	91	98	98	98	88	98	98
BIZ.T	Pearson Correlation	.375(**)	.264(*)	.241(*)	.416(**)	1	.302(**)	.153
	Sig. (2-tailed)	.000	.013	.024	.000		.004	.154
	N	88	88	88	88	88	88	88
BIZ.E	Pearson Correlation	.297(**)	.178	.617(**)	.462(**)	.302(**)	1	.237(*)
	Sig. (2-tailed)	.004	.079	.000	.000	.004		.019
	N	91	98	98	98	88	98	98
Explicit	Pearson Correlation	.617(**)	.588(**)	.317(**)	.463(**)	.153	.237(*)	1
	Sig. (2-tailed)	.000	.000	.001	.000	.154	.019	
	N	91	98	98	98	88	98	98

number of responses analyzed has become 244 responses, which is quite adequate for our study. (Roscoe 1975) summarizes the thumb rule for the sample size as follows:

- Sample sizes larger than 30 and less than 500 are appropriate for most of the researches.
- Minimum sample size must be 30 especially after breaking the sample into subsamples.

In multiple regression analyses it is important to have a subsample that is at least 10 times the number of variables.

In our cases we have excluded all samples of lesser than 30 responses specially when we broke the sample according to a judging criteria such as the size of the organization, or years of experience in Agile development.

Survey Validity and Reliability

Reliability of a measure is established by testing for both consistency and stability (Sekaran 2003). One of the strongest methods to test reliability is Cronbach's alpha, which tests whether the items comprising questions measuring the same variable positively correlate. In our questionnaire Cronbach's alpha was rated from 0.63 to 0.79,

Table 14. 3 to 5 years

		SQ	Tacit	TE.E	TE.T	BIZ.T	BIZ.E	Explicit
SQ	Pearson Correlation	1	.539*	.402*	.413*	.516*	.490*	.334*
	Sig. (2-tailed)		.000	.006	.004	.000	.001	.023
	N	46	46	46	46	45	46	46
Tacit	Pearson Correlation	.539*	1	.348*	.249	.418*	.549*	.429**
	Sig. (2-tailed)	.000		.015	.088	.004	.000	.002
	N	46	48	48	48	45	48	48
TE.E	Pearson Correlation	.402*	.348*	1	.270	.320*	.370 *	.308*
	Sig. (2-tailed)	.006	.015		.064	.032	.010	.033
	N	46	48	48	48	45	48	48
TE.T	Pearson Correlation	.413*	.249	.270	1	.588*	.220	.001
	Sig. (2-tailed)	.004	.088	.064		.000	.133	.997
	N	46	48	48	48	45	48	48
BIZ.T	Pearson Correlation	.516*	.418*	.320*	.588*	1	.353*	.104
	Sig. (2-tailed)	.000	.004	.032	.000		.017	.496
	N	45	45	45	45	45	45	45
BIZ.E	Pearson Correlation	.490*	.549*	.370*	.220	.353*	1	.533**
	Sig. (2-tailed)	.001	.000	.010	.133	.017		.000
	N	46	48	48	48	45	48	48
Explicit	Pearson Correlation	.334*	.429*	.308*	.001	.104	.533*	1
	Sig. (2-tailed)	.023	.002	.033	.997	.496	.000	
	N	46	48	48	48	45	48	48

** Correlation is significant at the 0.01 level (2-tailed).
* Correlation is significant at the 0.05 level (2-tailed).
How many years has your organization been doing agile? = 3-5 years

Table 15. 6 to 10 years

		SQ	Tacit	TE.E	TE.T	BIZ.T	BIZ.E	Explicit
SQ	Pearson Correlation	1	.598(*)	.686(**)	.659(*)	.217	.812(**)	.341
	Sig. (2-tailed)		.024	.007	.010	.477	.000	.233
	N	14	14	14	14	13	14	14
Tacit	Pearson Correlation	.598(*)	1	.294	.145	.521	.350	.206
	Sig. (2-tailed)	.024		.287	.606	.068	.201	.462
	N	14	15	15	15	13	15	15
TE.E	Pearson Correlation	.686(**)	.294	1	.311	-.360	.814(**)	.185
	Sig. (2-tailed)	.007	.287		.259	.227	.000	.510
	N	14	15	15	15	13	15	15
TE.T	Pearson Correlation	.659(*)	.145	.311	1	.294	.476	.094
	Sig. (2-tailed)	.010	.606	.259		.330	.073	.739
	N	14	15	15	15	13	15	15
BIZ.T	Pearson Correlation	.217	.521	-.360	.294	1	.004	.090
	Sig. (2-tailed)	.477	.068	.227	.330		.989	.770
	N	13	13	13	13	13	13	13
BIZ.E	Pearson Correlation	.812(**)	.350	.814(**)	.476	.004	1	.251
	Sig. (2-tailed)	.000	.201	.000	.073	.989		.368
	N	14	15	15	15	13	15	15
Explicit	Pearson Correlation	.341	.206	.185	.094	.090	.251	1
	Sig. (2-tailed)	.233	.462	.510	.739	.770	.368	
	N	14	15	15	15	13	15	15

which is considered acceptable to good indicator of the internal consistency reliability of the questionnaire.

The other issue is validity of the research, which can be distinguished to be of two types: external and internal. Both types of validity focus on the issue of causality between variables. Internal validity refers to testing the relation in a controlled lab experiment, where other variables are restricted. External validity refers to testing the relation in its natural setting without controlling other variables. Field experiment such as the research we have conducted helps in generalizing the results, without being able to determine the extent to which the variables are really contributing causality relationship. Because of the low internal validity of the panel of experts' survey

we have chosen to resort to the findings of an action research where we more able to control the variables.

In the following we discuss different types of validity; concurrent validity, criterion-related validity, and construct validity (Sekeran 2003)

Concurrent Validity

Concurrent validity refers to the ability to differentiate among individuals according to a predefined criterion. Unfortunately, we could not ensure concurrent validity as the differentiation between managers, quality assurance personnel, and business stakeholders was not possible on statistically significant basis.

Table 16. 11+ years

		SQ	Tacit	TE.E	TE.T	BIZ.T	BIZ.E	Explicit
SQ	Pearson Correlation	1	.055	-.847	-.207	.854	-.234	.623
	Sig. (2-tailed)		.945	.153	.793	.146	.766	.377
	N	4	4	4	4	4	4	4
Tacit	Pearson Correlation	.055	1	-.575	.942	.182	-.854	.488
	Sig. (2-tailed)	.945		.425	.058	.818	.146	.512
	N	4	4	4	4	4	4	4
TE.E	Pearson Correlation	-.847	-.575	1	-.342	-.765	.616	-.805
	Sig. (2-tailed)	.153	.425		.658	.235	.384	.195
	N	4	4	4	4	4	4	4
TE.T	Pearson Correlation	-.207	.942	-.342	1	-.155	-.652	.441
	Sig. (2-tailed)	.793	.058	.658		.845	.348	.559
	N	4	4	4	4	4	4	4
BIZ.T	Pearson Correlation	.854	.182	-.765	-.155	1	-.558	.273
	Sig. (2-tailed)	.146	.818	.235	.845		.442	.727
	N	4	4	4	4	4	4	4
BIZ.E	Pearson Correlation	-.234	-.854	.616	-.652	-.558	1	-.219
	Sig. (2-tailed)	.766	.146	.384	.348	.442		.781
	N	4	4	4	4	4	4	4
Explicit	Pearson Correlation	.623	.488	-.805	.441	.273	-.219	1
	Sig. (2-tailed)	.377	.512	.195	.559	.727	.781	
	N	4	4	4	4	4	4	4

Construct Validity

Construct validity tests whether the results obtained from a research fit the theories around which they have been built. This could be done through convergent validity and discriminant validity.

Convergent Validity

This could be established when the results of two researches agree with each other. We could establish such a validity measure through two ways. First our results concur with the results of Scott Ambler's findings in other survey, namely the documentation and modeling survey published on his website www.ambysoft.com.

Discriminate Validity

Here it is important to examine the relationship among variables presumed to be uncorrelated and make sure there is really no relationship. In our discussion the correlation among variables was low (less than 0.5) meaning that these are not significantly correlated, more over we tested the VIF (Variance Inflation Factor) factor which tended to be between 1 and 1.7, indicating very low covariance between all independent variables.

CONCLUSION

In this chapter, we have demonstrated the results of email-based panel of experts' survey. The

Table 17. Hypotheses of research and results of testing

Hypothesis	Substantiation
H10: There is no relation between software quality and the amount of tacit knowledge sharing used.	Rejected
H11: There is a positive relation between software quality and the amount of tacit knowledge sharing used.	Substantiated
H20: There is no relation between software quality and the amount of tacit knowledge sharing used within the team.	Rejected
H21: There is a positive relation between software quality and the amount of tacit knowledge sharing used within the team.	Substantiated
H30: There is no relation between software quality and the amount of explicit knowledge sharing used.	Rejected
H31: There is a positive relation between software quality and the amount of explicit knowledge sharing used.	Substantiated
H40: There is no relation between software quality and the amount of explicit knowledge sharing used within the team.	Rejected
H41: There is a positive relation between software quality and the amount of explicit knowledge sharing used within the team.	Substantiated
H50: There is no relation between software quality and the amount of explicit knowledge sharing used with business stakeholders.	Rejected
H51: There is a positive relation between software quality and the amount of explicit knowledge sharing used with business stakeholders.	substantiated
H60: There is no relation between software quality and the amount of tacit knowledge sharing used with business stakeholders.	Rejected
H61: There is a positive relation between software quality and the amount of tacit knowledge sharing used with business stakeholders.	Substantiated
H70: The size of organizations has no effect on the relation between software quality and the application of different knowledge sharing techniques.	Rejected

continued on following page

Table 17. Continued

Hypothesis	Substantiation
H71: The size of organizations has an effect on the relation between software quality and the application of different knowledge sharing techniques.	Substantiated: the bigger the organization, the more the need for explicit knowledge sharing whether within team or with business stakeholder
H80: Agile experience of the organization has no effect on the relation between software quality and the application of different knowledge sharing techniques.	Not rejected
H81: Agile experience of the organization has an effect on the relation between software quality and the application of different knowledge sharing techniques.	Cannot be Substantiated
H90: IT experience of the team has no effect on the relation between software quality and the application of different knowledge sharing techniques.	Not rejected
H91: IT experience of the team has an effect on the relation between software quality and the application of different knowledge sharing techniques.	Cannot be Substantiated
H10 0: the stakeholder type has no effect on the relation between software quality and the application of different knowledge sharing techniques.	Not Rejected
H10 1: the stakeholder type has an effect on the relation between software quality and the application of different knowledge sharing techniques.	Cannot be substantiated
H11 0: the stakeholders' collocation has no effect on the relation between software quality and the application of different knowledge sharing techniques.	Rejected
H11 1: the stakeholders' collocation has an effect on the relation between software quality and the application of different knowledge sharing techniques.	substantiated

survey was published in July 2008 on Scott Ambler's website www.ambysoft.com. There were over 300 respondents, but after applying quality measures we were left with 240 responses. Table 17 demonstrates the hypotheses of the research and the results of their testing:

Accordingly, the revised theoretical framework is shown in Figure 24.

REFERENCES

Harris, M. M., & Schaubroeck, J. (1988). A meta-analysis of self-supervisor, self-peer, and peer-supervisor ratings. *Personnel Psychology*, *41*, 43–62. doi:10.1111/j.1744-6570.1988.tb00631.x

Figure 24. Revised hypothetical framework

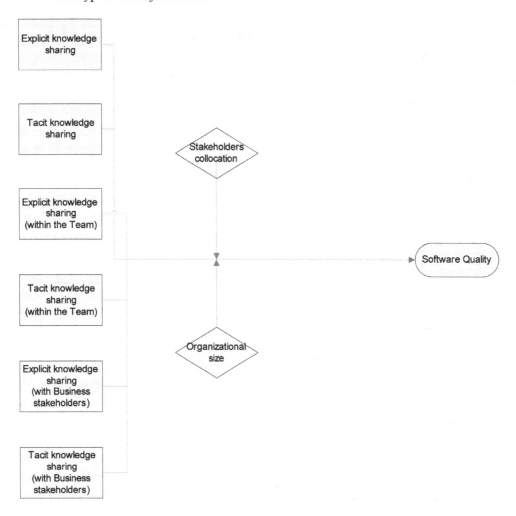

Hershel, R., & Jones, N. (2005). Business intelligence and knowledge management: The importance of integration. *Journal of Knowledge Management*, 44–55.

Miller, K., & Demaio, T. J. (2006). *Report of cognitive research on proposed American community survey disability questions*. Study Series ([), National Center for Health Statistics and U.S.Census Bureau.]. *Survey Methodology*, 2006–6.

Nonaka, I., & Takeuchi, H. (1995). *The knowledge-creating company*. New York, NY: Oxford University Press.

Pourkomeylian, P. (2001). *Software process improvement*. PhD. Thesis Retrieved from http://gupea.ub.gu.se/ dspace/ bitstream/ 2077/ 914/ 1/ pourkomeylian.pdf

Sekaran, U. (2003). *Research methods for business – A skill-building approach*. New York, NY: John Wiley & Sons, Inc.

Stroh, M. (2000). Qualitative interviewing. In Burton, D. (Ed.), *Research training for social scientists. A handbook for postgraduate researchers* (pp. 196–214). London, UK: Sage Publications.

Wiig, K. M. (1997). Knowledge management: An introduction and perspective. *Journal of Knowledge Management, 1*(1), 6–14. doi:10.1108/13673279710800682

KEY TERMS AND DEFINITIONS

Explicit Knowledge: The knowledge that is transmittable in formal, systematic languages. It can be articulated in formal languages, including grammatical statements, mathematical expressions, specifications, manuals and so forth. It can be transmitted across individuals formally and easily.

Explicit Knowledge Sharing: The use of explicit type of knowledge, such as documents, charts and the like.

Knowledge: "Justified true belief" which is subjective, difficult to codify, context-related, rooted in action, relational, and is about meaning. This differs from information as the later is objective and codified in many explicit forms such as documents, computer databases, images and the like.

Knowledge Management: The process an organization uses to identify, create, represent, share, and enable adoption of insights and experiences.

SECI Model: A model suggested by Nonaka and Tackuechi that suggests four transitions might occur: *Tacit to tacit (socialization):* the process of sharing experiences and thereby creating new tacit knowledge, such as shared mental models and technical skills; *Tacit to explicit (externalization):* the process of articulating tacit knowledge into explicit concepts; *Explicit to explicit (combination):* the process of systematizing concepts into a knowledge system, i.e. combining different bodies of explicit knowledge; *Explicit to tacit (internalization):* the process that is closely related to "learning by doing" in which a person tries to incorporate others explicit knowledge and hence transforms it into own tacit knowledge without the need to relive the experience.

Tacit Knowledge: The knowledge that is personal, context-specific, and resides in human beings minds, and is therefore difficult to formalize, codify and communicate. It is personal knowledge that is embedded in individual experience and involves intangible factors such as personal belief, perspective, and value system. Tacit knowledge is difficult to communicate and share in the organization and must thus be converted into words or forms of explicit knowledge.

Tacit Knowledge Sharing: The use of informal communication techniques to share knowledge, such as face –to- face communication.

Chapter 4
Knowledge Discovery Process Models:
From Traditional to Agile Modeling

Mouhib Alnoukari
Arab International University, Syria

Asim El Sheikh
Arab Academy for Banking and Financial Sciences, Jordan

ABSTRACT

Knowledge Discovery (KD) process model was first discussed in 1989. Different models were suggested starting with Fayyad's et al (1996) process model. The common factor of all data-driven discovery process is that knowledge is the final outcome of this process. In this chapter, the authors will analyze most of the KD process models suggested in the literature. The chapter will have a detailed discussion on the KD process models that have innovative life cycle steps. It will propose a categorization of the existing KD models. The chapter deeply analyzes the strengths and weaknesses of the leading KD process models, with the supported commercial systems and reported applications, and their matrix characteristics.

INTRODUCTION

The term 'Knowledge Discovery' (KD) or Knowledge Discovery in Data (KDD) was first coined in 1989. Fayyad defined knowledge discovery as it concerns with "the entire knowledge extraction process, including how data are stored and accessed, how to use efficient and scalable algorithms

to analyze massive datasets, how to interpret and visualize the results, and how to model and support the interaction between human and machine. It also concerns support for learning and analyzing the application domain" (Fayyad et al. 1996).

This means that data mining is simply one of the KD process's steps. Piatetsky-Shapiro explained the difference between knowledge discovery and data mining: "...data mining was used more by database and business folks. The term

DOI: 10.4018/978-1-61350-050-7.ch004

"knowledge discovery" (which I coined in 1989) was more popular among researchers in Artificial Intelligence. Both terms are used to describe the process of searching for useful knowledge in data, but [the term] data mining is much more popular" (Piatetsky-Shapiro 2000).

According to Fayyad et al. (1996), KDP is "the process of using the database along with any required selection, preprocessing, subsampling, and transformations of it; to apply data mining methods (algorithms) to enumerate patterns from it; and to evaluate the products of data mining to identify the subset of the enumerated patterns deemed knowledge".

The various models discussed in this paper are related to data mining and knowledge discovery. They vary in the number, iterations, activities, and structures of their stages. The paper includes analysis of the strengths and weaknesses of each of these methodologies. This paper's survey is different from two older surveys done by Kurgan and Musilek (2006) and Hofmann (2003) in the way it considers the leading KD process models. Our paper completes these two surveys with many of new KD process models presenting the evolutions of these models, and provides a characteristics matrix that summarizes the main differences among the considered models.

KNOWLEDGE DISCOVERY PROCESS MODELING CATEGORIZATION

The following are the proposed categories for Knowledge Discovery Process (KDP) modeling:

1. *Traditional KDP Approach.* This approach is widely used by most of KDP modeling innovators. Starting with Fayyad's et al. (1996) KDD process modeling, many of KDP modeling used the same process flow including most of the following steps: business understanding, data understanding, data processing, data mining/modeling, model evaluation, and deployment/visualization.
2. *Ontology-based KDP Approach.* This approach is the integration of ontology engineering and traditional KDP approach steps. Three directions were identified in this approach: Ontology for KDP, KDP for Ontology, and the integration of both previous directions (Gottgtroy 2007).
3. *Web-based KDP Approach.* This approach mainly deals with web log analysis. It is mainly similar to traditional KDP approach, but it has some unique steps to deal with log web data, see (Pabarskaite and Raudys 2007) and (Buchner et al. 1999).
4. *Agile-based KDP Approach.* This approach is the integration between agile methodologies and KDP traditional methodologies (Alnoukari et al. 2008).

THE LEADING KDP MODELS

The following leading KDP models have been chosen by the authors based on their innovation steps, and their applications in both academia and industry:

1. Knowledge Discovery in Databases (KDD) Process by Fayyad et al. (1996).
2. Information Flow in a Data Mining Life Cycle by Ganesh et al. (1996).
3. SEMMA by SAS Institute (1997).
4. Refined KDD paradigm by Collier et al. (1998).
5. Knowledge Discovery Life Cycle (KDLC) Model by Lee and Kerschberg (1998).
6. CRoss-Industry-Standard Process for Data Mining (CRISP-DM) by CRISP-DM (2000).
7. Generic Data Mining Life Cycle by (DMLC) by Hofmann (2003).
8. Ontology Driven Knowledge Discovery Process (ODKD) by Gottgtroy (2007).

9. Adaptive Software Development-Data Mining (ASD-DM) Process Model by Alnoukari et al. (2008).

The KDP models listed above will be discussed in details, stating their stages or tasks, indicating the strengths and weaknesses of each model. The authors will focus on the evolution of data mining and knowledge discovery process modeling.

The main measures used when evaluating the previous KDP models are the following:

1. *Data*: Defining the exact data sources (where the data is originated) such as: OLTP data bases, data warehouse, data marts, etc. Defining also the data destination (where the data is stored) such as: data repository, knowledge repository, etc. This measure is crucial in any KDP modeling as it defines its main inputs and outputs (Kurgan and Musilek 2006).

2. *Process*: Defining all process's steps or phases involved in the KDP model extended by the processes flows throughout the model's life cycle. The following process's steps have been identified as critical and are necessary to build a comprehensive KDP model: business understanding, data understanding, objectives/hypotheses setting, data preparation/ETL, modeling/data mining, evaluation, and deployment (Hofmann 2003). The naming and amount of the process's steps will be discussed throughout this section.

3. *People*: Defining the human resources involved throughout the KDP model. KDP model should address different kind of skilled peoples including: business analyst, data engineer, data miner, domain expert, knowledge engineer, and strategic manager (Hofmann 2003).

4. *Adaptive*: Defining how the KDP model could be adaptive to environment changes. This measure is crucial for applications (such as data mining and Business Intelligence) where requirements are uncertain or volatile.

5. *Knowledge*: Defining how the KDP model could enhance knowledge capturing and sharing. Knowledge is the core outcome of any KDP model. KDP model are evaluated by their ways to gain new knowledge, and their ways to store and maintain the discovered knowledge for future use.

6. *Strategy*: Defining how the KDP model could help formulating organizations' missions and long term objectives, and helping them in implementing and achieving their strategies.

KNOWLEDGE DISCOVERY IN DATABASES (KDD) PROCESS BY FAYYAD ET AL. (1996)

KDD was one of the first modeling process attempts toward formalizing KDP within a common framework (Cios et al. 2007).

Process Model Description

The Fayyad et al. (1996) KDD process model consists of the following five steps (or nine activities) (Figure 1):

1. *Data selection.* Consists of two sub steps. First, developing and understanding the application domain. Second, creating a target data set from a larger data store. Usually the data miner queries the existing data to select the data relevant to the discovery process. The outcome of this step is the Target Data.

2. *Data preprocessing.* Consists of dealing with noisy and missing data. It also ensures that the code values have coherent uniform meaning. This step ensures that KDD process model produces correct results. The outcome of this step is the Cleaned or Pre-processed Data.

Figure 1. KDD Process Model, adapted from Fayyad et al. (1996)

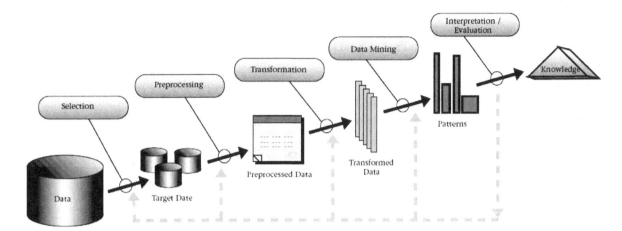

3. *Data Transformation.* This process is the final data processing phase before applying data analysis techniques. It consists of finding useful attributes by applying dimension reduction and transformation methods, and finding invariant representation of the data. The outcome of this process is the Transformed Data.

4. *Data Mining.* This process consists of three steps or sub tasks. First, choosing the data mining task by matching the goals defined in the first phase with a particular data mining method such as clustering, regression, classification, etc. Second, choosing the data mining algorithm(s) and selecting method(s) and parameters in order to search for patterns in data. Third, applying the data mining algorithm(s) in order to generate the data patterns in a particular representation form. The outcomes of this process are the Patterns and Models.

5. *Interpretation/Evaluation.* This process consists of two steps. First, interpreting mined patterns. It can possibly return to any of the previous steps for further iteration (indicated by dashed arrows). This step can also consist of visualization of the extracted patterns and models, or the data extracted from the

extracted models. Second, consolidating the discovered knowledge by incorporating it into the performance system, or simply documenting and reporting it to the desired parties. This step may include checking and fixing any potential conflicts with previously believed knowledge. The outcome of this process is the potential Knowledge.

Discussion

Fayyad's et al. (1996) KDD process model was one of the most popular and the most cited models. It is considered as the cornerstone of all the later KDD process models, as it defined the first KDD process main stages. It provides a comprehensive and a detailed KDD process steps with respect to data analysis and detailed data selection, preprocessing and transformation stages.

The main issue related to this model is that it lacks the business perspective (Cios et al. 2007). Other issues related to this model include: source is data only, no explicit needs for data warehousing or data marts (Hofmann 2003). According to Gartner (2000) the use of data warehouse/data mart provide a solid base of data which is ready to be used for the data mining stage, and offers faster execution of data mining projects. There is also no "deployment" stage which makes it difficult to evaluate and test results of the data mining stage, the knowledge discovered is not stored in order to be used in the future. Fayyad's et al. KDD process model lacks business perspective, also completeness and integrity in order to provide a successful data mining project (Hofmann 2003). It's difficult to adapt with requirements changes, no inner cycle until the end of evaluation stage. Finally this model ignores the involvement of any types of human resources.

Different KDD process models were created based on Fayyad's et al. (1996) KDD model. Feldens et al. (1998) proposed a simplified version of Fayyad's et al. KDD model. They suggested that KDD processes are based on the following main three steps (Figure 2): pre-processing, data mining, and post processing. The starting point for their model is the data warehousing or the legacy data. Collier et al. (1998) suggested an inspection stage after the evaluation process (Collier et al. 1998). They also allowed having inner loop between all process steps without going through the entire life cycle as Fayyad's et al. model. Both Feldens et al. (1998) and Collier et al. (1998) models were more specific in considering the data warehouse as the main source of data, and their models starting points.

INFORMATION FLOW IN A DATA MINING LIFE CYCLE BY GANESH ET AL. (1996)

The initial Information Flow in a Data Mining Life Cycle was developed by Ganesh et al. (1996), the process model was enhanced and extended by Kopanakis and Theodoulidis (1999).

Process Model Description

Ganesh et al. (1996) KD process model consists of the following six steps (Figure 3):

1. *Scrub, verify and summarize data.* The input of this stage is the data stored in operational databases. The data will be transferred into the data warehouse after scrubbing, verifying and summarizing operational data. Data quality in the data warehouse is constantly monitored and checked by the Data Analyst in order to ensure that warehouse data is cleaned, and standardized via data scrubbing.

2. *Selection of the training data sample.* Due to the huge data available in the data warehouse, subset of data is selected to form the training data set for the data mining algorithm. According to Ganesh et al. (1996) it is necessary to iterate this process with the model

Figure 2. KDD Process Model, adapted from Feldens et al. (1998)

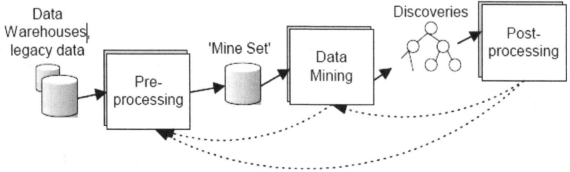

Figure 3. KD Process Model, adapted from Ganesh et al. (1996)

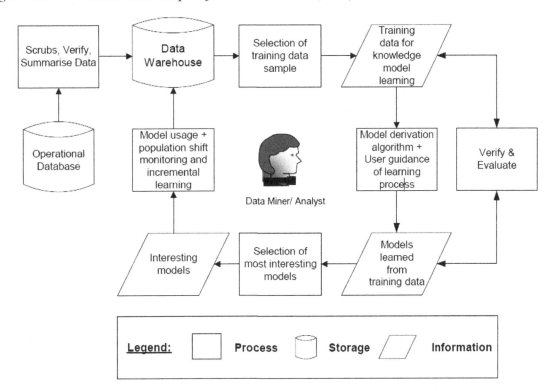

derivation algorithm (next process step) in order to find the suitable data sample.

3. *Model derivation algorithm.* Similar to data mining process that is viewed in this model as the derivation of an appropriate knowledge model of the patterns in the data that are of importance to the analyst or the user. The main advantage of this process is the use of the data analyst directions to decide different model's parameters which have been learned from the data.

4. *Verify and evaluate.* The data analyst verifies and evaluates the models learned from the training data according to different parameters including: accuracy and prevalence.

5. *Selection of most interesting models.* After generating the models, the data analyst chooses the most interesting models to be included in their application.

6. *Model usage + population shift monitoring and incremental learning.* The main focus of

this process step is to observe the updates on the database and to do a continuous validation of the patterns learned previously. This step will provide the business users with only the knowledge of the interesting models. According to Ganesh et al. (1996) some of the knowledge patterns are no longer valid after significant shift in the data warehouse, which leaves the place to develop new knowledge models based on the new data warehouse status.

Discussion

Critiques were made about Ganesh et al. KD process model (Hofmann 2003). The most important critique is that the data flow is not arranged and seems to be wrong at different steps, which makes it difficult to be implemented on data mining projects. Also the outcome of the whole life cycle is unclear; the knowledge models are stored in the data warehouse instead of a separate information and knowledge repository (IKR).

Data mining goals or objectives are not determined. It's vital for any data mining project to identify what the data mining process should discover. Also, this model has no deployment phase and the outcome of the whole life cycle is unclear.

Although this model has an explicit stage for data mining model verification and validation, it has no overall verification and validation stage.

People involvement in this model is only constrained to the data miner/analyst appearing in the diagram, although it was indicated that other types of users are also involved.

Kopanakis and Theodoulidis (1999) have extended this model by grouping Ganesh et al. (1996) steps into three stages:

1. Data preparation stage that includes scrubbing, verifying and summarizing data process which leads data into the data warehouse.
2. Model derivation stage that includes the selection of training data sample, model derivation algorithm, and verification and validation of the models learned from the training data.
3. Validation stage. This stage includes the selection and identification of the most interesting models that lead to create new knowledge. The selected models are continuously checked against the data warehousing models.

Although the categorization of Ganesh et al. (1996) process into three stages makes the model more clear and help assigning activities among various specialists, the updated model still have the same previous critiques.

SEMMA BY SAS INSTITUTE (1997)

This model was created by SAS institute and incorporated into its KD software platform SAS Enterprise Miner™.

Process Model Description

SEMMA process model is an acronym of its five steps:

1. *Sample.* This step consists of sampling the data by extracting a data set big enough to contain the significant information, and small enough to be processed quickly.
2. *Explore.* It consists of data exploration by searching for relationships, trends and anomalies to gain new knowledge.
3. *Modify.* The main focus of this step is the model selection process by creating, selecting and transforming the model variables.
4. *Model.* This step consists of modeling data to find data combinations or patterns that reliably predict the desired outcome.
5. *Assess.* This step consists of evaluating usefulness and reliability of the findings of the modeling steps.

Discussion

SEMMA steps can be seen as a practical implementation of Fayyad's et al. (1996) KDD process model (Azevedo and Santos 2008). By doing a comparison between KDD and SEMMA steps, we can easily confirm that they are equivalent. Sample is equivalent to Selection, Explore is equivalent to Pre-Processing, Modify is equivalent to Transformation, Model is equivalent to Data Mining, and finally Assess can be identified with Interpretation/ Evaluation. Due to this equivalence, SEMMA share the same limitations with the KDD process. SEMMA (1997) contains a case study in Churn Analysis that highlights SEMMA's limitations.

SEMMA steps are directly linked to the SAS Enterprise Miner software. This gives SEMMA the opportunity to be one of the top methodologies used for data mining applications.

SEMMA is considered as one of the leading KDP models due to its high rate usage. Usage of the models has been compiled using the recent poll conducted by KDnuggets (http://www.kdnuggets.com), which is a leading Web resource on DM. The poll from August 2007, which included 150 respondents, shows that 42% of respondents used the CRISP-DM model (Detailed discussion of this model will be conducted later in this paper), 19% used their own model, 13% used SEMMA, 7% used KDD process, 5% used their organization's specific model, 5% used Domain-specific methodology, and 9% used some other model or no model.

REFINED KDD PARADIGM BY COLLIER ET AL. (1998)

The refined KDD process model of Collier et al. (1998) is based on Fayyad et al. (1996) traditional KDD process model.

Process Model Description

Collier's et al. process model is based on the following eight steps (Figure 4):

1. Define the objectives
2. Select the relevant business data
3. Data quality analysis
4. Clean and transform data
5. Data mining
6. Acquire knowledge
7. Evaluate results
8. Deploy results or reiterate

Collier's et al. (1998) proposed model extends Fayyad et al. (1996) KDD process model with the following two important steps:

1. Define the objectives: in this step, business users propose the questions or goals to help in directing the KDD focus. Collier et al. (1998) were the first researchers that recognized the importance of defining the data mining project objectives as the first step in the KDD process. They recognized that without defining the project objectives, data analysis can become confusing and lead to wrong or ambiguous results. According to Collier et al. (1998), data mining can reveal and discover new business trends when used in conjunction with business understanding.

2. Deploy results or re-iterate: this is an additional step to the Fayyad's et al. (1996) traditional KDD processes. In this step, analyst can define instructions on what to do with the data mining findings. Collier et al. (1998) find that it is vital to define a set of actionable results based on the validated models.

Discussion

The main contribution proposed in Collier's et al. (1998) model is that it is based on the iterative life cycle of its eight steps. They suggested that iteration is more integrated in the KDD process model than the traditional model. Successive iteration can serve enhancing data mining outcomes. They are also the first who added two vital steps to the KDD process model: defining the objectives and deploying results or re-iterate.

Collier's et al. (1998) model has some limitations (Hofmann 2003): Data source is not explicitly identified, and the model does not easily respond to business's requirements changes. The model has no inner cycle until the end of deployment stage. The model also ignores the involvement of any type of human resources, and the knowledge discovered is not stored anywhere.

Figure 4. Refined KDD Process Model, adapted from Collier et al. (1998)

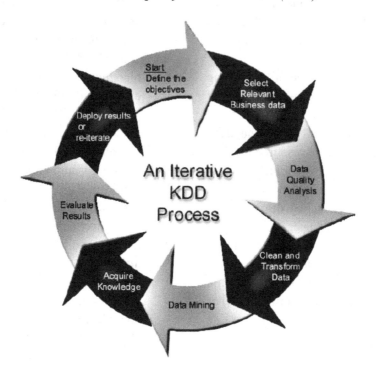

KNOWLEDGE DISCOVERY LIFE CYCLE (KDLC) MODEL BY LEE AND KERSCHBERG (1998)

Knowledge Discovery Life Cycle (KDLC) process model was created by Lee and Kerschberg (1998). KDLC model is mainly based on Fayyad's et al. (1996) KDD process model.

Process Model Description

KDLC process model is divided into six main steps or activities (Figure 5):

1. *Plan for Learning.* The focus of this activity is to plan for a set of experiments and formulate a set of hypotheses in order to discover knowledge. This activity is similar to data preparation activities (including data cleansing, data quality, data integration, etc) of Fayyad's et al. (1996) KDD and Collier et al. (1998) process models. The main difference is that data preparation steps were covered in more details in earlier models than KDLC model.

2. *Generate and Test Hypothesis.* This activity consists of generation hypothesis using investigative analysis, concept formulation, pattern definition and template specification via user queries. It also involves hypothesis testing by analyzing data (Lee and Kerschberg 1998). This activity is also similar to Fayyad's et al. (1996) KDD choosing the data mining tasks and algorithms activities.

3. *Discover Knowledge.* This activity is similar to data mining activity of Fayyad's et al. (1996) KDD process model. It involves the selection of the learning algorithms in order to discover knowledge and to transform it into human understandable structure such as decision trees.

Figure 5. Knowledge Discovery Life Cycle (KDLC) Process Model, adapted from Lee and Kerschberg (1998)

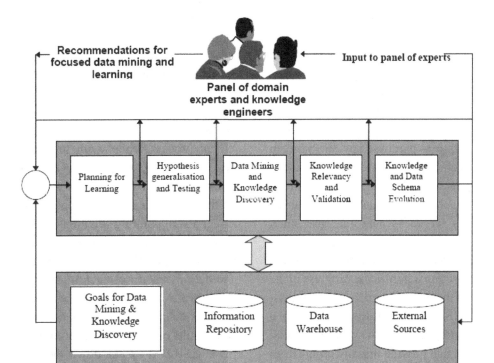

4. *Determine Knowledge Relevancy.* This activity involves the assessment of the discovered knowledge in terms of it relevancy, test cases coverage, and usefulness of the problem analyzed. Knowledge visualization, interpretation, and validation of this activity are similar to Fayyad's et al. (1996) KDD interpreting mined patterns activity.

5. *Evolve Knowledge/Data.* This activity deals with the evolution of the combined knowledge and data bases. As the knowledge is discovered from unambiguous data, domain knowledge, and learning algorithms, this activity is able to deal with knowledge lineage and derivation (Lee and Kerschberg 1998). The vital importance of this activity is its ability to manage the meta-information storage and maintenance in the information repository.

6. *Critique by a Panel of Experts.* This activity involves the assessment of the true meaning of the relevant discovered knowledge using the feedback of a Panel of Experts.\

Discussion

The main strengths of KDLC process model is that it is the first model that deals with the knowledge processing side. The newly discovered knowledge is checked and validated before storing it in a separate knowledge repository. Validation process is done using panel of experts in order to obtain valuable knowledge.

Kurgan and Musilek (2006) and Hofmann (2003) highlight some of the weaknesses of KDLC process model including: lacking sequential data and process flow, and ignoring data preparation and deployment stages.

Cross-Industry-Standard Process for Data Mining (CRISP-DM) by CRISP-DM (2000)

CRISP-DM was one of the first industrial data mining and knowledge discovery process models. It was developed in late 1996 by a large consortium of European companies including: Integral Solutions Ltd. (a provider of commercial data mining solutions purchased by SPSS Inc. in 1998), NCR (Teradata data warehouse provider), DaimlerChrysler (an automobile manufacturer), and OHRA (Dutch insurance company). The last two companies served as data and case study sources (Shearer 2000).

CRISP-DM version 1.0 was released in the year 2000, reflecting a significant progress in the development of the first standardized data processing model. CRISP-DM was fully supported by a special group named CRISP-DM SIG (Special Interest Group) that provide initially inputs from more the 200 users, data mining tools, and service providers.

CRISP-DM was initially tested by its supporting companies. DaimlerChrysler adapted it to develop its own customer relationship management (CRM) tool to improve customer marketing.

OHRA provided a valuable live environment for CRISP-DM testing. SPSS incorporated it in its Clementine commercial data mining workbench product.

Process Model Description

According to CRISP-DM (2000), CRISP-DM methodology is described in terms of a hierarchical process model with the following four levels of abstraction (Figure 6): in the top level, each process model consists of six phases, each of these phases consists of generic tasks that can cover all data mining situations, and intend to be stable and complete as possible. The specialized tasks level is the third level, where it describes the actions taken for each of the generic tasks. The top down level is the process instances. Each process instance records the actions, decisions, and results of an actual data mining engagement.

CRISP-DM breaks down the life cycle of a data mining project into the following six steps (Figure 7):

1. *Business Understanding.* The focus of this step is the understanding of the project objectives and requirements from business

Figure 6. CRISP-DM Hierarchical Process Model, adapted from CRISP-DM (2000)

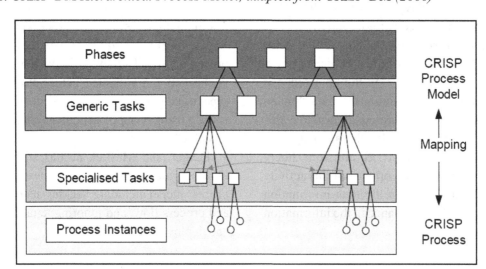

perspectives, and converting it into a data mining problem definition and a preliminary project plan. This first step is broken into the following activities:

- Determination of business objectives.
- Assessment of the situation.
- Determination of DM goals.
- Generation of a project plan.

2. *Data Understanding.* This step starts with data collection, and proceeds with all the activities that can help users become familiar with the data. It is broken into the following activities:

- Collection of initial data.
- Description of data.
- Exploration of data.
- Verification of data quality.

3. *Data Preparation.* This step covers all the activities needed to construct the final dataset that will feed into the modeling next phase. It can be divided into the following activities:

- Data selection.

- Data cleansing,
- Data construction.
- Data integration.
- Data formatting.

4. *Modeling.* The focus of this step is the selection and application of the appropriate modeling techniques. Parameters for the chosen modeling techniques are calibrated to obtain optimal values. Reiteration into the previous step is often required as some modeling techniques may require specific data format. This step can be divided into the following activities:

- Selection of modeling technique(s).
- Generation of test design.
- Creation of models.
- Assessment of generated models.

5. *Evaluation.* This step is vital as it ensures that the chosen model(s) achieves the business objectives properly. A key objective of this step is to determine if there are important business issues that have not been suffi-

Figure 7. CRISP-DM Phases, adapted from CRISP-DM (2000)

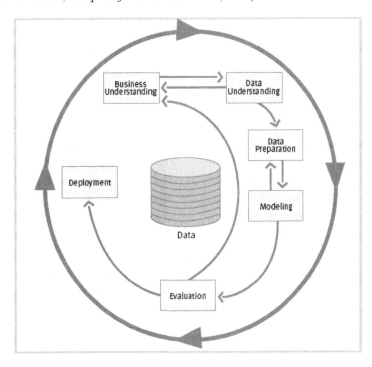

ciently considered. The evaluation step can be broken into the following activities:
- ◦ Evaluation of the results.
- ◦ Process review.
- ◦ Determination of the next step.

6. *Deployment.* The focus of this step is to organize and present the discovered knowledge in a way that the customer can use. This step is the endpoint of data mining project life cycle, and can be easy as the generation of data mining report or as difficult as implementing a repeatable data mining process across the organization. Deployment step can be divided into the following activities:
- ◦ Plan deployment.
- ◦ Plan monitoring and maintenance.
- ◦ Generation of final report.
- ◦ Review of the process substeps.

Discussion

Due to its support from a large consortium of European companies, CRIPS-DM was the most KD process model adopted in many data mining projects since its launch in the year 2000. References to knowledge discovery and data mining projects that used CRISP-DM process model include: (Maedche et al. 2000), (Gersten et al. 2000), (Pritscher and Feyen 2001), (Luan 2002), (Sund 2003), (Euler 2005), (Antons and Maltz 2006), (Caprace 2007), (Castellano et al. 2007), (Gunnarsson et al. 2007), (Bellazzi and Zupan 2008) and (Razali and Ali 2009).

CRISP-DM was the first KDD process model which explicitly launched the newly two important steps: business understanding and data understanding. According to Hofmann and Tierney (2007), these two steps are the cornerstone of any successful data mining projects as they can help digging more insights into the business objectives and current data availability. CRISP-DM is also characterized by clearly defined stages, in which each stage is divided into sub stages that provide the necessary details, with good documentation.

Although CRISP-DM is the most widely adopted KDD process model, it has many limitations. Different case studies highlight CRISP-DM limitations, see (Euler 2005), (Antons and Maltz 2006) and (Caprace 2007). These include: Source is data only; there is no explicit need for data warehousing or data marts. Deployment stage is a dead point, and ends the workflow since the final report is the end of the project. Knowledge discovered is not stored anywhere, and not used for any further investigation. CRISP-DM also ignores the involvement of human resources that are the cornerstone of any knowledge-based application (Hofmann 2003).

According to Gartner (2000), CRISP-DM documentation should be used as a framework rather than a methodology that can be immediately applicable. It also critiques CRISP-DM model as it's not able to support the following tasks:

- Identifying business decisions that could benefit from data mining.
- Evaluating quantity and quality of the source data.
- Choosing which of the many data mining steps is the most appropriate at any time.
- Exploiting insights from the analysis.
- Advising on changes in business practices.

One of the main limitations of CRISP-DM is in its linear and sequential life cycle model (Rennolls and AL-Shawabkeh 2008). Although feedback loops are mentioned, the model is dominated by the sequential nature, which does not appropriately characterize the dynamism of knowledge discovery. According to Rennolls and AL-Shawabkeh (2008), CRISP-DM has no real DM methodology as there is no methodology for the process of model selection.

Generic Data Mining Life Cycle by (DMLC) by Hofmann (2003)

Generic Data Mining Life Cycle (DMLC) was proposed by Hofmann (2003). The model is mainly based on CRISP-DM by avoiding the weaknesses of the previous models, especially the CRISP-DM model.

Process Model Description

DMLC model consists of nine steps grouped in the following three stages (Hofmann and Tierney 2007) (Figure 8):

1. *Hypotheses/Objectives preparation stage.* Consists of business understanding, data understanding and hypotheses/objectives definition steps.
2. *Data preparation stage.* Consists of select/ sample data, pre-process and transformation steps.
3. *Discovery and validation stage.* Consists of data mining, evaluation and deployment steps.

The model data store is based on the foundation of data warehouse/data mart and the information and knowledge repository (IKR).

Figure 8. Data Mining Life Cycle (DMLC) Phases, adapted from Hofmann and Tierney (2007)

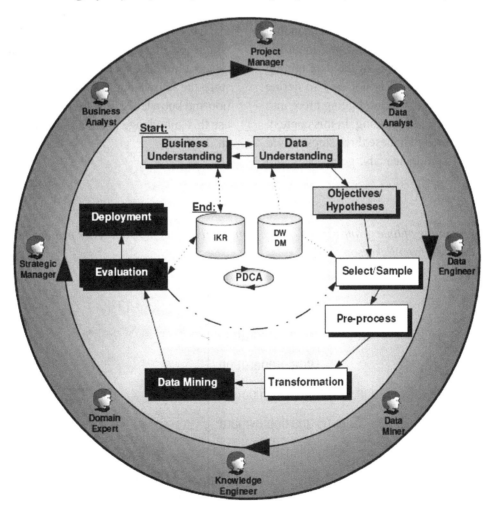

The model is circled by a list of human resources that have to be involved in the data mining project life cycle including: project manager, business analyst, data analyst, data engineer, data miner, knowledge engineer, domain expert, and strategic manager. The huge involvement of human resources in any data mining project maximizes the project outcome.

Discussion

Hofmann was one of the first KDD process modeler who raised the attention on the importance of the objectives/hypotheses preparation stage. He thought that the three steps: business understanding, data understanding and hypotheses/objectives definition should be seen as a whole. The logic behind this integration is clear as it is not possible to carry out the business understanding analyses if there is no initial thought about the hypotheses or the objectives of the data mining project, and vice versa, it is not easy to define the project objectives without digging more into business and data understanding. In this context, Hofmann suggested that these three steps should be approached simultaneously, going back and forth till the objectives/hypotheses are clearly set (Hofmann 2003).

Hofmann agreed with (Feldens 1998), (Eckerson 2007), (Inmon 2005) and (Turban et al. 2007) findings that the first two stages take most of data mining workload in order to ensure a successful data mining results (Figure 9). Feldens et al. (1998) even consider that these two steps take 80% of the overall workload.

DMLC main focus was to avoid the weaknesses of CRISP-DM model. This include: defining the start and end point of the KDD process, connecting the various processes flow through a sequential iteration, the detailed involvement of different types of human resources, and ensuring the quality and the correctness of each process using the PDCA methodology.

DMLC still have some weaknesses especially that it was built for large scale data mining projects which consider the huge involvement of different types of human experts. It is also unclear how to store the knowledge discovered in the information and knowledge repository (IKR), and how to use this knowledge to create and update business strategy.

Figure 9. Percentage of time groups spend on each phase in a predictive analytics project based on 166 responses, adapted from Eckerson (2007)

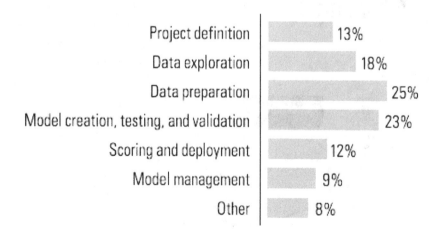

Ontology Driven Knowledge Discovery process (ODKD) by Gottgtroy (2007)

Ontology Driven Knowledge Discovery (ODKD) Process Model was proposed by Gottgtroy (2007). This process model was one of the first steps combining the prior knowledge (in terms of Ontology) and the process of knowledge discovery in an explicit and clear life cycle.

Many researches raised the importance of integrating between ontology engineering and KDD processes. Anand et al. (1995) work provides the first guidelines to reduce the data set needed for the knowledge discovery process using three types of domain knowledge. Owrang (2000) discusses the benefits of using the domain knowledge to constrain the search for beneficial knowledge by reducing the size of the data base needed to acquire this knowledge, reducing the size of the hypotheses by removing the unnecessary conditions, and finally reducing the list of operations

needed to provide the data required to validate the list of reduced hypotheses. Other researches proposed ontology guided methodologies to gain domain knowledge such as: (Yoon and Henschen 1999), (Phillips and Buchanan 2001), (Gottgtroy et al. 2003), (Svatek et al. 2005), (Svatek et al. 2006) and (Kuo et al. 2007).

Process Model Description

ODKD Model is based on both ontology engineering and CRISP-DM methodology. ODKD process model is composed of five phases in a hybrid life cycle. ODKD process model phases are the following (Figure 10):

1. *Ontology Preparation.* This is the initial phase that deals with the requirement gathering and data preparation tasks. It is subdivided into three pipelines:
    ◦   Domain understanding: Consists of two tasks: domain ontology selection

Figure 10. Ontology Driven Knowledge Discovery Process (ODKD) phases and tasks, adapted from Gottgtroy (2007)

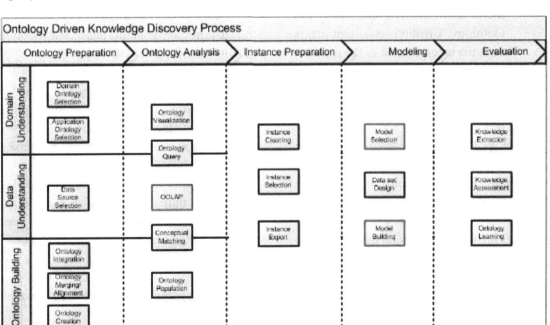

to select the knowledge that cover the problem perspective, and application ontology selection task that deals with the ontology assessment and selection, knowledge quadrant analysis, and knowledge representation mapping plan.

○ Data understanding: This phase deals with getting familiar with data after data collection based on the previous requirement gathering tasks. It also covers the steps needed to identify quality problems, and mapping data with the selected ontology.

○ Ontology Building: This is the last pipeline in ontology preparation phase. It consists of the following three tasks: Ontology Integration that deals with the integration between the selected ontology and business understanding in order to add a broader perspective to the problem domain. Ontology Merge/alignment to map concepts and relation between two Ontologies to form a new set of concepts and relations that represent the problem domain, and finally the Ontology Creation task that deals with the incorporation of the problem specific knowledge with the set of concepts and relations created in the previous Ontology Merge/Alignment task.

2. *Ontology Analysis.* This phase is related to the initial steps for ontology model discovery. It is subdivided into four pipelines: Ontology Visualization, Ontology Query, Conceptual Matching and Ontology Population. Ontology visualization and query steps are related to the exploration of the ontology model using visualization and search means, whereas conceptual matching and ontology population deal with the construction of the knowledge base.

3. *Instance Preparation.* This phase deals with all the activities related to constructing the optimal data set that will feed into the modeling phase. It is subdivided into three pipelines:

○ Instance cleaning: like data cleansing, this task deals with removing errors and detecting inconsistency from instance in order to improve the quality of instances that feed into the ontology modeling.

○ Instance selection: this task focuses on providing meaning to data and reducing features by understanding the domain.

○ Instance export: this task deals with the translation of the ontological model into a format that can be undertaken by the data mining algorithms, or exporting the knowledge base into a database format.

4. *Modeling.* In this phase, different modeling techniques are selected, applied and tested in order to validate the patterns found from different perspectives.

5. *Evaluation.* This phase deals with the validation of the knowledge extracted from the data mining modeling phase. It is subdivided into the following three pipelines:

○ Knowledge extraction: this task focus on transforming the knowledge discovered by the data mining model into the ontological model.

○ Knowledge assessment: this task focus on the analysis of the ontological model to validate the knowledge acquired or acquires more domain knowledge to maintain the knowledge base.

○ Ontology learning: this task deals with the assessed knowledge to update the current ontological model.

Discussion

Integrating ontology with knowledge discovery process has the aim to improve knowledge discovery in complex and dynamical domains (Gottgtroy et al. 2003). Three approaches are indentified concerning integration between ontology and KD. The first approach is the application of Ontologies to improve the KDP. The second approach focus on the application of data mining techniques to acquire knowledge from data. The third approach is the integration of the previous two approaches in order to bridge the gap between ontological engineering and knowledge discovery.

ODKD model is one of the first process models that attempt to integrate both approaches. ODKD model focuses on resolving the following issues related to the traditional KD processes (Gottgtroy et al. 2003) and (Gottgtroy 2007):

- Missing semantic and schema description as most of data warehouses schemas (such as star schema) lack the semantic direction description.
- Missing support for non-expert users. Most of non expert users do not have enough experiences on how to choose and apply the appropriate data mining tool, or to select the appropriate data set, or to formulate the appropriate data query.
- Lack effective, active knowledge updates. Most of the previous approaches do not explicitly fix the issues related to update the discovered knowledge effectively, or accumulate the new knowledge with the knowledge base.

Adaptive Software Development-Data Mining (ASD-DM) Process Model by Alnoukari et al. (2008)

Adaptive Software Development-Data Mining (ASD-DM) process model was proposed by Alnoukari et al. (2008). This model was the first to introduce agile methodologies into data mining process modeling. The basic idea behind this integration is that adaptive approaches are best fit when requirements are uncertain or volatile (this characterizes most of data mining applications); this can happen due to business's requirements changes, and rapid evolving markets. It is difficult to practice traditional methodologies in such unstable evolving markets.

Process Model Description

ASD-DM model consists of six steps grouped in the following three phases (Alnoukari et al. 2008) (Figure 11):

1. *Speculation.* Includes business and data understanding, and data preparations including ETL (Extract/Transform/Load) operations. This phase is the most important one as it takes considerable time and resources. This preparation phase will end by creating the enterprise data warehouse, and the required data marts and cubes.
2. *Collaboration.* Ensures the high communication in a diversity of experienced stakeholders in order to use the best modeling algorithm for predicative data mining process.
3. *Learning.* Testing and evaluating of such algorithms occur in this phase, the results will be discussed among the members of the project team. If the results are acceptable, a new release can be deployed in a form of predictive scoring reports, otherwise a new collaboration phase will be used in order to choose better data mining algorithm.

The cyclic nature of the whole framework can respond to the business dynamic changes, a new data sources can be added to the preparation phase, and the cycle will move again.

Figure 11. ASD-DM process model phases, adapted from Alnoukari et al. (2008)

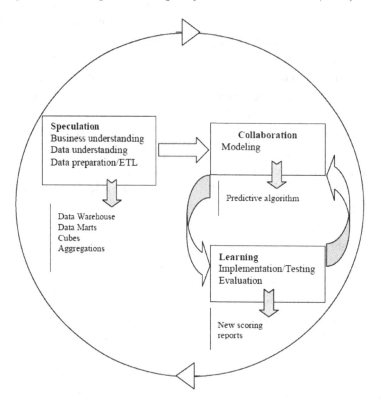

Discussion

ASD-DM process model was one of the first attempts to integrate agile modeling with KDD process modeling. The main focus of this model is to make it less costly to customize and adapt development processes. ASD agile modeling is best fit when requirements are uncertain or volatile, which makes it difficult to use traditional methodologies in such unstable evolving markets.

Speculation recognizes the uncertain nature of complex problems such as predictive data mining, and encourages exploration and experimentation. Predictive data mining problems require a huge volume of information to be collected, analyzed, and applied; they also require advanced knowledge, and greater business skills than typical problems, which need "Collaboration" among different stakeholders, in order to improve their decision making ability. That decision making ability depends on "Learning" component in order

to test knowledge raised by practices iteratively after each cycle, rather than waiting till the end of the project. Learning organizations can adapt more easily with ASD life cycle.

ASD-DM model was applied in different areas including: higher education, automotive manufacturing, and customer care, see (Alnoukari et al. 2008), (Diko et al. 2008) and (Alnoukari et al. 2009). ASD-DM previous mentioned case studies highlight some limitations such as: Data source is not explicitly identified, the model has no explicit deployment stage, the model also ignores the involvement of any type of human resources, and the knowledge discovered is not stored anywhere.

OTHER KDP MODELS

There are many other KDP models that have less significant impacts due to the fact that they are

Table 1. Other KDP models' steps summary

KDP Model	Ref.	KDP Approach	No of Steps	KDP Model Steps
Adriaans & Zantinge	(Adriaans and Zantinge 1996)	Traditional KDP Approach	6	Data Selection, Cleaning, Enrichment, Coding, DM, Reporting.
Berry & Linoff	(Berry and Gordon 1997)	Traditional KDP Approach	4	Identifying the Problem, Analyzing the Problem, Taking Action, Measuring the Outcome.
Feldens et al.	Feldens et al. (1998)	Traditional KDP Approach	3	Pre-Processing, Data Mining, Post-Processing.
Cabena et al.	(Cabena et al. 1998)	Traditional KDP Approach	5	Business Objectives Determination, Data Preparation, DM, Domain Knowledge Elicitation, Assimilation of Knowledge.
Edelstein	(Edelstein 1998)	Traditional KDP Approach	5	Identifying the Problem, Preparing the Data, Building the Model, Using the Model, Monitoring the Model.
Anand & Buchner	Buchner et al. (1999)	Web-based KDP Approach	8	Human Resource Identification, Problem Specification, Data Prospecting, Domain Knowledge Elicitation, Methodology Identification, Data Preprocessing, Pattern Discovery, Knowledge Post-processing.
Reinartz	(Reinartz 1999)	Traditional KDP Approach	7	Business Understanding, Data Understanding, Data Preparation, Data Exploration, Data Mining, Evaluation, Deployment.
Kopanakis & Theodoulidis	Kopanakis and Theodoulidis (1999)	Traditional KDP Approach	6	Scrub, verify and summarize data, Selection of the training data sample, Model derivation algorithm, Verify and evaluate, Selection of most interesting models, Model usage + population shift monitoring and incremental learning.
Han & Cercone	(Han and Cercone 2000)	Traditional KDP Approach	5	Original Data Visualization, Data Reduction, Data Preprocess, Pattern Discovery, Pattern Visualization.
Cios et al.	(Cios et al. 2000)	Traditional KDP Approach	6	Understanding the Problem Domain, Understanding the Data, Preparation of the Data, DM, Evaluation of the Discovered Knowledge, Using the Discovered Knowledge.
Han & Kamber	(Han and Kamber 2001)	Traditional KDP Approach	9	Learning the Application domain, Creating a Target Data Set, Data Cleaning and Preprocessing, Data Reduction and Transformation, Choosing Functions of DM, Choosing the Mining Algorithm(s), DM, Pattern Evaluation and Knowledge Presentation, Use of Discovered Knowledge.
Klosgen & Zytkow	(Klosgen and Zytkow 2002)	Traditional KDP Approach	7	Definition and Analysis of Business Problems, Understanding and Preparation of Data, Setup of the Search for Knowledge, Search for Knowledge, Knowledge Refinement, Application of Knowledge in Solving the Business Problems, Deployment and Practical, Evaluation of the Solutions.
Haglin et al.	(Haglin et al. 2005)	Traditional KDP Approach	7	Goal Identification, Target Data Creation, Data Preprocessing, Data Transformation, DM, Evaluation and Interpretation, Take Action steps.
Pabarskaite & Raudys	Pabarskaite and Raudys (2007)	Web-based KDP Approach	9	Data collection, Data cleaning, User identification, Session identification, Feature selection, Data transformation, Data combination, Mining the data, Result visualization.
Li & Ruan	(Li and Ruan 2007)	Traditional KDP Approach	6	Data Collection, Selection, Preprocessing, Transformation, Data Mining, Interpretation/Evaluation.
KDCK	Rennolls and AL-Shawabkeh (2008)	Ontology-based KDP Approach	5	Data Collection and Processing, Data Understanding, DM/Modeling, Knowledge Understanding, Business Understanding.

based on the models described in the previous paragraph, so the paper will not describe these KDP models in details. Table 1 summarizes these other KDP models and provides KDP model name, references, its approach, number of steps and the KDP steps for each of these models.

KDP MODELS: HISTORICAL OVERVIEW

Figure 12 shows most of the KDP models starting with Fayyad's et al. model. The innovative models (presented in bold) are considered the baseline for all the other KDP models. This diagram provides also an idea about the historical evolution of all the KDP models.

KDP MODELS: SUMMARY OF STRENGTHS & WEAKNESSES

Table 2 shows a detailed analysis of all the nine main KDP models described previously. Strengths and weaknesses of these models are based on KDP Model's innovation, simplicity, data source, people's involvement, discovered knowledge usage, stages, completeness, and model's dynamism.

Most of the nine KDP models follow a similar sequence of steps which are: domain understanding, data preparation, data mining, evaluation and deployment. Most of these models are based on the traditional KDP approach initiated by Fayyad et al. (1996) KDD model. Gottgtroy model is based on Ontology KDP approach, while Alnou-

Figure 12. KDP Models: historical evolution

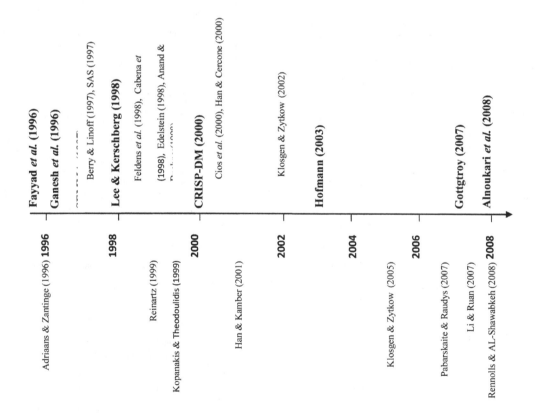

Table 2. List of the main KDP models' strengths and weaknesses

KD Process Model	KDP Approach	Strengths	Weaknesses
Fayyad et al.)1996(	Traditional KDP Approach	• Fayyad's et al. KDD model was the cornerstone of all the later KDD process models. • Simple and clear iterative stages. • Define the first KDD process main stages. • Detailed data selection, pre-processing and transformation stages.	• Source is data only, no explicit needs for data warehousing or data marts. According to Gartner (2000) the use of data warehouse/data mart provide a solid base of data that is ready to be used for the data mining stage, and offers faster execution of data mining projects. • No "deployment" stage which make difficult to evaluate and test results of the data mining stage. • No inner cycle until the end of evaluation stage. • Lack completeness and integrity in order to succeed a successful data mining project. • Lack business perspective. • Ignore the involvement of human resources. • Difficult to adapt with requirements changes. • Knowledge discovered is not stored anywhere.
Ganesh et al. (1996)	Traditional KDP Approach	• Involvement of human experts. • Good data preparation and use of data warehouse. • Verification and validation of the data mining model.	• Data flow is not arranged. • Data mining objectives are not determined. • No deployment phase and the outcome of the whole life cycle is unclear. • No overall verification and validation stage.
SEMMA (1997)	Traditional KDP Approach	• Reliable as the model is based on modern analytical practices. • Time and cost effective as it is based on samples of data.	• Same as Fayyad et al. (1996) process model weaknesses.
Collier et al (1998)	Traditional KDP Approach	• Based on iterative life cycle. • Identify the importance of adding the "Define the Objectives" step to the KDD processes life cycle. • Identify the importance of adding the "Deploy results" step to the KDD processes life cycle.	• Data source is not explicitly identified. • No inner cycle until the end of deployment stage. • Ignore the involvement of human resources. • Knowledge discovered is not stored anywhere.
Lee and Kerschberg (1998)	Traditional KDP Approach	• KDLC process model is the first KDD process model dealing with the knowledge processing side. • Newly knowledge discovered is stored in the information repository. • Involvement of human experts. • Definition of hypotheses. • KDLC main focus is on knowledge discovery, validation and evolution.	• No deployment stage. • Data flow is not arranged. • Ignores data preparation stage.
CRISP-DM (2000)	Traditional KDP Approach	• CRISP-DM model is the most widely used as a KDD process model for data mining projects. • Easy to understand and clearly defined stages. • Divided all phases into sub-phases that provide all necessary details. • Has good documentation.	• Source is data only, no explicit needs for data warehousing or data marts. • Deployment stage is a dead point, and ends the workflow since the final report is the end of the project. • Ignore the involvement of human resources. • Knowledge discovered is not stored anywhere.

continued on the following page

Table 2. Continued

KD Process Model	KDP Approach	Strengths	Weaknesses
Hofmann (2003)	Traditional KDP Approach	• Easy to understand and clearly defined stages. • Divided all stages into sub stages that provide all necessary details. • Use of different data sources: data warehousing/data marts, and information and knowledge repository. • Excellent involvement of human resources. • Knowledge discovered is stored in the information and knowledge repository (IKR).	• Not easy to be implemented as it needs huge resources. • Not clear how to store the knowledge discovered. • Poor documentation.
Gottgtroy (2007)	Ontology-based KDP Approach	• ODKD model is one of the first process models that attempt to integrate Ontologies and KDD processes. • Verification and validation of the knowledge extracted. • Support semantic and schema description. • Support active knowledge updates.	• Data flow is not arranged. • Not clear how to store the knowledge discovered. • Poor involvement of human resources.
Alnoukari et al. (2008)	Agile-based KDP Approach	• Alnoukari's et al. ASD-DM was the first model integrating agile modeling with KDD process modeling. • Simple and clear iterative stages. • Can respond easily to business's requirements changes and repaid evolving markets.	• Data source is not explicitly identified. • No explicit "deployment" stage. • Lack completeness and integrity in order to succeed a successful data mining project. • Ignore the involvement of human resources. • Knowledge discovered is not stored anywhere.

Table 3. KDP models supported commercial systems and reported applications

KDP Model	Model Name	KDP Approach	Supporting Commercial Systems	Reported Applications
Fayyad et al. (1996)	KDD	Traditional KDP Approach	MineSet™	Medicine, Engineering, Production, E-Business, Software.
Ganesh et al. (1996)		Traditional KDP Approach	N/A	N/A
SEMMA (1997)	SEMMA	Traditional KDP Approach	SAS Enterprise Miner™	Wide range of applications including: Marketing, Manufacturing, Sales, etc.
Collier et al. (1998)		Traditional KDP Approach	N/A	Medicine, Engineering, Marketing, Sales.
Lee and Kerschberg (1998)	KDLC	Traditional KDP Approach	N/A	N/A
CRISP-DM (2000)	CRISP-DM	Traditional KDP Approach	Clementine®	Wide range of applications including: Medicine, Engineering, Marketing, Sales, etc.
Hofmann (2003)	DMLC	Traditional KDP Approach	N/A	Transportation.
Gottgtroy (2007)	ODKD	Ontology-based KDP Approach	N/A	Biomedicine
Alnoukari et al. (2008)	ASD-DM	Agile-based KDP Approach	N/A	Higher Education, Automotive, Customer Care

kari et al. (2008) model is based on agile KDP approach.

by Clementine®, and SEMMA is supported by SAS Enterprise Miner™.

KDP MODELS: SUPPORTED COMMERCIAL SYSTEMS AND REPORTED APPLICATIONS

Table 3 shows KDP models that are supported by commercial systems. It clearly shows that only very few KDP models are supported by commercial systems. Fayyad's et al. KDD process is supported by MineSet™, CRISP_DM is supported

KDP MODELS: CHARACTERISTICS MATRIX

Table 4 shows the characteristics matrix for the nine innovative KDP models. This table summarizes the main differences between the main KDP models based on the following six measures: data, process, people, adaptive, knowledge, and strategy.

Table 4. KDP models' characteristics matrix

	Fayyad et al. (1996)	Ganesh et al. (1996)	SEMMA (1997)	Collier et al (1998)	Lee and Kerschberg (1998)	CRISP-DM (2000)	Hofmann (2003)	Gottgtroy (2007)	Alnoukari et al. (2008)
General									
KDP Model Name	KDD		SEMMA		KDLC	CRISP-DM	DMLC	ODKD	ASD-DM
Data Centric	√	√		√	√	√	√	√	√
Process Centric	√	√	√	√	√	√	√	√	√
People Centric					√		√	√	
Adaptive Centric		√		√	√	√	√		√
Knowledge Centric		√					√	√	
Strategy Centric							√		
Data Sources									
Data	√	√			√	√	√	√	
Data Warehouse/Data Marts		√			√		√		√
Other sources					√				
Process									
Number of steps	6	6	5	8	6	6	9	5	6
Human Resources									
Project Manager							√		
Business Analyst							√		
Data Analyst		√					√		
Data Engineer							√		
Data Miner		√					√		
Domain Expert					√		√		
Knowledge Engineer					√		√		
Strategic Manager							√		

The last three measures: adaptive, knowledge and strategy are introduced by the authors as they provide a clear comprehension on how KDP models adapt with requirements changes and rapid evolving markets, how KDP models utilize and store the discovered knowledge, and finally how KDP models support organization's strategy.

Table 4 clearly shows that most of the considered KDP models (except for DMLC, see Hofmann 2003) are not supporting all the previous measures.

CONCLUSION

In this paper, the authors provide a detailed survey on knowledge discovery process models. The paper provides a historical overview about most of the KDP models presented in the literature. The paper categorizes KDP models into four categories: Traditional, Ontology-based, Web-based and Agile-based approaches. Most of the KDP models starting with Fayyad et al. model follow the traditional approach. The paper provides a detailed discussion about nine of KDP models according to the innovative steps, usage rate and approaches related to each of these models. It also added three important measures for KDP model evaluation. These measures are: adaptive, knowledge, and strategy. These measures are added to the old measures proposed in previous surveys which are: data, people, and process centric Analysis of the strengths and weaknesses in each of these nine KDP models can help the authors to enhance their ASD-DM KDP model.

REFERENCES

Adriaans, P., & Zantinge, D. (1996). *Data Mining*. Harlow, UK: Addison-Wesley.

Alnoukari, M., Alzoabi, Z., & Hanna, S. (2008). Applying adaptive software development (ASD) agile modeling on predictive data mining applications: ASD-DM Methodology. In *IEEE Proceedings of International Symposium on Information Technology* (pp. 1083-1087).

Alnoukari, M., Sheikh, A. E., & Alzoabi, Z. (2009). Applying ASD-DM methodology on business intelligence solutions: A case study on building customer care data mart. In A. P. Abraham (Ed.), *The Proc. Data Mining 2009, IADIS Multi Conference on Computer Science and Information Systems (MCCMIS 2009)* (pp. 153-157).

Anand, S. S., Bell, D. A., & Hughes, J. G. (1995). The role of domain knowledge in data mining. In *Proceedings of the 4ᵗʰ International Conference on Information and Knowledge Management* (pp. 37-43).

Antons, C. M., & Maltz, E. N. (2006). Expanding the role of institutional research at small private universities: A case study in enrollment management using data mining. *New Directions for Institutional Research, 131*, 69–81. doi:10.1002/ir.188

Azevedo, A., & Santos, M. F. (2008). KDD, SEMMA and CRISP-DM: A parallel overview. In *Proceedings of the IADIS European Conference Data Mining* (pp. 182-185).

Bellazzi, R., & Zupan, B. (2008). Predictive data mining in clinical medicine: Current issues and guidelines. *International Journal of Medical Informatics, 77*, 81–97. doi:10.1016/j.ijmedinf.2006.11.006

Berry, M. J., & Gordon, L. (1997). *Data mining techniques: For marketing, sales, and customer support*. New York, NY: Wiley.

Buchner, A. G., Mulvenna, M. D., Anand, S. S., & Hughes, J. G. (1999). An Internet-enabled knowledge discovery process. In *Proceedings of the 9ᵗʰ International Database Conference* (pp. 13-27).

Cabena, P., Hadjinian, P., Stadler, R., Verhees, J., & Zanasi, A. (1998). *Discovering data mining: From concept to implementation.* Upper Saddle River, NJ: Prentice Hall.

Caprace, J. D., Losseau, N., Archambeau, D., Bair, F., & Philippe, R. (2007). A data mining analysis applied to a straightening process database. In *Proceedings of Computer Applications and Information Technology in the Maritime Industries (COMPIT'07)* (pp. 186-196).

Castellano, M., Mastronardi, G., Aprile, A., Minardi, M., Catalano, P., Dicensi, V., & Tarricone, G. (2007). A decision support system base line flexible architecture to intrusion detection. *Journal of Software, 2*(6), 30–41. doi:10.4304/jsw.2.6.30-41

Cios, K. J., Pedrycz, W., Swiniarski, R. W., & Kurgan, L. A. (2007). *Data mining: A knowledge discovery process.* Berlin, Heidelberg: Springer.

Cios, K. J., Teresinska, A., Konieczna, S., Potocka, J., & Sharma, S. (2000). Diagnosing myocardial perfusion from PECT bull's-eye maps—A knowledge discovery approach. *IEEE Engineering in Medicine and Biology Magazine, Special issue on Medical Data Mining and Knowledge Discovery, 19*(4), 17-25.

Collier, K., Carey, B., Grusy, E., Marjaniemi, C., & Sautter, D. (1998). *A perspective on data mining. Northern Arizona University.* USA: Centre for Data Insight.

CRISP-DM. (2000). *Step by step data mining guide.* CRISP-DM Consortium.

Diko, F., Alzoabi, Z., & Alnoukari, M. (2008). *Enhancing education quality assurance using data mining, case study: Arab International University systems. In 3rd.* European Quality Assurance Forum.

Eckerson, W. W. (2007). *Predictive analytics: Extending the value of your data warehousing investment.* Chatsworth, CA, USA: TDWI.

Edelstein, H. (1998). Data mining: Let's get practical. *DB2 Magazine 3*(2) 38-40.

Euler, T. (2005). Publishing operational models of data mining case studies. Workshop on Data Mining Case Studies, In IEEE *Proceedings of the International Conference on Data Mining* (pp. 99-106).

Fayyad, U., Piatetsky-Shapiro, & Smyth, G. P. (1996). From data mining to knowledge discovery in databases. *AI Magazine*, 37–54.

Feldens, M. A., Moraes, R. L., Pavan, A., & Castilho, J. M. (1998). *Towards a methodology for the discovery of useful knowledge combining data mining, Data warehousing and visualisation.* Universidade Federal do Rio Grande do Sul.

Ganesh, M., Han, E. H., Kumar, V., & Shekhar, S. (1996). *Visual data mining: Framework and algorithm development, TR 96-021.* University of Minnesota.

Gartner (2000). *Free methodology and process model for data mining released.*

Gersten, W., Wirth, R., & Arndt, D. (2000). Predictive modeling in automotive direct marketing: Tools, experiences and open issues. In *The 6th ACM SIGKDD International Conference on Knowledge Discovery and Data Mining* (pp. 398-406).

Gottgtroy, P. (2007). Ontology driven knowledge discovery process: A proposal to integrate ontology engineering and KDD. In *Proceedings of the 11th Pacific-Asia Conference on Information Systems* (pp. 1-7).

Gottgtroy, P., Kasabov, N., & Macdonell, S. (2003). An ontology engineering approach for knowledge discovery from data in evolving domains. In *Proceedings of the 2003 SIAM International Conference on Data Mining* (pp. 10-17).

Gunnarsson, C. L., Walker, M. M., Walatka, V., & Swann, K. (2007). Lessons learned: A case study using data mining in the newspaper industry. *Database Marketing & Customer Strategy Management, 14*(4), 271–280. doi:10.1057/palgrave.dbm.3250058

Haglin, D., Roiger, R., Hakkila, J., & Giblin, T. (2005). A tool for public analysis of scientific data. *Data Science Journal, 4*(30), 39–53. doi:10.2481/dsj.4.39

Han, J., & Cercone, N. (2000). RuleViz: A model for visualizing knowledge discovery process. In *Proceedings of the 6th ACM SIGKDD International Conference on Knowledge Discovery and Data Mining* (pp. 244-253).

Han, J., & Kamber, M. (2001). *Data mining: Concepts and techniques*. Morgan Kaufmann.

Hofmann, M. (2003). *The development of a generic data mining life cycle* (DMLC) (dissertation, School of Computing, Dublin Institute of Technology).

Hofmann, M., & Tierney, B. (2007). Development phases of a generic data mining life cycle (DMLC). In *Proceedings of the International Conference on Software Engineering Theory and Practice* (pp. 5-11).

Inmon, W. H. (2005). *Building the data warehouse*. John Wiley and Sons.

Klosgen, W., & Zytkow, J. M. (2002). The knowledge discovery process. In Klosgen, W., & Zytkow, J. M. (Eds.), *Handbook of data mining and knowledge discovery* (pp. 10–21). New York, NY: Oxford University Press.

Kopanakis, I., & Theodoulidis, B. (1999). *Visual data mining & modeling techniques. Centre of Research in Information Management (CRIM)*. UK: Department of Computation. University of Manchester Institute of Science and Technology.

Kuo, Y. T., Lonie, A., Sonenberg, L., & Paizis, K. (2007). Domain ontology driven data mining: A medical case study. In *Proceedings of the 2007 International Workshop on Domain Driven Data Mining* (pp. 11-17).

Kurgan, L. A., & Musilek, P. (2006). A survey of knowledge discovery and data mining process models. *The Knowledge Engineering Review, 21*(1), 1–24. doi:10.1017/S0269888906000737

Lee, S. W., & Kerschberg, L. (1998). A methodology and life cycle model for data mining and knowledge discovery in precision agriculture. In *IEEE International Conference on Systems* (pp. 2882-2887).

Li, T., & Ruan, D. (2007). An extended process model of knowledge discovery in database. *Journal of Enterprise Information Management, 20*(2), 169–177. doi:10.1108/17410390710725751

Luan, J. (2002). Data mining and knowledge management in higher education. In *AIR Forum*.

Maedche, A., Hotho, A., & Wiese, M. (2000). Enhancing preprocessing in data-intensive domains using online-analytical processing, In Y. Kambayashi, M. Mohania, & M. Tjoa (Eds.), *Data warehousing and knowledge discovery* (pp. 258-264). New York, NYL: Springer.

Owrang, M. M. (2000). Using domain knowledge to optimize the knowledge discovery process in databases. *International Journal of Intelligent Systems, 15*, 45–60. doi:10.1002/(SICI)1098-111X(200001)15:1<45::AID-INT3>3.0.CO;2-H

Pabarskaite, Z., & Raudys, A. (2007). A process of knowledge discovery from Web log data: Systematization and critical review. *Journal of Intelligent Information Systems, 28*, 70–104. doi:10.1007/s10844-006-0004-1

Phillips, J., & Buchanan, B. G. (2001). Ontology-guided knowledge discovery in databases. In *Proceedings of the 1st International Conference on Knowledge Capture*, Victoria, British Columbia, Canada.

Piatetsky-Shapiro, G. (2000). *Analytics and data mining: The key to successful CRM*. Retrieved on May 16, 2009, http://searchcrm.techtarget.com/webcastsTranscript/ 0,289691,sid11_gci%20510234,00.html

Pritscher, L., & Feyen, H. (2001). Data mining and strategic marketing in the airline industry. In *Proceedings of the 5th European Conference on Principles and Practice of Knowledge Discovery in Databases (PKDD'01)* (pp. 39-48).

Razali, A. M., & Ali, S. (2009). Generating treatment plan in medicine: A data mining approach. *American Journal of Applied Sciences*, 6(2), 345–351.

Reinartz, T. (1999). Focusing solutions for data mining. *Lecture notes in artificial intelligence*, 1623.

Rennolls, K., & AL-Shawabkeh, A. (2008). Formal structures for data mining, knowledge discovery and communication in a knowledge management environment. *Intelligent Data Analysis*, 12, 147–163.

SAS. (1996). From data to business advantage: Data mining, *SEMMA methodology and the SAS system (white paper)*. SAS Institute Inc.

SEMMA. (1997). *Data mining and the case for sampling (white paper)*. SAS Institute Inc.

Shearer, C. (2000). The CRISP-DM model: The new blueprint for data mining. *Journal of Data Warehousing*, 5(4), 13–22.

Sund, R. (2003). Utilisation of administrative registers using scientific knowledge discovery. *Intelligent Data Analysis*, 7, 501–519.

Svatek, V., & Rauch, J. (2006). Ontology-enhanced association mining. In M. Ackermann, B. Berendt, M. Grobelnik, A. Hotho, D. Mladenic,....G. Semeraro (Eds.), Semantics, *Web and mining* (pp. 163-179). Berlin-Heidelberg, Germany: Springer.

Svatek, V., Rauch, J., & Flek, M. (2005). Ontology-based explanation of discovered associations in the domain of social reality. In *ECML/PKDD05 Workshop on Knowledge Discovery and Ontologies* (pp. 75-86).

Turban, E., Aronson, J. E., Liang, T. P., & Sharda, R. (2007). *Decision support and business intelligence systems* (8th ed.). Upper Saddle River, NJ: Pearson Prentice Hall.

Yoon, S. C., & Henschen, L. J. (1999). Using domain knowledge in knowledge discovery. In *Proceedings of the 1999 ACM CIKM International Conference on Information and Knowledge Management* (pp. 243-250).

KEY TERMS AND DEFINITIONS

A Life Cycle (LC): A collection of phases through which a product, service or system goes through. Each phase, from problem identification through the implementation of the product, service, or system, depends upon the other phases to achieve a desirable outcome.

Agile Methodology: An iterative and incremental (evolutionary) approach to software development which is performed in a highly collaborative manner by self-organizing teams within an effective governance framework with "just enough" ceremony that produces high quality solutions in a cost effective and timely manner which meets the changing needs of its stakeholders.

Business Intelligence (BI): An umbrella term that combines architectures, tools, data bases, applications, practices, and methodologies. It is the process of transforming various types of business data into meaningful information that can help, decision makers at all levels, getting deeper insight of business.

Data Mining (DM): The process of exploration and analysis, by automatic or semi-automatic means, of large quantities of data in order to discover meaningful patterns and rules.

Data Warehouse (DW): A physical repository where relational data are specially organized to provide enterprise-wide, cleansed data in a standardized format.

Knowledge Discovery (KD): The process encompassing the entire data analysis life cycle, from the identification of data analysis goals and the acquisition and organization of raw data to the generation of potentially useful knowledge, its interpretation and testing.

Knowledge Management (KM): The acquisition, storage, retrieval, application, generation, and review of the knowledge assets of an organization in a controlled way.

Process Modeling (PM): The development of efficient, repeatable business processes that align with the overall business strategy of an enterprise.

Chapter 5
Agile Methodologies for Business Intelligence

Deanne Larson
Larson & Associates, LLC, USA

ABSTRACT

Agile methodologies were introduced in 2001. Since this time, practitioners have tried to create and apply Agile methodologies to many delivery disciplines. This chapter will explore the application of Agile methodologies and principles to business intelligence delivery. The practice of business intelligence delivery with an Agile methodology has yet be proven to the point of maturity and stability; this chapter will outline Agile principles and practices that have emerged as best practices and formulate a framework to outline how an Agile methodology could be applied to business intelligence delivery.

INTRODUCTION

The manifesto and principles for Agile Software Development (ASD) were published in 2001, and since then, the objectives and principles have been interpreted and applied to Business Intelligence (BI). The application to BI is natural, because of the iterative and incremental nature of BI development. The intent of this chapter is to provide practitioners an understanding of how the Agile ideals are applied to BI delivery. Beck, et al

DOI: 10.4018/978-1-61350-050-7.ch005

(2001) outlined the core ideals of the manifesto: individuals and interactions over processes and tools; working software over comprehensive documentation; customer collaboration over contract negotiation; and responding to change over following a plan. Ultimately, by following these ideals, software development becomes less formal, more dynamic, and customer focused.

Information Technology (IT) departments are faced with the circumstances of globalization and maintaining a competitive edge, which, in turn increases pressure to deliver high quality technology solutions faster. In this environment, the values of technology efforts are determined through how quickly payback and return on investment occur. BI efforts often include significant investment initially and ongoing to maintain value, thus inviting constant scrutiny on whether business value is gained. BI value measurement continues to be a struggle for organizations, mainly due to the challenge of directly attributing return to the investment in BI. BI plays the role of an enabler – enabling the organization to become smarter, work smarter, and make better decisions. The enabler role that BI plays makes it difficult to directly attribute a return on investment and after time, the use of information becomes routine and expected.

The information value chain is the process used to derive value from information and information from data; BI delivery is centered on the information value chain. Collecting raw data is the first step in the value chain; applying logic and business context to the data creates information; information is then consumed by BI users; decisions and actions are a result of the consumption of data; and ultimately decisions and actions provide business value. Understanding the information value chain is important in analyzing the benefits of Agile principles applied to BI delivery. BI delivery is not accomplished via traditional waterfall software development (although some organizations attempt this); it is more focused on data discovery and understanding how information is going to be used. This perspective drives how Agile principles should be applied to BI delivery – less focus on software development and more focus on information use.

The objectives of this chapter are fourfold. First, address the alignment between Agile principles and BI delivery. Second, analyze Agile methodologies and address the applicability to BI. Third, review the components and best practices of BI delivery. Last, propose an Agile framework for BI delivery.

BACKGROUND

Business Intelligence (BI) is defined by literature and scholars in similar ways. Noble (2006) defines BI as the ability to provide the business an information advantage; business doing what it has always done, but more efficient. Singer (2001) described BI as the value proposition that helps organizations tap into decision-making information that regular reporting does not provide. Singer outlined that BI requires tools, applications, and technologies focused on enhanced decision-making and is commonly used in supply chain, sales, finance, and marketing. Negash and Gray (2008) outlined BI more comprehensively. BI is a data driven process that combines data storage and gathering with knowledge management to provide input into the business decision making process. BI enables organizations to enhance the decision making process and requires processes, skills, technology, and data.

Being able to deliver BI in a manner that enables business collaboration, data to become information, and ease of use of information are the challenges. Delivery of BI is accomplished via a methodology. Creswell (2003) outlined that a methodology is set of processes, methods, and rules applied within a discipline. Successful BI methodology should focus on the information value chain and less on the development of software as is the focus of traditional information technology (IT) development. Research has demonstrated that waterfall lifecycles and traditional software development practices are not successful in BI. Software and hardware do not provide organizations value pertaining to BI; it is the use of information (Larson, 2009).

Common stumbling blocks that exist in BI projects include: fuzzy requirements; lacking an understanding about how data is created and used; data quality is not measured or known; source system constraints dictate design and service levels; developing based on perceptions of data; results are not demonstrated in a timely manner;

and working with a lack of trust between IT and business stakeholders (TDWI, 2008).

The application of Agile principles to BI is in its infancy stage. Agile ideals and principles were published by Beck, et al. (2001) and since this time, practitioners have focused on applying an Agile approach to BI. The challenges that BI projects face make the Agile approach an attractive answer due to the parallels that exist between them. By using an Agile approach, means the methodology is less formal, more dynamic, and customer focused. The dynamics required in BI delivery theoretically make an Agile approach a good fit with BI; however, practice with Agile ideals and principles have identified new stumbling blocks such focusing on a software development approach over the main deliverable of successful BI – the utility of information. These stumbling blocks will be identified and addressed throughout the rest of the chapter.

Agile Principles

Analyzing the Agile principles provides an understanding of how using an Agile approach matches well with BI delivery. To reiterate the principles: individuals and interactions over processes and tools; working software over comprehensive documentation; customer collaboration over contract negotiation; and responding to change over following a plan. Beck, et al. (2001) outlined that an Agile approach focuses more on the left side of the principle; however, the right slide (to the right of 'over') is not ignored.

Individuals and Interactions over Processes and Tools

Experienced individuals working together are more effective and build better systems than less experienced individuals using structured process and tools (Ambler, 2006). With BI, the system includes multiple components such as source systems, Extract, Transformation, and Load

(ETL) processes, databases, and front-end tools. The infrastructure of a BI system is the enabler to gaining value from organizational data. BI is less about the process and tools and more about the utility of information. Although the ideal discussed here emphasizes individuals and interactions over processes and tools, processes and tools are not eliminated from an Agile approach.

Process and tools are used to get the desired results, without burying the development lifecycle in needless bureaucracy. In Agile, a process will exist for defining releases, managing development, and ensuring quality results. The goal of the process is to guide development, foster collaboration and interaction, confirm expected results, and produce results and capabilities. Flexibility and encouraging change is the mantra of an Agile environment; however, controls still exist to provide working result. Tools such as a burn down chart or taskboard, for instance, provide the formalization and a modicum of control (Larson, 2009).

Working Software over Comprehensive Documentation

Documentation is valuable; however, the value is not the issue. Documentation has an inherent problem – usability. Documentation has been a dreaded aspect of traditional development methodologies. Documentation takes too much time to complete, tends to be out-of-date, and is rarely used after the initial deployment. Creating comprehensive documentation does not allow for quick delivery; however, not producing documentation can be more detrimental. For Agile, documentation needs be usable and add value. Documentation should less textual and more visible. Development artifacts in BI such as source to target mappings, diagrams, and models, are examples of valuable artifacts that are easy to use and maintain. Diagrams can provide a level of documentation that is adequate to support requirements, design, and development and are easy to maintain. A picture is worth a thousand words (Larson, 2009).

Customer Collaboration over Contract Negotiation

Practicing ongoing collaboration throughout any process adds value - communication is increased, expectations are consistently reaffirmed, and ownership of the end product is shared. Collaboration is emphasized in "interaction and individuals over process and tools" and fundamental to the success of Agile. Without pre-determined expectations, contracts can frame expectations but allow refinement and change. Contracts will in Agile exist and address enough detail to understand the framework of delivery. A contract created within an Agile approach focuses on enabling collaboration versus spending time documenting what should be delivered and when. The details surrounding requirements are not often known in enough detail to document. Collaboration between stakeholders addresses this via delivery by determining what the expectations are and increasing communication between stakeholders (Larson, 2009).

Responding to Change over Following a Plan

Inherently, management is about control and managers get apprehensive when a formal plan does not exist. Managing an effort with a plan implies that a change management process is in place. A change in project requirements means a change in scope, which impacts time, resources, and budget, the foundational aspects of project management. The traditional approach to managing a project is to follow the plan and discourage change. Change in traditional approaches is the exception and not the rule (Larson, 2009).

One of the objectives of Agile principles is removing bureaucracy from delivery of working software. The challenge with this approach is that when formality is removed from the delivery process, leaders become frustrated with the perceived loss of control. With Agile, the approach is to be prepared for change and respond accordingly.

Which poses the question - how is it possible to respond to change and keep a modicum of control? The need to meet milestones and deliver information capabilities based on commitments does not go away (Larson, 2009). This challenge will be addressed in the section outlining the best practices in BI Agile delivery.

Agile Methodologies

The manifesto and principles for Agile Software Development (ASD) were published in 2001, and since then, the objectives and principles have been interpreted and applied to new Agile methodologies. The popular approaches from which the manifesto and principles were derived – Extreme Programming (XP), SCRUM, Dynamic Systems Development Method (DSDM) – are in practice today with a modicum of success. The transition from traditional software development to an Agile methodology is not without challenges and not many organizations can prove the success of adopting this fairly new approach.

Kendall and Kendall (2005) posited that the traditional software development approach called the Software Development Lifecycle (SDLC) emphasized understanding, diagramming, and designing information systems. Agile approaches are focused more on people with the assertion that people are at the root of all errors and defects. Human creativity can take over when structured and formal processes fail to address system problems. Kendall and Kendall outlined that Agile methodologies only succeed when all the stakeholders collaborate. Last, Agile approaches only work well when the organizational culture supports collaboration and less structure.

Agile methodologies emphasize small incremental releases of a working feature or system deliverable. Each increment is delivered with the goal of improved quality. Less formality exists than in the structured approaches with less documentation. The focus of the Agile approach is more on people improving quality of systems through increased communication and collaboration (Kendall & Kendall, 2005).

Contrasting the SDLC to the Agile approach outlines key differences that should be considered in adoption. Traditional development has structured phases: requirements, design, development, test, and deploy, which are followed, each phase completing before moving to the next. Agile has iterative cycles that produce small releases of a feature or system component. Traditional development includes timelines that can extend to years before producing working software; Agile focuses on producing working software from smaller time-boxed releases. Traditional development includes larger teams of individual specialists versus Agile which emphasizes smaller teams of versatile programmers. Collaboration in traditional development happens intermittently during phases where Agile is focused on consistent collaboration between stakeholders.

The core practices of Agile methodologies include: small, short releases; a controlled work week (i.e. limited to a certain amount of hours); stakeholders physically located together; and a time-boxed project cycle (typically 60-90 days, although the cycle may be shorter depending on the deliverable) (Kendall & Kendall, 2005).

Small, Short Releases

Development teams will focus on shortening the time between releases meaning the scope of deliverables will be smaller. Small releases will include deliverables that address some of the features expected by stakeholders. For example, a menu screen for a system may allow a user to search on an attribute, but not on the full search criteria. The full search criteria will be added later. According to Kendall and Kendall (2005), "Short releases are intended to come out rapidly, in quick succession as the programmers finish them. Essential features will be developed first, and when actually released, the product will contain critical

features at first (p. 339)." The subsequent releases focus on small iterative improvements.

Small, short releases use iterations for development improvement and increments for managing scope. Increments deal with the staging and scheduling of deliverables which may occur at different rates. Iterations are time periods defined with the goal to revise and improve the deliverable. Increments are scheduled as part of a release plan tied to a program that outlines what information system capabilities are needed and when. Iterations happen within the increment. Iterations are time-boxed, therefore the results can be less or more than expected. If less than expected is delivered, the increment scope is adjusted accordingly (Larson, 2009).

Controlled Work Week

The culture of an Agile environment invests in maintaining the long-term health resources (Kendall & Kendall, 2005). Removing structure and placing more emphasis on stakeholder involvement can result in continuous development sessions with the same resources. The focus on the same stakeholders means each stakeholder has an intense work commitment. The loss of any one resource will have a larger impact on the release. Due to these characteristics of the Agile approach, controlling the work week becomes a priority to control resource stress and burnout. A controlled work week will assist in managing the long-term health of resources; without managing the work week intellectual tasks such as analysis and design could be diminished introducing more defects and lessening quality.

Stakeholders Located Together

The stakeholders in an Agile approach are the customers (user or sponsors of the system) and the technical resources. Technical resources could include project managers, analysts, programmers, designers, testers, or deployment personnel. With an Agile approach, smaller teams are used, which means the resources are multi-faceted. A technical resource would have the capability of completing analysis, design, and development.

With a smaller team, concepts such as pair-programming are used. Pair-programming is a core practice that consists of two programmers that work closely together to analyze, design, and develop a software deliverable. Throughout this process each programmer interacts collaboratively by clarifying logic and reviewing problems that arise. The benefits of this approach include catching defects early, enhancing creativity, and saving time in the development cycle. To get the most from using smaller teams, all stakeholders need to interact closely. In addition to the technical resources working closer together, customer stakeholders will also play a prominent role in the Agile approach. Customer expectations determine the success of the release; therefore customer input is critical in the development cycle.

Kendall and Kendall (2005) emphasized that communication between technical resources and the customer is essential during the Agile process. In order to support the Agile process, technical resources need to interact with the onsite customer. The interaction focuses on gaining an understanding of customer expectations and priorities and enables a way to foster the relationship between the customer and the technical resources.

In traditional software development, developers are not permitted to test their own code. The philosophy of this long-held belief is that developers considered their code to be a product of their own creation, thus code is personal and in some cases, "work of the artist". Developers would chose to see what they wanted to see. Developers were not considered objective enough to adequately test their code, therefore separate testers were traditionally used to complete test cases that verified the integration of components and final working system. Developers would complete unit tests of their code before passing the code on to test teams. In Agile, the philosophy of separating development

and test activities become a nonissue. Tests are completed directly between the developers and the customer. Self-testing, defined as developers testing their own code, has not been observed as an issue in the quality of software produced from an Agile approach (McAvoy & Butler, 2009).

Time-Boxed Efforts

By stipulating a timeframe when deliverables are completed, development teams in effect time-box deliverables. By creating a standard timeframe in which deliverables are completed, expectations are set that results will be observed by a specified date. Time-boxing provides two benefits. First, having a standard timeframe enables the technical teams to determine the scope of what can be completed and allows the scope of deliverables to be more manageable. Second, customers are able to see results and value is delivered sooner with a working system. The definition of a timeframe in an Agile approach is relative and may be different from organization to organization. A time-boxed effort will depend on the scope and the complexity of the project. Other considerations include the number of technical resources, availability and skills of the resources, and other factors specific to the situation (Kendall & Kendall, 2005).

At the heart of Agile is the focus on human interaction. For the core practices of Agile to be successful, the organizational culture has to embrace the empowerment of technical resources, be able to incorporate change easily, and be open to a less formal development approach. According to McAvoy and Butler (2009), another challenge to adapting an Agile development approach is the need for dynamic and versatile technical resources. Technical resources include individuals with technical expertise such as coding software; however, also included in this group are those who manage the effort. All resources involved in the Agile project have to be able to shelve their inherent systematic tendencies traditionally applied to information system development and be prepared

Figure 1. Comparison of business intelligence systems and transactional systems

Criteria	Business Intelligence	Transactional Systems
Requirements	Fuzzy Requirements (Use of Information)	Functional Requirements
Logic Focus	Business Logic Applied to Data	Process Logic for Application
Development Approach	Discovery and Iterative	Phased and Systematic
System Use	System for Information Use	System for Data Capture
Value	Value Derived from Information Quality and Use	Value Derived from Transaction Processing

to approach development more creatively for an Agile approach to be successful.

Ultimately, traditional development has characteristics that are more formal and structured which are perceived as less flexible, timely, and valuable. Traditional software development is the primary approach still practiced by IT departments; however, Agile is still being explored (McAvoy & Bulter, 2009). For Agile to be successful, an organizational culture shift needs to occur from practicing a systematic engineering development approach to focus more on smaller, versatile, teams working directly with customers.

Agile and Business Intelligence

One of the primary parallels between Agile and BI is the need for IT to work closely with the customer to discover expectations. BI is based on the utility of information which is not where traditional development efforts focus. Research has demonstrated that waterfall lifecycles and traditional software development practices are not successful in BI (TDWI, 2009). Traditional development focuses on delivering quality software, not on the utility of information. The software itself does not provide value to a business; it is the information used in the decision-making process that does.

The primary goal of a BI project is to enable the use of information. This perspective presents some challenges that cannot be adequately ad-

dressed using a traditional development approach. If the primary goal of BI is enabling the use of information, then scope of the BI project focuses on turning data into information. Software development is part of the data to information process; however, software development in BI is less about creating a working program to be used and more about application of business context to data. Software used in BI includes database management systems, data cleansing, data transformation, and analytical systems. The scope of development in BI includes more configuration and application of logic versus programmatic coding. In order to understand how to apply logic and configure the software, IT will need to comprehend the business use of data.

The differences between BI and transactional systems are demonstrated by analyzing how these systems are used and how that use provides value to an organization. Transactional systems are referred to as Online Transaction Processing (OLTP) systems where the primary purpose of the system is to automate a process and capture information. An example of an OLTP system would be a Point of Sales (POS) system used in retail stores. Figure 1 illustrates the characteristic differences between BI and transactional systems.

The criteria of requirements, logic focus, development approach, system use, and value provides context to do the comparison. With transactional systems, requirements are functional (how the system should function). BI systems, requirements are informational (what information is needed and how will it be used). Logic used in BI systems defines the business definitions of information attributes. Logic used in transactional systems pertains to how the business process is executed and what function needs to be supported. Although BI systems may be developed via a traditional approach, the analysis and development to understand the data is a discovery and iterative process. Transactional systems are addressed systematically, thus the approach is phased were one phase (i.e. requirements gathering) is completed prior to moving to the next. This phased approach is referred to as the waterfall approach.

System use and value, the last two criteria used in the comparison, outline the business perspective of the systems. BI systems are used to support analysis and decision-making, transactional systems are used to capture data during a business process. Value is derived differently for both systems. The value of BI systems is realized when information is used and the resulting action benefits the organization. Transactional systems provide value through the automation of business processes.

Focusing on the utility of information presents unique challenges not experienced in traditional software development. Transactional systems capture and store data in formats to promote system performance. Data, therefore, are not in a format that promotes use in a business context. BI systems are downstream from transactional systems, thus BI systems are consumers of transactional data Both of these issues are not typically experienced in transactional system development; however, each issue concerns the understanding and access to data, which in turn, impacts the ability to develop BI systems that provide value.

The challenges in BI development include: requirements that are fuzzy; lacking an understanding about how data is created and used; data quality is not known or measured; source system (often transactional systems) constraints impact

data availability; and working with incomplete metadata. Agile principles can address these challenges.

BI delivery tends to be a process where customer expectations are a cycle of discovery and refinement, hence the problem of fuzzy requirements. Turning data into information is not a simple process nor are requirements easy to determine even with the use of subject matter experts. BI begins with some key questions: What business questions need to be answered? What data sources qualify as the system of record? How will data be used? These questions are addressed through a discovery process that examines how data is created and how data is becomes information. BI systems include multiple components such as source systems, ETL, databases, and front-end tools. The infrastructure of a BI system is the enabler to gaining value from organizational data. "Individuals over interactions over processes and tools" support discovery (Larson, 2009).

Discovery implies an incremental and iterative approach. BI is naturally incremental and iterative; therefore, this aspect of the Agile manifesto aligns. Applying Agile to BI encourages collaboration between stakeholders which addresses several problems found in BI projects. First, an "us versus them" attitude tends to arise between IT and business stakeholders that stems from the application of technology to business; this attitude dissipates during collaboration. Second, no one stakeholder has a 100% understanding of the data and what it takes to provide valuable information; this becomes clear as collaboration progresses. Last, the *real* requirements are discovered through the sharing of knowledge versus relying solely on stakeholders' experience to define requirements (Larson, 2009). Collaboration is a success requirement for implementing BI which is emphasized in the ideal of "interaction and individuals over process and tools".

As mentioned prior, BI requires a discovery process where customer expectations are determined. Without pre-determined expectations, using contracts in BI would be challenging. BI projects need a framework of expectations which allow refinement and change. The objective is to focus more on collaboration versus spending time completing a detailed plan. Detailed plans are often difficult to create since only high-level planning information is known. Collaboration helps resolve this through determining what the expectations are and increasing communication between stakeholders. The Agile principles of "customer collaboration over contract negotiation" and "responding to change over following a plan" address challenges of BI systems.

BUSINESS INTELLIGENCE DELIVERY

Goals of BI Delivery

Yeoh and Koronios (2010) posited that a BI system is not a conventional IT system (i.e. transactional system); however, BI systems have similar characteristics to enterprise systems or infrastructure projects. BI system implementation is a complex activity involving hardware, software, and resources over the life of the system. The complexity of the BI system infrastructure increases with the scope. An enterprise BI system can include a data warehouse, integrated data structures, source systems, and large data volumes.

The literature and research on BI system success factors is limited; however, the available literature is consistent in several aspects. BI success focuses on a few main Critical Success Factors (CSF) categorized by organization, process, and technology (Yeoh & Koronios, 2010). Organizational CSFs consists of establishing a vision, outlining a business case for BI, and gaining leadership support for BI as a priority. Process CSFs focus on managing BI as an evolving ongoing program. Process CSFs include having a dedicated, skilled BI team for technical delivery as well as ongoing program and change man-

agement that focus on aligning BI with business goals. The technical category centers on two areas – data and infrastructure. Data and infrastructure CSFs consist of many factors related to stability and quality since these two areas are the major technical components of the BI systems (Yeoh & Koronios, 2010).

Analyzing the success factors provides insight into the goals of BI delivery. BI delivery consists of practices, methods, skills, and competencies required to create, implement, and sustain BI systems. The success factors will determine best practices in BI delivery. Yeoh and Koronios (2010) outlined that the CSF framework supported the perception of benefits expected by individual users and organizations of BI systems which was, "an interactive, business-driven, evolutionary continuum to support evolving business needs (p.25)." In simpler terms, BI delivery needs to support organic and evolutionary change, driven by the constant evaluation of information and user feedback. BI systems would be constantly optimized and improved based on an ongoing feedback loop. Based on the CSFs for BI and the differences between BI and transactional systems, Agile has synergies that address the nuances required for BI success.

Iteration and Incremental

One of the synergies that Agile has with BI is the short, small release and experts' recommendation that BI is best delivered in increments (Yeoh & Koronios, 2010). This incremental approach supports that fact that modern businesses are changing quickly and want to evaluate the impact of these changes. An incremental approach allows for management of risk, allows for more control, and enables customers to see tangible results.

Correct use of increments and iterations in BI begins with understanding that these concepts are not the same. Both concepts apply to BI delivery but in a different way. BI literature tends to use these concepts interchangeably. Iteration refers to the cyclic process of refinement to get to the best solution. Incremental is a staging and scheduling strategy where the scope of delivery is adjusted as necessary (Cockburn, 2008).

Increments deal with the staging and scheduling of deliverables which may occur at different rates. Iterations are cycles to revise and improve the deliverable. Increments are scheduled as part of a roadmap or release plan tied to an overall BI strategy that outlines what information capabilities are needed and when. Iterations will happen within the increment. Increments are time-boxed, therefore the results can be less or more than expected. If less than expected is delivered, increments are adjusted accordingly. Simply, increments manage the scope of the delivery and iterations are used to refine the quality of the deliverable. Deliverables can be code, models, diagrams, or any artifact created as part of the cycle.

The BI Lifecycle

A lifecycle is the progression of something from conception to end of life or when something no longer provides value. Lifecycles have phases that comprise the progression of conception to end; the BI lifecycle is no different. The BI lifecycle parallels the SDLC with similar phases; however, as outlined in the comparison of transactional systems and BI systems, the BI lifecycle is centered on the utility of information versus the development of software.

The phases in the SDLC tend to be common across many development lifecycles. These models include waterfall (common traditional approach), rapid prototyping, incremental, spiral, and build and fix. The major phases commonly observed across models can be described as planning, requirements, design, development, testing, implementation, and stabilization.

Planning centers on establishing goals and creating a high-level view of the project. The requirements phase refines the goals and determines the capabilities and functions required from the

project and for end users. In the design phase, desired capabilities are described and modeled in detail. Development activities focus on creating the capabilities and functions required by the project. Development activities can include coding, configuration, scripting, and unit testing. The testing phase includes validation and verification of functionality and interoperability. Implementation focuses on installation of the deliverables into a production environment. Last, stabilization includes all activities to maintain the system throughout the life of the system such as changes, corrections, and additions (Kay, 2002).

Discovery

During the discovery phase, the expectations of BI projects are not initially clear to stakeholders. Business users begin with the knowledge that information and analysis capabilities are needed, and IT professionals are ready to take down requirements without a clear starting point. For these reasons, the first phase is the discovery phase where stakeholders determine information requirements. Information requirements begin with defining business questions which provide insight into data sources, dimensions, and facts needed. Note: Discovery as part of the SDLC is not related to Discovery pertaining to Data Mining.

Design

Design in BI focuses heavily on modeling, but may start with establishing the architecture of the system. Architecture in BI is more than hardware infrastructure. BI architecture includes business, technical, process, data, and project components. BI business architecture centers on defining the drivers, goals, and strategy of the organization that drive information needs. BI project architecture describes the incremental methodology used for short, small releases. Process architecture includes the framework for data acquisition to data presentation. Data architecture address how data will be structured in data repositories, such as a data mart or warehouse. BI technology architecture includes hardware, BI software, and networks required to deliver BI projects. If the BI architecture is established, design will center on modeling data and processes to support information needs. Models created in this phase could include conceptual, logical, and physical data models as well as process models for ETL.

Development

BI development may include a wide array of activities. The primary focus of the development phase is to produce a working system that applies business context to data and presents information in a way that enables end users to analyze actionable information. Activities could include coding ETL, configuring logical layers in a BI tool, or scripting scheduling jobs. The scope of development can involve data acquisition to staging, staging to presentation, and presentation to the access and delivery of information.

Deploy

BI systems tend to be complex for many reasons. One reason for complexity is that BI systems have many independent components that require integration. Another reason is BI systems are impacted by continuous change. Because of this complexity, the BI deployment phase is formal and controlled. Activities in this phase focus on integration of new functionality and capability into production, and regression testing to verify that previously working functionality is not impacted. Deployment focuses on introduction of new components and maintaining the stability of the production BI system.

Value Delivery

The value delivery phase includes stabilization, maintenance, change management, and end user feedback. Successful BI systems generally have a long life and require program management to address change and maintain ongoing value. Due to continuous change and the dynamic uses of information, BI system value requires constant attention. Change impacting a BI system can initiate from source systems, business processes, software upgrades, new data integration, and organizational strategy. End user feedback provides an understanding of how information is used and the overall value gained from the BI system.

Synthesis of the BI Lifecycle and Agile

Three phases of the BI Delivery Lifecycle have characteristics where using an Agile approach may fit. The discovery, design, and development phases can benefit from iterative cycles, stakeholder collaboration, small time-boxed increments, and co-located resources. How these phases benefit from Agile is addressed in the BI Delivery Framework section.

Deployment and value delivery are phases that require formalization due to BI system complexity. Ensuring flawless integration and the quality of the BI system is crucial to its maintaining value. The Agile approach and principles are less applicable to deployment and value delivery and can be contradictory in this aspect of BI delivery.

Initially and through the development and design phases, using an Agile approach addresses the challenges of fuzzy requirements and goal of information utility by removing the rigidness of the traditional development approach. However, in the BI lifecycle stages of deployment and value delivery, lack of rigidness and formality can degrade the value of the BI system. For example, if change introduced in the production environment impacts data to information transformation, the quality of decision-making can be impacted. Some level of formality needs to be present to maintain BI system value.

Conversely, the incremental approach used in Agile can assist in deployment and value delivery.

Having smaller, shorter releases enables faster implementation and a smaller scope of regression testing. The next section details how Agile practices are applied to BI delivery.

Agile BI Delivery Framework

In theory, an Agile approach appears to fit well with BI delivery. Research on successful application of Agile practices to BI delivery is lacking. Industry consultants and software vendors are describing software and services that are "agile" for sales purposes as the theory of Agile is appealing. This author has compiled a BI Delivery Framework based on research and experience, which synthesizes Agile practices with BI delivery practices.

Valuable Practices

Discovery

What is emphasized with BI and Agile is the concept of discovery and this is the basis for what becomes the Agile BI lifecycle. Regardless subject matter experts availability, organizations don't know what they don't know about data or technology. For example, both data standardization and enterprise modeling can be an approach to data discovery; however, neither provides results quickly.

The expectations of BI projects are not always clear to stakeholders. End users know they need information and analysis capabilities and IT knows they need to deliver something. This phase is where discovery is highlighted the most. Outlining business questions are a best practice in gathering BI requirements. These questions immediately provide insight into data sources, dimensions, and facts needed.

Most of what can and cannot be delivered is determined by data quality and availability. Once data sources have been identified, the next step requires gaining an understanding of the data. Data profiling focuses on two phases – values

analysis and structure analysis. Data profiling provides data demographics and descriptive statistics such as: frequency distribution, high and low values, blank attributes and records, exceptions to domain values, dependencies between attributes, unknown constraints, mean, median, mode, and standard deviation. The knowledge gained from analyzing data demographics provides the basis for data quality metrics and can be used later in the lifecycle for modeling, development, and testing. Most importantly, assumptions about the data and information capabilities are removed. With this knowledge, information needs can be prioritized and increments planned (Larson, 2009).

Architecture

At the beginning of a BI program, the architecture needs to be established. Creating a flexible, scalable architecture is essential to supporting growth. Envisioning the architecture is the first step in Agile BI (Ambler, 2003). As mentioned in the BI lifecycle section, BI architecture includes the business, technical, process, data, and project architecture.

Envisioning the architecture begins with diagramming. Diagrams work well in Agile as they are easily altered and maintained versus text-based documents. Diagrams include data models, data flows, process flows, and infrastructure diagrams. With technical architecture, the deliverable can be a diagram outlining the different technologies required. A conceptual subject-level model can be the beginnings of the data architecture.

Diagrams are a beginning, but they don't prove out the architectural vision. Architecture decisions are ones that cannot be easily reversed once implemented. The approach of a reference implementation works well in the Agile paradigm. Like a prototype, a reference implementation is a working model but focuses on proving out the architecture. Reference implementations for ETL architecture, for example can demonstrate if service levels are possible and remove assumptions about the technology. A proof of concept (POC) is also another approach used in validating architectural decisions. POCs are often used in BI due to organizations using the best of breed approach. The best of bread approach is defined as organizations choosing independent tools, such as ETL and databases, which need to be integrated as part of the technical architecture. Although reference implementations and POCs are used in traditional software development, in Agile BI they become the rule (Larson, 2009).

Design

The activities completed in the design phase of the BI framework are modeling and mapping. These activities are iterative in nature and use the output of the discovery phase. Data profiling analysis and high-level architectural diagrams provide the context for design.

Modeling in this framework is focused on prioritized requirements, data demographics, and a stable scope for the increment. Business questions provide an understanding of how data will be used and data demographics assist the modeler in identifying business transactions, uniqueness, and primary/foreign key relationships. The modeling iteration is shortened through the use of data discovery early in the project. The modeling iteration may include a completed logical or physical model; however, due to the iterative cycles, the models may be a first pass. At a minimum, models will demonstrate behavioral and informational semantics. Models can represent sources and targets.

Mapping the data between source and target is an essential design activity. The source to target mapping will be evolutionary within the scope of the increment. The exercise of mapping confirms data understanding and discovers business, transformation, and cleansing rules.

By having models and source to target mappings, development on ETL and end user capabilities can begin. Refinements to the design can occur via development iterations. Subject matter experts from the business and IT collaborate to clarify and refine design throughout the increment.

Development

In an Agile environment, the goal of development is to deliver working software regularly. In BI, development deliverables can include ETL processes, analysis, or reporting capabilities. Different approaches to ETL exist such as Enterprise Application Integration (EAI), Enterprise Information Integration (EII), and Extract, Load, and Transform (ELT) which are out of scope for this research. Regardless of ETL approach, BI development includes an ETL deliverable.

Development iterations focus on the delivery of requirements; however, the requirements are not delivered the first cycle. Throughout the requirements and design iterations, stakeholders are working with the data to confirm understanding and remove assumptions. Development will produce software that enriches the data. The development iteration refines requirements and design through stakeholder collaboration. Stakeholders can confirm information results through validation of business rules and verification of output to alternate sources. Through development iterations, the scope that can be delivered in the allotted timeframe becomes clear. At the conclusion of the development phase, requirements and design are concluded for the increment and the development deliverables are ready to be tested.

Test

In the waterfall lifecycle, testing occurs after development and becomes the focal point of quality. This approach does not work due to the lateness in the lifecycle and the ability to correct major defects. With an Agile approach, testing occurs constantly through the interactions of stakeholders. Collaboration with stakeholders ensures results are verified during the lifecycle to produce higher quality results. Since BI systems tend to be complex, a formal change control process is recommended. Additionally, a regression test suite for the BI system is essential. With the fuzzy nature of information, it is possible to impact prior working functionality and not see the impact until after deployment.

Deploy

Complex BI systems require formal support and maintenance procedures to ensure the overall health of the system. This is where the flexible nature of Agile ends. New increments need a formal process to ensure existing operations and service levels are not impacted. Without a formal process, the risk of failure increases. Using an incremental approach allows a gradual and controlled deployment. In addition, introducing new functionality sooner allows stakeholders to recognize value and lessens the complexity of deployment.

Summary of the Agile BI Delivery Framework

The basis for the framework has been established through the analysis and synthesis of BI and Agile practices. The following conclusions are the basis for the framework.

- Complete a BI program charter to define constraints and outline the operating model. The charter assists in setting stakeholders' expectations on how an agile BI program will work and define the time-box approach.
- Start with the business information needs to provide context for scope. Outline business questions to be answered.
- Relaxing the formality in software development will initially be an issue in converting to an Agile BI life cycle. Using increments and iterations as a framework for controlling releases is a key success factor

in maintaining formality while enabling discovery and responses to change.

- Emphasize data discovery through requirements and design phase. Data profiling assists in removing assumptions about data sources and identifying data quality problems early in the life cycle. Profiling results can be used for multiple purposes in these phases.
- Use diagrams instead of comprehensive documentation. Artifacts need to have a high level of usability and be simple to maintain.
- Validate the BI architecture by using reference implementations and POCs. Architecture decisions are not easily reversed.
- Iterations need to be time-boxed in addition to increments.
- Define data validation and verification steps for the Agile BI life cycle. Business stakeholders will have expectations about when and how collaboration and interaction will occur. Data validation and verification should occur for development iterations.
- Testing is focused on confirming information results and capabilities throughout the life cycle. Data Profiling can assist in setting initial expectations and output can be reused to verify and validate information results.
- Regression testing should be completed for each change being introduced into production. The impact to existing information capabilities is not immediately visible.
- Change control for production environments must be formalized due to the natural complexity of BI environments.

Figure 2 depicts the framework for Agile BI Delivery.

Figure 2. Proposed agile BI delivery framework

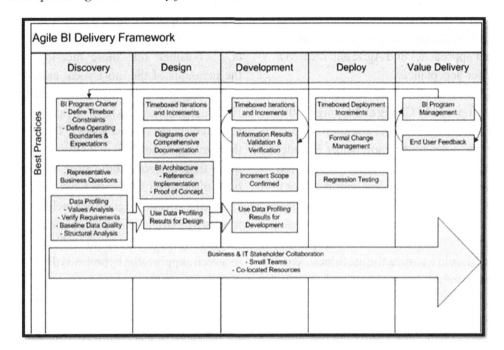

CONCLUSION

Recent Empirical Studies in Agile

This chapter has focused on adaptation of Agile principles to BI development and delivery. As previously mentioned, research in this area is lacking, especially in the area of BI. Although research is lacking, recent empirical studies related to Agile have emerged.

Dyba and Dingsoyr (2008) completed a review of empirical studies pertaining to Agile methodologies through 2005. Based on a search strategy, the study identified 1996 studies, but only 36 were classified as empirical. The 36 studies were grouped by four categories: introduction, social factors, perceptions, and comparative studies. The analysis of the 36 studies concluded that more research is needed to determine when Agile development methodologies should be applied. Claims from practitioners could not be supported based on the empirical studies found. Dyba's and Dingsoyr's conclusion included urging more

companies to participate in Agile studies and to focus on action research which would be highly relevant for an area such as Agile development.

Recent Agile (2007-2009) empirical research has been summarized by Ionel (2009). Ionel outlined that literature on implementing Agile approaches is limited. Implementation is a concern for IT managers. Literature provides the theory; however, practitioners are interested in implementation. Implementation concerns the management, technology, process, and people; therefore research on Agile implementation would be of more interest to practitioners.

Ionel (2009) identified acceptance of Agile methodologies as an issue that has surfaced in recent research. While research in the area of Agile approaches is increasing, adoption by practitioners is slow. Adoption continues to be slow because of lack of practitioner maturity and knowledge in the area of Agile. A barrier to adoption by IT managers is the acceptance that Agile approaches provide the benefits outlined by industry leaders. Ionel identifies a recent study by Chang and

Thong (2009) that outlines how to address the Agile approach acceptance. Chang and Thong (2009) analyzed literature on traditional software development approaches and Agile and created a framework for acceptance.

Ionel (2009) synthesized the conceptual framework proposed by Chang and Thong (2009) with other case studies. The common factors included in the conceptual frameworks include: ability (experience, training, support), motivation (organizational culture, career opportunities), opportunity (teamwork, communication, understanding). Combining the common factors with the characteristics of Agile can lead to acceptance. IT managers should examine the usefulness, ease of use, maturity of the organization, and compatibility with projects. Ionel emphasized the significance of the conceptual framework, "While this framework is yet to be empirically proved solid, it can be considered significant because it brings knowledge management as another perspective in examining acceptance of software development methodologies, on one hand, and because it synthesizes and critically analyses the previous literature on this subject (p.382)."

As part of Agile implementation, communication surfaces in recent literature as an important factor in Agile adoption. Communication makes software development more efficient; however, individuals involved in the software development process communicate from different perspectives (Ionel, 2009). Users will be focused on usability, customer are concerned about low maintenance costs, reliability, and quick delivery, maintenance groups want support documentation, and the development team are interested in the next technical challenge.

IT managers need to consider that communication is not a focus of Agile approaches. A paper by Pikkarainen, et al., (2008) provided insight into the importance of communication in the context of Agile approaches. Communications is extremely important between developers, project leaders, and stakeholders. SCRUM, one Agile approach, emphasizes daily standup meetings that are supposed to increase communication and reduce confusion; however, Pikkarainen, et al. outlined that these meetings can serve the demands of the most vocal customer which negatively impact the project. Another practice in Agile approaches is to have physically collocated resources in open work spaces. The perception is that having collocated resources enables clearer more frequent communication, but case studies have discovered that open work spaces can also cause distractions. Agile approaches tend toward limited formal and informal communication which can inhibit communications. Pikkarainen's, et al. research supports the hypothesis that the nature of Agile approaches (short increments of delivery) required a stronger emphasis on communication to be successful.

Salo and Abrahamsson (2008) have empirically studied Agile approaches such as SCRUM and XP. The findings of this study conducted in European embedded software organizations show that 77% of participants in the study who have used SCRUM have had positive experiences. The study found that 27% of participants used SCRUM regularly. Salo and Abrahamsson's research support that agile adoption is growing. Agile approaches are being used in software development. Large organizations such as Microsoft have started to use Agile which demonstrates the importance of this topic to IT managers.

Agile ideals fit well into the BI world, but successful application depends on understanding how the ideals apply and keeping focused on the information results. Agile addresses many of the common problems found in BI projects by promoting interaction and collaboration between stakeholders. Close collaboration between parties ensures clearer requirements, an understanding of data, joint accountability, and higher quality results. Less time is spent attempting to determine information requirements, and more time is devoted to discovering what is possible. Future research opportunities could include application of the Agile principles in practical case studies and an analysis of the best practices outlined in this chapter.

REFERENCES

Ambler, S. (2003). *Agile database techniques: Effective strategies for the agile developer*. New York, NY: John Wiley & Sons.

Beck, K., et al. (2001). *The agile manifesto for software development.Retrieved from*http://agilemanifesto.org/

Chan, F., & Thong, J. (2009). Acceptance of agile methodologies: A critical review and conceptual framework. *Decision Support Systems*, (46): 803–814. doi:10.1016/j.dss.2008.11.009

Cockburn, A. (2008). Using both incremental and iterative development. *The Journal of Defense Software Engineering.* May.

Dyba, T., Dingsøyr, T. (2008). Empirical studies of agile software development: A systematic review, Inform. Softw. Technol.

Ionel, N. (2009). Agile software development methodologies: An overview of the current state of research. *Annals of the University of Oradea* [Retrieved from Business Source Complete database.]. *Economic Science Series, 18*(4), 381–385.

Kay, R. (2002). Quick study: The software development lifecycle. *ComputerWorld.* May.

Kendall, J., & Kendall, K. (2004). Agile methodologies and the lone systems analyst: When individual creativity and organizational goals collide in the global IT environment. [Retrieved from Business Source Complete database.]. *Journal of Individual Employment Rights, 11*(4), 333–347. doi:10.2190/B6WV-TR2A-R42K-C87C

Larson, D. (2009). BI principles for Agile development: Keeping focused. [Retrieved from Business Source Complete database]. *Business Intelligence Journal, 14*(4), 36–41.

McAvoy, J., & Butler, T. (2009). A failure to learn by software developers: Inhibiting the adoption of an Agile software development methodology. [Retrieved from International Security & Counter Terrorism Reference Center database]. *Journal of Information Technology Case & Application Research, 11*(1), 23–46.

Negash, S., & Gray, P. (2008). Business intelligence. In Burstein, F., & Holsapple, C. W. (Eds.), *Handbook on decision support systems 2* (pp. 175–193). Berlin, Heidelberg: Springer. doi:10.1007/978-3-540-48716-6_9

Noble, J. (2006). The Core of IT. *CIO Insight. 15-17.*

Pikkarainen, M., Haikara, J., Salo, O., Abrahamsson, P., & Still, J. (2008). The impact of agile practices on communication in software development. *Empirical Software Engineering, 13*, 303–337. doi:10.1007/s10664-008-9065-9

Salo, O., & Abrahamsson, P. (2008). Agile methods in European embedded software development organizations: *A survey on the actual use and usefulness of extreme programming and scrum.* IET Software, 58-64.

Singer, T. (2001). Information engineering: The search for business intelligence. *Plant Engineering.* November. 34-36.

The Data Warehouse Institute. (2009). TDWI requirements gathering: *Getting correct and complete requirements for BI systems.* www.tdwi.org

Yeoh, W., & Koronios, A. (2010). Critical success factors for business intelligence systems. [Retrieved from Business Source Complete database]. *Journal of Computer Information Systems, 50*(3), 23–32.

ADDITIONAL READING

Abrahamsson, P., Salo, J., & Ronkainen, J. (2008). *Agile software development methods: Review and analysis, VTT Technical report.*

Abrahamsson, P., & Salo, O. (2004). Empirical evaluation of Agile software development: The controlled case study approach. In the *Proceedings of the 5th International Conference on Product Focused Software Process Improvement*, Keihanna-Plaza, Kansai Science City in Kyoto-Nara area, Japan.alo and Pekka Abrahamsson.

Chan, F., & Thong, J. (2009). Acceptance of agile methodologies: *A critical review and conceptual framework. Decision Support Systems*, (46): 803–814. doi:10.1016/j.dss.2008.11.009

Dyba, T., & Dingsøyr, T. (2008). Empirical studies of agile software development: A systematic review. *Information and Software Technology*. doi:10.1016/j.infsof.2008.01.006

Graves, R. (2005). Business intelligence tools: The smart way to achieve compliance. *DM Review, 15*(12), 16. Retrieved from http:// www.information-management.com

Griffin, J. (2007a). *Putting the business back into business intelligence initiatives*: The notion that BI projects are IT projects must be left behind. *DM Review, 17*(2), 15. Retrieved from http://tdwi.org/ pages/ publications/ business-intelligence-journal.aspx

Griffin, J. (2007b). The big shift in business intelligence. *DM Review, 17*(8), 22. Retrieved from http:// tdwi.org/ pages/ publications/ business-intelligence-journal.aspx

Guntamukkala, V., Wen, H., & Tarn, J. (2007). An empirical study of selecting software development life cycle models. [Retrieved from Business Source Complete database.]. *Human Systems Management, 25*(4), 265–278.

Hedgebeth, D. (2007). Data-driven decision making for the enterprise: An overview of business intelligence applications. *Vine, 37*(4), 414–420. doi:10.1108/03055720710838498

King, W. R. (2006). The critical role of information processing in creating and effective knowledge organization. *Journal of Database Management, 17*(1), 1–15. doi:10.4018/jdm.2006010101

Ocampo, M. A. (2007). Overcoming the barriers to business intelligence success. *DM Review, 17*(9), 24. Retrieved from http:// web.ebscohost.com.ezproxy.apollolibrary.com

Richardson, J., Schlegel, K., Hostmann, B., & McMurchy, N. (2008). *Magic quadrant for business intelligence platforms, 2008.* Gartner RAS Core Research Note G00154227.

Smalltree, H. (2007). *Gartner Business Intelligence summit 2007: Redefining BI.* Retrieved from http://searchdata management.techtarget.com/ news/ article/ 0,289142,sid91_gci1247220,00.html

Sriram, R. S. (2008). Business intelligence in context of global environment. *Journal of Global Information Technology Management, 11*(2), 1.

Tarter, C. J., & Hoy, W. K. (1998). Toward a contingency theory of decision making. *Journal of Educational Administration, 36*(3), 212. doi:10.1108/09578239810214687

Wang, X., Lane, M., Conboy, K., & Pikkarainen, M. 2009. Where agile research goes: starting from a 7-year retrospective (report on agile research workshop at XP2009). *SIGSOFT Softw. Eng. Notes* 34, 5 (October 2009), 28-30. DOI=10.1145/1598732.1598755 http:// doi.acm.org/ 10.1145/ 1598732.1598755

KEY TERMS AND DEFINITIONS

Business Intelligence: A data driven process that combines data storage and gathering with knowledge management to provide input into the business decision making process. Business Intelligence enables organizations to enhance the decision making process.

Data Warehouse: An integrated, subject-oriented, non-volatile, time-variant data store. A data warehouse can also be considered a union of all data marts. Data warehouses are used to support business intelligence.

Extract, Transformation, and Load (ETL): The process used to capture data from sources, apply transformation rules (filter, select, derive, translate, convert), and load data into a target data store.

Information Technology: The use of software, hardware, and infrastructure to manage and deliver information. Organizations have information technology departments that focus on managing information as an asset. Information technology departments manage the infrastructure used to deliver information.

Information Utility: The process of using information for decision making, knowledge extraction, or for other management activities.

Metadata: Are all the information that is used to define and describe contents, definitions, operations, and structures within an organization's system architecture. Metadata are required by users to understand data meaning and context. Metadata can be categorized into business, technical, and process metadata.

Proof of Concept (POC): A demonstration in principle, whose purpose is to verify that a concept or theory is feasible.

Online Transaction Processing (OLTP): Refers to a class of systems that facilitate and manage transaction-oriented applications.

Chapter 6
BORM:
Agile Modelling for Business Intelligence

Martin Molhanec
Czech Technical University, Czech Republic

Vojtěch Merunka
Czech University of Life Sciences, Czech Republic

ABSTRACT

The business intelligence system gradually became of vital importance for many organizations nowadays. But unfortunately, the traditional static modelling may not be able to deal with it. One solution is to use an agile modelling that is characterized with better flexibility and adaptability. The introduced BORM (Business and Object Relation Modelling) method is just an object-oriented and process-based analysis and design methodology, which has proved to be effective in the development and simulation of large and complex business systems such as business intelligence represents. This chapter describes BORM method and presents it on an application example created in Craft. CASE analysis and modelling tool. At the beginning the authors introduce fundamental principles of BORM method and explain the most important concepts of the method. Finally the authors make clear the method in more detail by means of simple and descriptive, but nontrivial, example from real practice.

INTRODUCTION

As Ventana Research (2006) stated, "*Most organizations use BI and BPM technologies to serve separate purposes that seldom overlap. For the most part, BI deployments don't focus on process, and BPM technology doesn't provide metrics or an aggregate view of business. This situation reflects the predominant view that these are different technologies that each stands alone, delivering value to the business each in its own way.*" The modelling of business intelligence nowadays is such a case, it is still so concentrated on traditional data modelling for creating of data warehouses, but the modelling of flexible business processes is repressed.

DOI: 10.4018/978-1-61350-050-7.ch006

The business intelligence applications still face failures in determining the process model adopted. As the world becomes increasingly dynamic, the traditional static modelling may not be able to deal with it. But our business projects not only became larger, but also began to place considerable emphasis on integration with already existing information systems. More advanced techniques of business process analysis such as *Business Process Modeling Language* (BPML, 2009), *Business process Modeling Notation* (BPMN, 2010) have been created. Unfortunately, they do not meet fully analyst requirements from viewpoint of software developers.

Our approach – BORM (*Business and Object Relation Modelling*) tries to fill in the gap between "Business and IS" and minimize the failure rate of information systems through the application of object-oriented process modelling before the system is built. There are some recent works that confirm our idea to use process models as the skeleton of a unified approach to model and analyze business and IT (Margaria & Steffen, 2009).

Further, the business intelligence systems needs appropriate tools for timely decision making. The BORM method comprises the unique ORD (*Object Relation Diagram*) graphic tool amalgamating state transition and activity diagrams together. This holistic approach strongly supports the main concept of the BORM method formulating an opinion that data and processes are very closely interconnected together. Furthermore, this approach is notably supported by Craft.CASE (Craft.CASE 2009) tool containing a simulator of ORD which allows running simulation scenarios including step-by-step operation. This way the BORM method helps to do a timely decision making in the frame of business intelligence systems.

That is why we introduce BORM method as an object-oriented and process-based analysis and design methodology, which has proved to be effective in the development of business intelligence systems. The effectiveness gained is largely due to a unified and simple method for presenting necessary aspects of the relevant business model, which can be simulated, verified and validated for subsequent software implementation. Also the BORM method makes extensive use of business process modelling towards the area of software engineering.

This chapter describes BORM and demonstrates it on an application example from real business engineering created in Craft.CASE analysis and modelling tool.

BACKGROUND

One of the biggest problems of creating a good business model lies in the initial stages of model development cycle. The initial stages of business modelling methodologies are concerned with two tasks.

The first is the specification of the requirements for the system.

The second is the construction of an initial business model; this model is often called an essential or conceptual model and is built out of the set of the domain specific objects known as essential or conceptual objects.

We must not forget that both these tasks should be carried out with the active participation of the stakeholders, in order to ensure that the correct system is being developed. Consequently, any tools or diagrams used at these early stages should be meaningful to the stakeholders, because many of them are not "*software engineering literate*". Finally, these diagrams must not deform or inadequately simplify the requirement information.

The most frequent technique for requirements' specification in nowadays software development methodologies is *Use Case modelling* as a part of UML (2009) standard. The Use Case method has been created by Jacobson (1992) and is concerned with the identification of external actors, which interact with the software part of the system. This means that is necessary to know the system boundary and distinguish between entities, which are internal and external to that boundary. It is an experience of authors that the correct identification of the system boundary is a "*non-trivial*" task, which often requires significant understanding of the proposed system and consequently can only successfully take place at the end of the requirements specification stage.

The most widespread modelling tool today – UML is not suitable for the first stages of analysis, where business processes need to be recognized. This modelling inability is documented in (Simone and Graham, 1999). Indeed, UML diagrams are too complex for the business community as they often contain too much detail concerning potential software implementations. This means classes, inheritance, public/private methods, attributes, link classes, etc. (Fowler, 1997).

It is our experience based on several real information system projects we did for private Czech companies that proves Ambler's statement (Ambler, 1997) about the correct identification of the system boundary is a 'non-trivial' task, which often requires significant understanding of the proposed system and consequently can only successfully take place at the end of the requirements specification stage. Some deficiencies in this approach are also highlighted by Barjis (2007). There are many views on the effectiveness of Use Cases and related tools as a first stage in System Design. For example, Simons and Graham (Simone and Graham, 1999) describe a situation where Use Case modelling obscures the true business logic of a system. Because of standard UML-based tools are too oriented at the world of programming concepts, other methods for business logic and process modelling appeared:

The basic grammar of some other process modelling tools is based on Petri Nets. The strengths of this approach are that it is both graphical and has strong mathematical basis. A practical implementation of Petri Nets is EPC diagram of Aris method (EPC, 2010).

Other techniques are based on miscellaneous varieties of flowchart diagrams. This approach is the oldest diagramming technique used in computer science. It was primarily used for visualizing the sequences of operations in computer programs. Today, flowcharts are frequently used to model business processes. A practical implementation of flowcharts is workflow diagram used in Proforma Workbench or FirstStep Business CASE Tools. Indisputably, it is also a kind of the Activity Diagram of UML (Fowler, 1997).

The third technique used here is the use of state machines. These have the theoretical background (Shlaer and Mellor, 1992), as well as Petri Nets. A practical implementation of state machines is state-chart diagram in UML, for example. Though, the sequence diagram of UML has features of state machines as well.

The overview of all main approaches for modelling business logic and processes mentioned above is presented in Table 1.

The business community needs a simple yet expressive tool for modelling; able to play an equivalent role to that which was played by the Entity-Relation Diagrams, Data-Flows Diagrams or Flow-Charts over the past decades. One of the strengths of these approaches was that they contained only a limited set of concepts (about five) and were comprehensible for problem domain experts after a few minutes. But unfortunately UML approach lost this power.

One of other alternatives for business modelling more suitable than UML is BORM method (Knott, 2003). Especially the BORM process diagram and the way, how to start business system analysis in simple but precise method going smoothly from business analysis and simulation to detailed UML software design based on MDA principle. Moreover, the possibility to simulate a complicated business process predetermines BORM as suitable tool for modelling and simulating complex business processes as a part of business intelligence.

Table 1. The most used business modeling approaches

Approach	Theory behind	Advantages	Disadvantages
EPC – Aris	Petri Nets	Very popular in Europe, perfectly supported by Aris CASE Tool, easy and comprehensible method for domain experts.	Weak relation at subsequent software development techniques, slow analysis, low expressiveness of large models.
UML Activity Diagram or BPMN	Flowchart	Industry standard, supported by many CASE tools with UML (Unified Modeling Language) or BPMN (Business Process Modeling Notation).	Too software-oriented, difficult to understand by domain experts.
UML sequence and state-chart diagram	Finite state machine	Industry standard, supported by many CASE tools with UML (Unified Modeling Language).	Too software-oriented, difficult to understand by domain experts.
Workflow Diagrams	Flowchart	Easy and comprehensible method for domain experts, perfectly supported by many business CASE Tools.	Weak relation at subsequent software development techniques, not very popular in Europe where Aris takes the dominant place.

BORM: AGILE MODELING FOR BUSINESS INTELLIGENCE

Development of the BORM methodology started in 1993. At that time, several *"first generation"* object or semi-object-oriented analysis methods (OMT, Martin-Odell, Booch, Coad-Yourdon, Jacobson, etc.) already existed. These methods were, and still are, very useful for the development of hybrid software systems. However, these methods also possess two fundamental weaknesses which made them inappropriate for their own development requirements.

Firstly these existing methods did not offer sufficient support for development using a pure object-oriented language like Smalltalk. When developing systems in Smalltalk the authors often used constructs of the language like polymorphism between objects without any inheritance or object dependency, which were not supported and could not be expressed in any of these existing development methodologies. Also in the diagrammatic notations they provided it was impossible to represent most pure object-oriented algorithm. Such algorithms may often be described as mutual asynchronous communications (message passing) between objects, which as the result of receiving messages invoke internal methods with a consequential change in their state.

Secondly, these existing methodologies initially commenced with the construction of a set of classes showing inheritance and aggregation hierarchies. While this is an effective way of expressing the structure required for subsequent coding in an object-oriented language, it is not however effective in illustrating the problem domain. This is because the "object oriented nature" of these diagrams is difficult for domain experts, not educated in computer science concepts, to understand. Consequently such diagrams cannot be used in describing proposed solutions to clients.

BORM Fundaments

BORM is a unified approach to business and IT system modelling. For more on the BORM method let see (Knott, 2003). BORM is based on the spiral model for the development life cycle as described in (Boehm, 1981). One loop of the object-oriented spiral model contains stages of strategic analyses, initial analyses, advanced analyses, initial design, advanced design, implementation and testing.

The first three stages are collectively referred to as the expansion stages. Expansion ends with the finalizing of detailed analysed conceptual model, which fully describes the solution to the problem from requirements point of view.

The remaining stages are called as consolidation stages. They are concerned with the process of developing from "*expanded ideas*" to a working application. During these the conceptual model is step by step, transformed into a software design.

Three Areas of BORM Modeling in MDA perspective

MDA (Model-Driven Approach) is a software development methodology. It provides a set of guidelines for the structuring of specifications, which are expressed as step-by-step transformed models. It was created by the Object Management Group (OMG) in 2001 and is the most used software methodology based on the UML (Unified Modeling Language, 2009). BORM can be regarded as a special kind of MDA. In the MDA terminology, we can describe BORM as:

The CIM (Computer-Independent Model) modelling, according to the BORM method, is a visualization of the environment in which a project is being executed. It deals primarily with business process models. Its aim is to understand and describe a problem and find a solution. A well-made CIM model enables proper descriptions of settings for information system to be made; a necessary condition for a designed solution. This part of BORM having the special BORM process diagram used for the organizational modelling and simulation is discussed in this paper.

PIM (Platform-Independent Model) modelling, according to the BORM method, is a visualization of the required information system in software engineering concepts. The UML (Unified Modeling Language) standard has an important role. There is a set of transforming rules (Merunka, 2008) from BORM model to the conceptual UML model (Knott, 2000).

The PSM (Platform-Specific) model is a revised form of the PIM model which, unlike

PIM, enables specific software implementation, since it includes specific properties of the target environment and reused artefacts of the IT architecture, etc. There is also a set of transforming rules from PIM UML models to the PSM UML models (Knott, 2000).

Business Engineering: Business Models

The first part of the method (CIM) covers the organizational modelling. It transforms a project assignment into a model described by miscellaneous hierarchies, process participants, process scenarios, various diagrams and generated reports. The main instrument of verification and validation is the process simulator, which is currently implemented in the Craft.CASE tool (2009).

For the following purposes, it is possible to use this part of BORM without any relation to a software engineering phase or organizational structure improvement.

Projects documenting processes and organizational structure. These are, for instance, projects whose aim is knowledge management, creating training materials, knowledge visualization, etc.

Projects for preparing the groundwork for selection procedures for organizational consultancy, or other consultancy services.

Projects for preparing the groundwork for selection procedures for the delivery of information systems, or other software engineering projects.

Business Engineering: Business Scenarios

BORM was initially developed as an object-oriented method for the analysis and design of object-oriented software systems. The process, described by Satzinger (1996), starts from an informal problem specification and provides both methods and techniques, to enable this informal specification to be transformed into an initial set of interacting objects. The tools and techniques developed for requirement analysis and used in the initial phases of BORM, provide an independent method for business process modelling as part of business process reengineering. The authors find that this independent method, referred to as BOBA (BORM Object Behaviour Analysis) is frequently used alone.

One advantage of this approach is that it provides a close interactive interchange between the developers and members of the user's organization. As well as identifying initial objects, BOBA elicits from the domain experts, detailed descriptions of their requirements which are fed back to them via easily understood descriptions of the proposed system's behaviour using a number of tables and graphs.

The problem specifications from which the process starts are obtained from relevant parties in the problem domain by interviewing. This determines a list of required system functions, which are essentially Use Cases. From this list, a set of system scenarios is formed. BOBA scripts always include at least the four sections shown in Table 2.

BORM BUSINESS DIAGRAM

The BORM method uses an original diagram for business process modelling and subsequent simulation. The diagram conveys together information from three separate UML diagrams: state, communication and sequence. It has been founded that it is clearly understood by business

stakeholders. Main principles of the BORM process diagram are:

Each subject participating in a process is displayed in its states and transitions.

The diagram expresses all the possible process interactions between process participants.

The business process itself consists of a sequence of particular communications and data flows among participating subjects.

In other words, BORM process diagrams are graphical representations of interconnected Mealy-type finite state machines of particular subjects. Visual simulation of a business process is based on market-graph Petri net. This is a very powerful, yet simple diagram. The full set of BORM process diagram is shown in Figure 1.

BORM APPLICATION EXAMPLE: PUBLIC REGIONAL MANAGEMENT SYSTEM

One of the recent BORM applications of organizational modelling and simulation was the project of improvement the decision-making on the level of mayors and local administrations. It offers the possibility to model and simulate real life situations in small settlements. The project activities were for modelling, simulation and reengineering processes related to the regional government processes of small towns and villages, and the subsequent development of supporting information systems addressing life situations of local people.

Table 2. Scenario structure in BORM

Section name	Description
initiator	A brief verbal description of the beginning of the scenario including any inputs or entry conditions. It also describes the first event or first activity of some element within the process.
action	A verbal description of the process itself.
participants	The set of those members of the system, which are required for the action. It is often the case that the same participants may be present in several processes of the modelled system.
result	A brief verbal description of the end and outputs of the scenario.

Figure 1. BORM diagram symbols

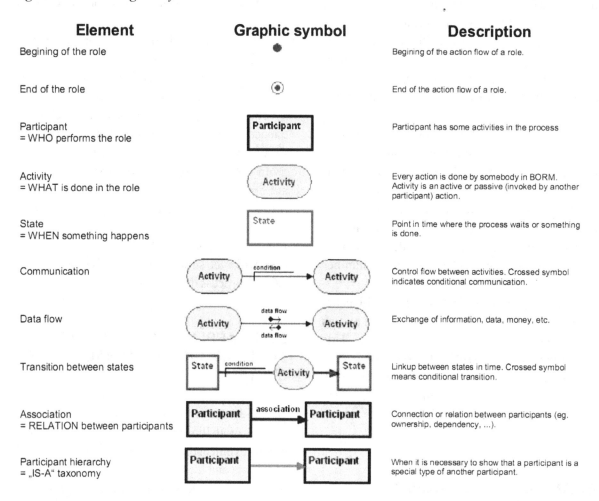

Element	Graphic symbol	Description
Begining of the role		Begining of the action flow of a role.
End of the role		End of the action flow of a role.
Participant = WHO performs the role	Participant	Participant has some activities in the process
Activity = WHAT is done in the role	Activity	Every action is done by somebody in BORM. Activity is an active or passive (invoked by another participant) action.
State = WHEN something happens	State	Point in time where the process waits or something is done.
Communication	Activity — condition → Activity	Control flow between activities. Crossed symbol indicates conditional communication.
Data flow	Activity — data flow / data flow → Activity	Exchange of information, data, money, etc.
Transition between states	State — condition → Activity → State	Linkup between states in time. Crossed symbol means conditional transition.
Association = RELATION between participants	Participant — association → Participant	Connection or relation between participants (eg. ownership, dependency, ...).
Participant hierarchy = „IS-A" taxonomy	Participant → Participant	When it is necessary to show that a participant is a special type of another participant.

Nowadays we have to solve many problems related to the small settlement development and expansion, landscape care and over-all efforts to improve the quality of life and the level of democracy while preserving the conditions of the sustainable development (addressing living standard, cultural and historic value, agricultural and industrial production, transport infrastructure construction, tourism potential, etc.).

One of the specific problems that our approach can be applied to is the urban sprawl as it is stressed by Frumklin (2004). The cause of the urban sprawl in the small settlement development is the fact that the elected members of local administrations (e.g. mayors and clerks) are not (and as the logic states they cannot be) fully educated in all the details of law, state and local administration agenda and their effects on living in the settlements. They don't know how to use fully the legislation in favour of the settlements and usually depend on a misleading interpretation provided by their governing bodies and more often by another subjects (usually privately involved in the process in question and thus biased).

Urban sprawl is a phenomenon that emerged in the last decades in the advanced industrial countries (USA, France, and Great Britain) and recently also in our country. Inhabitants of af-

Figure 2. BORM process model: a building permission example

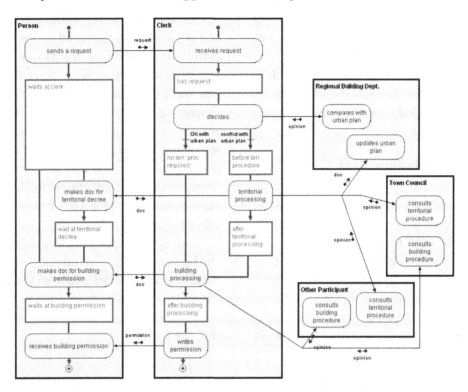

fected settlements usually perceive the urban sprawl positively at first, mainly because of the lobbying. It can be described as an uncontrolled expansion of certain kind of urban build-up into the free landscape caused by favourable land prices, demand for cheap but modern estates, etc. Duany (2001) notes a harmful absorption of original small settlement structures, which causes following negative effects:

Pawning of infrastructure development of the original settlement. New inhabitants fulfil themselves and shop only at the place of their work in a metropolis and the settlements are just a kind of sleeping accommodation for them. New inhabitants' lack of interest in contributing to the settlement development leads to misusing of democratic principles of the self administration against the original local inhabitants and inevitably to the rise of social segregation between the original and the new inhabitants.

Urban sprawl causes disruption of the cultural and historical value of the settlement, disruption of the ecological stability of the area, deconstruction of the transport infrastructure, loss of touristic attractiveness etc.

Loss of the quality agricultural soil.

Modeling and Simulation

In the first instance the legislation and local officials' knowledge related to the processes and agendas of the urban planning of the landscape areas and small settlements with regards to the new housing and building law and regional management trends in the European Union was analyzed. The resulting BORM business diagram of the process of obtaining building permission is shown in Figure 2.

This approach of using process models and their visual simulation helps the officials (especially in the smallest settlements) to clarify the legislation and shows them possible ways of its usage. These models and their visual simulation show how the BORM can be used to improve the process of decision-making on the level of mayors and local administrations. It offers the possibility to model and simulate real life situations in small settlements. One concrete simulation step is shown in Figure 3.

Craft Case Modelling Tool

The BORM method is supported only by Craft. CASE (Craft.Case, 2009) tool which provides all instruments for CIM (as business models) and PIM (as conceptual models) modelling, including their mutual interconnection and the possibility to

undertake thorough testing. The Craft.CASE can be used in process and organizational consultancy and in analytical projects and information system drafts while identifying requests on newly – designed systems; also in component modelling and service oriented architecture. Craft.CASE supports concept transformations via business process simulators, instance-level modelling and set of transformation rules describing how to derive subsequent concepts from previous ones. Moreover, in each step of the method, Craft.CASE keeps consistency between two layers of a model; subjects and behaviours.

Craft.CASE supports concept transformations via business process simulators, instance-level modelling and set of transformation rules describ-

Figure 3. A simulation step example performed by Craft.CASE tool

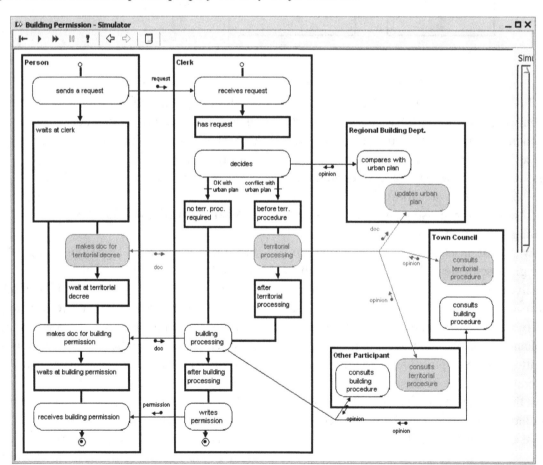

ing how to derive subsequent concepts from previous ones. Moreover, in each step of the method, Craft.CASE keeps consistency between two layers of a model; subjects and behaviours. Thanks to meta-model background and system internal procedures, there is rigidly checked, whether all subjects from the first layer (e.g. classes, object states, packages etc.) have corresponding behaviours from the second layer (e.g. scenarios, use-cases, operations etc.) and vice versa. More information about Craft.CASE such as its programming facilities, meta-model etc. is described in (Merunka et al., 2008).

FUTURE RESEARCH DIRECTIONS

As mentioned above; there exists the gap between the view of business stakeholders and the view of software engineering builders and architects. A situation when modelling of business goes another way and independently from modelling of information systems is highly undesirable. BORM is a method, which combines in the non-traditional form some already existing concepts especially activity and state model together. Nevertheless there are some directions for evolution of BORM method based on the specific recommendation of BORM users. The most requested are:

The transformation of BORM models into commonly used UML models is more or less only about the support of the UML exporting standard XMI. This project has been already recently started.

The transformation into the Petri-net models is almost explored, because the Craft.CASE business process simulator is implemented on the same algorithm as animation of Petri nets. The only thing which must be yet formalized and standardised is the appropriate semantic convention of mapping BORM concepts into Petri-Net concepts.

Unfortunately, the transformation into BPMN is more complicated, because there are BORM concepts, which do not have any direct mapping

into BMPN and vice versa. But the permanently ongoing process of the BPMN development and step-by-step integration with the UML concepts brings BORM method the possibility in the near future, when BPMN will be better elaborated and more integrated with the UML, to unite with BPMN as well.

CONCLUSION

An experience with business clients shows that they prefer to see and understand and simulate each important relationship between/among flows of material, finance, resources, and information, but in one coherent model. Therefore clients appreciate BORM approach, especially the BORM process diagram, instead of using separate activity, state-transition, and sequence and communication diagrams of the same business situation. Clients say that such way of analysis gives them complex and context view of issues they did not see before. Clients appreciate BORM models having collection of business elements and their relationships being visualized and simulated together. Moreover, several clients applying miscellaneous legacy process modelling tools for historical reasons (e.g. EPC-based ARIS, for example) still prefer to analyze and design processes using BORM and later they convert the results into their legacy systems.

The highest value of BORM is generated by the way of modelling, which covers two different worlds: business engineering and software engineering. Further, BORM is a comprehensible tool for the collaboration between software developers and problem domain experts.

Furthermore, the next evolution of BORM method will strongly concentrate on elaboration of BORM compatibility and portability with the most contemporary modelling concepts as are UML, BPMN and Petri Nets as mentioned above.

Finally, the chapter cover briefly entire BORM method as unique step by step transformation approach. Some details were stressed in order to better understand the basic principles of the method.

REFERENCES

Ambler, S. (1997). *Building object applications that work, your step–by–step handbook for developing robust systems using object technology.* Cambridge, UK: Cambridge University Press/ SIGS Books. doi:10.1017/CBO9780511584947

Barjis, J. (2007). Developing executable models of business systems. In *Proceedings of the ICEIS - International Conference on Enterprise Information Systems* (pp. 5-13). INSTICC Press (2007).

Boehm, B. W. (1981). *Software engineering economics.* Englewood Cliffs, NJ: Prentice-Hall.

Craft.CASE (2009). *Business process modeling,* Retrieved July 15, 2010, from http:// www. craftcase.com

Duany, A. (2001). *Suburban nation: The rise of sprawl and the decline of the American dream.* New York, NY: North Point Press.

EPC – Event-driven Process Chain. *(2010).* Retrieved 30 July 2010, from http:// en.wikipedia. org/ wiki/ Event-driven_process_chain

Fowler, M. (1997). *UML distilled: Applying the standard object modelling language.* Reading, MA: Addison Wesley.

Frumkin, H., Frank, L., & Jackson, R. (2004). *Urban sprawl and public health: Designing, planning, and building for healthy communities.* Washington, DC, USA: Island Press.

Jacobson, I. (1992). *Object–oriented software engineering – A use case driven approach.* Boston, MA: Addison Wesley.

Knott, R. P., Merunka, V., & Polak, J. (2000). Process modelling for object oriented analysis using BORM object behavioral analysis. In *Proceedings of 4th International Conference on Requirements Engineering ICRE 2000,* Chicago, USA, IEEE Computer Society Press.

Knott, R. P., Merunka, V., & Polak, J. (2003). The BORM methodology: A third-generation fully object-oriented methodology. In *Knowledge-Based Systems,* Elsevier Science International New York, ISSN 0950-7051 (2003)

Margaria, T., & Steffen, B. (2009). *Continuous model-driven engineering.* IEEE Computer, October 2009.

Merunka, V., Brozek, J., & Nouza, O. (2008). Automated model transformations using the C. C. language. In *Proceedings of the International conference EOMAS 2008,* Montpellier, France, Springer LNBIP.

Process Modeling Language, B. (2009). Retrieved July 15, 2010, from http:// en.wikipedia.org/ wiki/ Business_Process_Modeling_Language

Process Modeling Notation, B. (2010). Retrieved July 15, 2010, from http:// en.wikipedia.org/ wiki/ Business_Process_Modeling_Notation

Satzinger J. W., & Orvik T. U. (1996). *The object-oriented approach - Concepts, modeling and system development.* Boyd&Fraser (1996)

Shlaer, S., & Mellor, S. (1992). *Object lifecycles: Modelling the world in states.* Yourdon Press.

Simone, A. J. H., & Graham, I. (1999). 30 things that go wrong in object modeling with UML, chapter 17. In H. Kilov, B. Rumpe, I. Simmonds (Eds.), *Behavioral Specifications of Businesses and Systems* (pp. 237 – 257). Berlin_Heidelberg: Kluwer Academic Publishers.

The UML standard. OMG – The Object Management Group (2009). ISO/IEC 19501. Retrieved July 15, 2010, from http:// www.omg.org

Ventana Research. (2006). *Business intelligence meets business process management.* Retrieved 30 July 2010, from http:// www.techsoli.com/ pages/ resources/ pdfs/ Ventana-BI_and_BPM.pdf

ADDITIONAL READING

Barjis, J., & Reichgelt, H. (2006). *A Petri Net Based Methodology for Business Process Modeling and Simulation.* In the proceedings of the Fourth International Workshop on Modeling, Simulation, Verification and Validation of Enterprise Information Systems (MSVVEIS), Paphos, Cyprus, May 23-24, 2006. ISBN: 972-8865-49-X

Catell, R. G. G. (1994). *The object database standard – ODMG93.* Morgan Kaufman Publishers.

Eriksson, H., & Penker, M. (2000). *Business modeling with UML.* John Wiley and Sons.

Kotonya, G., & Sommerville, I. (1999). *Requirements Engineering: Processes and Techniques.* John Wiley and Sons.

Scholz-Reiter, B., Stahlmann, H.-D., & Nethe, A. (1999). *Process modelling.* Springer.

Scholz-Reiter, B., & Stickel, E. (1996). *Business process modeling.* Springer.

Shlaer, S., & Mellor, S. (1992). *Object Lifecycles: Modeling the World in States.* Yourdon Press.

KEY TERMS AND DEFINITIONS

AGILE: Agile software development is a recent concept of software engineering process based on iterative development. The term was born in 2001 when the "Agile manifesto" was published.

BPML: Business Process Modeling Language is a meta-language for modelling of business process. At present time is replaced by BPDM (Business Process Definition Meta-model) by OMG.

BPMN: Business Process Modeling Notation is a graphical notation for description of business processes created in 2005. At present (2010) is maintained by Object Management Group (OMG). BPMN is easy understandable by business stakeholders.

FSM: A finite-state machine is a mathematical abstraction of system behaviour based on following concepts: states of the system, transitions between the states and actions fired by the transitions.

MDA: Model Driven Architecture is a recent software development approach based on rigorous usage of modelling in all phases of software development. At present time is hold by OMG.

OMG: Object Management Group is a consortium engaged in standardisation for object oriented systems. At present time holds and manages the following standards: CORBA, UML, BPMN, MDA, SysML and other.

OOP: Object oriented programming is recent programming paradigm based on following concepts: object, class, inheritance, association, message, encapsulation, polymorphism and other.

UML: Is general purpose modelling language created by James Rumbaugh, Grady Booch and Ivar Jacobson in 1994. It is not a software engineering method by itself, but many new software engineering methods have been created based on it.

Chapter 7
Agile Approach to Business Intelligence as a Way to Success

J. Fernández
Technical University of Catalonia, Spain

E. Mayol
Technical University of Catalonia, Spain

J.A. Pastor
Universitat Oberta de Catalunya, Spain

ABSTRACT

In this chapter we present an overview of several methodological approaches used in business intelligence (BI) projects, as well as data warehouse projects. This study reveals that some of them reveal weaknesses, since they are not specifically defined for BI projects, and thus they do not fit specific BI project characteristics or user requirements. These may be the main cause explaining that there is not a broadly accepted BI methodology by practitioners. Even though the goal to find the "best BI methodology" is difficult (or impossible) to meet, we think that any best-class BI methodology may follow an agile approach to better fit BI project characteristics and practitioners' requirements. In this sense, we have analysed BI project characteristics as well as agile principles defined in the Agile Manifesto, and we have identified a strong relationship between these two sources. In this chapter, we show this strong relationship between the so-called critical success factors for BI projects and the Agile principles. Therefore, based on our analysis, we consider that successful BI methodologies must follow an agile approach.

INTRODUCTION

Nowadays, we are in the rise of the so-called Business Intelligence (BI) movement and nearly all organizations make some effort to create and improve their decision-making processes and systems. A lot of new BI projects appear constantly, but the overall experience in the last years is no so good. Something usually goes wrong in the execution of BI projects, since most BI projects (85%) failed to achieve their goals (Fayyad, 2003).

Business Intelligence is still a very young area (Preston, 2007), where we have found thirteen

DOI: 10.4018/978-1-61350-050-7.ch007

different methodological approaches to manage a BI project (Chowdhary & Bhaskaran et Al, 2006; Chowdhary et Al, 2006; Afolabi & Thiery, 2006; Stefanoc & List, 2005; Rowan, 2003; Bäck, 2002; Brohman et al, 2000; Moss, 2001; March & Hevner, 2005; Guo et al, 2006; Dori et al,2005; Kaldeich & Oliveira, 2004; Niu & Zhang, 2008), and most of them have been defined during the last 10 years. But, which are the reasons of this surprising high failure rate in front of the high amount of methodological alternatives?

In fact, we could say that the wide diversity and heterogeneity of methodological approaches for BI projects shows the immaturity that still exists in this area. Thus, to choose a BI methodology is not an easy task, and Thomann & Wells (2000) state that each BI project and each organization must choose the specific methodology that better fits to the project and organization characteristics in order to have more possibilities to success.

The main confusion about BI projects (Jourdan et al, 2008) arises when BI is considered only a product. BI is both a process and a product. As a process, BI is a set of methods and activities that organizations must perform to develop useful information and knowledge (or "intelligence") to survive and thrive in a global and IT based economy. As a product, BI is the information system that allows organizations to predict their behaviour and to take decisions about their future.

Agile methodologies (Agile Manifesto, 2001) are experimenting a great popularity and they have been adopted in different areas. Their use seems to provide good results in the current high competitiveness economy, through quick development and high adaptation to the organization. Agile methodologies focus on the creation of value to the business user, and they may help to integrate information systems in the core of the user's business processes. Therefore, agile methodologies seem to be a right answer to align IT with the business, which is in fact, one of the BI goals.

BACKGROUND

BI is a somewhat ambiguous term that encompasses different acronyms, tools, and disciplines: OLAP, Data Warehousing, Datamarts, Datamining, Executive Information Systems, Decision Support Systems, Neural Networks, Expert Systems, Balanced Scorecards, and many others. It is difficult to give an exact definition of all the terms under the BI umbrella, since they are very interrelated and sometimes there are confused and used indistinctly. Even if BI is a multifaceted concept and supports different interpretations, all of them have three characteristics in common: they provide information to control business activity, they give support to decision making processes and the information provided by BI is business language oriented.

BI provides *information to control business activity* regardless of where the information is stored. BI is an important component of the overall management information system, which controls the proper operation of business processes and activities. In a classical organization (see Figure 1) transformation or operational processes are affected by external events and environment perturbations (market changes, substitute products, new legislation, etc.). Under these situations, operational processes usually require some kind of control, adaptation and correction. Without this supervision, business processes may tend towards disorganization and chaos.

Business control is performed, for example, by means of some performance indicators. These indicators are properly quantified to analyse and evaluate the achievement of organizational objectives. Therefore, it is a mechanism to find out if something is going wrong, or if something can be improved in the organization. Business activities and processes generate and consume information during their execution. Part of this information (operational information) is consumed in the short term, but most of it is stored in some mostly-transactional system (ERP, CRM,

Figure 1. Organization as a system

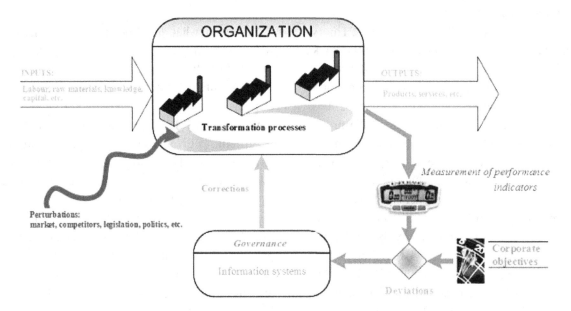

SCM, etc.) until it is used for tactical (mid-term) or strategic (long-term) decision-making processes.

Operational information must be aggregated and made available to the control system in a timely manner, regardless of the operational system from which it comes. Therefore, it will be possible to modify and optimize organization processes. The levels of aggregation and required standardization of heterogeneous data sources will be higher as more strategic and decisional processes are addressed. This decisional nature of the process justifies the next core dimension or characteristic of BI: *decision-making support*.

BI does not only provide information to the users, it allows the users to manage, browse and analyse information of organizational behaviour. Therefore, it is useful to find causes of problems and to identify improvement opportunities. Analysis is fundamental for decision-making activities. Decisions are not made on the basis of a single source of information. Various information sources are weighed up and interrelated; you might say that the information is "alive". Information analysis

is what enables the user to make better business decisions.

Additionally, it is not possible to make effective business decisions if we do not talk the same business language. Regardless of where the information is stored and how it may have been transformed or aggregated, the key point is to provide this information to business users in their own language. They should understand the causes and consequences of their decisions, they must be comfortable with their decision, and they will not require re-interpretation of information provided using the terms they are familiar with. In this sense, BI must be *information orientated towards the language of business users*. In this way, user work is easier and the decision-making required to improve processes and to gain competitiveness is speeded up.

We might therefore define BI as the system that provides the information required to control business processes and to take effective business decisions.

However, there is an additional characteristic inherent to BI, and perhaps the most important characteristic to shape the need for BI Governance in the future. This is that BI must be focused on enabling business users to make decisions with semantically appropriate information.

The high competitiveness in our actual world requires information systems to be quickly developed and easily adapted to the organization. In this crazy race to survive in the market, the first thing most organizations discard, in order to have a rapid development, is precisely a comprehensive analysis. In other words, to speed development we think we can replace an exhaustive analysis by a light analysis or simply forget analysis. This is undoubtedly the big mistake, since we can indeed have a system developed quickly, but it will surely be a system full of errors, unmanageable, non maintainable and without real value for the organization.

Since it is difficult to change the global market rules then, specification and development methodologies must be adapted to this changing environment. The most important key success point is to obtain a quick result, with strong visualization tools and with an intuitive use of information. Therefore, in this changing environment it is not a bad idea to consider a methodology based on agile principles, which is based on short development cycles and an incremental enhancement of system features at each iteration cycle. In fact, it is on this kind of changing environments, where agile methodologies had been developed.

In the literature, there have been a lot of discussions and debates (Highsmith, 2001; Highsmith, 2002; Glass, 2001) to determine whose are the best methodologies. But agile methodologies are neither the "ultimate solution" to all problems of BI development. They can be (and are) applied in most organizations and in fact, we can adapt these methodologies without losing the rigor of classical methodologies. However, to apply agile methodologies, it is necessary a first important and crucial step: the organization must understand what "agile" means and must be ready to embrace this kind of methodology.

BI is the "brain" of the management information system. Therefore, the system must grow quickly and consistently, as the organization evolves and new needs are required. Organizations adapt to the changes in their environment, and this adaptation must be done quickly. Therefore, it seems logical to think that BI systems must take advantage of agile methodologies to accelerate organization evolution. We think that agile methodologies may enable organizations to evolve in an effective, efficient and, of course, ... agile way.

What Does a BI Methodology Need?

Due to the above mentioned diversity and heterogeneity of methodological approaches, to choose a methodology is not easy task. Therefore, it is necessary to know in advance what are the main characteristics of a BI project and which are the requirements that a BI methodology must satisfy.

Larissa T. Moss and Shaku Atre (2003) identifies 16 development steps and more than 900 task to do in the lifecycle of a BI project. This is the largest methodological roadmap applied to decision support systems, and the most referenced by BI practitioners. But this methodology is only a documented BI roadmap to be used as a guide. On the other hand, as Brousseau et al. (2006) say: "The job of a manager is, above all, to make decisions. At any moment in any day, most executives are engaged in some aspect of decision-making: exchanging information, reviewing data, coming up with ideas, evaluating alternatives, implementing directives, following up."

The most successful managers and executives become increasingly open and interactive in their leadership styles, and more analytic in their thinking styles, as they progress in their careers. In this sense, to reach this leadership and analytical fitness, they require a methodology and a BI system that "provides them information to support decision making at right time, at right people and that is understandable." However, BI system developers and IT managers must remember that: a BI project is not their personal project; a BI project belongs to the organization; that they must be sure it provides value to the organization; and it must be addressed to the right people at the right moment.

Then, what kind of methodology is needed? This is not an easy question because to think and make decisions is not an easy task either. Larissa Moss (2005) offers the 5 features that a methodology should satisfy for this type of decisions systems. We also include two more features to this list (the last two) by considering the decision-making process needs. Thus, we expect of a BI methodology to be:

C1. Change Oriented: A BI methodology must be more orientated to facilitate and manage change than to the achievement of a final product. Since the market, the provided services and the business processes change constantly, then the methodology must give effective support to manage this change in a dynamic way.

C2. Cross-functional: A BI methodology must be executed by a multidisciplinary team. Information does not belong to a single department, it is a resource of all the organization, and everyone must be involved in its provision and use. Processes of an organization are not isolated in only one department, they usually cross several department boundaries. Therefore, to control and manage the main processes of the organization it is necessary to follow a cross-functional and multidisciplinary approach.

C3. Multi-project: A BI methodology must be able to manage several (sub-)projects at once and in parallel (ETL, cleansing data, reporting, queries, dashboards, scorecards, data-mining, etc.). Sekine et al. (2009) proposed a two-phase method dealing with business processes for aligning BI projects with business goals: the first phase extracts and checks the adequacy of hypotheses for

achieving business goals and, in the second phase, actions needed to implement the hypotheses are defined and clarified.

C4. Task exhaustive: A BI methodology considers all tasks to be taken into account. Not having all of them in mind could induce to forget some critical task, and then, it would be necessary to redo some work, with the inherent lose of efficiency and completeness.

C5. Focus in critical path: A BI methodology must use critical paths for management. This means that it must specially focus on critical tasks that would change the planning. Then, re-planning is only necessary when this path is affected.

C6. People focus: In any organization some people make the decisions; other people actually perform, control, and decide on processes. All of them are focused on the management of structures and processes in a continuous way. We need effective mechanisms to foster relations between the people in the organization. We need to focus on people. We need to add a third additional component to "structures" and "processes". This component is the "relational mechanism". This mechanism will ensure the active participation and collaboration of key users from business and IT in interdisciplinary teams. These teams are those that will ensure to provide value to the organization and guarantee its use.

C7. Alignment with business needs: A BI methodology must control the alignment of IT development with business needs to provide value (see Figure 2). Development must be linked with business change and also with business strategy. Ensuring IT alignment with the business has traditionally been viewed as the job of the Chief Information Officer (CIO). However, successful IT/business alignment entails more than the executive level communication and strategic translation. It is necessary to

Figure 2. Creation of value from Business Intelligence systems

involve all people. Traditionally, organizations have structured the alignment strategy around the CIO who, when s/he address the need to govern the decision-making systems, may becomes a bottleneck which prevents organization from narrowing the IT/Business gap. Everything must go through him/her, and s/he is responsible to translate business objectives into specific IT objectives that are exclusively carried on by the IT managers. In order to close this gap and to provide true value to the project, it is necessary to stay in contact with business people. We need to have control about the actual impact of our project in the every day life in our organization, and to include control tasks in the BI methodology. One solution may be to have regular meetings with all levels of decision makers related to our project, until IT structure is efficiently interlinked with business structure. When it is not possible to see the difference between the two structures, then we have bridged the IT/Business gap once for all. The IT/Business gap can be bridged by putting IT and business people working together into the same groups. The decision maker must play an active role within the IT groups developing BI systems. The initiatives generated by teamwork, the interdisciplinary process monitoring groups, and the joint sessions of BI system review, must be a routine part of the project work. In this way, Marjanovic (2010) argues that further opportunities for business value

creation could be discovered through systematic analysis of the non-technical aspects of BI and Business Process Management integration, especially in terms of strategy alignment, human-centred knowledge management and ongoing improvement of BI supported processes.

Review of BI Methodological Approaches

The life cycle of a BI project (Moss & Atre, 2003; Brousseau et al,2006; Moss, 2005; Gangadharan et al, 2004) involves multiple phases, with many of them being cyclic and running in parallel. Some methodological approaches have identified more than 900 tasks to be implemented and managed properly. Therefore, it is not so easy to identify "the best" BI methodology, perfect in all its aspects. There are many methodological approaches in the scientific literature, most of them are good in some aspect, but not so good in others. Therefore, we do not know which is "the best" methodology to deal with a BI project.

In this section we discuss about the most representative approaches used to deal with BI projects. We review the strengths and weaknesses of 14 methodologies that have been implemented and documented in BI projects. We describe how these methodologies try to solve the most problematic specific issues of BI projects, and the aspects that are not explicitly considered by these approaches.

The basic scheme that we will use to summarise each methodology review focus in the following aspects:

- *Basic approach*: Which are the key principles that each methodological approach supports? Which is the origin of the approach? Which are the concepts underlying each approach?

- *Methodologies*: Examples of methodologies that follow each approach. If there are many, what are the methodologies with the same purpose or leitmotiv?

- *Strengths*: What are the most successful points of each approach?

- *Weaknesses*: What are the main limitations of each approach?

1.   Traditional Analysis Approach

Basic Approach: In the traditional waterfall process, the basic approach involves translating user needs into software requirements by using an analysis step. Later, user requirements are transformed to a design architecture, which is implemented and tested. At the end, the software is delivered to users.

Methodologies: Plan-Driven (like Rational Unified Process) and Requirement-Driven Methodologies (Rowan, 2003).

Strengths: This approach is the precursor of most of existing methodologies, since it is based on the origins of software engineering. This approach had been applied in many projects and under several distinct situations, therefore such methodologies are well known since they had been tested and proved broadly.

Weaknesses: Many attempts to apply methodologies based on requirements have done, but they have failed to implement BI systems. The root of the problem is that decision-making is always a semi-structured and rapidly changing process, while these methodologies assume a stable environment with minor changes and a

definite structure. This approach might not be able to handle appropriately frequent changes on current and future demands of users. Moreover, the difficulty for users to describe and explain how they make their decisions may be a problem to use this methodological approach.

2.   User Driven Approach

Basic Approach: BI methodologies that follow this approach are based on an early prototype construction based on the business objectives. Given these objectives, users will define their information needs, queries that will be requested to the BI system, and the maintenance and future development requirements (Engström et al, 2000). In Afolabi & Thiery (2006) the importance of the role and participation of the business users in the construction of BI systems is stated, not only when the system is defined, but basically during all cognitive stages of the decision making process of the user (observation, elemental abstraction, reasoning, symbolization and creativity.) Through these studies, we may infer that a BI system should be constructed based on the type of queries the user will request (query adaptation) and the type of responses that the system must provide (response adaptation) (Schuff et al, 2005). Therefore, as we have more knowledge of how users "understand and process" the information, more capable we are to design a BI system. See for example, the Knowledge Warehouse designed by Nemati et al. (2002).

Methodologies: Demand-Driven, User-Driven and Prototype-Driven methodologies.

Strengths: The most important advantage of this approach is its complete orientation towards the system's use and the user needs. The requirements are not completely defined to start with, and thus these methodologies seeks to show the user a working prototype (Yang et al, 2006; Huynh & Schiefer, 2001) to try to capture the best possible business needs (Winter & Strauch, 2006). These methodologies seek a well-defined user interface, after trying to understand the user and the issues that s/he has to respond wrt. the business, especially the strategic questions (Rouibah & Ouldali, 2002). Many of the current projects that have been reported as successful by practitioners and software vendors are a combination of methodologies based on requirements management and on prototyping. Therefore, one success factor is precisely the user involvement and alignment with the real business needs.

Weaknesses: A weakness of this approach is to assume that all users know the business strategy and that they act consistently with it, when in fact it is not always the case. Therefore, mainly those users that make decisions are those that must lead the BI system creation process.

3. Data-Driven Approach

Basic Approach: This approach is based on the hypothesis that "users lie, data don't". This approach is focused on the analysis of business data with a higher rate of access, data that is queried more frequently, and how are different data related. This "most useful" data guides the BI system design process.

Methodologies: (Rowan, 2003).

Strengths: The strength of this approach is based on the appreciation that "data does not lie, let's use it". If a dataset is requested to build a BI system, it means that this data is needed. Following this approach, we can have a clear idea of what information is necessary for the user to achieve some functionality.

Weaknesses: Data-driven approaches like (Rowan, 2003) leave the users and the business objectives out of consideration, but focus only on data usage. The problem is that this strategy could not properly identify the business, i.e. the necessary control information, when this is not highly accessed. Additionally, this methodology may not be adequate to identify future business needs.

4. Data Value-Chain Approach

Basic Approach: This approach is based on the BI Value Chain. In fact, this approach is an evolution of the data-driven approach focused specifically on those data that generates greater value for the business.

Methodologies: (Brohman et al, 2000).

Strengths: The main strength of this approach is that it considers the business needs focussing on the data that add value to the business, and leaves out that data with access but without any business value.

Weakness: This approach inherits the same limitations mentioned for the data-driven approach.

5. Process-Driven Approach

Basic Approach: This approach focuses on the analysis of how business processes are performed in the organization. A control process guides this approach, because if we have control over our own process we can provide value.

Methodologies: (Rowan, 2003).

Strengths: The main strength of this methodology is its process orientation. Business processes must be controlled to ensure the daily operation and competitiveness of the organization. Therefore, processes must be monitored or linked by the BI system for them to be improved and controlled.

Weaknesses: In organizations, people manage processes and there are often dissonances between what processes define, the business needs and what people decide. Isolating processes without taking into account cross-functional relationships may give us a false view of the organization operation. Moreover, if we only focus on processes we cannot give a global landscape. Besides, customers do not perceive the organization processes, they only perceive provided services, and thus a service-orientation might be a better approach.

6.   Event-Driven Approach

Basic Approach: The Event-Driven approach proposes to split business processes in three views: Data, Function and Organization, all three connected to each other through events. Stefanov and List (2005) propose to extend this model with BI objects and BI data connectors, as a way to fill the gap between business and BI systems.

Methodologies: Stefanov and List (2005).

Strengths: The main strength is that it is an attempt to analyse the organization in a cross-functional way and also includes support functions to the processes.

Weaknesses: The weak point is that this approach is too complex to be implemented and it requires much effort and high maturity models in the organization.

7.   Object-Process Driven Approach

Basic Approach: This is a methodological variation halfway between Event-Driven and Process-Driven. An example is the OPM Driven Approach (Dori et al.,2005) in which objects and processes are equally important and managed in a similar way.

Methodologies: (Dori et al.,2005)

Strengths: This approach can be regarded as another step to completeness and complexity of BI methodologies.

Weakness: In some cases, it is difficult to implement in real complex organizations.

8.   Joint Approach

Basic Approach: The Joint Approach focuses on the identification of a cross-functional architecture. The key point is that processes are transversal to the organization, since more than one functional unit participates in their execution. Therefore, there are several crossing boundaries, many gaps, and many joints (March & Hevner, 2005). Precisely, in those joints is where it is necessary to focus the effort. Managing all this information altogether implies a big effort that requires the support of a BI system to do it more efficiently.

Methodologies: (March & Hevner, 2005).

Strengths: The key point of this approach is on how accurate is the identification of information gaps that usually occur in the boundaries between functional units. Is in such joint points where specialized information systems and people usually fail; therefore, considering this joint points in the methodology is one of the strengths of this approach.

Weaknesses: The weak point of this approach relies in the difficulty to define processes or services to manage and control the information and coordinated reasoning in these joint points.

9.   Goal-Driven Approach

Basic Approach: This approach focuses on goals of the organization and its processes. It is based on the analysis of the interaction between customers/providers and business users to achieve that goal. IT is based on providing value to the customers to generate value to the organization, but it is not possible to generate value without the provider's participation. The BI system architecture is defined as result of the analysis of information needs and relationships between them. Therefore, it is necessary to define the strategic goals and try to make the main effort to improve the relationships between customers and providers with the organization.

Methodologies: (Rowan, 2003).

Strengths: The strength of this approach is that it is based on the company's strategic objectives and in its real needs.

Weaknesses: This approach must consider strategic objectives of the organization, but the problem may appear if control processes do not consider explicitly the operational and tactical business objectives. The BI system provides support functions to control the organizational processes, but when organization strategy is mistaken or tactical and operational objectives are unknown, this approach is not so successful as it is expected.

10. Triple-Driven Approach

Basic Approach: Guo et al (2006) consider that current BI methodologies are still immature to be applied in an isolated manner. Therefore, they propose a combination of the best ideas of Goal-based, Data, and User Driven approaches, creating the Triple-Driven approach. They conclude that these three approaches are perfectly compatible.

Methodologies: Guo et al (2006)

Strengths: They combine the specific strengths of each methodology.

Weaknesses: They reduce their weakness, but maintaining some of their limitations.

11. Model Driven Approach

Basic Approach: The Model Driven BI (Chowdhary et al, 2006) methodology seeks to bridge the business and the IT department. Its purpose is to provide the basis for developing quick solutions, which evolve easily and with a high flexibility. The underlying idea is to develop a model to simplify business complexity and then, to transform and deploy it in different system architectures, preferably in service-oriented architectures (SOA).

Methodologies: (Chowdhary et al, 2006)

Strengths: Model Driven Development (MDD) has been widely applied in several areas, such as software reuse, re-engineering, reverse design of user interfaces, etc. Benefits of the MDD approach may include time reduction in software development, quality improvement and quality maintenance. It is a simple evolution of prototyping that makes more emphasis on semantic transformation.

Weaknesses: The approach is too technology dependent. It is not easy to simplify business complexity, and it is not easy to deploy SOA architectures in real business situations.

12. Cognition-Driven Approach

Basic Approach: In this approach (Niu & Zhang, 2009) manager situation awareness (SA) and mental models are developed and enriched. These models are used to define naturalistic decision making processes based on traditional BI systems. Mental models are also used to supervise information retrieval and presentation processes. The final decision-making process is based on a recognition decision model, previously primed.

Methodologies: (Niu & Zhang, 2009)

Strengths: The strongest point in this approach is that mental models will significantly increase the probability to make good decisions and to have a good performance. The manager situation awareness is represented and analyzed to define decision maker's knowledge needs, and his/her knowledge perception and comprehension.

Weaknesses: The main weakness of this approach is that it is necessary to know the analytic reasoning and mental models of the decision maker. And these mental models are unstructured, fuzzy and not easy to define. Therefore, there is a gap between the data warehouse and decision maker cognition process.

13. Adaptive Business Approach

Basic Approach: The Adaptive Business Approach (Bäck, 2002) is based uniquely on what is relevant to the business. It focuses on problems of the business to adapt to market changes and the data necessary to address this situation. The expected output of a BI system must either be a concrete solution to the problem or more knowledge about the problem to continue reasoning.

Methodologies: (Bäck, 2002)

Strengths: The strongest point of this approach is that it focuses on change. Organizations are affected by marked changes and therefore they may become vulnerable; so focussing on change may allow making more accurate decisions about the future and the organization to evolve.

Weaknesses: The weakness of this approach is that sometimes, processes with lesser business value require to be also supported in order to execute our main (most value added) processes.

14. Agile Approach

Basic Approach: The Agile Manifesto (2001) defines four values that agile methodologies should follow: "*... to value: Individuals and interactions over processes and tools. Working software over comprehensive documentation. Customer collaboration over contract negotiation. Responding to change over following a plan. That is, while there is value in the items on the right, we value the items on the left more.*"

Methodologies: Agile Modeling, Agile Unified Process (AUP), Dynamic Systems Development Method (DSDM), Essential Unified Process (EssUP), Extreme Programming (XP), Feature Driven Development (FDD), Open Unified Process (OpenUP), Scrum, etc.

Strengths: This approach can help us to search for a better BI methodology, contributing easily in five of the seven characteristics that a BI project must have, and that we identified in the previous section: (C1) Change Oriented, (C2) Cross-functional, (C3) Multi-project, (C6) People-focused and (C7) Alignment with business needs. At this point, we can guess that this may be a good way of doing things: changing and adapting more to the people and organizations that want to face BI projects.

Weaknesses: Little academic work (Fernández, Mayol & Pastor, 2008) has been done wrt. this approach, even though practical experiences are growing day by day. One of the first references that propose the use of agile methodologies is an informative paper appeared in 2001 of just two pages in which, L. Moss (2001), co-author of a BI greatest methodological guide (Moss & Atre,

2003), says that it would be possible to use agile methodologies with rigor in BI projects. No further remarkable references appeared until 2007. But, from 2007 a lot of references and proposals appeared until today. Only for your reference at July 2010, Google retrieves 106.000 results to the keywords "Agile Business Intelligence". If we make the same search in Google Academic we only found 17 results, showing a great gap between practitioners and researchers in this topic.

Therefore, could the Agile approach be a good BI methodological approach? Is in fact as good as it seems? Is it a good way to find the ultimate methodology to assure BI projects success? We do not know, but we will try to show there is a strong relationship between Agile approach characteristics and BI projects success factors. Therefore, it may be a big step in the good direction.

To show it, we will first analyse what does an Agile Methodology adoption imply and, after that, we will review BI Critical Success Factors to try to show they are strongly correlated.

THE MEANING OF AN AGILE APPROACH

The high current market competitiveness needs information systems to be quickly developed and well adapted to the business. But in this crazy race to rapid development, the first thing discarded is an in-deph comprehensive analysis of the organization, replacing it by a more shallow analysis. This is undoubtedly the big mistake, we have a system developed quickly but what probably full of errors, unmanageable and difficult to be maintained.

Since it is difficult to change global market rules, the alternative consist to adapt specification and development methodologies to this changing environment full of pressures. In this context, it is crucial for success to obtain a system that can be seen, displayed and used very quickly. The methodology has to be agile and dynamic, so you

Table 1. Agile values

VA1	The individual and their interactions rather than the process and tools.
VA2	Develop software that runs more than to get a good documentation
VA3	Collaboration with the customer rather than negotiating a contract.
VA4	Respond to the changes that follow a planning

must have a short development cycle in which it is possible to enhance the features in each iteration. To satisfy this aim, Agile Methodologies have been defined (Table 1). These methodologies are based to provide these four values to the projects:

VA1. The individual and their interactions rather than the process and tools

The key tool of software engineering and development is the human brain. Journeys of 14 hour per days of work are in detrimental to the quality of the final product. One person alone cannot make a project; s/he needs an environment in which to develop their work and a team with which to collaborate. These interactions should also be taken care of. A key factor for success is to build a good team (technically and collaboratively) that knows how to build their own development environment. A common mistake is to build the environment first and expect the team will adapt to it. This strategy reduces effectiveness. It is preferably that the team set up the environment based on their needs and personal characteristics.

Moreover, interaction between the team and the end-users must be as smooth as possible, preferably with the user being a member of the team. In fact, both parts have the common goal to make the project work and be useful to the business. If this interaction runs satisfactorily, aspects as the choice of the tool and the development process are less important to determine the project success.

VA2. Develop software that runs more than to get a good documentation

One of the advantages of good system documentation is to have it available when you have to change something in a system. A good up-to-date documentation on each modification lets you know the actual status of implementation and supports to make the appropriate changes, but few people with the external pressures of time and money update the documentation accordingly. Usually when someone has to fix or redesign something wrong in a system, s/he concentrates on quickly making the modification because it is very possible that end-users are waiting (even angry) and the organization is losing money. In these cases, the developer does not look the documentation in detail and, when the error is fixed, s/he does not update the documentation.

In the Agile approach it is a priority to avoid these mistakes. It promotes to focus development time to ensure that software works correctly and that has been tested thoroughly, reducing as much as possible useless documentation that will not be up-to-date. The unwritten rule of the agile approach is not to produce superfluous documents, but only those necessary to make an immediately and important decision during the development process. These documents should be short and concise, forgetting such aspects that do not contribute to the understanding of the problem.

VA3. Collaboration with the customer rather than negotiating a contract

In the last few years, Information Technology Consulting has often become a contest between the provider and the client who hires it. On the one hand the client tries to make the greatest number of features with the same money, and on the other, the consultant tries to perform only the functions originally contracted. In follow-up meetings of the project is easy to hear phrases like "this change does not enter into the contract" generally answered by the typical "I have no more budget." At the end of such projects the consultant becomes a hybrid between an analyst and an attorney that must develop legal skills to be safeguarded in case of a legal dispute.

Therefore, for a successful project, the complicity and the continuous contact between the client and the development team is essential. The client must be and feel part of the team. In this way both parts understand the difficulties of the other and, consequently, they may work together to solve them.

VA4. Respond to changes more than following a plan

Organizations are changing constantly, adapting to market needs and reorganizing their work-

flows to be more efficient. It is difficult therefore, that during the development of a project, it is not affected by changes on the information needs of the organization. Moreover, economic possibilities of the organization can influence the project by enlarging or reducing it. There are many factors that may alter our initial project plan, and if it is not adapted to these changes the risk that system becomes is useless increases. The ability to respond to changing requirements, technology, budget or strategy is undoubtedly a success factor.

Agile Principles

The Agile Manifesto distinguishes also twelve principles that characterize an agile process. Those twelve principles (listed in Table 2) had not been sufficiently implemented in more traditional approaches. Traditional approaches consider them in some way, but without enough emphasis. Agile approaches focus in more depth in these principles, trying to solve the main gaps of software development methodologies.

Table 2. Agile principles

P1 (Continuous **delivery of value**)	I. Our highest priority is to satisfy the customer through early and continuous delivery of valuable software
P2 (Welcome changes)	II. We welcome changing requirements, even late in development. Agile processes harness change for the customer's competitive advantage.
P3 (Frequently deliveries)	III. Deliver working software frequently, from a couple of weeks to a couple of months, with a preference to the shorter timescale
P4 (Working together)	IV. Business people and developers must work together daily throughout the project.
P5 (Motivated individuals)	V. Build projects around motivated individuals. Give them the environment and support they need, and trust them to get the job done. .
P6 (Face-to-face conversation)	VI. The most efficient and effective method of conveying information to and within a development team is face-to-face conversation.
P7 (Working software)	VII. Working software is the primary measure of progress.
P8 (Sustainable development)	VIII. Agile processes promote sustainable development. The sponsors, developers, and users should be able to maintain a constant pace indefinitely
P9 (Attention to excellence)	IX. Continuous attention to technical excellence and good design enhances agility.
P10 (Simplicity)	X. Simplicity (the art of maximizing the amount of work not done) is essential
P11 (Self-organizing teams)	XI. The best architectures, requirements, and designs emerge from self-organizing teams
P12 (Reflects and adjusts)	XII. At regular intervals, the team reflects on how to become more effective, then tunes and adjusts its behaviour accordingly.

SUCCESS AND FAILURE IN BUSINESS INTELLIGENCE

Review of BI Critical Success Factors

As we have said, agile methodologies are taking positions in BI projects. But are they a definite solution? Are they a valid approach to manage BI projects? Does agility guarantee BI project success?

In order to answer these questions we first need to take into account critical success factors (CSF) of BI projects. A study by Monash University (Fayyad, 2003) concludes that 85% of BI projects have failed to achieve one of its objectives. What does it determine success and failure of such systems?

To introduce these success factors, we have grouped them by the approach made by its authors. Therefore, we group them in the following categories:

1. CSF relative to BI tools
2. Organizational CSF
3. CSF relative to knowledge management
4. Intangible CSF
5. CSF about people and leadership
6. CSF from academic and scientific literature

1. CSF Relative to BI Tools.

Are BI tools failing? Azvine et al. (2005) tell us that current BI tools have been failing in these three main points:

- Displaying and reporting what happened
- Understanding rationale of the past
- Predicting what will happen

If it really depends on BI tools, then do not worry about what kind of methodology to use. The truth is that Azvine's vision might be too

alarmist. But in fact BI tools have a large deficit in the last two points.

2. Organizational CSF.

One of the basic features for BI system success is undoubtedly the organizational culture and organizational maturity level. Creating and managing a culture of measurement needs time. Quinn (2003), in the white paper "Establishing a Culture of Measurement, A Practical Guide to BI" provides five rules for success (CSF) and another 5 for the failure (CFF) of BI projects, which are summarized in Table 3.

3. The CSF relative to knowledge management.

Another point to consider when determining the success of BI solutions is how the knowledge of the Information Systems Department is managed. Becker, Vilkov & Brelage (2004) list the shortfalls in knowledge management in the departments of BI. The first one is the difficulty in defining appropriate structures for locating information. Where is the document? What does it contain? 30% of the documents with information are stored and handled in isolated personal computers or laptops, therefore limiting its accessibility to other users in the organization. The second deficiency identified by these authors is the difficulty of accessing to the personal knowledge of each employee of the organization. This knowledge acquisition requires time and money of the company in training initiatives, but it is very difficult to reuse. If we also consider a high employee turnover, losses are considerable.

4. Intangible CSF.

A successful BI solution involves a purely intangible part that must also be evaluated. Counihan, Finnegan and Sammon (2002) stated the difficulty of evaluating strategic information systems, especially in their intangible issues.

Table 3. CSF and CFF Quinn (2003)

Quinn-CSF1	Rule 1: Understanding users.
Quinn-CSF2	Rule 2: Using the paradigm of Clicks.
Quinn-CSF3	Rule 3: Distinguish between users, information producers and information consumers.
Quinn-CSF4	Rule 4 Establish a culture of measurement.
Quinn-CSF5	Rule 5 BI construction is a strategic decision of the entire company.
Quinn-CFF1	Reason 1: The skills and desires of the users are underestimated.
Quinn-CFF2	Reason 2: The emphasis in the wrong phase of the cycle.
Quinn-CFF3	Reason 3: The information is not self-explainable, there is no case of semantics.
Quinn-CFF4	Reason 4: We don't have established a culture of measurement.
Quinn-CFF5	Reason 5: BI projects have been implemented unevenly tactical.

Moreover, Gibson, Arnott and Jagielska (2004) identified six criteria for assessing the intangible benefits of BI systems:

- Determine the criticality of intangibles issues
- Separate the user requirements from internal intangible issues
- Show the importance of intangibles to the company's managers
- Categorize the intangibles to make their evaluation easier
- Manage to have a rapid success (quick win)
- Measure the compliance level of intangibles

5. CSF about people and leadership.

Another factor to take into account that may determine the success or failure of BI systems is the profile of the people involved in implementation and development, especially in project leadership. Educations, experience, and so on, are factors that may have a direct influence to the project success. Faulkner and MacGillivray (2001) identified 12 success factors (Table 4) that must satisfy the leader of the project.

Chenoweth, Corral and Demirkan (2006) state that interaction between technology and the corporate social context clearly determines the success or failure of a data warehouse. At the same time, this interaction may determine the extent and evolution of a BI system.

In this sense, they propose seven key interventions, shown in Table 5, as a list of basic questions to consider and in their order of execution.

Notice that user is the centre of everything; however user implication on the project determines clearly project success or failure.

6. CSF from academic and scientific literature

A more extensive list of CSF may be obtained with a review of scientific and academic literature. In this section we summarize the most relevant proposals. These CSF are not centred in any specific Business BI issue as previous lists. In this case they are more general, but as relevant and critical as the others.

Solomon (2005) gives us a guide of things to consider when we implement a BI solution or a Data Warehouse (Table 6).

Larissa Moss (2005) offers 10 mistakes to avoid in the management of BI and Data Wharehouse projects (Table 7).

Briggs & Arnott (2002) and Briggs (2004) propose the critical success factors in Table 8 for decision-making systems.

Wixon and Watson (2001) identified the factors shown in Table 9 as the most relevant.

Table 4. Success factors for project leader of BI (Faulkner and MacGillivray, 2001)

Code	
F & M-CSF1	1.- To reflect rather than act on the values of the company
F & M-CSF2	2.- To focus project goals on the most urgent needs of the organization.
F & M-CSF3	3.- To identify business needs and provide user friendly tool support to business people.
F & M-CSF4	4.- To make plans for success adapted to how the organization evaluates success.
F & M-CSF5	5.- To being a child of three years: ask the reason for everything.
F & M-CSF6	6.- To consider the project as the major innovation for the organization
F & M-CSF7	7.- To dialogue, dialogue and dialogue!!
F & M-CSF8	8.- To integrate and involve business executives and managers as co-leaders of "their own" project
F & M-**CSF9**	9.- To be proactive, foresee resistance to change and become a champion of the BI cause
F & M-CSF10	10.- To learn from others.
F & M-CSF11	11.- To evaluate and consider risk and cost of do not using Business Intelligence Tools
F & M-CSF12	12.- To have a open mind and a global vision of BI evolution into the organization

Table 5. Interventions of (Chenoweth et al., 2006)

Code	
CHENOW-INT-1	1 .- Does top management support the project?
CHENOW-INT-2	2 .- Do users support the project?
CHENOW-INT-3	3 .- Do users access to a wide range of data?
CHENOW-INT-4	4 .- Do users need restrictive tools?
CHENOW-INT-5	5 .- Do users understand the relationship between data warehouse and business processes?
CHENOW-INT-6	6 .- Do users perceive the IT department support in their daily tasks?
CHENOW-INT-7	7 .- Are there one or more power users?

Table 6. Solomon(2005)

Code	
Solom-CSF-1	1.- Define service level agreements and reporting requirements with users
Solom-CSF-2	2.- Identify the source systems
Solom-CSF-3	3.- Plan a data quality
Solom-CSF-4	4.- Choose the design model adequately
Solom-CSF-5	5.- Choose appropriate ETL tool
Solom-CSF-6	6.- Perform incremental loads whenever possible
Solom-CSF-7	7.- Choose properly the DBMS and BI platform
Solom-CSF-8	8.- Make a process for reconciling data
Solom-CSF-9	9.- Reschedule often
Solom-CSF-10	10.- Consider user support

Table 7. Moss (2005)

MOSS-CFF-1	1.- Lack of methodology.
MOSS-CFF-2	2.- Inadequate working equipment.
MOSS-CFF-3	3.- Insufficient involvement of business users
MOSS-CFF-4	4.- Inadequate stages.
MOSS-CFF-5	5.- Lack of project planning.
MOSS-CFF-6	6.- A failure of Quality Assurance and preproduction tests
MOSS-CFF-7	7.- Inadequate testing.
MOSS-CFF-8	8.- Consideration of the volume of erroneous debugging data.
MOSS-CFF-9	9.- Ignore the metadata.
MOSS-CFF-10	10.- Being a slave of project management tools.

Table 8. Briggs (2002, 2004)

Code	
Brigg-CSF-1	1.- Project Sponsorship
Brigg-CSF-2	2.- Manage user expectations
Brigg-CSF-3	3.- Use of prototypes
Brigg-CSF-4	4.- Find a quick win
Brigg-CSF-5	5.- Choose a measurable problem of the organization
Brigg-CSF-6	6.- Model and design of Data Warehouse
Brigg-CSF-7	7.- Select a suitable Business Case
Brigg-CSF-8	8.- Link to business strategy
Brigg-CSF-9	9.- Select tools carefully
Brigg-CSF-10	10.- Involve End User
Brigg-CSF-11	11.- Manage Organizational Change
Brigg-CSF-12	12.- Consider the organizational culture
Brigg-CSF-13	13.- Focus on Data Management
Brigg-CSF-14	14.- Consider Scalability and Flexibility
Brigg-CSF-15	15.- Transmission of knowledge in outsourced projects
Brigg-CSF-16	16.- Use standards to reduce complexity
Brigg-CSF-17	17.- Consider previous experience of team members
Brigg-CSF-18	18.- Consider End User Support

Table 9. Wixon and Watson (2001)

Code	
W & W-CSF-1	1.- Management Support
W & W-CSF-2	2.- Existence of a Project Leader
W & W-CSF-3	3.- Use Adequate resources
W & W-CSF-4	4.- User participation
W & W-CSF-5	5.- Team Skills
W & W-CSF-6	6.- Data Sources

A few years after, Watson & Wixon (2007) added three new CSF (Table 10).

Sammon and Finnegan (2000) propose 10 basic commandments (Table 11).

Weir et al. (2003) proposed a set of best BI practices (Table 12).

Abdullaev & Ko (2007) analyse lessons learned from several experiences on BI construction (Table 13).

Ko & Addullaev (2008) propose challenging points during the development of BI projects (Table 14).

Yeoh, Gao & Koronios (2007) build new recompilations of CSF (Table 15).

Table 10. Watson & Wixon (2007)

Code	
W & W-CSF-7	1.- Information and analytics as part of the organization's culture.
W & W-CSF-8	2.- Business and BI strategies alignement.
W & W-CSF-9	3.- Effective BI governance.

Table 11. Sammon and Finnegan (2000)

Code	
S & F-CSF-1	1.- Initiative linked to a business need
S & F-CSF-2	2.- Sponsorship Management
S & F-CSF-3	3.- Management of user expectations
S & F-CSF-4	4.- Cross-Functional Project
S & F-CSF-5	5.- Quality Data
S & F-CSF-6	6.- Model Flexibility
S & F-CSF-7	7.- Data management
S & F-CSF-8	8.- Automatic data extraction processes
S & F-CSF-9	9.- Knowledge
S & F-CSF-10	10.- Tools

Table 12. Weir et al. (2003)

Code	
WEIR-BP-1	1.- Make incremental charges
WEIR-BP-2	2.- System construction must be adaptable
WEIR-BP-3	3.- Manage user expectations
WEIR-BP-4	4.- Projects managed jointly by users and technicians
WEIR-BP-5	5.- Direct contact with the business
WEIR-BP-6	6.- Do not seek perfection

Table 13. Abdullaev & Ko (2007)

Code	
ABDU-LL-1	1 .- Centralization of data in a corporate data warehouse and its aggregation on several specialized data marts enable quick and reliable access to any requested information.
ABDU-LL-2	2.- The definition of reporting standards for corporate-wide use makes the exchange of information between departments much clear and consistent.
ABDU-LL-3	3.- Some predefined report models has to be implemented in order to provide decision makers the functionality to add or subtract necessary elements and build ad hoc reports
ABDU-LL-4	4.- There should be network of responsible people to align specifications of standard reports with local needs and to facilitate the implementation of BI project.
ABDU-LL-5	5.- There should be strong commitment from company's board of directors toward standing ready to resolve any conflicts and changes occurred during the project development.
ABDU-LL-6	6.- Integration of "Six Sigma" techniques into the IT infrastructure of the company will result in robust BI system.
ABDU-LL-7	7.- The IT infrastructure has to be raised on a single platform which is provided by well known companies.

Table 14. Ko & Addullaev (2008)

Code	
KO-CP-1	1.- Not internal requirements, but market and customer requirements.
KO-CP-2	2.- Dedicated business representation from each department.
KO-CP-3	3.- Availability of skilled team members.
KO-CP-4	4.- Unique BI development methodology.
KO-CP-5	5.- Thorough project planning..
KO-CP-6	6.- Data standardization
KO-CP-7	7.- Date quality control.
KO-CP-8	8.- Existence of metadata.
KO-CP-9	9.-Implementation of only required tools.

RELATIONSHIP BETWEEN AN AGILE APPROACH AND CRITICAL SUCCESS FACTORS IN BUSINESS INTELLIGENCE PROJECTS

The purpose of our analysis in to try to identify a clear relationship between BI Critical Success Factors and the Agile Principles identified in the Agile Manifesto. If this correlation exists, and depending on how strong it is, we may conclude that an Agile Methodology may be or not a good approach to manage and construct BI Projects in any organization.

To analyse the relationships between CSF and Agile Principles, first of all we have classified and grouped all CSF, best practices and recommendations enumerated en the previous section in three basic groups:

- *Primary factors* (PF): those proposed by more than five authors.
- *Secondary factors* (SF): those proposed by between two and five authors.
- *Author factors*: those who have only been identified by a single author. These factors are not considered in our analysis.

Since primary and secondary factors are proposed by different authors and with different names or semantics, in tables 16 and 17 we summarize

Table 15. Yeoh, Gao & Koronios (2007)

Code	
YGK-CSF-1	1.- Committed top management support
YGK-CSF-2	2.- Adequate resources are provided
YGK-CSF-3	3.- A high-level champion from business side.
YGK-CSF-4	4.- Formal user involvement throughout the lifecycle
YGK-CSF-5	5.- Formal education, training and support are in place
YGK-CSF-6	6.- Well-established business case
YGK-CSF-7	7.- Strategic BI vision that is integrated with company initiatives
YGK-CSF-8	8.- Project scope is clearly defined
YGK-CSF-9	9.- Adoption of incremental delivery approach
YGK-CSF-10	10.- Project scheduled to deliver quick-wins
YGK-CSF-11	11.- Team possess the right mix of skills
YGK-CSF-12	12.- Use of external consultant at early phase
YGK-CSF-13	13.- Committed business domain expertise
YGK-CSF-14	14.- The team is cross-functional
YGK-CSF-15	15.- Stable source systems are in place
YGK-CSF-16	16.- Establishment of a strategic, scalable and extensible technical framework
YGK-CSF-17	17.- Prototype is used as proof of concept
YGK-CSF-18	18.- High quality of data at source systems
YGK-CSF-19	19.- Information area readiness
YGK-CSF-20	20.- Business-led establishment of common measures and classifications
YGK-CSF-21	21.- Metadata model is sustainable for scalability
YGK-CSF-22	22.- Business-led data governance

these factors with a unique name and code. With this, we reduce the number of CSF to consider and we also facilitate the understanding of each one. First column indicates a code to each factor, second column refers to the specific code on our previous literature review, and the last column proposes a consensus name to refer to the CSF.

Codes follow this rule: PF for Primary Factor, SF for Secondary Factor. Additionally, each code contains a number indicating the number of appearances in the scientific literature review of the previous section, a dash and a sequential number. For example, code PF8-1 is the first primary factor with 8 occurrences.

In Figure 3, we show a graphical distributional primary and secondary CSF with respect the number of occurrences in the literature review of the previous section. Average of primary factors is 9.4 occurrences, while for secondary ones the average is 3.4. Range of values for primary factors is [15, 6] and for secondary ones is [5, 2]. Observe also in the right image of Figure 3 that primary factors correspond nearly to 66% of all identified CSF, while secondary factors represent 33%. Therefore, our analysis will be representative if we consider uniquely primary and secondary factors.

ANALYSIS OF THE RELATIONSHIPS

In Table 18, we show a table in which at each cell we indicate a plus symbol (+) if there is positive relationship between a CSF (row) and an agile

Table 16. Primary factors

Code	Authors	Factors
PF15-1	SOLOM-CSF-2;W&W-CSF-6;SOLOM-CSF-3;SOLOM-CSF-8;BRIGG-CSF-13;S&F-CSF-5;S&F-CSF-7;MOSS-CFF-9;S&F-CSF-8; KO-CP-6;KO-CP-7;KO-CP-8;YGK-CSF-18;YGK-CSF-20;YGK-CSF-21	Data management
PF11-1	SOLOM-CSF-9;MOSS-CFF-1;MOSS-CFF-4; Quinn-CFF2;MOSS-CFF-5;MOSS-CFF-10;KO-CP-4;KO-CP-5;YGK-CSF-8;YGK-CSF-9;YGK-CSF-17	Project management and methodology
PF10-1	Quinn-CSF1;F&M-CFF3; Quinn-CFF1; CHENOW-INT-3;CHENOW-INT-4;BRIGG-CSF-2; S&F-CSF-3;WEIR-BP-3;ABDU-LL-4;YGK-CSF-13	Understand and manage business users needs
PF9-1	BRIGG-CSF-1;W&W-CSF-1;S&F-CSF-2; Quinn-CSF5;CHENOW-INT-1;W&W-CSF-2;ABDU-LL-5;YGK-CSF-1;YGK-CSF-3	Management support
PF8-1	F&M-CFF2;BRIGG-CSF-4;BRIGG-CSF-5;BRIGG-CSF-7;S&F-CSF-1;WEIR-BP-5;BRIGG-CSF-8;YGK-CSF-10	Achieve early project success
PF7-1	Solom-CSF-5;Solom-CSF-7;Brigg-CSF-9;S&F-CSF-10;ADBU-LL-7;KO-CP-9;YGK-CSF-16	Careful choice of tools
PF6-1	F&M-CFF8;MOSS-CFF-3;BRIGG-CSF-10;W&W-CSF-4;WEIR-BP-4; YGK-CSF-4	Users are involved in the project

Table 17. Secondary factors

Code	Authors	Factors
SF5-1	W & W-CSF-3;MOSS-CFF-2;W&W-CSF-5;YGK-CSF-2;YGK-CSF-14	Appropriate work equipment
SF5-2	Quinn-CSF4; Quinn-CFF4; Brigg-CSF-12;W&W-CSF-7;YGK-CSF-20	The organizational culture
SF5-3	Brigg-CSF-6; S & F-6-CSF;Solom-CSF-4;ABDU-LL-1;KO-CP-2	Data warehouse design model
SF4-1	Brigg-CSF-17;S&F-CSF-9;KO-CP-3;YGK-CSF-11	Prior knowledge of team members
SF3-1	CHENOW-INT-2; Solom-CSF-10; Brigg-CSF-18	Users support the project
SF3-2	YGK-CSF-7;W&W-CSF-8;W&W-CSF-8	BI Strategy / BI Governance
SF2-1	F & M-CFF9; Brigg-CSF-11	Organizational change management
SF2-2	WEIR-BP-1; Solom-CSF-6	Incremental loads
SF2-3	ABDU-LL-2;ABDU-LL-3	Reporting definition

principle (column). If the relationship is negative, it is indicated with a minus symbol (-). If we do not identify a clear relationship between them, we leave the cell empty. The last column and the last row accumulate the total amount of positive and negative relationship for each agile principle and each critical success factor.

To determine the relationship nature (ie. sign) between CSF and agile principles we have used our experience on more than 50 deployments of BI projects in Spain during the last 10 years. Moreover, we also consider the agile principles definitions from the Agile Manifesto, the CSF descriptions provided by the literature, and experiences documented in the literature.

Table 18. Relationships between CSF and Agile Principles

	P1	P2	P3	P4	P5	P6	P7	P8	P9	P10	P11	P12	Sum.
PF15-1									+				1
PF11-1	+	+	+	+	+	+			+		+	+	9
PF10-1	+	+		+		+							4
PF9-1								+					1
PF8-1	+		+	+						+			4
PF7-1		-											-1
PF6-1	+	+		+	+	+		+					6
SF5-1					+				+				2
SF5-2		+		+				+			+		4
SF5-3		-							+		+		1
SF4-1				+									1
SF3-1	+	+		+	+								4
SF3-2									+		+	+	3
SF2-1		+	+										2
SF2-2													0
SF2-3		-		+									0
Sum.	5	3	3	8	4	3	0	3	5	1	4	2	41

Figure 3. Items by primary factors and secondary factors

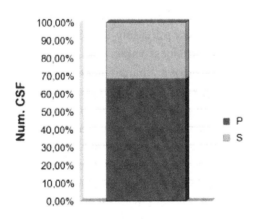

To show how relationships between CSF and agile principles has been identified, we will analyse in more detail the specific relationships between Primary Factors and Agile Principles that we have indicated in the seven first rows of table 18.

PF15-1 Data Management

I this case, only one clear positive relationship has been identified between the "Data Management" CSF and the agile principle of "Putting attention to excellence" (P9).

In fact, BI projects are fundamentally good data management tools that provide functionalities to perform data quality evaluation, data profiling and data transformation and distribution. Therefore, putting special attention to have a good design in data management, will help to achieve excellence in BI projects. A poor data design may move the project towards its failure.

PF11-1 Project Management and Methodology

As we mentioned at the beginning of the chapter, a BI methodology is expected to facilitate change management (C1), to be executed by a cross-functional or multidisciplinary team (C2), to help in the management of several projects (C3), to be task exhaustive (C4), to focus on critical path management (C5) and on people (C6), and finally to be aligned with business needs. Taking into account such characteristics, we identify several relationships with respect the following Agile Principles:

- P1 (Continuous delivery of value): Project management must guarantee to deliver value to the organization in a continuous and early way. Delivering this value through the used methodology allows doing a value-guided project management, and therefore, contributing to the alignment of project management to business objectives (C7).
- P2 (Welcome changes): In this case, if a BI methodology must manage change (C1) in a easy way, it contributes to see changes not a difficulty for the project, but an opportunity.
- P3 (Frequently deliveries): Making deliveries frequently contributes to foresee changes in business needs (C1, C7) and to improve the communication between cross-functional work teams (C2).
- P4, P5, P11 (Working together, Motivated people and Self-organizing teams): By promoting that business people and developers work together, the methodology will be people oriented (C6), when team configuration and worker needs are one important key issue of the methodology.
- P6 (Face to face conversation): Face to face conversations and frequent deliveries between team members promote to consider people as a key issue of the methodology (C6).
- P9 (Attention to excellence): Putting special attention to functional and technical excellence, good data design and detailed analysis of all processes of the organiza-

tion, will facilitate to manage the BI project more accurately (C4) and the business objectives.

- P12 (Reflects and adjusts): When teams make periodical review sessions to analyse how they are working and to adapt, the project will be more effective or efficient. Thus these teams are contributing to drive more easily the global project management to critical paths (C5).

PF 10-1 Understand and Manage the Business Users Needs

One of the most important aspects of the BI systems is to be designed to support the business user needs. Thus, in the development and implementation of the system, the development team must understand and manage properly the business needs and the decision maker requirements.

- P1 (Continuous delivery of value): BI system users are often managers and executives that make decisions to satisfy tactical or strategic goals of the organization. Therefore, the BI system must give support in this task providing the information with higher business value.
- P2 (Welcome changes): Decision-making is a non-structured process and a rapidly changing process. Therefore, the BI project must be managed so that it accepts and admits changes on the process while it supports or the information needs it satisfies.
- P4 and P6 (Working together and Face-to-face conversation): When business users and developers are organized in multidisciplinary teams where communication and collaboration is fluid, then it is easier for the BI project team to understand and manage more properly the business user needs, and in fact to be more aligned with the business objectives.

PF9-1 Management Support

- P8 (Sustainable development). Sponsors, developers, and business users must be really involved in the BI project and they should collaborate in a sustainable environment. Therefore, it is possible to improve management support when the system provides value to the organization.

PF8-1 Achieve Early Project Success

A possible way to have an early success of the project is to focus on the most urgent business needs. That is, to focus on those needs that must be satisfied as well and as soon as possible. Therefore, the organization regards the BI project as successful project.

- P1 and P3 (Continuous and frequently delivery of value). As the BI project delivers value to the business users in a continuous, frequent and early way, the organization may better manage its more critical and urgent business needs.
- P4 (Working together). The strategy to configure mixed teams (with technical and business professionals) clearly facilitates the concentration into the more immediate and early tasks to satisfy the most critical and urgent organization needs. However, this team configuration also contributes to have a more fluid relationship and a more effective working environment.
- P10 (Simplicity). Also positive, because the art of maximizing the amount of work not done, can change our behaviour to achieve rapid success.

PF7-1 Careful Choice of Tools

Organizations are a complex net of processes that must be managed properly to be competitive. However, BI must provide management support by providing strategic and tactical information to help decision maker to analyse and take the most appropriate decision in each situation. This support is provided by means of a set of BI tools.

- P2 (Welcome changes). Once an organization has selected the BI tools to support decision-making process, it is not easy to change them. Moreover, when a team is familiar with one tool, it is difficult to convince them to change it. It is also for this change aversion that BI tool must de selected carefully, taking into account the semi-structured and rapidly changing nature of the decision making process. Therefore, we consider that there is a negative relationship between the agile principle and the critical success factor.

PF6-1 Users are Involved in the Project

- P1 (Continuous delivery of value). To have the decision maker involved to the team facilitates to know his/her needs quickly and it is easier to satisfy them. Therefore, as soon the team has some user request, then it can decide to handle it immediately and deliver as soon as possible to the user. In this way, the project team may delivery continuously little doses of value to the user.
- P2, P4 (Welcome changes and Working together). To have decision makers involved in the project team working together with technicians facilitates to understand more quickly organization needs and to propose changes to have a greater competitive advantage. Therefore, the rest of people may be more easily convinced about the inherent business value and then they may accept these changes.
- P5, P6 (Motivated individuals and face-to-face conversations). To involve decision makers in the project team facilitates to

have all team members more motivated to develop the BI project. At the same time, this time configuration facilitates the face-to-face conversation and collaboration between the members of the team.

- P8 (Sustainable development). Sponsors, developers, and business users participating into the same BI project team facilitates to have a sustainable environment, and therefore, to have a more solid development team with users and developers involved.

MAIN CONCLUSIONS OF THE ANALYSIS

A quick look to the table 18 allows us to identify that all 12 agile principles have some kind of relationship with the BI critical success factors, except for principle P7 "Working Software". Moreover, only the SF2-2 factor ("Incremental Loads") is not related with any agile principle. Therefore, a quick analysis of table 18 allows us to state that 91.66% of the agile principles are linked to critical success factors of BI; and that 93,75% of critical success factors are related to some agile principles. Moreover, they are concerned to 100% of primary factors and 88.88% of secondary factors. So, the first conclusion that we obtain from this analysis is that *there is a clear relationship between agile principles and BI critical success factors.*

Given this clear relationship, and considering the last column and row of the table 18, notice that 100% of agile principles have a clear positive correlation with some BI critical success factor, and vice versa. There is only one exception for critical success factor PF7-1 ("Careful choice of tools"), but this negative correlation is with only principle P2 ("Welcome changes"). Thus, the second conclusion we may obtain from this analysis

is that the *relationship between agile principles and BI critical success factors is clearly positive.*

Table 18 allows us to be more precise in the characterization of the relationship between agile principles and critical success factors of BI projects. All negative correlations are with respect to the "welcome changes" (P2) agile principle. Moreover, most positive relationships are for principles P1, P4 and P9. Therefore, the third conclusion that we obtain from our analysis is that an *agile methodology applied to Business Intelligence projects should emphasize "Early and continuous delivery of value", "Business people and developers must work altogether" and "Put attention to good design and technical excellence". But at the same time, it must establish careful controls with respect to "changes".*

Taking into account negative relationships between agile principles and BI critical success factors, notice that all of them refer to only three critical success factors: "Careful choice of tools" (PF7-1), "Data Warehouse design model" (SF5-3) and "Reporting definition" (SF2-3). But only the first one has a global negative relationship with an agile principle. BI tools are not as flexible and adaptable as the non-structured and rapidly changing nature of the decision-making process. Thus the fourth conclusion of our analysis is that *business intelligence tools may not facilitate, to some extent, the application of a methodological approach based on continuous changes. Therefore, when BI tools are evaluated this risk must be taken into account.*

These four conclusions confirm our initial hypothesis and the main purpose of this chapter. There is a very strong and positive relationship between agile approaches and success factors in BI projects. So, we may state that *"Following an Agile Approach to manage a Business Intelligence Project may be a more safe way towards BI project success".*

CONCLUSION

With the rise of the Business Intelligence in the last years, all organizations make efforts to create or improve their decision-making processes and systems. A lot of new Business Intelligence projects appear constantly, but the experience is not so good. Organizations are doing something wrong because a lot of BI projects (85%) fail to achieve their goals.

A wide diversity and heterogeneity of methodological approaches to manage BI projects shows the state of novelty and inexperience that still exists in this area. To choose a BI methodology is not an easy task. Implementation and management of a business intelligence project may involve multiple phases and more than 900 tasks. Therefore, it is not so easy to identify a methodology that is so good in all aspects and dimensions.

Agile methodologies have experimented a great popularity recently and have been adopted in different areas. This kind of methodologies seems to have good results by focusing in quick development and high adaptation to the organization, helping in aligning IT and business. They focus on the creation of value to the business user, and they integrate information systems in the core of the business processes. Basic principles that guide this approach were defined in the Agile Manifesto.

In this chapter we have presented and analysed the Critical Success Factors of Business Intelligence projects. On the other side, we have collected all Agile Principles that guide Agile development methodologies. Finally we have analysed the relationships between these two sources, respectively BI success factors and agile principles, to try to evaluate how adequate may be to use an Agile Approach to manage Business Intelligence projects.

After our analysis, we have identified a clear positive relationship between Agile Principles and Critical Success Factors of Business Intelligence projects. Moreover, an Agile methodology applied to Business Intelligence projects should emphasize customer's satisfaction through early and continuous delivery of valuable software; should promote the participation of developers and business people in the same project team; should enhance agility with a continuous attention to technical excellence and good design. However, it is necessary to make careful control to manage changes during the entire project.

These results confirm our initial hypothesis that there is a strong relationship between agile approaches and success factors in business intelligence projects. So, we may state that *"Following an Agile Approach to manage a Business Intelligence Project may be a more safe way towards BI project success"*.

ACKNOWLEDGMENT

This work has been partly supported by the Spanish Ministerio de Ciencia y Tecnología under project TIN2008-00444/TIN. I would like to thank referees and to Núria Roca for their comments on previous versions of the chapter.

REFERENCES

Abdullaev, R. S., & Ko, I. S. (2007). A study on successful business intelligence systems in practice. *Journal of Cases on Information Technology*, *2*(2), 89–97.

Afolabi, B., & Thiery, O. (2006). *Using users' expectations to adapt business intelligence systems*. Retrieved July 2010 from http:// arxiv.org /ftp/ cs/ papers /0608/ 0608043.pdf

Agile Manifesto. (2001). Retrieved July 2010 from http:// www.agilemanifesto.org

Azvine, B., Cui, Z., & Nauck, D. D. (2005). Towards real-time business intelligence. *BT Technology Journal*, *23*(3), 214–225. doi:10.1007/ s10550-005-0043-0

Bäck, T. (2002). Adaptive business intelligence based on evolution strategies: Some application examples of self-adaptive software. *Inf. Sci.*, *148*(1-4), 113–121. doi:10.1016/S0020-0255(02)00283-9

Briggs, D. (2004). A critical review of literature on data warehouse systems success/failure *(Working Paper. No. 2004/01). Melbourne, Australia. Decision Support Systems Laboratory, Monash University.*

Briggs, D., & Arnott, D. (2002). Decision support systems failure: An evolutionary perspective *(Working Paper. No. 2002/01). Melbourne, Australia. Decision Support Systems Laboratory, Monash University.*

Brohman, M. K., Parent, M., Pearce, M., & Wade, N. (2000). The business intelligence value chain: Data-driven decision support in a data warehouse environment: An exploratory study. *HICSS 2000.*

Brousseau, K. R., Driver, M. J., Hourihan, G., & Larsson, R. (2006). El estilo de toma de decisiones de los directivos experimentados. *Harvard Deusto Business Review, May 2006.*

Chenoweth, T., Corral, K., & Demirkan, H. (2006). Seven key interventions for data warehouse success. *Communications of the ACM, 49*(1), 114–119. doi:10.1145/1107458.1107464

Chowdhary, P., Bhaskaran, K., Caswell, N. S., Chang, H., Chao, T., Chen, M., & Zeng, L. (2006). Model driven development for business performance management. *IBM Systems Journal, 45*(3), 587–605. doi:10.1147/sj.453.0587

Chowdhary, P., Mihaila, G. A., & Lei, H. (2006). Model driven data warehousing for business performance management. *ICEBE, 2006,* 483–487.

Counihan, A., Finnegan, P., & Sammon, D. (2002). Towards a framework for evaluating investments in data warehousing. *Information Systems Journal, 12*(4), 321–338. doi:10.1046/j.1365-2575.2002.00134.x

Dori, D., Feldman, R., & Sturm, A. (2005). An OPM-based method for transformation of operational system model to data warehouse model. *SwSTE, 2005,* 57–66.

Engström, H., Chakravarthy, S., & Lings, B. (2000). A user-centric view of data warehouse maintenance issues. *BNCOD, 2000,* 68–80.

Faulkner, A., & MacGillivray, A. (2001). A business lens on business intelligence – 12 tips for success. *ODTUG 2001.*

Fayyad, U. M. (2003). *Tutorial report. Summer school of DM.* Monash Uni Australia.

Fernández, J., Mayol, E., & Pastor, J. A. (2008). *Agile business intelligence governance: Su justificación y presentación.* Retrieved July 2010 from http:// www.uc3m.es/ portal/page/ portal/ congresos_jornadas/ congreso_itsmf/ Agile%20 Business%2 0Intelligence%2 0Governance.pdf

Gangadharan, G. R., & Swami, S. N. (2004). Business intelligence systems design and implementation strategies. *ITI 2004* (pp. 139-144).

Gibson, M., Arnott, D., & Jagielska, I. (2004). Evaluating the intangible benefits of business intelligence: Review & research agenda. *IFIP TC8/WG8.3 International Conference 2004* (pp. 295-305).

Glass, R. L. (2001). Agile versus traditional: Make love not war. *Cutter IT Journal, 14*(12), 12–18.

Guo, Y., Tang, S., Tong, Y., & Yang, D. (2006). Triple-driven data modelling methodology in data warehousing: A case study. *DOLAP, 2006,* 59–66.

Highsmith, J. (2001). The great methodologies debate: Part 1. *Cutter IT Journal, 14.*

Highsmith, J, (2002). The great methodologies debate: Part 2. *Cutter IT Journal, 15.*

Huynh, T. N., & Schiefer, J. (2001). Prototyping data warehouse systems. *DaWaK, 2001,* 195–207.

Jourdan, Z., Rainer, R. K., & Marshall, T. E. (2008). Business intelligence: An analysis of the literature. [ISM]. *IS Management*, *25*(2), 121–131.

Kaldeich, C., Oliveira, E., & Sá, J. (2004). Data warehouse methodology: A process driven approach. *CAiSE*, *2004*, 536–549.

March, S., & Hevner, A. R. (2005). Integrated decision support systems: A data warehousing perspective. *Decision Support Systems*, 2005.

Marjanovic, O. (2010). Business value creation through business processes management and operational business intelligence integration. *HICSS*, *2010*, 1–10.

Moss, L. T. (2001). Business intelligence methodologies, Agile with Rigor. *Cutter IT Journal*, *14*(12), 19–26.

Moss, L. T. (2005). Ten mistakes to avoid for data warehouse projects managers. *TDWI'S best of Business Intelligence, 3*, 16-22.

Moss, L. T., & Atre, S. (2003). *Business intelligence roadmap: The complete project lifecycle for decision support applications*. Boston, MA: Addison Wesley Longman.

Nemati, H. R., Steiger, D. M., Iyer, L. S., & Herschel, R. T. (2002). Knowledge warehouse: An architectural integration of knowledge management, decision support, artificial intelligence and data warehousing. *Decision Support Systems*, *33*(2), 143–161. doi:10.1016/S0167-9236(01)00141-5

Niu, L., & Zhang, G. (2008). A model of cognition-driven decision process for business intelligence. *Web Intelligence*, *2008*, 876–879.

Preston, R. (2007). Business intelligence still in its infancy. *Information Week*. Retrieved July 2010 from http:// www.informationweek.com/ story/ show Article.jhtml? articleID=1 96801521

Quinn, K. R. (2003). Establishing a culture of measurement, a practical guide to BI. *White Paper Information Builders, 2003*.

Rouibah, K., & Ould-ali, S. (2002). PUZZLE, a concept and prototype for linking business intelligence to business strategy. *JSIS*, *11*, 133–152.

Rowan, J. (2003). Design techniques for a business intelligence solution. *Auerbach Publications 2003*.

Sammon, D., & Finnegan, P. (2000). The ten commandments of data warehousing. *The Data Base for Advances in Information Systems*, *31*(4).

Schuff, D., Corral, K., & Turetken, O. (2005). Comparing the effect of alternative data warehouse schemas on end user comprehension level. *ICIS05* Retrieved July 2010, from http:// citeseerx.ist.psu.edu/ viewdoc /download;jsessionid= 0136B9AAC27DC2F065A3 910CDC2D1591 ?doi=10.1.1.84.1805 &rep=rep 1&type=pdf

Sekine, J., Suenaga, T., Yano, J., Nakagawa, K., & Yamamoto, S. (2009). A business process-IT alignment method for business intelligence. *BMMDS/EMMSAD 2009* (pp. 46-57).

Solomon, M. D. (2005). Ensuring a successful data warehouse initiative. *ISM Journal winter 2005* (pp. 26-36).

Stefanov, V., & List, B. (2005). Bridging the gap between data warehouses and business processes: A business intelligence perspective for event-driven process chains. *EDOC*, *2005*, 3–14.

Thomann, J., & Wells, D. L. (2000). Implementing data warehousing methodology- Guideline for success. Retrieved July 2010 from http:// www.decisionpath.com:8180/ docs_downloads/ DW%20 methodology% 20article%203.pdf

Weir, R., Peng, T., & Kerridge, J. M. (2003). Best practice for implementing a data warehouse: A review for strategic alignment. *DMDW 2003*.

Winter, R., & Strauch, B. (2003). A method for demand-driven information requirements analysis in data warehousing projects. *Proceedings of the 36th Hawaii International Conference on System Sciences (HICSS'03)*.

Wixom, B. H., & Watson, H. J. (2001). An empirical investigation of the factors affecting data warehouse success. *MIS Quarieriy, 25*(1), 17–41. doi:10.2307/3250957

Wixom, B. H., & Watson, H. J. (2007). The current state of business intelligence. [COMPUTER]. *IEEE Computer, 40*(9), 96–99.

Yang, W., Hou, P., Fan, Y., & Wu, Q. (2006). The research of an intelligent object-oriented prototype for data warehouse. *ICIC, 2006*(1), 1300–1305.

Yeoh, W., Gao, J., & Koronios, A. (2007). Towards a critical success factor framework for implementing business intelligence systems: A Delphi study in engineering asset management organizations. *CONFENIS, 2007*, 1353–1367.

KEY TERMS AND DEFINITIONS

Agile Methodologies: Software development methodologies based on iterative development, where requirements and solutions evolve through collaboration between self-organizing cross-functional teams and a business approach that aligns development with customer needs and company goals.

Analysis: (in this context): A category of applications and technologies for collecting, managing, processing and presenting data for business analysis and management purposes.

Business Intelligence: Business intelligence (BI) is a broad category of applications and technologies for gathering, storing, analyzing, and providing access to data to help enterprise users make better business decisions. BI applications include the activities of decision support systems like, query and reporting, online analytical processing (OLAP), statistical analysis, forecasting, data mining, etc.

CSF: Critical Success Factor (CSF) is any event that must occur for the project to meet its goals and objectives.

Data Warehouse: A collection of data, from a variety of sources, organized to provide useful guidance to an organization's decision makers.

Dashboard: Present a range of different indicators on the one page, like a dashboard in a car. However, this approach should allow users to customise their dashboard view, and set targets for various metrics. It's common to have traffic-lights defined for performance (red, orange, green) to draw management attention to particular areas.

Reporting: Information organized in a narrative, graphic, or tabular form, prepared on ad hoc, periodic, recurring, regular, or as required basis. Reports may refer to specific periods, events, occurrences, or subjects, and may be communicated or presented in written or on-line form using BI Platforms.

Chapter 8
Enhancing BI Systems Application through the Integration of IT Governance and Knowledge Capabilities of the Organization

Samir Hammami
The International University for Science and Technology, Syria

Firas M. Alkhaldi
King Saud University, Saudi Arabia

ABSTRACT

Over years, research in Management Information Systems (MIS) has resulted in significant implications for organizations in a wide variety of areas by using socio-technical perspective, which has helped to deliver more business focused solutions. This study reports the results of an empirical examination of the effect of IT governance framework based on COBIT and Organizational Knowledge Pillars in enhancing the IT Governance framework (Business / IT Strategic alignment, Business value delivery, risk management, Resource management, performance measurement) to enhance the business intelligence application and usability within the organization. Quantitative method is adopted for answering the research questions. A questionnaire was used for data collection after contacting several companies, in addition confirmatory factor model and structural equation model were developed and tested and the overall results of the empirical investigation supported the general framework. Using confirmatory factor analysis techniques, the effects of the combination between IT governance factors seen by ITGI and organizational knowledge pillars of the firm on BI Systems application in it were tested and confirmed and the models were also verified. Several statistical methods were used for data analysis; moreover different statistical tools as software packages were employed such as SPSS 17 and EQS 6.1. The study proposes that knowledge management (KM) and IT Governance framework are vital organi-

DOI: 10.4018/978-1-61350-050-7.ch008

zational abilities that support business intelligence application; it also observes that combination of IT governance framework with organizational knowledge within the firm can enhance the organization's BI system application and usability, and its goal is to advance the understanding of the relationships among these factors. The study develops and tested two main hypothesizes: (1) IT Governance framework supports business intelligence application. (2) Organizational knowledge, in turn, leads to support business intelligence application.

INTRODUCTION

Since the mid 1990s of the last decade, the economic theories focused on knowledge based economy as the major trend in which it became the vehicle of the world wide economy. Furthermore businesses in the new century are facing high levels of competition from not only from the local companies but also from foreign ones as a result of globalization, in addition to high increasing speed of technological developments in this digital economy. Here is it seems that there is a tremendous need by organizations around the world to take advantage of the information revolution particularly the field of information systems applications to maximize the benefit out of the invested recourses in information technology by them. Conventionally the development of any system is organized in to several stages that begin with the alignment with business goals until reaching the implementation phase passing through the planning and designing stages. Additionally it is crucial to assess whether the final results meet all different requirements needed in order to increase shouted performance. To do so business must implement business intelligence systems which are applications that meet the large heterogeneous requirements in order to help the decision maker to take his decision by offering the right information at the right time in the right place. Recent trends in this area show an interest in knowledge management (KM) as the possible solution provider to the issue rose previously. Many authors as presented in section 6 argued that KM can provide competitive advantages. Also

this study will demonstrate that there is a lack of theoretical studies on development of relationships among BI systems and KM capabilities, and. IT governance In addition to a systematic empirical investigation of these relationships.

BACKGROUND

The knowledge-based view (KBV) theory looks at the organization as a combination of several assets and resources and explains how organizations can get added value from these assets and resources (Grant & Chen, 2005). in addition Styhre (2004) claimed that the organization should be viewed as a site of continuous development and integration pool of all resources like physical, financial and human resources, because of that, two of the main intangible assets of the firm (IT capabilities and knowledge capabilities) are not reflected in the financial indicators although the impact of IT in globalization is evident. Furthermore the role of humans was always important, but it is clear that management experiences are nearly poor in developing countries so it's hard to attain a competitive advantage without the existing of mature management and the know-how experiences (Le Chien Thang et. el., 2007). Following this notion and based on Aristotle's dictum to enhance the utilization of the organization's capabilities, Avison & Fitzgerald (2006) incline that is better to build the widest possible information system for the whole organization rather than building it for particular isolation functions depending, so the integration here is a necessity as indicated by (Haag & Cummings, 2008), in addition Newell, el. al., (2003) confirmed that it is possible to apply business intelligence system in a form of information system and Knowledge Management (KM) systems on the organization which can be simultaneously have a good effect, although this outcome is not automatic, and should be fostered.

Information technology/systems need solid vision and robust planning since IT/IS is viewed as the means not as desired end, notably, it should be in line with culture, values and needs of the organization (Commonwealth Telecommunications Organization, 2002), Another important issue is Knowledge Management (KM) as one of the key progress factors in organizations, is that it involves explicit and persistent representation of knowledge of dispersed groups of people in the organization, so as to improve the activities of the organization because knowledge management is an vital issue in human resource management and enterprise organization, and also user engagement in the company project one of the most important benchmarks is the as seen by (Hwang & Thorn, 1999).

BUSINESS INTELLIGENCE AND HUMAN FACTOR

Business intelligence system is at the heart of the management information system of any organization that seeks well inform performance, and as indicated by Bounabat, (2005); and Wu & Wang, (2007) it is very essential to improve the overall company performance and it is designed to support organization-wide processes. This impose that organization should employ a central data repository to provide all users with a consolidated view to provide them with valuable information as to improve the executive decision making and to decrease time and cost and to increase the efficiency of the organization (Arinze and Anandarajan, 2003; Laudon & Laudon, 2010) so as stated by Plaza & Rohlf, (2008) it has become

a strategic instrument that allows organizations to rise above the restrictions of legacy systems.

Baltzan & Phillips (2008) and Haag & Cummings (2008) they define several characteristics of BI systems which are flexibility, reliability and performance in addition to alignment and the understanding of IT staff of business goals, where flexibility could be define as the ability to meet all types of business requirements changes, reliability is ensuring that all systems are functioning correctly and providing accurate information, and performance is to how quickly a system performs a certain process and transaction.

Organizations used to invest large resources in BI Systems, Sedera, et. al. (2004) justifies that as top managers would expect positive outcomes for the organization as a result. Soto-Acosta & O'Cerdan, (2009) argued that empirical finding show a positive relationship between business strategies and firm performance, so it is confirmed that is the non-planned existence of technologies is not positively associated with firm performance, in addition Brown (2006) claimed that strategic information systems planning is the most important key to achieve success for information systems managers which depends on a deep analysis of the organization environment. The closer link of the IS strategy and business strategy which helps smooth the progress of acquisition and deployment of information technology that is harmonizing with the organization's competitive requirements as seen by number of authors such as (Grovera & Segarsb, 2005; Baets, 1992; and Henderson & Venkatraman, 1999; Das, et. Al., 1991; Lederer & Sethi, 1988; Henderson, et. At., 1987; Bowman et. Al., 1983; King, 1988; and Chan, et. Al., 1997). According to Grovera & Segarsb, (2005) and Lederer & Sethi, (1988) business and IS planners should make an intensive effort to better analyze the internal operations of the organization in terms of its processes, procedures, and technologies.

The existence of IT experts, professionals and knowledgeable workers is the focal point of BI system success achieving the people oriented approach in business and it is a high valuable goal of the organization (Timbrell & Jewels, 2002; and Rao, 2000). The above statement is in line with the views of Luftman, et. al., (2004) where they argued that there are several skills required in a successful IT professionals like understanding the business vision and issues, team working, ability to self development in addition to their IT skills and ability to learn from the projects and knowledge around, the workers are one of the critical success factor of the organizational projects success. IT human resource contributes to system analysis and design in addition to human resources planning (Grant & Chen, 2005; Timbrell & Jewels, 2002; and Rao, 2000). In summary business intelligence systems is a combination of attributes that represent flexibility, reliability performance, system alignment, system analysis and people understanding of business goals.

ORGANIZATIONAL KNOWLEDGE

Knowledge is considered as a Key to sustainable competitive advantage, and it is considered as power which flows from the top down (Lewis, 2006). Organizational Knowledge is seen as an enterprise wide business practices that focus on knowledge processes (Alkhaldi 5Cs; constructing, capturing, codifying/decodifying, communicating and capitalizing), Building and maintaining knowledge infrastructure both soft and hard, aligning organizational Structure and polices with knowledge initiatives. It can be partly seen as a result of social and economic consequences of information technology development. The combination of Knowledge capabilities and information system strategy as in business intelligence system is vital and it has been considered by McGinnis & Zhenyu, (2007) as the business process to achieve the alignment between the business strategy and the information technology relatedness within the organization. It is very crucial to improve the suc-

cess rates of information systems wide angle of the organization, so the new goal should be making organization reach the level where the important work will be the knowledge work.

KNOWLEDGE MANAGEMENT

Knowledge management aims at enhancing the quality of business activities by managing and supporting various formal information existing inside and outside an enterprise so it could be considered as a business process not a technology so new knowledge was constructed as a result of business processes, and it is one of the most important corporate assets. Moreover Malhotra (2004) argued that there are knowledge gaps between technology inputs, knowledge processes, and business performance, also Nickols (2000) asserted that KM involve and about; what is done, how it is done, and how well it is done. Clearly, then, one critical link between KM and business results is through business processes. The impact of KM on key business results might be the greatest through its potential for improving the performance of business processes. Accordingly, it implies that the design or redesign of business processes should be an important feature in comprehending of where and how knowledge plays a role in the performance of the process. In turn, this can be carry out by recognizing the nature of knowledge needed to make the decisions or take a specific actions that make up the process, as well as addressing considerations related to the knowledge produced by those decisions and actions. Fleming (1996) asserts that if Knowledge cannot be communicated and shared with others, it is nearly useless. It becomes most useful and actionable when it's shared throughout an organization, Here these state and "type" of knowledge communication should be referenced to the management level that it is serving, for example; strategic level (the organization needs to be able to analyze and plan its business in terms of the knowledge it currently has and the knowledge it needs for future business processes), the tactical level (the organization is concerned with identifying and formalizing existing knowledge, acquiring new knowledge for future use, archiving it in organizational memories and creating systems that enable effective and efficient application of the knowledge within the organization). And the operational level (knowledge is used in everyday practice by professional personnel who needs access to the right knowledge, at the right time, in the right location).

According to Nickols (2000) for a business processes to make profits, add value, knowledge assets is needed, which is the knowledge concerning markets, products, technologies and organizations, that a business has or needs to have. Knowledge management is not only about managing these knowledge assets but also managing the processes that act upon the assets as well. These processes (Alkhaldi 5Cs) as previously mentioned include: constructing, capturing, codifying/decodifying, communicating and capitalizing. Therefore, Knowledge management involves the identification and analysis of available and required knowledge assets, knowledge asset related processes, the subsequent planning and control of actions, to develop both the assets and the processes so as to fulfill organizational objectives. McGinnis & Zhenyu (2007) claimed that there is a poor research about the issues concerned the post implementation of information systems, and this statement indicates that continuous improvement efforts should be done on the system to achieve the expected success of implemented system by the cycle of analysis, design, construction and deployment and this argument is in line with Nonaka's SECI model as seen in Nonaka & Konno (1998) that knowledge will enhance and the system implementation and add new insights to its success.

ORGANIZATIONAL KNOWLEDGE PILLARS

As indicated by a number of authors that intention to share knowledge is considered as one of the most important factors of KM capability (Bock, et. al., 2005; Jarvenpaa & Staples, 2000; Yang & Wan, 2004; and Hsu, 2006). In addition to developing knowledge strategies that aligned to business strategy and defining knowledge resources, many authors also believe that concentrating on the organizational values and continuous learning is as vital as intention to the organizational success, (Krogh, et.al., 2001; Janev & Vranes, 2005; Gottschalk, 2005; Chan & Rosemann, 2001; Yang J.-T., 2007). Tan (2002) proposed that the organizational and information infrastructures should be developed with an understanding culture to reach the success of business strategies. Breschi, et. al., (2003) proposed that the knowledge is the main factor which affects the infrastructure in the organizations in addition to culture as argued by (Tan, 2002), which could not happened randomly and it is a result of the organizational learning processes, that induce a sharing climate and fostering it to make sharing part of organization culture (Bock, et. al., 2005; Davy, 2006; Yang & Wan, 2004; and Hsu, 2006). In order to achieve basic objectives, of available resources like men, machines, methods, money and information systems, all should be brought together, here comes the importance of the organizational structure that facilitate the relationship between stakeholders, so organizational structures can facilitate KM processes through a specialized form of a structures and roles that specifically support KM processes when the organization depends on communications between employees, and knowledge sharing to create new knowledge. Thus, this dimension reflects the capability of structural knowledge managements of organizations (Becerra-Fernandez, et. al., 2004; Subramaniam & Youndt, 2005; Chuang, 2004; Yang & Wan, 2004; and Adenfelt & Lagerstrom, 2006).

Organizational culture is described by many authurs (Lucas, 2005; Huotari & Iivonen, 2004; Lewis, 2006; Davy, 2006; Escrig-Tena & Bou-Llusar, 2005; Nabuco, et.al., 2006; and Malhotra, 2005) as shared values, beliefs or perceptions held by employees within an organization or organizational unit and reflects the norms and beliefs that guide the behavior of the organization's members. Moreover, attributes of an enabling organizational culture include understanding of the value of KM practices, management support for KM at all levels, incentives that reward knowledge sharing, and encouragement of interaction for the creation and sharing of knowledge. In summary the organizational management pillars are Intention to share knowledge, knowledge management plan development, organizational structure, and organizational culture.

IT GOVERNANCE FRAMEWORK

IT field nowadays is more dynamic than before, managers and developers are continuously challenged to deliver more powerful, flexible and efficient systems and processes to keep pace with the evolving business requirements and regulations. Information technology is one of the most important resources in any organization (ITGI, 2008) and governance becomes at the heart of enterprises, so the role of IT in the overall governance of a business is increasingly becoming a key to competitive advantage (Hamaker, 2005; and Grembergen, 2004). Top management should realize the significant impact that IT have on the success of the enterprise management hopes for the way IT is operated and the probability of its being leveraged successfully (ITGI, 2007). IT resource is going further than the angle of a service resource and goes toward a source of the sustainable competitive advantage (Drnevich, et. al., 2006). IT Governance can be seen as an integral part to corporate governance, and it can be defined as an expression used to explain the

use of organizational processes to make decisions about how to get and deploy IT resources and competencies (Weill, 2004; and Meredith, 2008) and achieving Better Decisions through IT (Thompson & Stolovitsky, 2009) or it can be defined as stated by ISACA, (2002) "the Information Systems Audit and Control Association" a structure of relationships and processes to direct and control the enterprise in order to achieve the enterprise's goals by adding value while balancing risk versus return over IT and its processes.

PURPOSE AND PROCESS OF IT GOVERNANCE

The purpose of IT governance is to direct IT activities, to ensure that IT's performance is aligned with the enterprise and realize the promised benefits, and it is see as an enabler for the enterprise by taking advantage of opportunities and maximizing benefits. IT governance is also about making sure that the IT resources are used responsibly and IT-related risks are managed properly. IT governance involves participation of several individuals such as team leaders, managers, executives, board of directors and stakeholders.

Setting strategy, managing risks, allocating resources, delivering value and measuring performance, and the stakeholder values is seen as the activities that are at the heart of the governance responsibilities, which drive the enterprise and IT strategy. The overall goals of IT governance activities are to understand the issues and the strategic importance of IT, to ensure that the enterprise can sustain its operations and to ascertain that it can implement the strategies required to extend its activities into the future. IT governance practices aim at ensuring that expectations for IT are met, IT's performance is measured, its resources are managed and its risks are mitigated. The IT Governance Institute, (2003) indicated that IT governance process begins with setting the enterprise's IT goals, and then provide first direction, then a continuous circle is established so performance is measured and compared to objectives, resulting in redirection of activities where necessary and change of objectives where appropriate.

INFORMATION TECHNOLOGY GOVERNANCE FRAMEWORK (COBIT)

According to ITGI (2007) COBIT identifies 34 IT processes and control objectives that are generally used by IT organizations. For each of these 34 processes, a link is made to the business and IT goals that are supported (Luftman et. al., 2004; ITGI, 2007), in addition COBIT provides a complete set of requirements for each IT process to allow managers to improve business value or decrease risk, organizational structures, procedures, practices, and policies (Voon & Salido, 2009). COBIT can help an enterprise to appreciate and comprehend the status of its own IT systems and to decide what level of management and control the enterprise should provide, through the maturity models that enable benchmarking and identification of necessary capability improvements, performance goals and metrics for the IT processes, that measure how these processes meet business and IT goals based on balanced scorecard principles (ITGI, 2007). COBIT is an IT governance framework that allows managers to bridge the gap between control requirements, technical issues and business risks (Ahuja, 2009), and support IT governance by providing a common control framework that ensures the following (National Computing Centre, 2005).

IT Governance Pillars by COBIT

Control Objectives for Information and related Technology (COBIT) is an IT governance framework and supporting tool set that lets managers to bridge the gaps amongst control requirements, technical issues and business risks. COBIT enables clear policy development and good practice for IT control throughout enterprises. It emphasizes regulatory compliance, helps enterprises increase the value attained from IT, enables alignment and simplifies implementation of the COBIT framework's concepts. COBIT is intended for use by business and IT management as well as IT audit and assurance professionals; therefore, its usage enables the understanding of business goals and communication of good practices and recommendations to be made around a commonly understood and well-respected framework (ISACA, Information Systems Audit and Control Association, 2009).

IT/Business Strategic Alignment

Given the limited and few MIS researches that deals with strategic alignment link between IT and firm performance as indicated by Masa'deh, et. at., (2008), where they claimed that most research in strategic alignment model (SAM) is focusing on ensuring the linkage of business and IT plans; defining, maintaining and validating the IT value proposition; and aligning IT operations with enterprise operations.

IT strategy plans must be formed and shaped to aid the organization in the fulfillment of long and short term business objectives. Each IT plans should be linked to specific organizational goals, where goals may be seen as improved in customer contact management, expand e-commerce services, or improve operating speed with better software integration. The supporting IT plan could define implementation and support for a new business goal. Its role is that of requirements' facilitator and custodian. The true strategic value of IT will be determined in the minds of the business executives and should be a concern to them if its influence is to overriding other non-IT business objectives. The IT strategy will be composed of plans for data, software applications, technology, personnel, and facilities. IT/Business alignment is very vital for business continuity (Watson et.

al., 1997), and there is a need for more research that concentrates on the antecedent factors that lead to the alignment between IT investment that influence firm performance (Masa'deh, et. at., 2008). So to start with IT strategy and operations should be aligned and integrated with business goals and operations (IT Governance Institute, 2003), then strategy and goals should be translated into operational tasks (ITGI, 2003), in addition to that as stated by ITGI (2003) a clear commitment from the top management for major IT projects should exist, moreover, the execution of IT strategy should be done against IT standards and policies, finally the existence of clear trend to depend on IT capabilities to do the daily operations.

Business Value Delivery

ITGI (2003) Reported that Business Value Delivery is about executing the value proposition throughout the delivery cycle, ensuring that IT will deliver the promised benefits against the strategy, focusing on optimizing costs and proving the intrinsic value of IT. The crucial principles of IT value are the on time and within budget delivery of appropriate quality, which achieves the benefits that were promised. Because of the size of investment and the uncertainty of the outcome, top management and boards fear to start major IT investments. For effective IT value delivery to be achieved, both the actual costs and the return on investment need to be managed (ITGI, 2003). To achieve expectations of business and executive managers relative to IT responsibility of IT investments should be shared between the business and (ITGI, 2003). In addition IT budget and its investment plan should be realistic and integrated into the overall goals and financial plan of the organization and financial reporting has accurate accounting (ITGI, 2003). Moreover, service levels should be approved previously and they need to be controlled continuously, and a trend to identify and acquire new IT services should exist. Accordingly, the value of IT should

be assessed, clarified and demonstrated, and the existence of seeking for new ways to proactively increase IT value contribution is very important (ITGI, 2003). Finally, strong IT project management disciplines should be applied.

Resource Allocation

Allocation is about the optimal investment in, and the proper management of critical IT resources: applications, information, infrastructure and people. Key issues relate to the optimization of knowledge and infrastructure (IT Governance Institute, 2003). A key to successful IT performance is the optimal investment, use and allocation of IT resources (people, applications, technology, facilities, data) in servicing the needs of the enterprise. Most enterprises fail to maximize the efficiency of their IT assets and optimize the costs relating to these assets (IT Governance Institute, 2003). According to ITGI (2003) management boards need to address appropriate investments in infrastructure and capabilities by ensuring that:

- The responsibilities with respect to IT systems and services procurement are understood and applied
- Appropriate methods and adequate skills exist to manage and support IT projects and systems
- Improved workforce planning and investment exist to ensure recruitment and, more important, retention of skilled IT staff
- IT education, training and development needs are fully identified and addressed for all staff
- Appropriate facilities are provided and time is available for staff to develop the skills they need.

And also the Boards need to ensure that IT resources are used wisely by ensuring that:

Figure 1. Business intelligence pillars, IT governance pillars and organizational knowledge pillars

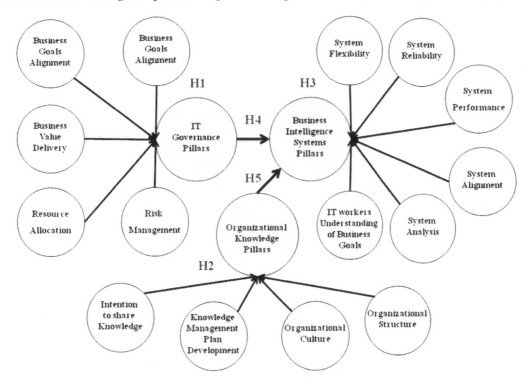

- Appropriate methods and adequate skills exist in the organization to manage IT projects.
- The benefits accruing from any service procurement are real and achievable.

Risk Management

Risk management as one of the key activities performed in the organizational which have been recognized as critical elements in influencing the productivity and innovation in companies (Drucker, 1999). Risk Management requires risk awareness by senior corporate officers, a clear understanding of the enterprise's appetite for risk, understanding of compliance requirements, transparency about the significant risks to the enterprise and embedding of risk management responsibilities into the organization.

Performance Measurement

In spite of the importance of performance measurement, there is no single universally accepted definition. Performance measurement can be describe as a process for the monitoring, assessing, and reporting of accomplishments to assist better management, but it can also include the broader notions of productivity, economy, efficiency, effectiveness, impact, quality, timeliness, and safety. Performance measurement can be directed toward either individual or collective performance or a combination of both (Bevir, 2007), in addition performance measurement with COBIT answer the following question: how well is the IT function supporting business requirements. Tracks and monitors strategy implementation, project completion, resource usage, process performance and service delivery, using, for example, balanced scorecards that translate strategy into action to achieve goals measurable beyond conventional accounting. According to ITGI (2007) Effective and timely measures aimed at addressing these top management concerns need to be promoted by the governance layer of an enterprise. Hence, boards and executive management need to extend governance, already exercised over the enterprise, to IT by way of an effective IT governance framework that addresses strategic alignment, performance measurement, risk management, value delivery and resource management. Simply put, IT governance and the effective application of an IT governance framework are the responsibilities of the board of directors and executive management. IT governance is an integral part of enterprise governance and consists of the leadership and organizational structures and processes that ensure that the organization's IT sustains and extends the organization's strategies and objectives. IT governance framework, such as Control Objectives for Information and related Technology (COBIT) can be a critical element in ensuring proper control and governance over information and the systems that create, store, manipulate and retrieve it.

The Model

Based on the above literature review the proposed model is shown in Figure 1. Hypotheses are shown in Table 1.

OPERATIONALIZATION OF VARIABLES

The purpose of this section is to describe the data collection method used, the various techniques used to test the research hypotheses as presented before, and it also It discusses reliability statistics of the sample, the descriptive statistics and the results of the confirmatory model analysis.

Sample

The sample used in this study consists of 179 respondents representing various organizations in both private and public sector in Syria. The sample was non random (purposeful), selected among many organizations which have fulfill two criteria, firstly it should have working information system; secondly it should have it own IT department. Given these condition a unique dataset were produced and were used to test the research model of this study.

The secondary Data were generated for this study from the empirical investigation through a survey method designed to test the validity of the model and research hypotheses. In addition the primary data were obtained from the literature written about the constructs of the proposed model, statistics and cases, and tracking and analyzing the existing organizations.

Measures

Dependent construct in this study are business intelligence systems, organizational knowledge and IT governance, and all of these constructs representing a latent factor, which has a number of attributes. On the other hand, IT governance, organizational knowledge are considered independent constructs.

Descriptive, relational, associational statistics were used to satisfy the research objectives and hypothesis testing, the analysis of the measurement models and results in this research went through two phases: the first phase was the descriptive analysis using SPSS 17 software, and the test conducted were factor analysis which were used to validate and measures the internal consistency of a constructs. Different methods used to measure the degree to which the distributions of the sample data to be in line with the normal distribution theory; such as Standard deviation, Skewness and Kurtosis. The second phase was examining the hypotheses by applying the partial least squares

Table 1. Study Hypothesis

Hypothesis 1: **There is a significant relationship between IT Governance and its components (Business Goals Alignment, Business Value Delivery, Resource Allocation, Risk Management and Performance Measurement).**	H1a: Strong Alignment between IT and Business Goals is positively associated with IT Governance application.
	H1b: Greater presence of Business Value Delivery through IT is positively associated with IT Governance application.
	H1c: Greater presence of good Resource Allocation of IT is positively associated with IT Governance application.
	H1d: Greater presence of good IT Risk Management is positively associated with IT Governance application.
	H1e: Greater presence of good IT Performance Measurement is positively associated with IT Governance application.
Hypothesis 2: **There is a significant relationship between Organizational knowledge and its components (Intention to share Knowledge, Knowledge Management Plan Development, Organizational Culture, Organizational Structure)**	H2a: Greater presence of Intention to share Knowledge is positively associated with knowledge management application rate.
	H2b: Greater presence of Management Plan Development is positively associated with knowledge management application rate.
	H2c: Focusing on Organizational Collaboration Culture is positively associated with knowledge application rate.
	H2d: Convenient organization's Structure is positively associated with knowledge application rate.
Hypothesis 3: **There is a significant relationship between Business Intelligence System and its components (System Flexibility, System Reliability, System Performance, System Alignment, System Analysis and IT workers Understanding of Business Goals)**	H3a: High Flexibility is positively associated with Business Intelligence System application.
	H3b: High Reliability is positively associated with Business Intelligence System application.
	H3c: High Performance is positively associated with Business Intelligence System application.
	H3d: Greater System Alignment with organizational goals is positively associated with Business Intelligence System application.
	H3e: Greater Understanding by IT workers of Business Goals is positively associated with Business Intelligence System application.
Hypothesis 4: There is a significant relationship between IT Governance and Business Intelligence System within the organization.	
Hypothesis 5: There is a significant relationship between Organizational Knowledge Management Business Intelligence Systems within the organization.	

method using (EQS 6.1) to analyze the collected data. In this method the interaction between each set of indicators and their underlying construct were found and analyzed. Accordingly the results all hypothesizes testing were accepted.

Measurement Model Validity

To validate measurement model in the proposed model, three types of validity were achieved: first; content validity, second; convergent validity, and finally discriminate validity. Content validity was used to insure the consistency between the mea-surement items and the relevant literature. This was done through pilot-testing the instrument. Secondly convergent validity was obtained by testing composite reliability and average variance extracted from the measures (Hair et.al., 1998). Finally the researcher confirmed the discriminate validity of instrument by checking the square root of the average variance extracted as recommended by (Fornell & Larcker, 1981).

Table 2. Multi-variant normality test

Descriptive Statistics							
	N	Mean	Std. Deviation	Skewness		Kurtosis	
	Statistic	Statistic	Statistic	Statistic	Std. Error	Statistic	Std. Error
Intention	179	3.28	1.044	-.432-	.182	-.544-	.361
Plan	179	3.00	1.049	-.089-	.182	-.559-	.361
Culture	179	3.13	.918	-.214-	.182	-.524-	.361
Structure	179	3.14	1.004	-.419-	.182	-.791-	.361
Flexibility	179	3.61	1.191	-.393-	.182	-.994-	.361
Reliability	179	3.87	.985	-1.010-	.182	.908	.361
Performance	179	3.53	1.029	-.646-	.182	-.187-	.361
Alignment	179	3.37	1.054	-.478-	.182	-.359-	.361
Analysis	179	3.23	1.032	-.224-	.182	-.539-	.361
Understanding	179	3.51	.926	-.427-	.182	-.049-	.361
ITBA	179	3.4637	.76037	-.431-	.182	-.090-	.361
ITVD	179	3.3575	.78653	-.260-	.182	-.334-	.361
ITResM	179	3.3948	.76963	-.399-	.182	-.164-	.361
ITRiskM	179	3.2402	.83540	-.400-	.182	-.346-	.361
ITPerM	179	3.4581	.74929	-.391-	.182	-.337-	.361
Valid N (listwise)	179						

Normality

The main purpose of Normality is to measure the degree to which the distributions of the sample data match up the normal distribution, which looks similar to a bell shape. Normal distribution is the most popular method used to explain symmetrical, bell-shaped curve, which has the greatest frequency of scores in the middle, with smaller frequencies towards the extreme. In addition Standard deviation can be used to measure the normality of the variable's data, when standard deviation is less than one it indicates normality. Moreover skewness and kurtosis values are very important indicators for normality. Skewness is a measure to indicate the symmetry. Kurtosis is a measure to test if the data are peaked or flat in accordance to a normal distribution. From the results illustrated in table 2, it can concluded that the sample meets the normality conditions

Structural Equation Modeling

Structural Equation Modeling (SEM) is the second generation of data analysis methods that is used for testing the statistical conclusion validity i.e. "testing the degree to which researches meet recognized standards for high quality statistical analysis" (Gefen et al., 2000). SEM is more preferable over the first generation statistical methods such as regression, another thing SEM facilitates analyzing the measurement errors of the observed variables as part of the model, and also combining the factor analysis with the hypotheses testing in the same analysis. The outcome is a more accurate analysis of the proposed research model and, most of the time, makes a better methodological assessment means. SEM methods offer better information about the degree to which the data support the research model than in regression methods (Gefen et al., 2000).

The Model Components

This proposed model comprises of three constructs as described below:

- IT Governance was modeled as a first order construct comprised of the five first-order dimensions: (1) IT/Business Alignment, (2) Business Value Delivery, (3), Risk Management (4), Resource Allocation and (5) Performance Measurement.
- Organizational Knowledge was modeled as a second order construct comprised of four first-order dimensions: (1) Intention to share Knowledge, (2) Plan (3) Culture and (4) Structure.
- Business Intelligence Systems was modeled as a third order construct comprised of the five first-order dimensions: (1) Flexibility, (2) Reliability, (3) Performance, (4) Alignment, (5) Analysis and (6) IT workers Understanding of Business Goals.

Fit Statistics

Goodness-of-fit measures the degree to which the actual or observed input matrix is predicted by the proposed model. Goodness-of-fit measures can be classified into three types as follows:

1. Absolute fit measures (AFM): assess the overall model fit; these measures include:
   - Chi-square (X^2) accompanied by the model's degree of freedom and its probability, Chi-square compares the proposed model to a saturated model; the model does fit the data when the probability (p) is greater than or equal 0.5 (Alkhaldi F. M., 2007)
   - Goodness-of-fit index (GFI): Compares the proposed model to no model, it ranges from 0 - 1.0, and

when its value is above 0.90 this means good fit.
   - The Root Mean Squared Error of Approximation (RMSEA) which estimates of discrepancy per degree of freedom in the model. The values are recommended to be less than 0.08 (Alkhaldi F. M., 2007).
2. Incremental fit measures (IFM): allow the comparison between the proposed model and the competing models and it used to assess the incremental fit of the model compared to the null model; The IFM measures include:
   - Tucker-Lewis Index (TLI).
   - Comparative Fit Index (CFI).
   - Incremental Fit Index (IFI).

The value of these three measurements should be greater than 0.9 to indicate good fit (Alkhaldi F. M., 2007).

3. Parsimonious Fit Measures (PFM): "adjust" the measures of fit to compare between models with different numbers of estimated coefficients so that the amount of fit achieved by each estimated coefficient can be determined".

These measures include the normed fit index X^2/df (the adjusted Chi-square by the degree of freedom), (Alkhaldi F. M., 2007) said that:

- If value is > 5 then Model does not fit data
- If value is between 2 – 5 then model may fit
- If value is < 2 fair fit of model to data

The proposed model was analyzed using SEM. The confirmatory modeling approach was carried out to examine the significant of the research model using EQS 6.1 Software. The results were as shown in Table 3.

Table 3. Shows benchmarks and values of the model fit indicators

ABSOLUTE FIT MEASUREMENT			
Index names	abbreviation	Accepted level	Model Calculated Values
CHI Square	X^2	-	83.156
Degree of freedom	df	-	65
X^2/df	X^2/df	≤ 2 (fair fit)	1.28
Probability	P	$P \geq 0.05$	.06404
Bentler-Bonett Normed Fit Index	NFI	≥ 0.9	.942
Bentler-Bonett Non-Normed Fit Index	NNFI	≥ 0.9	.978
Comparative Fit Index	CFI	≥ 0.9	.986
Bollen's Fit Index	IFI	0 to1	.987
Goodness of fit index	GFI	≥ 0.9	.945
Adjusted Goodness of fit index	AGFI	≥ 0.9	.898
Root Mean-Square Residual	RMR	Close to 0	.041
Standardized RMR	SRMR	≤ 0.05	.045
Root Mean-Square Error Of Approximation	RMSEA	≤ 0.1	.040

Table 3 also shows the values derived from the research model. As shown in table 7.2, Chi-square value is significant at 0.05 significance level, X2 (.05 = 83.156, P = 0.06), and all other fit measures point to that the revised model is accepted as GFI = .945, RMSEA = .040, IFI = .987, CFI = .986, and X2/df = 1.28. Therefore, the model was accepted and adopted for testing the hypothesis of this study.

Structural Model Testing

Several techniques were used to assess the hypotheses of the model. The first method is the overall coefficient of determination (R square value) which is a measure of the entire structural equation; second the standardized estimation coefficients (beta). This beta can closely approximate the magnitude of the effect, when the value of beta closes to zero, it means that the relationship is weak, but when the value of beta increased, this means the relationship is strong.

Table 4 shows the results of the evaluation test for the data used in building research model.

BI Systems Sub model Measurement Analysis

Measurement BI Systems sub model stands for the first question in the research which discusses the existence of a significant relation between BI systems and its pillars (Flexibility, Reliability, Performance, Alignment, Analysis and Experts). To test direct significant relationships between the six pillars and BI systems, Standardized Beta was used as indicator for this relationship. Referring to table 4, it is obvious that a positive significant relationship between BI and each pillar does exist. The value of t-test is examined in order to test hypotheses and analyzing the systems structural model. It is noticed from table 3 that t-values between BI and its pillars are significant at .05, so this indicate that all of them are part of BI systems.

KM Sub Model Measurement Analysis

Measurement KM sub model stand for the second question in the research which discusses the ex-

Table 4. Test statistics

Test statistics - Measurement Models					
Regression path		**Standardized Beta (β)**	**t - test**	**R²**	**Significance @ .05**
BI Systems Sub model					
Flexibility	BI	.426	9.161	.182	√
Reliability	BI	.659	8.214	.435	√
Performance	BI	.780	7.216	.609	√
Alignment	BI	.781	6.965	.610	√
Analysis	BI	.698	7.432	.488	√
Understanding	BI	.576	8.772	.331	√
KM Sub model					
Intention	KM	.618	8.159	.381	√
Plan	KM	.735	6.870	.541	√
Culture	KM	.631	8.038	.398	√
Structure	KM	.680	7.583	.462	√
IT Gov Sub model					
ITBA	ITGOV	.778	7.266	.605	√
ITVD	ITGOV	.770	7.566	.593	√
ITResM	ITGOV	.796	6.891	.633	√
ITRiskM	ITGOV	.749	7.878	.560	√
ITPerfM	ITGOV	.781	6.841	.609	√

istence of a significant relation between KM and its pillars (Intention, Plan, Culture, and Structure). To test direct significant relationships between the three pillars and KM, Standardized Beta was used as indicator for this relationship. Referring to table 5, it is obvious that a positive significant relationship between KM and each pillar does exist. The value of t-test is examined in order to test hypotheses and analyzing the structural model. It is noticed from table 5 that t-value between KM relatedness and are significant @ .05, so this indicate that all of them are part of KM.

ITGOV Sub Model Measurement Analysis

Measurement IT Gov sub model stand for the third question in the research which discusses the existence of a significant relation between IT Governance and its pillars (IT/Business Alignment, Business Value Delivery, Resource Management, Risk Management and Performance Measurement). To test direct significant relationships between the five pillars and ITGOV, Standardized Beta was used as indicator for this relationship. Referring to table 5, it is obvious that a positive significant relationship between ITGOV and each pillar does exist. The value of t-test is examined in order to test hypotheses and analyzing the structural model. It is noticed from table 5 that t-value between ITGOV and its pillars are significant at .05, so this indicate that all of them are part of ITGOV.

Analysis of Structural Model

Structural model consists of three segments.

Table 5. Structure statistics

Test statistics - Structure Model				
Hypo. No.	**Path**		**Standardized Beta (β)**	**Significance @ .05**
H4	ITGOV	BI	.760	√
H5	KM	BI	.070	√

BI = 0.76 * ITGOV + 0.07 * KM

First segment: which stand for the fourth question of the research which discusses the significant relation between BI systems and ITGOV. To test direct significant relationships between the two constructs, Standardized Beta was used as indicator for this relationship. Referring to table 5, it is obvious that a significant relationship between BI and ITGOV does exist.

Second segment: stand for the fifth question in the research which discusses the significant relation between KM and BI systems, standardized Beta was used as indicator for these relationships. Referring to table 5, it is obvious that a significant relationship between KM and BI systems.

The structural model fit was accepted, as Chi-square value is not significant at 0.05 significance level, (CHI-square = 83.156 based on 65 degrees of freedom, and the probability value for the chi-square statistic is 0.667

Each hypothesis was tested, analyzed and the overall results of the empirical investigation have supported the general framework that was presented in the research model.

CONCLUSION

The main purpose of this study is to explore the importance of enhancing the IT Governance in business environment. The outcomes of the statistical analyses are used in order to situate a practical suggestion that companies can carry out to enhance business intelligence systems implementation. Each hypothesis was tested, analyzed and the overall results of the empirical investiga-

tion have supported the general framework that was presented in the research model. Based on the findings of this research, number of recommendations and results are presented that aim at developing the awareness about the importance of business intelligence systems, IT governance and organizational knowledge.

The study aimed to suggest based on the various relationship findings illustrated in statistical results of the proposed model a means to enhance understanding of the concept of Business intelligence systems and its importance by enhancing the combination of IT governance in the firm and the knowledge capabilities (KM) and their role in business environment. Additionally this research describes the pillars of IT governance, particularly IT business Alignment, IT value delivery, IT resource management, IT risk management and IT performance management used by COBIT as a framework. This research clearly highlight the imperative needs to build the right culture that keeps looking at Information technology as a tool and not as a goal, also to adopt specialized frameworks to assess the contribution of information technology in the whole business. This study finding were based on coherent model that integrates a number of models into one model that describes the importance of KM pillars with business intelligence systems and its pillars and also why it should be one of the important issues in business environment culture.

This study provides comprehensive statistical discussion about the methods and techniques that can be used to have right and suitable implementation of business intelligence systems, and

Table 6. Results of hypothesis testing

Hypo. No.	Hypothesis	Result
H1	**ITGOV**	**Accepted**
H1a	IT/Business Alignment	Accepted
H1b	Business Value Delivery	Accepted
H1c	Risk Management	Accepted
H1d	Resource Allocation	Accepted
H1e	Performance Measurement	Accepted
H2	**KM**	**Accepted**
H2a	Intention	Accepted
H2b	Plan	Accepted
H2c	Culture	Accepted
H2d	Structure	Accepted
H3	**BI**	**Accepted**
H3a	System Flexibility	Accepted
H3b	System Reliability	Accepted
H3c	System Performance	Accepted
H3d	System Alignment	Accepted
H3d	System Analysis	Accepted
H3e	IT workers Understanding of Business Goals	Accepted
H4	**ITGOV - BI**	Accepted
H5	**KM - BI**	Accepted

increase the awareness of the importance of these systems. Finally, there was no previously detailed research available on the topic of IT Governance combination with knowledge capabilities of the organization to enhance the business intelligence systems. This research discusses all these factors in details.

In summary, this research investigates the relationship between business intelligence systems, Organizational Knowledge and IT Governance was explained. The results indicated that IT Governance and Organizational Knowledge can enhance the business intelligence systems of the organizations but with different ratios. IT governance can strongly enhance business intelligence systems but the organizational knowledge supports it weakly, the reason might simply refer to the fact that knowledge concept is still new studied

environment or not applied in the correct way in the sampled organizations. Model was introduced to help understanding the areas where the sampled organizations need to focus on and try to enhance the mechanism of their work in order to achieve the goals of this research and also urge these organizations to apply correctly the discipline of knowledge management.

RESEARCH LIMITATIONS

The research's limitations are summarized as follows:

- First, this study focused on medium and small firms which are working in Syria. Although the study's concepts are potentially applicable in large firms too, further research is needed to determine if the results hold in the context of smaller firms. Until such research is conducted, caution must be exercised in generalizing the results to large firms.

- Limited number of theoretical framing in term of previous studies that related KM, IT governance and their Role in enhancing BI.

FUTURE RESEARCH DIRECTIONS

This research was implemented to explain the importance of KM and IT governance in enhancing BI systems. Further studies should be directed to investigate the followings:

- Researches can be applied to different aspects related to IT governance frameworks.
- Researches for the KM pillars should be given more consideration
- It is recommended to carry out this study on more companies' especially international and multi-business companies.

REFERENCES

Adenfelt, M., & Lagerstrom, K. (2006). Enabling knowledge creation and sharing in transnational projects. *International Journal of Project Management, 24*, 191–198.

Ahuja, S. (2009). *Integration of COBIT: Balanced scorecard and SSE-CMM as a strategic Information Security Management (ISM) framework*. Purdue University.

Alkhaldi, F. M. (2007, August). Factor analysis exploratory and confirmatory type. *Al-Manhajyah* .

Arinze, B., & Anandarajan, M. (2003, February). A framework for using OO mapping methods to rapidly configure ERP Systems. *Communications of the ACM, 46*(2), 61–65.

Avison, D., & Fitzgerald, G. (2006). *Information Systems development*. New York, NY: McGraw-Hill.

Baets, W. (1992). Aligning Information Systems with business strategy. *The Journal of Strategic Information Systems, 1*(4), 205–213.

Baltzan, P., & Phillips, A. (2008). *Business driven Information Systems*. New York, NY: McGraw-Hill/Irwin.

Bevir, M. (Ed.). (2007). *Encyclopedia of Governancegovernance*. California, USA: SAGE Publications, Inc.

Bock, G.-W., Zmud, R. W., Kim, Y.-G., & Lee, J.-N. (2005). Behavioral intention formation in knowledge sharing: Examining the roles Of extrinsic motivators, social-psychological forces, and organizational climate. *Management Information Systems Quarterly, 29*(1), 87–111.

Bounabat, B. (2005). Rising to the digital challenge: Lessons from Mediterranean Enterprises. In Chapelet, B. (Ed.), *CentreTIME: Grenoble Ecole de Management* (pp. 167–228). Grenoble, France: CentreTIME, Grenoble Ecole de Management.

Bowman, B., Davis, G., & Wetherbe, J. (1983). Three stage model of MIS planning. *Information & Management, 6*(1), 11–25.

Breschi, S., Lissoni, F., & Malerba, F. (2003). Knowledge-relatedness in firm technological diversification. *Research Policy*, (32): 69–87.

Brown, I. T. (2006). Testing and extending theory in strategic Information Systems planning through literature analysis. In M. Khosrow-Pour, *Advanced Topics in Information Resources Management, 5*, 282-318. Hershey, PA, USA: Idea Group Publishing.

Chan, R., & Rosemann, M. (2001). Managing knowledge in enterprise systems. *Journal of Systems and Information Technology*, 5(2), 37–54.

Chan, Y. E., Huff, S. L., Barclay, D. W., & Copeland, D. G. (1997). Business strategic orientation, Information Systems strategic orientation, and strategic alignment. *Information Systems Research*, 8(2), 125–150.

Chuang, S. H. (2004). A resource-based perspective on knowledge management capability and competitive advantage: An empirical investigation. *Expert Systems with Applications*, 459–465.

Crawford, S. (2008). *EMA's 2008 Survey of IT governance: Risk and compliance management in the real world*. Enterprise Management Associates.

Das, S. R., Zahra, S. A., & Warkentin, M. E. (1991). Integrating the content and process of strategic MIS planning with competitive strategy. *Decision Sciences*, 22(5), 953–984.

Davy, C. (2006). Recipients: The key to information transfer. *Knowledge Management Research & Practice*, 4, 17–25.

Drnevich, P. L., Hahn, J., & Shanley, M. (2006). Toward a strategic perspective of Information Technology. In Walters, B., & Tang, Z. (Eds.), *IT-enabled strategic management: Increasing returns for the organization* (pp. 16–37). Hershey, PA, USA: Idea Group Publishing.

Escrig-Tena, A. B., & Bou-Llusar, J. C. (2005). A model for evaluating organizational competencies: An application in the context of a quality management initiative. *Decision Sciences*, 36(2), 221–257.

Fleming, N. (1996). *Coping with a Revolution: Will the Internet change learning? Gottschalk, P. (2005). Strategic knowledge management technology*. Hershey, PA, USA: Idea Group Publishing.

Grant, G., & Chen, Y. H. (2005). Measuring enterprise systems capabilities: A dynamic capability study. *The 9th Pacific Asia Conference on Information Systems, PACIS 2005* (pp. 1520-1526). Bangkok, Thailand: Electronic Commerce Research Center, National Sun Yat-sen University.

Grembergen, W. V. (2004). *Strategies for Information Technology governance*. Hershey, PA, USA: Idea Group Publishing.

Grovera, V., & Segarsb, A. H. (2005). An empirical evaluation of stages of strategic Information Systems planning: Patterns of process design and effectiveness. *Information & Management*, 42, 761–779.

Haag, S., & Cummings, M. (2008). *Information Systems essentials*. New York, NY: McGraw-Hill Irwin.

Hamaker, S. (2005). Enterprise governance and the role of IT. *Information Systems Control, 6*.

Henderson, J. C., Rockart, J. F., & Sifonis, J. G. (1987). Integrating management support systems into strategic Information Systems planning. *Management Information Systems*, 4(1), 5–24.

Henderson, J. C., & Venkatraman, N. (1999). Strategic alignment: Leveraging Information Technology for transforming organizations. *IBM Systems Journal*, 38(2-3), 472–484.

Hsu, I.-C. (2006). Enhancing employee tendencies to share knowledge—Case studies of nine companies in Taiwan. *International Journal of Information Management*, 26, 326–338.

Huotari, M.-L., & Iivonen, M. (2004). *Trust in knowledge management systems in organizations* (Khosrow-Pour, M., Ed.). Hershey, PA, USA: Idea Group Publishing.

Hwang, M. I., & Thorn, R. G. (1999). The effect of user engagement on system success: A meta-analytical integration of research findings. *Information & Management*, 35(4), 229–336.

ISACA, Information Systems Audit and Control Association. (2002). *Is Auditing Guideline IT Governance Document G18.* Information Systems audit and control association. USA: ISACA, www.isaca.org.

ISACA, Information Systems Audit and Control Association. (2009). *IT Standards, Guidelines, and Tools and Techniques for Audit and Assurance and Control Professionals.* USA: ISACA, www.isaca.org.

IT Governance Institute. (2003). *Board briefing on IT governance. Board briefing on IT governance* (2nd ed.). IL, USA: Rolling Meadows.

ITGI. (2003). *Board briefing on IT governance.* IL, USA: IT Governance Institute.

ITGI. (2007). *COBIT 4.1 Framework control objectives management guidelines maturity models. The IT governance institute.* IL, USA: The IT Governance Institute.

ITGI. (2007). *IT governance using COBIT® and Val IT: Student book* (2nd ed.). United States of America: IT Governance Institute.

ITGI. (2008). *IT GOVERNANCE ROUNDTABLE: IT GOVERNANCE FRAMEWORKS.* IT Governance Institute.

ITGI. (2009). *VAl IT 2.0 Based on COBIT.* USA: IT Governance Institute.

Janev, V., & Vranes, S. (2005). The role of knowledge management solutions in enterprise business processes. *Journal of Universal Computer Science, 11*(4), 526–545.

Jarvenpaa, S. L., & Staples, D. S. (2000). The use of collaborative electronic media for information sharing: An exploratory study of determinants. *The Journal of Strategic Information Systems, 9*, 129–154.

King, W. R. (1988). How effective is your information systems planning. *Long Range Planning, 21*(5), 103–112.

Krogh, G. V., Nonaka, I., & Aben, M. (2001). Making the most of your company's knowledge: A strategic framework. *Long Range Planning, 34*, 421–439.

Laudon, K. C., & Laudon, J. P. (2010). *Management Information Systems: Managing the digital firm* (10th ed.). Upper Saddle River, NJ: Prentice Hall.

Lederer, A. L., & Sethi, V. (1988). The implementation of strategic Information Systems planning methodologies. *Management Information Systems Quarterly, 12*(3), 444–461.

Lewis, R. D. (2006). *When cultures collide: Leading across cultures.* Boston, USA: Nicholas Brealey International.

Luftman, J. N., Bullen, C. V., Liao, D., Nash, E., & Neumann, C. (2004). *Managing the Information Technology resource.* New Jersey, USA: Pearson Printice Hall.

Malhotra, Y. (2004). Integrating knowledge management technologies in organizational business processes: Getting real time enterprises to deliver real business performance. *Journal of Knowledge Management, 9*(1), 7–28.

Masa'deh, R., Hunaiti, Z., & Yaseen, A. A. (2008). An integrative model linking IT-business strategic alignment and firm performance: The mediating role of pursuing innovation and knowledge management strategies. *Communications of the IBIMA, 2*, 180–187.

Masing, E. (2009). *Aligning IT with business goals.* Information management and SourceMedia, Inc.

McGinnis, T. C., & Zhenyu, H. b. (2007). Rethinking ERP success: A new perspective from knowledge management and continuous improvement. *Information & Management,* (44): 626–634.

McNurlin, & Sprague. (2006). *Information Systems management in practice 7E.* USA: Pearson Printice Hall.

Meredith, R. (2008). Information Technology governance and decision support systems. *Proceeding of the 2008 Conference on Collaborative Decision Making: Perspectives and Challenges* (pp. 175-186). Centre for Decision Support and Enterprise Systems Research, Monash University.

Nabuco, O., Koyama, M. F., Pereira, E. D., & Drira, K. (2006). Agent-based system for discovering and building collaborative communities . In Ghaoui, C. (Ed.), *Encyclopedia of human computer interaction* (pp. 12–17). Hershey, PA, USA: Idea Group Inc.

National Computing Centre. (2005). *IT governance developing a successful governance strategy: A best practice guide for decision makers in IT.* London, UK: National Computing Centre.

Newell, S., Huang, J., Galliers, R., & Pan, S. (2003). Implementing enterprise resource planning and knowledge management systems in tandem: Fostering efficiency and innovation complementarity. *Information and Organization,* (13): 25–52.

Nickols, F. (2000). *Knowledge management (KM) and process performance implications for actions.*

Nonaka, I., & Konno, N. (1998). The concept of 'Ba': *Building a foundation for knowledge creation, 40*(3), 40–54.

Plaza, M., & Rohlf, K. (2008). Learning and performance in ERP implementation projects: A learning-curve model for analyzing and managing consulting costs. *International Journal of Production Economics, 115,* 72–85.

Rao, S. S. (2000). Enterprise resource planning: Business needs and technologies. *Industrial Management & Data Systems, 100*(2), 81–88.

Sedera, D., Gable, G., & Chan, T. (2004). Knowledge management as an antecedent of enterprise system success. *Americas Conference on Information Systems, AMCIS,* New York, NY.

Soto-Acosta, P., & O'Cerdan, A. L. (2009). Evaluating Internet technologies business effectiveness. *Telematics and Informatics, 26,* 211–221.

Styhre, A. (2004). Rethinking knowledge: A Bergsonian critique of the notion of tacit knowledge. *British Journal of Management, 15,* 177–188.

Subramaniam, M., & Youndt, M. A. (2005). The influence Of intellectual capital on the types of innovative capabilities. *Academy of Management Journal, 48*(3), 450–463.

Tan, F. B. (2002). The integral role of Information Technology in achieving business strategy success . In Tan, F. B. (Ed.), *Advanced topics in global information management* (pp. 42–62). London, UK: Idea Group Publishing.

Thompson, W., & Stolovitsky, N. (2009). *Seeing the big picture: A corporate guide to better decisions through IT.* Technology Evaluation Centers.

Timbrell, G. T., & Jewels, T. J. (2002). Knowledge re-use situations in an enterprise systems context. *Issues and trends of Information Technology management in contemporary organisations* (pp. 296-299). Seattle, Washington, USA.

Voon, P., & Salido, J. (2009). *MOF to COBIT/Val IT comparison and cross-implementation guide.* Microsoft.

Watson, R. T., Kelly, G. G., Gilliers, R. D., & Brancheau, J. C. (1997). Key issues in Information Systems management: An international perspective. *Journal of Management Information Systems, 13*(4), 91–115.

Weill, P. (2003, October). How top performers govern IT. *CISR research briefing, 3*(3A).

Weill, P. (2004). Don't just lead, govern: How top-performing firms govern IT. *MIS Quarterly Executive*, *3*(1), 1–17.

Wu, J.-H., & Wang, Y.-M. (2007). Measuring ERP success: The key-users viewpoint of the ERP to produce a viable IS in the organization. *Computers in Human Behavior*, *23*, 1582–1596.

Yang, J.-T. (2007). Knowledge sharing: Investigating appropriate leadership roles and collaborative culture. *Tourism Management*, *28*, 530–543.

Yang, J.-T., & Wan, C.-S. (2004). Advancing organizational effectiveness and knowledge management implementation. *Tourism Management*, *25*, 593–601.

KEY TERMS AND DEFINITIONS

Business Intelligence (BI): A wide term referring to applications used to take advantages from the discovery and analysis of the organizational data to enable the managers at all levels to make better and efficient decisions depending on better supplied information.

COBIT: (The Control Objectives for Information and related Technology): An IT Governance framework created by ISACA (the Information Systems Audit and Control Association) and ITGI (IT Governance Institute) in 1996, and has several versions.

Intention: What the individual do upon the effect of his culture and environment with a specific purpose to do so.

IT Governance: A part of the overall organizational governances, and it's primary goal is to focus on the information technology systems, and make sure that any IT investment in the organization is aligned with the business goals and strategies.

Knowledge Management: The processes applied to govern, manage and take advantages from knowledge as an organizational asset.

Organizational Culture: The values, norms and assumptions of organizational members that reflect in their behaviors.

Organizational Knowledge: The combined knowledge built and created by individuals through memories and practiced projects in the organizational context to achieve its goals.

Chapter 9
ASD-BI:
A Knowledge Discovery Process Modeling Based on Adaptive Software Development Agile Methodology

Mouhib Alnoukari
Arab International University, Syria

ABSTRACT

Business Intelligence applications are of vital importance for many organizations. These applications still face failures in determining the process model adopted. In this chapter, we are proposing a new knowledge discovery process model named "ASD-BI" that is based on adaptive software development (ASD) agile methodology. ASD-BI process model was proposed to enhance the way of building business intelligence and data mining applications.

The main contribution of this chapter is the demonstration that ASD-BI is adaptive to environment changes, enhances knowledge capturing and sharing, and helps in implementing and achieving organization's strategy. ASD-BI process model will be validated by using a case study on higher education.

INTRODUCTION

Software is considered as an important industry since more than 40 years. Software is intangible and more easily adapted than a physical product.

DOI: 10.4018/978-1-61350-050-7.ch009

Software development process was one of the most important research targets as it mainly affects software project success or failure.

The main three core areas affecting any software project are: quality, cost, and time. The challenge is to produce high quality software in time constrained market with the minimum cost.

Traditional software development processes are characterized by rigid control mechanisms with heavy documentation which make it difficult to validate a successful combination between quality, cost, and time.

Agile methods may make it less costly to customize and adapt development processes. Agile processes focus on code rather than documentation (Keith, 2006). According to the "Manifesto for Agile Software Development" (ALLIANCE, 2001), agile process philosophy is based on the following four values:

- Individuals and interactions over processes and tools
- Working software over comprehensive documentation
- Customer collaboration over contract negotiation
- Responding to change over following a plan

Agile modeling has many process centric software management methods, such as: Adaptive Software Development (ASD), Extreme Programming (XP), Rational Unified Process (RUP), Lean Development, SCRUM, and Crystal Light methods.

Agile methods share the same properties by focusing on people, results, minimal methods, and maximum collaboration. Agile approaches are best fit when requirements are uncertain or volatile; this can happen due to business dynamism, and rapid evolving markets. It's difficult to practice traditional methodologies in such unstable evolving markets, thus agile methodologies were developed as a solution to software development processes in an uncertain environments (high speed, high change) (Highsmith, 2000; Keith, 2006; Abdullah, Holcombe, & Gheorge, 2006).

ASD agile method (developed by Jim Highsmith) is one of adaptive approaches (Pressman, 2001). ASD is based on the idea of developing adaptive systems (i.e. Chaos theory) from which

agile and adaptive processes were arise (Highsmith, 2000; Keith, 2006). ASD considers outcomes are unpredictable, and planning is paradox. ASD is not a methodology for doing software project, but rather it is an approach that could be adopted by organizations in an unpredictable environment (Keith, 2006).

ASD replaces the static Plan-Build-Revise lifecycle, with the dynamic Speculate-Collaborate-Learn life cycle (Figure 1).

"Speculate" replaces "Plan" as planning is too deterministic in an unpredictable world.

"Collaboration" replaces "Build" as ASD's processes recognize the role of people in producing successful products. Collaboration can make people more creative, and help producing creativity answers in an unpredictable environment.

"Learning" replaces "Revise" as ASD recognizes that knowledge can be gained through experience.

RELATED WORKS

To our knowledge, there is no other work that applies agile methodologies on knowledge discovery process modeling. Therefore, we describe in this section works with different approaches but related to our work in some manner.

Knowledge Discovery Process (KDP) modeling are mainly categorized into the following main four categories: traditional KDP, Ontology-based, web-based, and agile-based approaches.

TRADITIONAL KDP APPROACH

This is the most used approach for knowledge discovery modeling. Starting with (Fayyad, Piatetsky-Shapiro, & Smyth, 1996) model, most of the KDP modeling follows its same steps. This model was one of the first attempts towards formalizing the KDP modeling within a common framework (Cios, Pedrycz, Swiniarski, & Kurgan,

Figure 1. Adaptive software development (ASD) phases, adapted from Pressman (2001)

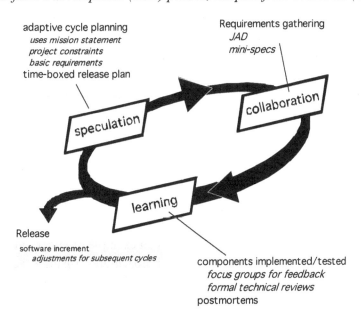

2007). Fayyad's et al. KDP model consists of the following five processes: data selection, data preprocessing, data transformation, data mining, and interpretation/evaluation. Although this model is the cornerstone of the other traditional process models, and provides detailed data preparation activities, it lacks business perspectives (Cios, Pedrycz, Swiniarski, & Kurgan, 2007), and uses data only as the main data sources without any explicit use of data warehouses/data marts. It also lacks of explicit "Deployment" stage, the knowledge discovered in not stored anywhere for future use, and it ignores the human resources involvement.

Many other KDP models were created based on Fayyad's et al. model. (Feldens, Moraes, Pavan, & Castilho, 1998) model is a simplified version of KDP modeling based on the following three stages: pre-processing, data mining, and post processing. (Collier, Carey, Grusy, Marjaniemi, & Sautter, 1998) model adds an inspection stage after evaluation, and allowed having inner loop between all processes without going through the entire life cycle. The previous two models use

data warehouse as the main data source for their processes life cycle.

(Ganesh, Han, Kumar, & Shekhar, 1996) model consists of six processes in an unordered data flow. It was one of the first models that noticed the importance of adding expert peoples into the KDP modeling by adding a data miner/analyst to their model. (Kopanakis & Theodoulidis, 1999) extends this model by grouping its processes into three main stages: data preparation, model derivation, and validation stages.

(Lee & Kerschberg, 1998) six processes' model added the knowledge dimension by storing the discovered knowledge into a separate knowledge repository. A panel of experts is used to validate the discovered knowledge in order to obtain a valuable knowledge.

(CRISP-DM, 2000) model is the most adopted KDP model in many data mining projects, and one of the first models towards KDP standardization. It is supported by a large consortium of European companies including: Integral Solutions Ltd. (a provider of commercial data mining solutions purchased by SPSS Inc. in 1998), NCR (Teradata data warehouse provider), DaimlerChrysler (an automobile manufacturer), and OHRA (Dutch insurance company). Business understanding and data understanding are the two important added steps. However, this model still lacks the explicit use of data warehouse/data marts; the deployment stage is a dead point which makes it difficult to adapt with environment changes; knowledge discovered in not stored anywhere; and it ignores the involvement of human resources.

(Hofmann, The Development of a Generic Data Mining Life Cycle (DMLC), 2003) completes CRISP-DM model by adding the objectives/hypotheses setting step, and defined clearly the data sources and peoples involvement in his KDP model.

Many other KDP models are based on the traditional approach including: (Adriaans & Zantinge, 1996), (Berry & Gordon, 1997), (SAS, 1997), (Edelstein, 1998), (Reinartz, 1999), (Kopanakis & Theodoulidis, 1999), (Han & Cercone, RuleViz: A Model for Visualizing Knowledge Discovery Process, 2000), (Han & Kamber, 2001), (Klosgen & Zytkow, 2002), (Haglin, Roiger, Hakkila, & Giblin, 2005), (Li & Ruan, 2007), and (Rennolls & AL-Shawabkeh, 2008) model.

Ontology-Based KDP Approach

This approach is based on the integration of the traditional KDP approach and Ontology engineering. The following three dimensions are indentified in this approach: Ontology for KDP, KDP for Ontology, and the integration of both previous directions. (Gottgtroy, Kasabov, & Macdonell, 2003) process model is an example of the Ontology-based KDP approach.

Web-Based KDP Approach

This approach is similar to the traditional KDP approach, but it has some unique steps to deal with web log data. (Anand & Buchner, 1998), (Buchner, Mulvenna, Anand, & Hughes, 1999),

and (Pabarskaite & Raudys, 2007) process models are examples of web-based KDP approach.

Agile-Based KDP Approach

This approach is the integration between the traditional KDP approach and agile methodologies. The main goal of this approach's processes is to make the knowledge discovery process more adaptive and agile. (Alnoukari, Alzoabi, & Hanna, Applying Adaptive Software Development (ASD) Agile Modeling on Predictive Data Mining Applications: ASD-DM Methodology, 2008) is an example of integrating the traditional KDP approach and Adaptive Software Development (ASD) agile methodology.

WHY ASD AGILE METHODOLOGY CAN FIT WELL WITH BUSINESS INTELLIGENCE APPLICATIONS?

In this section, we will analyze the main characteristics of agile methodologies. The goal is to compare these methodologies in order to choose one of them to be used in business intelligence and data mining applications.

Table 1 is based on (Stojanovic, Dahanayake, & Sol, 2003) work, and it compares between agile methodologies based on set of criteria including: Key characteristics, special features, and fitness for BI applications.

ASD methodology can be fit well for Business Intelligence applications as "Speculation" phase recognizes the uncertain nature of complex problems such as predictive data mining, and encourages exploration and experimentation. Further more Business Intelligence requires huge volume of information to be collected, analyzed, and applied; it also requires advanced knowledge, and greater business skills than typical problems, which need "Collaboration" among different stakeholders, in order to improve their decision making ability (Alnoukari, Alzoabi, & Hanna,

Table 1. Agile methodologies comparisons and BI fitness

	Key characteristics	Special features	BI fitness
ASD	Adaptive, collaborative teamwork, learning, mission-driven.	Non-linear overlapping lifecycle phases, component based	Suggested
XP	Customer-driven, frequent release, pair programming, testing focus.	User stories, refactoring, test-first development, project velocity	Not suggested: need extra resources (pair programming), preferred for small projects only.
SCRUM	Small teams, iterations (sprints) 7-30 days cycle,	Daily short meeting (15 minutes), demos after each increment.	Not suggested: applicable for small and medium projects only.
DSDM	Similar to XP and/or ASD, fitness for business purpose.	Use of prototyping, several small teams (2-6 people)	Not suggested: needs several small teams, applicable for small projects only.
FDD	Five basic process steps, short iterations, feature-centered	Combining features and object modeling, scalable	Not suggested: needs management practice support
Crystal family	Family of methods, adaptable to different project size and complexity	Features and values common to the whole family, small teams, 1-3 months cycle, face-to-face communication	Not suggested: not completed yet.
Agile Modeling	Applying agile principles and practices to modeling	Can fit well into different processes (XP or RUP)	Not suggested: not completed yet.
Extreme Modeling	Integrating model-based and XP principles	Tool support needed, models testable and executable	Not suggested: not completed yet.

2008). Finally, decision making ability depends on "Learning" component in order to test knowledge raised by practices iteratively after each cycle, rather than waiting till the end of the project. Learning organizations can adapt it more easily with ASD life cycle (Highsmith, 2000).

ASD-BI Knowledge Discovery Process Model

ASD-BI is a new proposed knowledge discovery model. This model is built in a way to consider the strengths of the previous models, and avoid their weaknesses. A summary of strengths and weaknesses of the main knowledge discovery process models was presented in a survey conducted by the authors (Alnoukai, El Sheikh, & Alzoabi, 2009).

In the following sections, the chapter describes ASD-BI process model in details, starting with the model's data sources and data destination (the authors used this term to distinguish it from the data source term as data destination is mainly the explicit knowledge that would be organized and stored in the knowledge repository), followed by detailed description for the model's processes and phases, and the human resources involved in this model. The authors then present the role of ASD-BI model in enhancing knowledge capturing and sharing, and how it helps organizations in implementing and achieving their strategies. Adaptive dimension was already discussed in the previous section.

ASD-BI Data Sources and Data Destination

Data sources are crucial for any BI application. Data sources have to be clearly identified in the knowledge discovery process model used for BI project implementation.

Few KD process models raised the importance of specifying their data sources. Most of these KD process models used the term "data" in their process life cycle (Fayyad, Piatetsky-Shapiro, & Smyth, 1996; CRISP-DM, 2000; Gottgtroy, Kasabov, & Macdonell, 2003). Others didn't even mention any information about the data source used in their process models (Collier, Carey, Grusy, Marjaniemi, & Sautter, 1998).

The use of data warehouse/data marts is of vital importance and inevitable for building BI applications (Inmon, 2005; Turban, Aronson, Liang, & Sharda, 2007). Very few of KD process models included them in their process life cycles (Ganesh, Han, Kumar, & Shekhar, 1996; Feldens, Moraes, Pavan, & Castilho, 1998; Ganesh, Han, Kumar, & Shekhar, 1996; Alnoukari & Alhussan, 2008). Turban separates between the data warehouse which is "a physical repository where relational data are specially organized to provide enterprise-wide, cleansed data in a standardized format" and the data mart which is "a departmental data warehouse that stores only relevant data" (Turban, Aronson, Liang, & Sharda, 2007).

ASD-BI data model is using data warehouse/data marts as the core data source for any BI application. The data stored in the data warehouse/data marts are provided from the different operational and legacy systems and data (including external data) the BI project is using as the source systems data. ETL tools are used to extract, transform, and load data from the source systems data into the data warehouse/data marts (Turban, Aronson, Liang, & Sharda, 2007).

Metadata is very important in any BI project as it describes tables and their relation to each other. Metadata explains "how, why, and where the data can be found, retrieved, stored and used in an information management systems" (Pant, 2009). According to (Inmon, 2005), without metadata the workload of the data mining project would increase considerably. Metadata is an important way to understand data, as it provides a way to store semantics about the entire individual attributes as well as their values and restrictions. This means that metadata is the cornerstone for any BI project (Hofmann, 2003). Metadata repository is "where all the metadata information about source, target, transformations, mappings, workflows, sessions and business terms is stored" (Pant, 2009).

ASD-BI metadata repository is a separate data storage that is used to describe the data stored in the data warehouse/data marts. It has all the necessary information to respond to the user queries. It contains also the final representation of the data browsers the users are able to ask about.

Knowledge repositories (KR) are used to store explicit knowledge of organizational knowledge. Different services can be associated to KR including (Housel & Bell, 2001): generation of new knowledge in forms that can be stored in the repository, capturing new knowledge, organizing items in the repository, managing access to the KR, and retrieving knowledge from the repository.

Knowledge repository is mainly based on the concept of metadata. Metadata is used for the selection and application of the data mining method, as well as interpretation of the method results (Hofmann & Tierney, 2007).

ASD-BI knowledge repository is used to store and maintain the knowledge discovered for future use. It depends mainly on the metadata repository for the selection of the data mining method or modeling, and the interpretation of the knowledge discovered. ASD-BI knowledge repository is used as a data source to use the knowledge stored for business understanding and objectives/hypotheses settings. It is also used as a data destination to store the explicit knowledge discovered during the knowledge discovery process.

ASD-BI knowledge repository simply holds business rules and previously achieved data mining results, whereas ASD-BI metadata repository focuses on the semantics of data.

ASD-BI Processes and Processes Categorization

ASD-BI process model uses the same list of CRISP-DM processes in addition to the important Objectives/Hypotheses settings process. The list of ASD-BI processes includes: business understanding, data understanding, objectives/hypotheses setting, data preparation/ETL, modeling/data

Figure 2. ASD-BI Process Model, a detailed overview

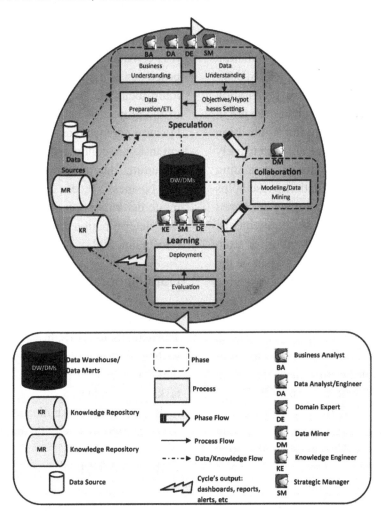

mining, evaluation, and deployment. A survey conducted by the authors on knowledge discovery process models concludes that the previous processes have been identified as critical (Alnoukai, El Sheikh, & Alzoabi, 2009).

Categorizing the processes into phases adds more understandability and tasks organization, cooperation, and learning. Processes categorization would help analyzing individual phases separately, setting milestones, and assigning the needed resources for each task (Hofmann, 2003). (Feldens, Moraes, Pavan, & Castilho, 1998) divided data mining life cycle into three main stages: pre-processing, data mining, and post-processing.

(Kopanakis & Theodoulidis, 1999) defined the following three categories in their knowledge discovery modeling: data preparation, model derivation, and validation stages.

ASD-BI process model keeps the same ASD agile method categorization. The following phases are the main processes categories for ASD-BI model (Figure 2).

Speculation

In this phase, we conduct all the project initiation tasks including: determining the objectives, mission and requirements of each cycle, determining the optimal number of cycles and timebox for each cycle, making preliminary size and scope estimation, and identifying the high risk items early in the project (Highsmith, 2000). ASD-BI speculation phase includes all the processes that lead to business and data understanding and data preparation and processing. As speed is the main measure in using ASD adaptive approach, Joint Application Development (JAD) sessions are extensively conducted in this phase for data understanding and gathering. ASD-BI speculation phase helps determining the optimal number of cycles based on the overall project objectives, requirements, estimates and resources. The duration of each cycle varies from two to eight weeks based on the overall project schedule and the project's degree of uncertainty. Each cycle (except for cycle 0 as it involves only project's preparation deliverables) delivers a demonstrable set of project outputs (analytical reports, dashboards, etc) for customer review process, though the outcome of each cycle should be visible and tangible (Highsmith, 2000). The outcome of this phase is the data processed, cleansed and ready for use in the modeling and data mining processes. This phase is the most important one as it takes considerable time and resources. This preparation phase will end by creating the enterprise data warehouse, and the required aggregations, data marts and cubes. ASD-BI speculation phase consists of the following four BI processes: business understanding, data understanding, objectives/hypotheses settings, and data preparation. (Highsmith, 2000) suggested that the first three processes should be seen as a whole. The logic behind his suggestion is that it is not that easy to define the project objectives without digging more into data and business understanding. The authors propose that data preparation process can also be seen as integrated with these three processes in the speculation phase, as the outcomes of this initial phase are to define the project objectives with the data processed for the modeling/data mining process. The description for each of these steps is as the following:

Business Understanding

This is the starting point of ASD-BI process model. It is considered to be one of the most important processes as it affects the overall BI project. The main focus of this process is the understanding of the project objectives and requirements from business perspectives (CRISP-DM, 2000). Different tasks are conducted during this process phase including: determination of business objectives and business success criteria, situation's assessment, determination of the BI application goals, and determination of the business basic rules (Hofmann, 2003).

Data Understanding

This is another vital phase in any BI application. The main focus is to help users to become familiar with the data in order to address all the data issues that can appear in the next processes. Different tasks are conducted during this process phase including: initial data collection, data exploration, data description, and data quality verification.

Objectives/Hypotheses Setting

This process uses the outcomes of the previous two steps to formulate the BI application objectives and hypotheses. This process was first considered by (Collier, Carey, Grusy, Marjaniemi, & Sautter, 1998). They reveal the fact that the objectives used in conjunction with business understanding can successfully highlight new business insights. This was also confirmed by (Turban, Aronson, Liang, & Sharda, 2007)

Data Preparation/ETL

This is the last and the heaviest process between all the other processes. The term ETL (Extract/Transform/Load) is mostly used with BI projects, whereas data preparation is commonly used with knowledge discovery processes. This process conduct all the activities required to construct the dataset needed for the modeling/data mining phase. The list of activities and tasks includes: data selection, cleansing, construction, integration, and formatting (CRISP-DM, 2000).

Collaboration

This phase deals with the issues concerning the components delivery concurrency and collaboration. It ensures the high communication in a diversity of experienced people, how people interact, and how to manage the interdependencies critical issues (Highsmith, 2000). ASD-BI collaboration phase includes the use of the team members' broad-based knowledge. This can be used for example to choose the best modeling algorithm for predicative data mining process, or to use different modeling algorithms for the same problem, and provide them for customer review process. The main focus of this phase is collaborative problem solving and sharing tacit knowledge. ASD-BI collaboration phase consists only of the modeling/data mining process.

Modeling/Data Mining

The focus of this process is the selection of the appropriate modeling method or data mining algorithm for the project's BI problem. Data mining is the core component of any BI project. Different data mining algorithms can be used according to the project objectives. The list of data mining methods includes: classification, clustering, association, sequencing, and forecasting. The aim of this process is conducting analysis tasks using different or a combination of data mining models including: decision trees, neural networks, memory based reasoning, etc (Fayyad, Piatetsky-Shapiro, & Smyth, 1996; Turban, Aronson, Liang, & Sharda, 2007).

Learning

In this phase, we focus on quality review. Different perspectives are used for quality review including: customer, technical, practices and project's status (Highsmith, 2000). Customer feedback and visibility is the main focus of the learning phase. This can be handled using customer focus group which are similar to JAD sessions but with the goal to review the application itself. According to (Highsmith, 2000), customer focus groups are more formal cycle milestones. Technical reviews are also key important activities to deliver quality products. Postmortem sessions and project status reviews are needed to evaluate each cycle's progress and the whole project status. ASD-BI learning phase consists of two process steps:

Evaluation

This is a vital process that ensures that the modeling method or the data mining model choice was appropriate for achieving the project's objectives. Many authors consider that evaluation process would help choosing useful hidden patterns from a huge number of patterns resulting from data mining algorithms (Fayyad, Piatetsky-Shapiro, & Smyth, 1996; Collier, Carey, Grusy, Marjaniemi, & Sautter, 1998). ASD-BI model already defined the project objectives clearly, which make the main focus of this step is to evaluate the chosen model and the results, or compare between different data mining algorithms results. Technical reviews, customer focus groups, postmortem sessions are the key factors for the evaluation process. The correct results of the modeling or data mining methods are stored in the knowledge repository (KR) even if they are not relevant to the BI projects' objectives, as they may be used in any future BI projects.

Deployment

This is the endpoint of each ASD-BI cycle. The knowledge discovered by the modeling/data mining step should be organized and presented in a way that the customer can use. BI projects can have different ways to present the discovered knowledge such as: analytical reports, dashboards, alerts, etc. Project status review activities are conducted after each cycle's deployment in order to evaluate the current cycle results, and to prepare for the next cycle activities.

ASD-BI: Human Resources Involvement

BI projects require qualified and skilled people (Hofmann, 2003). Most of the KD process models ignore the human resources involvement in their processes life cycles. (Ganesh, Han, Kumar, & Shekhar, 1996) consider the use of data analyst and data miner in their KD process model. (Lee & Kerschberg, 1998) consider the use of domain expert and knowledge engineer in their KDLC process model. (Hofmann, 2003) was one of the first researchers who stressed the importance of involving human resources in KD process models. He used a wide range of skilled people in his DMLC model life cycle including: project manager, business analyst, data engineer, data miner, domain expert, knowledge engineer, and strategic manager (Hofmann, 2003).

ASD-BI process model involves the following human resources in its different life cycle phases: business analyst, data analyst/engineer, data miner, domain expert, knowledge engineer, and strategic manager. ASD-BI process model considers people involvement as crucial for BI applications. The previous listed people are defined as jobs and skills to be achieved not specific personnel. ASD-BI people involvement is different from project management resources which require different type of peoples including: project manager, developer, tester, etc.

ASD-BI different human resources are defined as the following:

- *Business analyst* is the person who is responsible of understanding the different aspects of the assigned business (Hofmann & Tierney, 2007). He/She should have skills in both business and IT, and has enough experience on BI applications. His core role is building the project's hypotheses or objectives in cooperation with the data analyst/engineer, domain expert, and strategic manager. Business analyst role was identified in the (Hofmann, 2003) process model. Business analyst has a crucial role in the ASD-BI speculation phase.

- *Data analyst/engineer* is the database/ data warehouse expert person. He/She is responsible for analyzing the current data sources, and has enough experience to design and construct the corresponding data warehouse/ data marts. He/She is also responsible for data governance, data architecture, metadata repository, data integration, and data quality. Although some researches separated data analyst/engineer job into different two jobs of data analyzing, data engineering (Hofmann, 2003), the authors find that separation is not beneficial as they require the same human capabilities and experiences. Data analyst/engineer role was identified in the (Ganesh, Han, Kumar, & Shekhar, 1996; Hofmann, 2003) process models. Data analyst/engineer has a crucial role in the data understanding, data preparation steps in the ASD-BI speculation phase.

- *Domain expert* is the subject expert person with a relevant background in the specified subject matter (Lee & Kerschberg, 1998). He/She has an important role in supporting the job of all the other BI resources by using his knowledge in assuring that the BI project is setting the right objectives/hypotheses, getting the right and beneficial outcomes, and specifying the good knowledge to be stored in the knowledge repository (KR). Domain expert's is role in knowledge externalization and socialization. Though domain expert has to work closely with all the other resources especially business analyst, data miner, knowledge engineer, and strategic manager. Domain expert role was identified in the (Lee & Kerschberg, 1998; Hofmann, The Development of a Generic Data Mining Life Cycle (DMLC), 2003; Gottgtroy, Kasabov, & Macdonell, 2003) process models.

- *Data miner* is the core person in ASD-BI process model. He uses the data provided from the data analyst/engineer for the generation of data mining algorithm or model (Ganesh, Han, Kumar, & Shekhar, 1996). Data miner has to be a skilled person with good experiences in statistics, data bases, and data mining methods and algorithms. Data miner role was identified in the (Ganesh, Han, Kumar, & Shekhar, 1996; Hofmann, 2003) process models. He works closely with the data analyst/engineer and domain expert.
- *Knowledge engineer* has the role of assuring that knowledge is obtained, transferred, and stored in a structural way in the knowledge repository (KR). He has a crucial role of getting the benefits of building an enterprise BI application by enhancing the organizational knowledge. Knowledge engineer role was identified in the (Kopanakis & Theodoulidis, 1999; Hofmann, 2003) process models.
- *Strategic manager* ensures the BI application's role in building and achieving business strategy. The role of business and competitive intelligence in formulating organization's mission and long term objectives and designing strategies was lately

clarified by (Albescu, Pugna, & Paraschiv, 2008). This strategic role has to be conducted by the strategic manager with the support of all the other BI resources, mainly the business analyst, domain expert, and knowledge engineer. Strategic manager role was identified only in the (Hofmann, 2003) DMLC process model.

ASD-BI: The Knowledge Dimension

ASD-BI process model concentrates on human-based techniques in communicating knowledge such as on-site customer, customer focus groups, daily short meetings, and postmortem sessions. The model's main focus is to maximize the knowledge transferred and shared among various stakeholders of the BI project.

All of the ASD-BI principles are shared with other agile methodologies principles (such as ASD, XP, and Agile modeling) including: on-site customer, planning, small releases, metaphor, coding standards, continuous integration, and planning game.

Knowledge capturing happens informally through the use of principles like: on-site customers and customer focus group.

Knowledge sharing among all project stakeholders happens through social activities, such as short meetings and postmortem sessions.

ASD-BI involvement of knowledge engineer is crucial in assuring that knowledge is obtained, transferred, and stored in a structural way in the knowledge repository (KR).

ASD-BI: The Strategy Dimension

BI technologies provide organizations with the ability to take advantages of available information – internal and external. Competitive Intelligence, a concept introduced by Porter (1980), is considered as one of the application domains of business intelligence (Baars & Kemper, 2007).

(Albescu, Pugna, & Paraschiv, 2008) proposed a model integrating Business and Competitive Intelligence technologies that can help formulating organization's mission and long term objectives, and designing strategies from which to choose.

ASD-BI process model considers that Business Intelligence and Competitive Intelligence are the same. They only differ in the data sources type. Business Intelligence data sources are usually internal databases, or flat files. Competitive intelligence is generally based on external data sources, such as customer surveys, product brochures, competitors' financial reports, government publications, and patent databases. These data sources are usually available in electronic forms, and can be accessed by using Internet technologies.

ASD-BI process model focuses on the strategic dimension of using Business Intelligence and Data Mining applications. It heavily involves a strategic manager in order to formulate the BI application's objectives and hypotheses that can help formulating organization's strategy. The BI application's outcomes could also reveal new sources of competitive advantage, and help organizations becoming flexible in order to meet market changes.

APPLYING ASD-BI IN BUILDING BI APPLICATION ON HIGHER EDUCATION: ARAB INTERNATIONAL UNIVERSITY CASE STUDY

Using BI application for educational system is a new growing research discipline. Business Intelligence can improve quality in higher education system. Most of higher education procedures such as assessment, evaluation, and counseling require knowledge. Knowledge can be extracted from huge educational data sets using data mining. Business Intelligence applications can help both instructors and students to improve the quality of education.

Data mining is the core component of any educational Business Intelligence application where pedagogic strategies can be experimented and evaluated. The main objective of using data mining in educational system is to improve learning (Romero and Ventura 2007).

Data mining techniques extract hidden patterns from huge educational data sets. The discovered hidden patterns enhance the procedures of decision making especially producing more advanced plans for directing students.

Data mining techniques used for educational systems include (Romero and Ventura 2007, Shyamala and Rajagopalan 2006, Smith 2005): clustering, classification, association rules, decision trees, linear regression, and neural nets.

University lecturers and management can have deep insights of the need of different groups of students by means of data mining methods especially clustering method (such as TwoStep and K-means) (Romero and Ventura 2007).

Data mining analysis can also help in better allocation of resources and staff, manage students' outcomes, and improve effectiveness of alumni development. Data mining results can be used for further steps like adjustment of timetable based on students' desires, this means that two courses with high association correlation don't overlap in the timetable, also these two courses should be enrolled in the same semester, and not wait for one or two semesters.

These are some of the questions that can be answered and analyzed using data mining methods. Data mining methods can be used in higher education to:

- Predict next semester GPA for each student
- Identify the students likely to drop out
- Provide counseling for students in timely manner
- Identify students at risk of failures, in order to provide extra help
- Classify students' results

- Identify students who are taking the most "credit hours"
- Identify courses that attract more students

Reponses to these issues can help improve educational quality by maximizing educational system efficiency, increasing student success and learning outcomes, and decreasing students drop outs (Shyamala and Rajagopalan 2006).

AIU (Arab International University) is a new private university in Syria. It is 5 years old, the university began to find difficulties in managing the huge data deployed from its different information systems. The academic, financial, and HR systems are at the core of the university daily operations. As most of the university information systems were provided by different sources, there was an urgent need to integrate data from all these sources into one data warehouse in a manner that could help the university in making use of all data to assure quality.

The following paragraphs describe in detail a walkthrough of ASD-BI process modeling in building AIU-BI application:

Speculation

This is the longest and most important phase as it consists of the core tasks related to business and data understanding and preparation. It also defines the overall project hypotheses and objectives. The outcome of this phase is the AIU Enterprise Data Warehouse containing three data marts: academic, financial and HR data marts. The data warehouse was built in an adaptive way in order to be able to integrate new future data sources.

Business Understanding

AIU currently consists of six faculties with more than 4500 students and about 500 courses delivered per semester. AIU is following the credit hours academic system. English is the language used for education in this university. Business understanding process required JAD sessions. The main objective of these sessions was to understand the three main systems: academic, financial, and HR with the aid of a domain expert in each of these systems. It also helps elaborating the initial hypotheses and goals in each of the previous three fields. The core scope of AIU-BI project is to enhance the procedures of decision making especially producing more advanced plans for directing students, and to enhance the procedures of admission, registration and payments. Six cycles were initially identified with a time box of about eight months for the total project duration. First cycle was identified as the most crucial cycle. It involves determining the main project objectives, building the AIU Enterprise Data Warehouse, and deploying the first dashboards, and KPI (Key Performance Indicators) academic reports. The second cycle's goal was to get feedback from the AIU managers about the first set of academic dashboards and reports, and updating them according to their notes. The other two consecutive cycles were to provide KPI dashboards and reports about the financial system. The last two cycles conducted the HR KPI analyses. Cycle's duration was varied from two to eight weeks. The first cycle was the longest and took about eight weeks. The project was identified as a medium size BI project according to its objectives and the overall data size. Resources needed were optimized due to the agility of ASD-BI used methodology. Three full time people were assigned to build the AIU-BI project in eight months. The first author played the role of business analyst, knowledge manager, and strategic manager. The other two resources played the roles of data analyst/engineer, and data miner. Three other part time people were identified from the university staff and played the role of domain experts in the domain of academic, financial and HR. AIU-BI project's team was an on-site team to enhance knowledge sharing between all the team's members, and speed up the project's cycle development by scheduling daily status meetings between this team and AIU focus group.

Data Understanding

The data gathered to produce the AIU-BI application are the: academic data (registration, examination, enrollment, etc), financial data (student fees, staff salaries, orders, sales, etc.), and HR data (staff personal information). The data analyst/engineer role was to dig more into the current databases to become familiar with the data to address all the issues that can be raised during the next processes, get deep insights about the databases structures, and propose the AIU data warehouse design and implementation.

Hypotheses/Objectives Setting

The main focus of this process step was to use the outcomes of the previous two steps in order to identify the AIU-BI project objectives. Business and data understanding can reveal new business insight. Identification of the project's objectives was done through daily JAD sessions with the collaboration of business analyst, strategic manager, data analyst/engineer and domain experts. The main goals of this project are to: enhance the university's procedures, increase income by determining profitability patterns, analyze students demographic information, enhance education quality, increase the number of students, and highlight the drawbacks in any of the university's processes.

Project's objectives identification is done using a list of KPIs. KPIs provide deep insights into the university's success factors, and help in measuring progress. KPIs are ways to align BI with the business overall goals and strategy. AIU KPIs include vital statistical information such as: admission trends, registration trends, profit values, relative faculties' performance, real-time registration statistics, real-time staff statistics, real-time students' payments, etc.

A list of dashboards was also identified including:

- Total number of current accepted students per faculty.
- GPA Average per faculty.
- Total number of current students per faculty.
- Total number of registered courses per faculty.
- Total number of registered hours per faculty.
- Average credit hours registered per faculty.
- Percentage of current student payment per faculty.
- Total payment amount per faculty.
- Total students payment cut off.
- Total expenses per faculty.
- Total number of current academic staff per faculty.
- Total number of current admin staff per faculty.
- Total number of required academic staff per faculty.
- Total number of required admin staff per faculty.

A list of analytical reports was identified including:

- Total number of admitted students compared with the previous years.
- GPA average compared with the previous years.
- Distribution of admitted students according to specific period zones per faculty.
- Distribution of admitted students according to week days, cities, nationalities, and countries.
- Total number of new students leaving the university per faculty.
- Correlation between registered hours & AGPA, secondary school average & AGPA, registered hours & English level,

English level & secondary school average, and registered hours & secondary school average per faculty.

- Total number of opened groups, groups>45, groups<15 per faculty.
- Number of registered students per English level, per faculty.
- Percentage for each English level per faculty.
- Average number of students in each group per faculty.
- Percentage for each English level per faculty.
- Total number of students benefitting from financial decreases per type, per faculty.
- Percentage of courses income per faculty.
- Percentage of faculties' income per total income.
- Percentage of academic staff per students per faculty.
- Distribution of academic staff per scientific level (PhD, M.Sc., etc).

A list of data mining reports was identified including:

- Predicting student's admission number according to different period zones per faculty.
- Predicting student GPA, faculty average GPA, and university average GPA.
- Association rules between courses per faculty.
- Clustering students according to their AGPA and English level.
- Classification of students according to their letter grade.
- Predicting the list of students likely to drop out.
- Predicting the list students at risk of failures.
- Classification of courses which attract more students.

- Predicting faculties' income for the next semester.
- Classification of faculties' income according to courses.
- Classification of faculties' expenses according to courses.
- Classification of faculties' academic staff per age.
- Classification of faculties' academic staff per scientific degree.

Data Preparation/ETL

This is the main part of the speculation phase as it deals with the data extraction from the project's data sources, completes all the transformation operations, and migrate the cleansed data into the data warehouse. Data sources are from Oracle and SQL Server data bases. AIU enterprise data warehouse was built using Oracle 11g Enterprise Edition. The Bottom-Up approach is the methodology used for the data warehouse creation in order to be adaptive and be able to include additional data sources in the future. Three data marts were created for the academic, financial and HR data. Academic and HR data marts are of galaxy architecture with multiple fact tables, whereas financial data mart is of snow flake architecture. Relationships between these three data marts are created using students' and faculties' identifiers. Data extraction from academic and HR databases were done using Oracle database link with a low level of granularity, Oracle Transparent Gateways for Microsoft SQL Server was used to extract data from the financial database with a low level of granularity. Incremental strategy was used to update the data warehouse. Academic data extraction is done after closing each academic semester, financial data extraction is done by the end of each fiscal year, whereas the HR extraction is done on a monthly basis. Data transformation is applied using a staging area in order to be able to deal with the Bulk Update strategy. Data loading is conducted between the staging area and the AIU

Enterprise Data Warehouse. ASD-BI metadata repository is built during this phase. It describes all the data stored in the AIU data warehouse/data marts, and has all the necessary information to respond to user queries. ASD-BI metadata repository is composed of the following three layers: the physical layer that contains information about the AIU data warehouse/data marts, the business model layer that holds information about the data warehouse/data marts from business view to build the data browsers, and the presentation layer that is responsible for presenting the data stored in the business layer in an easy and simple way using the data browsers. ASD-BI metadata repository is the cornerstone for building the ASD-BI knowledge repository. It stores initially all the business rules that are necessary for the BI project, and helps for the selection and application of the data mining method, and the interpretation of the method's results. It also stores the knowledge discovered during the knowledge discovery process.

Collaboration

This is the core phase of the ASD-BI process model. It contains modeling/data mining process step which is the engine of any BI application. It requires an extensive knowledge sharing between diversity of skilled people in order to choose the best modeling/data mining method that could help achieving the problem objectives.

Modeling/Data Mining

Data mining is the core component of any BI project. Different data mining algorithms are used in order to satisfy many of the project's objectives. Different modeling/data mining methods were applied including: prediction, clustering, classification, and association rules. Predicting students cumulative GPA was implemented based on Attribute Importance technique that use all the attributes needed to compute the GPA ordered according to their importance. Support

Vector Machine (SVM) algorithm was chosen between different other algorithms as it is the best algorithm for predicting a continuous value such as GPAs. Predictive confidence for GPA prediction was about 70%. Clustering methods were applied for different project's problems such as classifying students' GPAs according to their completed credit hours. K-means algorithm was chosen as it is able to deal with medium volume of data. Association rule method was applied for solving the best suggested list of courses for each student's registration. Apriori algorithm was chosen to perform "market basket analysis" to discover relationships or correlations among a set of subjects in each AIU faculty. Results of these modeling/data mining methods will be discussed in detail later in the learning phase.

Learning

This is the quality assurance phase. It deals heavily with the quality of the modeling/data mining results. Each ASD-BI model cycle delivers a demonstrable set of project outputs including: dashboards, analytical reports, and alerts. AIU focus group is assigned for customer review and feedback sessions. Evaluation and deployment are the two important processes that characterize the learning phase. Sharing knowledge is the main outcome of this phase as it involves a lot of discussions between skilled people from both AIU and ASD-BI development team.

Evaluation

This process deals with the customer feedback and visibility of the modeling/data mining results. AIU focus group has the responsibility of evaluating the chosen model results, or comparing between different data mining methods, or proposing new project outputs based on the obtained results. Technical reviews are conducted during this step in order to assure that the results obtained are of high quality.

Figure 3. AIU Students classified according to their accumulative GPA and their english level

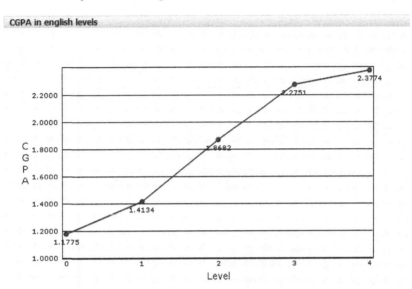

Deployment

This is ASD-BI cycle's endpoint. The modeling/ data mining process accepted outcomes are presented for customer review in different ways: dashboards, analytical reports, alerts, etc. Postmortem sessions and project status reviews are conducted to evaluate each cycle's progress and the whole project's status. Discussion with the customer through AIU focus group provides important feedback after each cycle. This makes the model flexible and adaptive, and reduces the optimal number of cycles needed to complete the project. In the following sections, the authors present a list of AIU-BI project outputs that characterize the role of Business Intelligence and Data Mining in supporting higher education's decision makers:

- Correlation of students' level of English and overall performance. This report helped a lot in evaluating the current system used in the English Language Center in the university and resulted in major changes in the system. (Figure 3) shows that there is

strong correlation between students' level of English and accumulative GPA. This report had an important effect at the AIU strategy by updating the courses offering in the following semesters. All students with low level in English (levels 0 to 2) have to follow one full English courses semester. This strategic decision enhances the overall performance of the university.

- Correlation of students' performance in different subjects. The AIU-BI project's tries to find some correlation between students' performance in different subjects and provides an indicator of how students should select the subjects for enrollment. For example, the system showed that some strong correlation (around r2 = 0.67) exists between "Business Ethics" and "Organizational Behavior" courses despite the fact that none is a prerequisite for the other. So academic advisors were told to encourage students to enroll for "Business Ethics" after they have passed "Organizational Behavior". This indicator

Figure 4. Business Administration students clustered according to their accumulative GPA and their credit hours

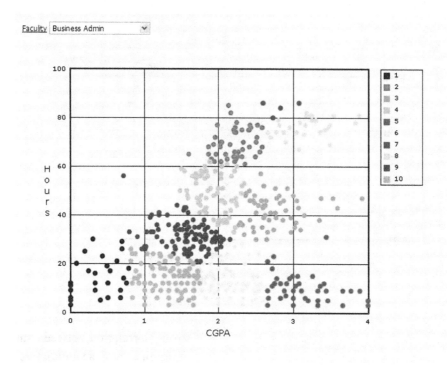

promises a great aid when curriculum is to be redesigned later on.

Market basket analysis report helps in preparing the time table for each semester. The resultant time table would contain a set of highly interrelated courses that students require. This means that two courses with high association correlation don't overlap in the time table, also these two courses should be enrolled in the same semester, and not wait for one or two semesters. This analysis helps achieving one of the main AIU strategic goals by enhancing the total number of enrolled courses. This has an immediate financial revenue increase.

Clustering each faculty's students according to their cumulative GPAs, and their completed hours help the university's academic advisors focus on special groups, especially the group of students that are likely to drop out (Figure 4). Correlation between credit hours and AGPA changes shows

a clear picture about the optimal number of the credit hours the students would take to increase their AGPA. Figure 5 Shows that this ranges between 2-12 and 20-22 hours. This provides the AIU decision makers with the reasons to find out how to help students to enhance their AGPAs while getting the required credit hours in each semester (which varies between 16-19 hours).

Analysis of the total number of students' presence per different time ranges per days helps AIU achieving one of its strategic goals by enhancing services provided to its students and optimizing costs (Figure 6). Such analysis helps AIU preparing the optimal plans for transportation, restaurants, library services, and others. The immediate effect of using this report was reducing the transportation costs by 30%. Currently all AIU plans depends mainly on this analytical report.

Predicting students GPAs is one of the important outcomes of AIU-BI project. Different algorithms were used for prediction. Evaluation of the

Figure 5. Credit hours relation to AGPA changes

Credit Hours Relation to AGPA Changes

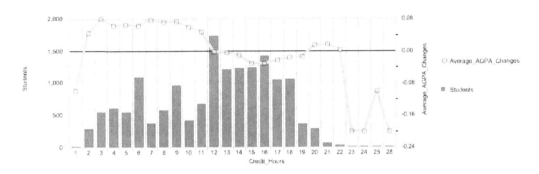

Figure 6. Total number of students' presence per different time ranges per week days

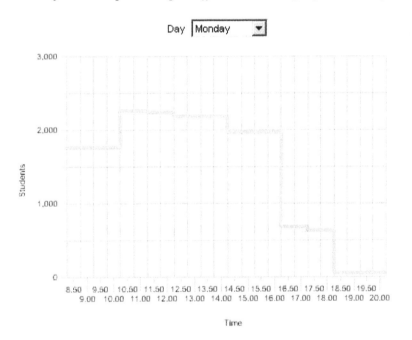

results for each algorithm permit choosing the best method with the highest predictive confidence. SVA algorithm was chosen with more than 70% predictive confidence (Figure 7 shows GPA prediction deviation errors). This also helps predicting the average GPA per each faculty, which would help AIU preparing plans to enhance the overall performance.

Other different financial and HR reports and dashboards help AIU decision makers analyzing the current status, and preparing plans to enhance performance. Figure 8 shows a financial dashboard that presents the percentage of the actual students' payments. Other dashboards provide information about the total payments per faculty, net profit per faculty, financial analysis during the last four years, and many other reports. Some of these

Figure 7. GPA prediction deviation errors chart

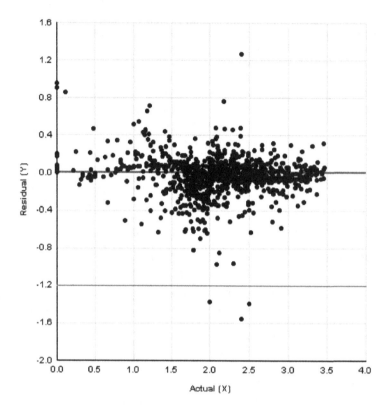

Figure 8. Actual payments percentage

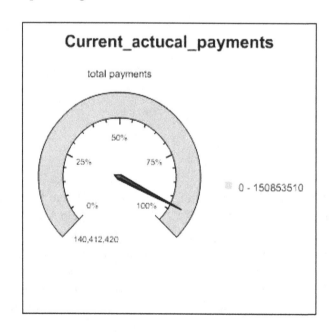

reports were updated according to AIU demand. Updates and accomplishment of any new requirements were done during the consecutive cycles. ASD-BI process model provides the framework to fulfill any new changes in a high speed way. AIU-BI project was mainly successful due to its flexibility and adaptability.

CONCLUSION

In this chapter, we proposed a new knowledge discovery process model named "ASD-BI". ASD-BI is based on ASD agile methodology in order to fulfill the main requirements of building BI application, which are agile and adaptive. ASD-BI process model takes in consideration the strengths and weaknesses of the previous knowledge discovery process models that are presented in a survey conducted by the authors (Alnoukai, El Sheikh, & Alzoabi, 2009).

ASD-BI process model is mainly based on six dimensions: data, process, people, adaptive, knowledge and strategy. Other models focus mainly at most on the first three dimensions. The authors' model focuses extensively on knowledge capturing and sharing, and helps organizations implementing and achieving their strategies.

The case study conducted using the proposed model demonstrated high flexibility in building BI applications, with higher cost effectiveness in terms of resources and duration.

Throughout the life cycle of a Business Intelligence project many different disciplines are involved to ensure successful implementation. This includes data warehousing, data mining, project management, agile methodology, and among others, business analysis. The main objective of this chapter is to develop an agile knowledge discovery process model and apply it on higher education. Although this objective was completed, there still some limitations especially in the way building the knowledge repository.

Future work can be carried out in the area of building the knowledge repository, storing and organizing the extracted knowledge, and using Ontologies to combine the prior knowledge (in terms of Ontology) and the process of knowledge discovery in an explicit and clear life cycle.

REFERENCES

Abdullah, S. S., Holcombe, M., & Gheorge, M. (2006). The impact of an agile methodology on the well being of development teams [San Bernardino, CA, USA: Empire Software Eng.]. *Empirical Software Engineering, 11*(1), 143–167.

Adriaans, P., & Zantinge, D. (1996). *Data Mining*. Boston, MA: Addison-Wesley.

Agile Alliance. (2001). *Manifesto for agile software development*. Available at http://www.agilealliance.org

Albescu, F., Pugna, I., & Paraschiv, D. (2008). Business intelligence & knowledge management – technological support for strategic management in the knowledge based economy. *Informatica Economică, 4*(48), 5–12.

Alnoukari, M., & Alhussan, W. (2008). Using data mining techniques for predicting future car market demand. In *IEEE Proceedings of International Conference on Information & Communication Technologies*, Damascus, Syria (pp. 929-930).

Alnoukari, M., Alzoabi, Z., & Hanna, S. (2008). Applying adaptive software development (ASD) agile modeling on predictive data mining applications: ASD-DM methodology. In *IEEE Proceedings of International Symposium on Information Technology*, Kuala Lumpur, Malaysia (pp. 1083-1087).

Anand, S. S., & Buchner, A. (1998). *Decision support using data mining*. London, UK: Financial Times Pitman Publishers.

Azvine, B., Cui, Z., & Nauck, D. (2005). Towards real-time business intelligence. *BT Technology Journal, 23*(3), 214–225.

Baars, H., & Kemper, H. G. (2007). Management support with structured and unstructured data- An integrated business intelligence framework. *Information Systems Management, 25*, 132–148.

Bäck, T. (2002). Adaptive business intelligence based on evolution strategies: Some application examples of self-adaptive software. *Information Sciences, 148*(1-1), 113-121.

Berry, M. J., & Gordon, L. (1997). *Data mining techniques: For marketing, sales, and customer support.* New York, NY: Wiley.

Boddy, D., Boonstra, A., & Kennedy, G. (2005). *Managing Information Systems: An Organisational Perspective* (2nd ed.). Harlow: Pearson.

Buchner, A. G., Mulvenna, M. D., Anand, S. S., & Hughes, J. G. (1999). An Internet-enabled knowledge discovery process. In *Proceedings of the 9th International Database Conference,* Hong Kong, (pp. 13-27).

Cios, K. J., Pedrycz, W., Swiniarski, R. W., & Kurgan, L. A. (2007). The knowledge discovery process. In *Data mining: A knowledge discovery process* (p. 606). Berlin, Heidelberg: Springer.

Cody, W. F., Kreulen, J. T., Krishna, V., & Spangler, W. S. (2002). The integration of business intelligence and knowledge management. *IBM Systems Journal, 41*(4), 697–713.

Collier, K., Carey, B., Grusy, E., Marjaniemi, C., & Sautter, D. (1998). *A perspective on data mining. Northern Arizona University.* USA: Centre for Data Insight.

CRISP-DM. (2000). *CRISP-DM 1.0 – Step by step data mining guide.* CRISP-DM Consortium.

Drnevich, P. L., Hahn, J., & Shanley, M. (2006). Toward a strategic perspective of Information Technology. In Walters, B., & Tang, Z. (Eds.), *IT-enabled strategic management: Increasing return for the organization* (pp. 16–37). Hershey, PA, USA: Idea Group.

Edelstein, H. (1998). Data mining: Let's get practical. *DB2 Magazine, 3*(2), 38-40.

Fayyad, U., Piatetsky-Shapiro, G., & Smyth, P. (1996). Knowledge discovery and data mining: Towards a unifying framework. *2nd International Conference on Knowledge Discovery and Data Mining (KDD-96)* (pp. 82-88). USA: AAAI Press.

Feldens, M. A., Moraes, R. L., Pavan, A., & Castilho, J. M. (1998). *Towards a methodology for the discovery of useful knowledge combining data mining, data warehousing and visualisation.* Brazil: CNPq/Protem-cc Fase III (SIDI Project), Universidade Federal do Rio Grande do Sul.

Ganesh, M., Han, E. H., Kumar, V., & Shekhar, S. (1996). *Visual data mining: Framework and algorithm development. Technical Report TR 96-021.* University of Minnesota.

Gartner. (1996). Retrieved June 05, 2009, from http:// www.innerworx.co.za/ products.htm.

Girija, N., & Srivatsa, S. K. (2006). A research study- Using data mining in knowledge base business strategies. *Information Technology Journal, 5*(3), 590–600.

Gottgtroy, P., Kasabov, N., & Macdonell, S. (2003). An ontology engineering approach for knowledge discovery from data in evolving domains. In *Proceedings of the 2003 SIAM International Conference on Data Mining,* San Francisco, CA.

Grembergen, W. V., Haes, S. D., & Guldentops, E. (2004). Structures, processes and relational mechanisms for IT governance. In Grembergen, W. V. (Ed.), *Strategies for Information Technology governance.* Hershey, PA, USA: Idea Group.

Haglin, D., Roiger, R., Hakkila, J., & Giblin, T. (2005). A tool for public analysis of scientific data. *Data Science Journal*, *4*(30), 39–53.

Han, J., & Cercone, N. (2000). RuleViz: A model for visualizing knowledge discovery process. In *Proceedings of the 6ᵗʰ ACM SIGKDD International Conference on Knowledge Discovery and Data Mining* (pp. 244-253). Boston, MA, USA: ACM.

Herring, J. P. (1988). Building a business intelligence systems. *The Journal of Business Strategy*, 4–9.

Highsmith, J. (2000). Retiring lifecycle dinosaurs: Using adaptive software development to meet the challenges of a high-speed, high-change environment. *Software Testing & Quality Engineering*, 22-28.

Hofmann, M. (2003). *The development of a generic data mining life cycle (DMLC)*. School of Computing, Dublin Institute of Technology.

Hofmann, M., & Tierney, B. (2007). Development phases of a generic data mining life cycle (DMLC). In *Proceedings of the International Conference on Software Engineering Theory and Practice*, 5-11.

Housel, T., & Bell, A. (2001). *Managing and measuring knowledge*. Boston, MA: McGraw-Hill.

Inmon, W. H. (2005). *Building the data warehouse*. Hoboken, NJ, USA: John Wiley and Sons.

Jermol, M., Lavrac, N., & Urbancic, T. (2003). Managing business intelligence in a virtual enterprise: A case study and knowledge management lessons learned. *Journal of Intelligent & Fuzzy Systems*, 121–136.

Jourdan, Z., Rainer, R. K., & Marshall, T. E. (2007). Business intelligence: An analysis of the literature. *Information Systems Management*, *25*, 121–131.

Katz, J. D. (2002). The integral role of Information Technology in achieving business strategy success: Managing the information resources of global competitors. In Tan, F. B. (Ed.), *Advanced topics in global information management* (pp. 42–62). Hershey, PA, USA: Idea Group.

Keith, E. R. (2006). *Agile software development processes - A different approach to software design*. Retrieved May 29, 2009, from Agile Alliance: http://www.agilealliance.org/ show/1099

Kerdprasop, N., & Kerdprasop, K. (2007). Moving data mining tools toward a business intelligence system. *Transactions on Engineering, Computing and Technology*, *19*, 117–122.

Klosgen, W., & Zytkow, J. M. (2002). The knowledge discovery process. In Klosgen, W., & Zytkow, J. M. (Eds.), *Handbook of Data Mining and Knowledge Discovery* (pp. 10–21). New York, NY: Oxford University Press.

Kopanakis, I., & Theodoulidis, B. (1999). *Visual data mining & modelling techniques. Centre of Research in Information Management (CRIM)*. UK: Department of Computation, University of Manchester Institute of Science and Technology.

Lange, K. (2006). Differences between statistics and data mining. *DM Review*, *16*(12), 32–33.

Lee, S. W., & Kerschberg, L. (1998). A methodology and life cycle model for data mining and knowledge discovery in precision agriculture. *IEEE International Conference on Systems, Man, and Cybernetics (SMC '98)*, San Diego, CA, USA (pp. 2882-2887).

Li, T., & Ruan, D. (2007). An extended process model of knowledge discovery in database. *Journal of Enterprise Information Management*, *20*(2), 169–177.

Mannila, H. (1997). Methods and problems in data mining. In F. Afrati, & P. Kolaitis (Eds.), *International Conference on Database Theory.* Delphi, Greece: Springer-Verlag.

Marren, P. (2004). The father of business intelligence. *The Journal of Business Strategy, 25*(6), 5–7.

Michalewicz, Z., Schmidt, M., Mich, M., & Chiriac, C. (2006). *Adaptive business intelligence.* Springer.

Nayak, R., & Qiu, T. (2005). A data mining application: Analysis of problems occurring during a software project development process. *International Journal of Software Engineering and Knowledge Engineering, 15*(4), 647–663.

Negash, S. (2004). Business intelligence. *Communications of the Association for Information Systems, 13,* 177–195.

Okuhara, K., Ishii, H., & Uchida, M. (2005). Support of decision making by data mining using neural system. *Systems and Computers in Japan, 36*(11), 102–110.

Pabarskaite, Z., & Raudys, A. (2007). A process of knowledge discovery from Web log data: Systematization and critical review. *Journal of Intelligent Information Systems, 28,* 70–104.

Pant, P. (2009). *Essential Components of a Successful BI Strategy.* Information Management Special Reports.

Pérez-Valls, M., Ortega-Egea, J. M., & Úbeda, J. A. (2006). Relationship between new Information Technologies and flexible organizational forms. In Walters, B., & Tang, Z. (Eds.), *IT-enabled strategic management: Increasing return for the organization* (pp. 68–92). Hershey, PA, USA: Idea Group.

Porter, M. E. (1979). How competitive forces shape strategy? *Harvard Business Review,* 137–145.

Power, D. J. (2007). *A brief history of decision support systems.* Retrieved May 28, 2009, from DSSResources.COM: http://DSSResources. COM/ history/ dsshistory.html

Pressman, R. S. (2001). *Software engineering a practitioner's approach.* New York, NY: McGraw Hill.

Rawlings, I. (1999). Using data mining and warehousing for knowledge discovery. *Computer Technology Review, 19*(9), 20–22.

Reinartz, T. (1999). *Focusing solutions for data mining.* Lecture notes in artificial intelligence, 1623.

Rennolls, K. (2005). An intelligent framework (O-SS-E) for data mining, knowledge discovery and business intelligence. In *IEEE Proceedings of the 16th Workshop on Database and Expert System Applications,* 715-719.

Rennolls, K., & AL-Shawabkeh, A. (2008). Formal structures for data mining, knowledge discovery and communication in a knowledge management environment. *Intelligent Data Analysis, 12,* 147–163.

Sabherwal, R., & Chan, Y. E. (2001). Alignment between business and IS strategies: A study of prospectors, analyzers, and defenders. *Information Systems Research,* 11–33.

SAS. (1997). From data to business advantage: *Data mining, SEMMA Methodology and the SAS System (White Paper).* SAS Institute Inc.

Shariat, M., & Hightower, R. (2007). Conceptualizing business intelligence architecture. *The Marketing Management Journal, 17*(2), 40–46.

Stojanovic, Z., Dahanayake, A., & Sol, H. (2003). Modeling and architectural design in agile development methodologies. *EMMSAD, 03,* 1–10.

Stolba, N., & Tjoa, A. M. (2006). The relevance of data warehousing and data mining in the field of evidence-based medicine to support healthcare decision making. *Enformatika, 11*, 12–17.

Tang, Z., & Walters, B. (2006). The interplay of strategic management and Information Technology. In Walters, B., & Tang, Z. (Eds.), *IT-enabled strategic management: Increasing returns for the organization* (pp. 1–15). Idea Group.

Turban, E., Aronson, J. E., Liang, T. P., & Sharda, R. (2007). *Decision support and business intelligence systems* (8th ed.). Upper Saddle River, NJ: Pearson Prentice Hall.

Watson, H. J., Wixom, B. H., Hoffer, J. A., Anderson-Lehman, R., & Reynolds, A. M. (2006). Real-time business intelligence: Best practices at Continental Airlines. *Information Systems Management*, 7–18.

Wee, C. H., & Leow, M. L. (1994). Competitive business intelligence in Singapore. *Journal of Strategic Marketing, 1*, 112–139.

Weiss, S. M., Buckley, S. J., Kapoor, S., & Damgaard, S. (2003). Knowledge-based data mining. [Washington, DC: ACM.]. *SIGKDD, 03*, 456–461.

KEY TERMS AND DEFINITIONS

Agile Methodology: An iterative and incremental (evolutionary) approach to software development which is performed in a highly collaborative manner by self-organizing teams within an effective governance framework with "just enough" ceremony that produces high quality solutions in a cost effective and timely manner which meets the changing needs of its stakeholders.

A Life Cycle (LC): A collection of phases through which a product service or system goes through. Each phase, from problem identification through the implementation of the product, service, or system, depends upon the other phases to achieve a desirable outcome.

Business Intelligence (BI): An umbrella term that combines architectures, tools, data bases, applications, practices, and methodologies. It is the process of transforming various types of business data into meaningful information that can help, decision makers at all levels, getting deeper insight of business.

Data Mining (DM): The process of discovering interesting information from the hidden data that can either be used for future prediction and/or intelligently summarizing the details of the data.

Data Warehouse (DW: A physical repository where relational data are specially organized to provide enterprise-wide, cleansed data in a standardized format.

Knowledge Discovery (KD): The process encompassing the entire data analysis life cycle, from the identification of data analysis goals and the acquisition and organization of raw data to the generation of potentially useful knowledge, its interpretation and testing.

Knowledge Management (KM): The acquisition, storage, retrieval, application, generation, and review of the knowledge assets of an organization in a controlled way.

Process Modeling (PM): The development of efficient, repeatable business processes that align with the overall business strategy of an enterprise.

Chapter 10
Measurement of Brand Lift from a Display Advertising Campaign

Jagdish Chand
Yahoo! Inc, USA

ABSTRACT

Brand Marketing is a form of advertising where advertiser tries to raise awareness and create affinity of brand name with consumers. If the advertisements are able to create brand awareness, consumer will be more likely to buy the product offered by the brand as compared to other, when there are multiple choices presented to the consumer. But measuring the lift in brand awareness as a result of marketing campaign is a tough problem.

In this chapter we will describe an advanced business intelligence system we built at Yahoo to measure the lift in brand awareness driven from the display advertising campaigns on Yahoo network. It helped us to show to the advertisers that display advertising is working in lifting awareness and brand affinity.

INTRODUCTION

Marketing is as old as the first business on earth. Once you build a business, you need to advertise to connect your business with customers. The process of connecting a business to customers is called marketing. *Marketing is the process by which companies create customer interest in prod-*ucts or services. (Kotler, Armstrong, Wong, and Saunders, 2008) American Marketing Association defines marketing as *"the activity, set of institutions, and processes for creating, communicating, delivering, and exchanging offerings that have value for customers, clients, partners, and society at large."* (American Marketing Association, 2007) The vehicle for doing marketing is called an advertisement. A wave of advertisements to market a specific aspect of the business is called

DOI: 10.4018/978-1-61350-050-7.ch010

a marketing campaign. There is huge amount of money is spend on the marketing campaigns every year. E.g. Kantar Media reports that, *"Total advertising expenditures in the first quarter of 2010 rose 5.1 percent from a year ago and finished the period at $31.3 billion."*(Daddi, 2010)

The advertisements are delivered to the consumer through the media frequently consumed by the consumer. As media consumption patterns changed, the best medium to deliver advertisements to consumers has changed with time. Advertisements have moved from big billboards to newspapers, newspapers to the radio and television and online to the Internet. As these multiple channels compete for the marketing dollar, each channel needs to prove to the marketer that money spent via these channels helps the marketer to achieve his or her marketing goals.

There are two types of advertisers: Direct Marketers and Brand Marketers. Direct Marketers like to reach consumers directly with an offer of call to action. A call to action can be an offer to buy something at a certain price, sign up for a service or to make a call to the advertiser to get some information. Business dictionaries define the call to actions as, *"The portion of an advertisement or marketing effort that requests that a consumer perform a specific action."* (Business Dictionary, 2010) Direct marketing campaigns in the Internet world are executed mainly by using search keyword associated advertisements or by sending e-mails directly to consumers. In contrast to Direct Marketers, Brand Marketers run marketing campaigns to raise awareness of their brand. There is no call to action associated with their advertisements. Their message is to emotionally connect the brand with the consumer. Having the consumer emotionally connected with the brand, it is more likely that the consumer will buy a product provided by that advertiser when there are more than one choices present during any buying decision. Brand marketing campaigns run on prime TV networks and in the Internet world

are executed mainly using the display or video advertisements on prime networks such as Yahoo.

As evident from the description above, it is very easy to measure the effectiveness of a direct marketing campaign by measuring the responses to the calls to action. But measuring the effectiveness of a brand campaign using Display Advertising is a difficult problem to solve, because you have to measure the lift in the emotional engagement of the user.

In this chapter we will describe an Advanced Business Intelligence System; we built at Yahoo to measure the Brand Lift driven from the display advertising campaigns on Yahoo network. It helped us to show the advertisers that display advertising is working in lifting brand awareness and brand affinity. This information enables our sale team to drive repeat business and increased spend from our large brand advertises.

Background

Yahoo advertising Analytics is a system to provide deep analytics to top Yahoo Advertisers. As a part of development of this system, we needed to build a system to measure the lift in brand awareness after a user is exposed to a Display advertising campaign. In order to measure the lift in brand awareness, we needed to find some proxy by which to measure brand awareness. This had to be in the form of some action performed by the users which indicated the user is aware of the brand and is more likely to choose the offer provided by that brand name when multiple choices are present. We chose following two proxies for the brand awareness:

Keyword Search

When a user performs a search for a keyword associated with a brand on a search engine like Yahoo or Google, he expresses a need at that point of time for a product or service offered by that brand. By performing a search, he may be either be researching that product or looking for the vendors that sell products from the target brand. So by performing the search user is proving that he is aware of the brand. Hence searching on the keyword related to the brand can be considered proxy to the brand awareness. If a user starts searching more for the brand related keywords after getting exposed to the display ad campaign, it can be used to measure the lift in the brand awareness from the given campaign.

Click on Sponsored Search Advertisement

Sponsored search ads are part of search engine marketing or SEM, a vehicle for direct marketing. SEM is defined as, *"The act of marketing a web site via search engines, whether this be improving rank in organic listings, purchasing paid listings or a combination of these and other search engine-related activities."*(Sullivan, 2010). In this type of marketing, advertiser bids a price in order to have their ad displayed in conjunction with algorithmic search results whenever a user searches for a keyword related to a product offered by the advertiser. However, the advertiser gets charged only if a user clicks on its advertisement. For a given keyword usually 5 to 10 sponsored search ads are displayed. As described earlier, when a user goes to search engine and types in a product related keywords, he expresses a need or desire to buy or learn about the product. In this case keywords may not be directly related to the brand but generic as car, which is of interest to all auto advertisers. The sponsored search ads, which appear above the search results, are from the providers of the products which are related to the keyword being searched & compete to satisfy that user's requirement. If a user clicks on the search ad offered by an advertiser when multiple ads from competitors are present, it may be because the user is aware of the brand. He is choosing the ad from a competing set of ads and

can be considered equivalent of buying a product when multiple competing products are present. So click on the sponsored search ad can be considered a proxy to the brand awareness and if a user start clicking more on the search ads after getting exposed to the search ad campaign, it can be used to measure the lift in brand awareness from the given display ad campaign.

In addition to above two proxies, there can be more industry specific proxies for the brand awareness. E.g. for the advertiser from automobile industry, car comparison and research on the cars offered by the advertiser, on Yahoo! Auto site can be considered as measure of brand awareness. For an advertiser in consumer product and electronics category, research by user on the products, offered by the advertiser, on Yahoo! Shopping site can be considered a proxy to brand awareness. For the advertiser in the entertainment category, activity of checking the show time or viewing the trailer of the advertised movie on Yahoo! Movies can be considered as measure of awareness for advertised movie. But to start with we chose above said two proxies, keyword search and click on sponsored search ads, as proxies for brand awareness. The system was designed in such a way that, in future, it can be extended to include other brand awareness proxies. In the remaining of this chapter will refer these proxies to brand awareness as conversions. A conversion is an overloaded term and can be used in different contexts. But in this chapter, a conversion refers to a proxy to the brand awareness.

To measure the lift in brand awareness, we first identify the conversions which can be associated with the brand of a given advertiser. Once the conversions have been identified, the system measures the lift in the conversions, amongst the users who have been exposed to Display Advertisement campaign from that advertiser. The next section describes the algorithm and system in more detail to measure the lift in brand awareness.

Options to Compute Brand Lift

Once the proxies to the brand awareness were identified, we had competing solutions to measure the lift in brand awareness. This section describes these solutions at high level as well as pros and cons of each.

Ideal Solution

The ideal way to do the brand lift calculation is through controlled experiments or A/B testing. *A/B testing or bucket testing is a method of marketing testing by which a baseline control sample is compared to a variety of single-variable test samples in order to improve response rates. (Wikipedia, 2010)* This requires a small (but statistically significant) hold-out set of users who qualified for the campaign but are deliberately not exposed to the campaign. This group of users will form the control group. The test group will be a set of users who qualified for the campaign and were exposed to it. By measuring the difference in the brand awareness between these two groups, we can measure the brand lift driven from the display advertising campaign. This solution requires that the end to end ad serving infrastructure supports A/B testing and the Sales Team sets these tests before the campaigns start running. At the time of system development, ad serving infrastructure was not ready to support an end to end A/B testing. Even if the ad serving infrastructure support were present, it is quite error prone for sales team to configure these tests before the start of a campaign. Hence even though this was the best option, it could not be pursued further.

Pre and Post Campaign Tracking

Under this option, the system would identify a set of users who qualify for a given Display Campaign, and then measure their brand awareness before the start of the campaign. When the campaign starts, the system measures the brand awareness of the users who are now exposed to the campaign. The difference between the pre-campaign and post-campaign brand awareness of the user's who were exposed to the campaign can be used to measure the lift in brand awareness driven from that Display Ad campaign. This method, although looks attractive at high level, has one big issue. The measurement of brand awareness is done across different times and time can be very big factor in level of conversion activity. E.g. users may have more search activity for flowers during the mother's day or Valentine's Day. Similarly users may search heavily for cars during the president's day sale event and increased activity may not have any correlation with the ad campaign. Due to this reason of time bias, this option was rejected.

Synthetic A/B Testing

When a user accesses a Yahoo! web page, the web page requests the Yahoo! ad server to serve an ad to the user. The ad server decides to choose one ad from thousands of competing ads based upon the requesting web page, profile of the visiting user and campaign's targeting profile. In the synthetic A/B testing method, the system simulates the process used by the ad server to choose the ad to be shown to the user. The system first looks at all the users who visited the Yahoo! network on a given day and then identifies the set of users who could have been exposed to a display campaign as they met all of its targeting criteria. The Campaign targeting criteria are set of rules an advertiser has specified for a campaign. For e.g. an advertiser running ads for sports cars can set the rule that his ad campaign be showed to only the users who are Male in the age group of 18-35, living in Silicon Valley and have shown interest in Sports car. So if the advertiser was the only advertiser targeting this segment of users and purchased a sufficient number of ad impressions, he could have reached all of these users. But in reality only a subset of these users will be exposed to the advertiser's campaign due to other competing campaigns as well as the limit on the advertiser's budgets. From this population of campaign qualified users, we build the test and control group as follow:

- The set of users who are exposed to the campaign make the test group.
- The set of users who qualify but are not exposed to the campaign make the control groups.

The difference in the level of brand awareness among these two groups can be used to measure the Brand Lift. This method is the closest to the real A/B testing as described in first option and was implemented in our system to measure the brand lift. We will describe this method and system built to compute this method in more detail in the following sections.

Algorithm for Synthetic A/B Testing to Compute Brand Lift

One Important factor in computing the Brand Lift from the Display Ad campaign is the memory window or conversion window. A conversion / memory window is defined as the time duration during which the user retains the impact of a campaign after getting exposed to it. In our case, we chose the conversion window as 28 days. Based upon the conversion window of 28 days, here is the high level algorithm to compute the Brand Lift for a single campaign as described in figure 1.

On a given day, compute the set of users who came to the Yahoo Network and met a certain engagement threshold (N). We defined engagement in terms of number of page views consumed by a user. We decided to set a minimum threshold to ensure that a user has had enough chance to get ads served by the Yahoo! ad server.

For all the users in N, find the subset of users who were candidate for getting exposed to a given campaign at least one day in last 28 days (campaignCandidate(N)). A candidate for a cam-

paign is defined as a user whose profile matches with the campaign's targeting profile and he visited the network locations specified as part of the campaign's targeting on a given day.

Compute total number of conversions from the campaignCandidate(N) users campaignCandidateConv(N)) .

Compute the number of conversions from the users exposed to the campaign by building a click stream from last 28 days campaign data (campaignConvExposed(N)) and today's conversion data. In order for an exposure to the campaign to get counted against a conversion, the campaign exposure event needs to happen before the conversion event itself.

From all the campaign candidates from last 28 days campaignCandidate(N), select the users who were exposed to the campaign at least one day in last 28 days (CampaignExposed(N)).

Lift for a given campaign can be computed as:

$Lift(Campaign)=$

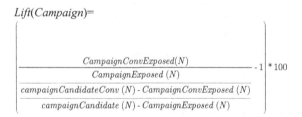

$$\left[\frac{\dfrac{CampaignConvExposed(N)}{CampaignExposed(N)}}{\dfrac{campaignCandidateConv(N) - CampaignConvExposed(N)}{campaignCandidate(N) - CampaignExposed(N)}} - 1 \right] * 100$$

Average Lift across n days is computed as:

$$AvgLift(campaign)= \frac{\sum_{t}^{n}=1\left(l_i * n_i\right)}{\sum_{t}^{n}=1n_i}$$

Where n_i the total is number of candidate on the given day i and l_i is the lift from the campaign on that day.

The algorithm in Figure 1 is for one campaign. The biggest challenge in implementing this system is to scale the system to account for the thousands of campaigns running everyday alongside the new campaigns starting each day. There are millions of users who visits the Yahoo Network every day and get exposed to thousand

Figure 1. Synthetic A/B testing algorithm for computing the Brand Lift. Cookies stand for users.

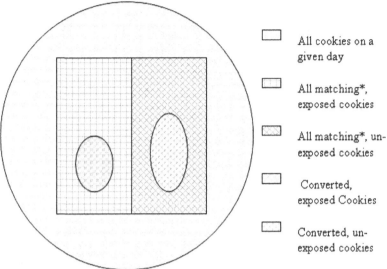

* Matching profile for the past 27 days + 1 conversion (given) day. The profile being matched is as targeted by the 'lifting' campaign.

$$\text{Lift}_{\text{Campaign}} = \left(\frac{\Box \big/ \boxplus}{\Box \big/ \boxtimes} - 1 \right) \times 100\%$$

of ad campaigns from different advertisers, thus generating billions ad impressions & generating terabytes of data. Computing this metrics for each campaign at scale over 28 days of data is a big challenge. The following section describes the system implementing this algorithm. In the image below, the term cookies refers to users.

System to Compute the Brand Lift Based Upon the Algorithm in Figure 1

In Yahoo all user activity data is collected by a Data warehousing system built upon proprietary technologies and stored in the tables sorted by user id and activity timestamp. In addition to other activities, this data also contains the information about a user's exposure to display and search ad

campaigns. Most of these tables are partitioned into multiple files using the hash of user id. The system conceptually described in Figure 2 is a distributed system which runs on the cluster of 30 8-CPU machines with most of the components having a Hadoop like Map/Reduce functionality.

Here are the different parts of the system that run daily to compute the Brand Lift across thousand of campaigns.

Conversion Definition and Mapping

The system provides a UI, where lets the sales team define their conversions and then associate them with the appropriate advertisers. A conversion, as described earlier, is an activity which can describe the brand awareness of a user. A conversion is associated with an advertiser, not

Figure 2. System design of the brand lift computation system

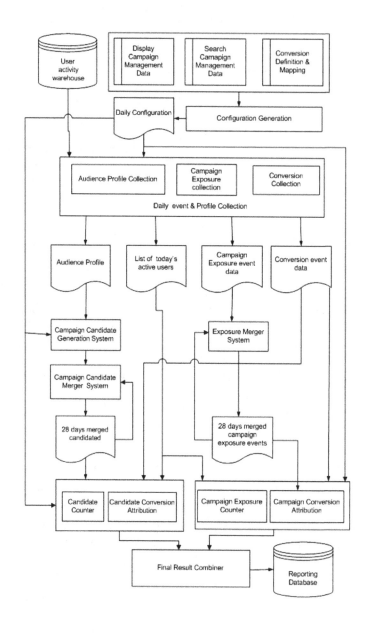

with any specific campaign. Because conversions are proxies to the advertiser brands, hence they do not change from campaign to campaign. Once a conversion is mapped at the advertiser level, all campaign from the advertiser automatically get mapped to this conversion. As discussed earlier there are two types of conversions:

Keyword Search

This conversion definition for a given advertiser is created by selecting the set of the keywords, associated with the advertiser's brand and its product. The system provides a UI for the sales team to create these groups of keywords and associate them with the advertiser.

Sponsored Search Ad Click

This conversion type comprises of campaign ids of sponsored search campaigns running for a given advertiser in the sponsored search ad system. An advertiser is the common link between the campaigns running on display & search side. All the sponsored search ad campaigns for a given advertiser automatically get mapped as conversions for display ad campaigns for computing the brand lift.

In future, when we add new conversion types, this system will be enhanced to create those definitions and mappings

Configuration Generation System

This system generates the configuration information for other components. This System interacts with three systems: Display Campaign Management, Sponsored Search Campaign Management and Conversion Definition & Mapping System to generate the configuration information for computing the daily brand lift for all the active display campaigns in last 28 days. The System generates following information:

- List of Display Campaigns which are active today and their targeted audience profile.
- List of Display campaigns which were active at least one day in last 28 days.
- Definition of all conversions.
- Mapping between display ad campaigns and conversions driven from advertiser level mapping.

Audience Profile Collection System

This component first makes a list of all the users, who met the activity threshold today on the Yahoo

network. Next, the system builds the set of profile attributes for these users with the help of a user profile system. The profile attributes are the same set of attribute as used by the display ad serving system to make ad serving decision. These profile attributes can be classified as:

- **Behavioral**: Computed by the Behavior Targeting system by mining user activities on Yahoo Network. Examples of these attributes are interest in Music, Sports and Real State etc.
- **Demo**: These attributes are self declared attributes of the user e.g. age, gender etc.
- **Geo:** Geo is the geographic location of user when he/she visited the Yahoo network today.
- **Yahoo Network Location:** The pages or sites visited by users today on Yahoo network, where ad server could have served an ad to user.

The system collects all these attributes from various inputs sources and then creates a single output feed with the following format:

- Userid - id used to identify a user
- Geo/Demo profile attributes
- Behavior attributes
- Pages visited today: For e.g. Y!Auto, Y!Music etc.

The output feed is sorted by user id and split across multiple files based upon a hash of user id. This split, across all components, helps in running the system as a distributed system across multiple machines.

Candidate Generation System

The input to this component is Audience profile generated by the Audience Profile Collection System and list of campaigns and their audience targeting profile created by the Configuration generation system. For each user, system matches user's profile with the targeting profile for all of today's active campaigns. The output of the matching algorithm is another feed which comprises of a user & the list of campaigns which this user could have been exposed to. In other words, if a campaign's profile matches to the user's profile, user is deemed to be a candidate for that campaign. The output of this system is of the form:

- Userid
- Date
- campaignID1, campaignID2, campignID3 (candidate for these campaign)

Again this output is also sorted by the userid and split across multiple files with pre defined number of splits based upon the hash of userid.

Campaign Exposure Collection System

This component generates the campaign exposure data for all the active campaign and users, who have network activity above the pre defined threshold. The input to this system is the list of active campaigns for today as generated by the Configuration Generation System as well as data from the proprietary data warehouse. The system reads today's data from the warehouse and extracts all campaign exposure events which belong to the active campaigns. Output of this system looks like:

- Userid
- Timestamp of the exposure
- Campaign ID
- Event Type (view, click)

The output is sorted on the userid and timestamp and split across multiple files with pre defined number of splits based upon the hash of userid.

Conversion Collection System

The input to this system is the data warehouse, list of conversion ids mapped to the campaigns active in last 28 days and definition of all the conversions. The system reads the data from the warehouse and extracts all the conversion for the conversion ids specified in the input file. Conversions can come from multiple sources: the user search activity and sponsored search campaign clicks can be in different source table of the warehouse – and hence the system may need to extract & merge the data from these sources into one output. This design gives the flexibility to add new type of conversions and conversion sources in future. Output of this component is:

- Userid
- Timestamp of conversion
- ConversionID

The output is sorted by userid and timestamp and split across multiple file using the hash of userid.

Candidate Merger System

The input to this system is today's output of candidate generations system and yesterday's output of itself. For the given user, system builds the set of campaign for which this user was a candidate in the last 28 days. If a user was candidate for more than one day, candidature from the latest date is selected. E.g. if a user was candidate for given campaign on dayx and dayx-y, then system will keep the records that user was candidate on datex and record datex-y is removed. Because the system only needs to find out that user was candidate of the campaign at least one day in 28 days, keeping the latest date is sufficient. If after merging, user was candidate for a given campaign only before 28 days, and then the candidature for that campaign is removed from the user candidate set. Output of this component this is:

- Userid datex campaign1 campaign2 campaign3…
- Userid datex-1 campaign4 campaign5 campaign6
- Userid datex-27 campaignx campaign

Where a campaign id for given user can appear only once. The output is sorted by userid and date and split across multiple file using the hash of userid.

Campaign Exposure Merger System

The input to this system is today's output of Campaign exposure collection system, today-28 days output of campaign exposure collection system and yesterday's output of itself. The system generates click stream of user campaign exposure events using following steps:

For all users, subtract the activity of the to-day-28 day from the yesterday merged data. If for a given user, count of ad views or click is zero from a given campaign, that campaign is removed from the click stream.

In the output of previous step, last 27 days data, if a user was exposed to a campaign multiple times or clicked on ad related to campaign multiple times, only latest click and view event is kept in the click stream with latest timestamp. But count of views and clicks is aggregated. E.g. if user was exposed to campaign 10 times before yesterday and again exposed to campaign yesterday at 23:59 pm. Only campaign exposure event from yesterday 23:59 PM is kept in the click stream but ad view count is set to 11.

Campaign exposure events from today are added to the user click stream without any aggregation. This will be important when we count conversions from the user exposed to the campaign and will be explained in more detail the conversion attribute system.

The output of the system is:

- Userid timestamp campaignID #view 0 (view record for campaign))
- Userid timestamp campaignID 1 # clicks (click record for campaign)

The output is sorted by userid and timestamp and just like other dataset is split across multiple files.

Campaign Exposure Counter Systems

The input to this component is output of Campaign exposure merger system and active list of user for today who have activity above required threshold on the network. The component computes the total unique users for each campaign who were exposed to the campaign in last 28 days using the following algorithm:

Filter the campaign exposure merger output for only those users who have activity above certain threshold, today on the Yahoo network.

From the filtered data compute the number of unique users for each campaign using the map/reduce like system.

Output of this system is:

- Campaign ID
- #users

Campaign Candidate Counter System

The input to this component is output of Candidate merger system and active list of user for today who have activity above required threshold on the network. The component computes the total unique users for each campaign, who were candidates for the campaign at least one day in last 28 days and have today's activity on the Yahoo Network above certain threshold using following algorithm:

Filter the candidate merger output for only those users who have activity above certain threshold. This gives all the active campaign candidates who visited the network today with some minimum activity.

From the filtered data compute the number unique users for each campaign candidate using the map/reduce like system.

Output of this system is of the format:

- Campaign ID (candidate)
- #users

Candidate Conversion Attribution System

This system attributes today's conversions to users who were active today on the network and were candidate of the given campaign at least one day in last 28 days. The input to this component is output of the conversion collections system and Candidate Merger System. This system joins the conversions with the Candidate data from last 28 days and computes the number of conversions from the campaign candidates using the following algorithm:

Join the input of the conversion collection system and candidate merger system and only select those users who have both conversion and candidate. Conceptually(it happen in memory) output of this step may looks like;

- Userid advertiserid candidate_row campaign1, campaign2, campaign3,..
- Userid advertiserid conversion_row conversion1,conversion2,conversion3

Once the candidates with conversions are identified for the campaigns from a given advertiser, system computes the crosstab between the conversion and candidate using map/reduce like system. Where mapper builds the output like "candidate ID conversion ID 1" for each user then aggregate the pairs locally and reducer aggregates the output by pairs from all mappers. One map run for each file split. As describes earlier all the

data is split by hash of the user, so it is possible to join multiple data set per split basis.

Output of this system is:

- Campaign ID
- Conversion ID
- #conversions

Conversion Attribution System

This system attributes the conversions for an advertiser, to the display campaigns from the same advertiser on the basis of the exposure that the users who converted had. The exposure to the display campaigns needs to happen before the time of the conversion. It is for this reason that we do not aggregate the campaign exposure events for the day in the exposure merger system. For e.g. if a user was exposed to the campaign at 10:00 am in the morning and 11:00 pm in the evening, by aggregating we could have only kept the event from 11:00 pm. However, if user did the conversion activity at 2:00 pm, we could not have been able to attribute that conversion to the campaign.

The input to this component is output of the conversion collections system and Campaign Exposure Merger System. The system joins these two data sets and builds a click stream in which campaign exposure events and conversion events for a given user are grouped by advertiser and sorted by the timestamp using following algorithm:

Merge the input from the conversion collections system and exposure merger system and only select those users who have both conversion and campaign exposure events.

Once the users with campaign exposures and conversions have been identified, rollup the conversion and campaign events to their advertiser and then build the click stream by sorting the events using the userid, advertiser id and timestamp. This will bring the all the campaign and conversion events for a given user and advertiser together sorted by the time of their occurrence.

Format of the click stream looks like:

- User-id
- Advertiser-id
- Timestamp
- Event type (campaign or conversion)
- Event ID (conversion or camapaign)
- #campaign views (0 in case of conversion event)
- #campaign clicks (0 in case of conversion event)

After the click stream of conversions and campaign exposure events has been built, the system runs the attribution engine to attribute the campaign exposure to the conversions. Attribution engine is also a map/reduce kind of system, where the mapper does the conversion attribution for one user at a time and then the reducer aggregates the output from all the mappers to create the final output. Here is algorithm used by the map side of attribution engine to attribute the conversions to the campaigns:

Set up three in-memory data structures:

- A Hash table, campaignExposureHash with key as campaign ID and value as a structure containing the ad views and clicks from the campaign.
- A last campaign exposure structure with two fields:
  - Campaign ID of last click event, clickCampaignID
  - Campaign ID of last view event, viewCampaignID
- A Hash table, AttributionHash with
  - key: the pair of campaign ID and conversion ID
  - value: structure consisting following members:
- attributions
- Assists
- Ad views
- Ad clicks

Start reading the click stream for a given user and advertiser.

If the type of current event being read is a campaign, update the campaignExposureHash with the ad views or clicks for the campaign. Depending on the of campaign event, update the value of clickCampaignID or viewCampaignID with the current campaign id of the event.

If the type of current event being read is conversion, then do the attribution and generate the output as follow:

- If the clickCampaignID is not 0, it becomes the attributed campaign id for this conversion.
- If the clickCampaignID is 0, then viewCampaignID becomes the attributed campaign id for this conversion.
- All the other campaign IDs in the campaignExposureHash become assists for this conversion and attributed campaign ID becomes main driver for this conversion. For computing brand lift, we only consider assists but attributed campaigns can be used in other reports.

For all the campaigns in the campaignExposureHash, generate the output as follow:

- Campaign ID
- Conversion ID
- #attribution (1 if it is the attributed campaign id, otherwise 0)
- #assist (value will be always 1)
- #campaign views consumed before the conversion
- #campaign clicks before conversion

The output of the previous step is then stored or updated in the AttributionHash keyed on campaign id and Conversion id pair as follow:

- If the pair does not exist in the hash table, add the pair and associated value structure to the hash table with value from current attribution.

- If pair exists, then take the existing value structure and update it as follow:
  - Update the values of #attribution and #assists by adding the new values. E.g. if the current value for attribution in the structure was 20, after this update it will become 21 if it was attributed campaign ID, otherwise will remain 20.

Ad views and clicks are not added to the existing values; rather the existing values in the structure are replaced by the values from the current attribution. This is because these are cumulative values. For e.g. if the user had been exposed to 20 ad views for a campaign before the first conversion, the value in existing structure for ad views will be 20 for this conversion and campaign pair. If the user gets exposed to 10 additional ad views before the next conversion, the total ad views will be 30 for the campaign. If we were to just add ad views to the existing value, the total will read 50 ad views for 2 conversions. But actually it took 30 ad views to achieve 2 conversions. That is why the ad views are replaced and not added.

Finally when the userid, advertiser id pair changes in the click stream, all the keys and values in the AttributionHash are streamed out and in memory structures are reset to an empty state. The attribution output is then aggregated per mapper and given to the reducer to generate the final output. All the in memory data structure resets to original values.

Final output of the Conversion Attribution system looks like:

- Campaign ID
- Conversion ID
- #attribution
- #assists

- #campaign views
- #campaign clicks

Output of this component, in addition to brand lift computation, can be used for multiple other reports in the system, which is outside the scope of this chapter.

Final Result Combiner

This component takes the output of Conversion Attribution, Candidate Conversion Attribution, Candidate Counter and Campaign Exposure counter and produces the final result ready to be loaded in the database and being reported. Output of this components looks like:

- Advertiserid
- Campaign ID
- Conversion ID
- #candidate user Count (from Campaign Candidate Counter System)
- #Exposure user count (from Campaign Exposure Counter System)
- #attribution (from Conversion Attribution System)
- #assists (from Conversion Attribution System)
- #candidate conversion (from Candidate Conversion Attribution System)
- #campaign view (from Conversion Attribution System)
- #campaign clicks (from Conversion Attribution System)

Database and WS API

The output of the Final Result combiner is loaded into the database. A Web service API then reads the data from the database and reports the daily and aggregated lift metrics for a given campaign using the formula described in the algorithm section.

FUTURE DIRECTIONS

Although this system is a pretty good start to measure the brand lift driven from the display brand campaigns, there are multiple enhancement being planned to make candidate and campaign exposure population look alike beyond just the campaign targeting attributes. One of the ideas is to segment the user by their level of the activity on Yahoo network. Other enhancement is on same line, but measures the level of engagement on the conversion domain. E.g. if we are using search as conversions, we want to make sure that both exposed and unexposed have similar level of activity on Yahoo search.

SIMILAR SYSTEMS TO MEASURE THE BRAND LIFT

In the absence of an automated advanced BI system such as the one described above, brand lift from an advertisement campaign is measured by computing the brand recall metrics. *Brand Recall is the extent to which a brand name is recalled as a member of a brand, product or service class, as distinct from brand recognition. (Wikipedia, 2010)*

The brand recall metrics is computed by conducting a survey before & after an advertisement campaign's run period. If the brand recall is greater in the post advertisement campaign survey as compared to the pre advertisement campaign survey, then that difference is the metric which provides the lift from the brand campaign. One example of such a system is the Brand Survey Lift, which is provided by the Comscore, Inc to its advertisers. Comscore describes this system as follows - *"AdEffx Brand Survey Lift™ (BSL) is the industry's most comprehensive and trusted survey solution for measuring a campaign's branding effectiveness.".(ComScore, 2010)* Another example of a similar survey based system is called Adometer, which is offered by Dynamic Logic. Adometer is defined by the Dynamic Logic

as: *"Now, more than ever, marketers are looking for ways to optimize their advertising campaigns based on real-time results, enabling creative and media changes to be made while the campaign is still live. Dynamic Logic's quick-response solution, called Adometer®, allows for an early "check" on an online campaign's performance using real-time attitudinal and demographic data."(Dynamic Logic, 2010)*

Although these are good to have third party systems and are widely used for measuring the effectiveness of big spend brand campaigns, they suffer from the same problem as the options we explored to compute the Brand Lift. For e.g. just like ideal A/B testing option, these system also need some set up for each campaign before the campaign starts running. This makes them very expensive, hard to scale as well as prone to manual error. Similarly, just like pre and post campaign tracking issues we explored, these surveys also ignore a very important factor, the time.

Based upon the above analyses, the system described & built by Yahoo! is far superior in both in terms of quality of metrics computations as well as manageability as compared to the survey based systems offered by other competing solutions. It can compute a high quality Brand Lift metric for a large set of campaigns without any manual intervention.

CONCLUSION

In this chapter we described the methodology to measure the lift in Brand Awareness from a Display Ad campaign and a system to compute this metric. This system is a great help to any sales team, when they are working with advertisers to show them the value of their marketing investments and want to get bigger return business. With little effort this system can also be extended beyond online display advertisement campaign to other marketing methods.

REFERENCES

American Marketing Association. (2007). Definition of marketing. *American Marketing Association*. Retrieved July 24, 2010, from http:/ www.marketingpower.com/ AboutAMA/ Pages/ DefinitionofMarketing.aspx.

Business Dictionary. (2010). Call to action. *Business Dictionary*. Retrieved July 24, 2010 from http:// www.businessdictionary.com/ definition/ call-to-action-CTA.html

ComScore. (2010). Brand survey lift. *ComScore, Inc*. Retrieved November 13, 2010 from http:// www.comscore.com/ Products_Services/ Product_Index/ Brand_Survey_Lift

Daddi, B. (2010). Kantar Media reports U.S. advertising expenditures increased 5.1% in the 1st quarter of 2010. *Kantar Media News*. Retrieved July 24, 2010, from http:// www.kantarmediana. com/ news/ 05262010.htm

Dynamic Logic. (2010). Adometer. *Dynamic logic, Inc*. November 13, 2010 from http:// www. dynamiclogic.com/ na/ products/ Adometer/

Kotler, P., Armstrong, G., Wong, V., & Saunders, J. (2008). *Marketing defined. Principles of marketing* (5th ed., p. 7). Upper Saddle River, NJ: Pearson Education, Prentice Hall.

Sullivan, D. (2010). Search engine marketing definition. *Search Engine Land*. Retrieved July 25, 2010 from http:// searchengineland.com/ does-sem-seo-cpc-still-add-up-37297.

Wikipedia. (2010). A/B testing definition. *Wikipedia, the free encyclopedia*. Retrieved July 24, 2010 from http:// en.wikipedia.org/ wiki/ A/ B_testing.

Wikipedia. (2010). Brand awareness. *Wikipedia, the free encyclopedia*. Retrieved November 13, 2010 from http://en.wikipedia.org/wiki/ Brand_awareness

KEY TERMS AND DEFINITIONS

Advertisement: Vehicle for doing the marketing. It can be a message written on billboard or a video message played on TV or interactive graphical images displayed online on internet.

Advertiser: Company who is running the marketing campaign.

Brand Awareness: Positive impact of the brand on consumer, which bias user buying decision in favor of brand, when multiple competing products are present in a buying decision,

Conversion: A desired activity performed by the user after receiving the marketing message from the advertiser.

Conversion Attribution: The process of giving credit to a marketing campaign for a conversion.

Conversion Window: A time period in which a user still retains the impact of the marketing message and conversions happening in this time period can be attributed to the marketing message.

Conversion Window: A time period in which a user still retains the impact of the marketing message and conversions happening in this time period can be attributed to the marketing message.

Marketing: activity of getting the word out about a product or company to the targeted consumers.

Marketing Campaign: A set of advertisements across multiple channels used to market some specific product of the company is calling marketing campaign.

Chapter 11
Suggested Model for Business Intelligence in Higher Education

Zaidoun Alzoabi
Arab International University, Syria

Faek Diko
Arab International University, Syria

Saiid Hanna
Arab International University, Syria

ABSTRACT

BI is playing a major role in achieving competitive advantage in almost every sector of the market, and the higher education sector is no exception. Universities, in general, maintain huge databases comprising data of students, human resources, researches, facilities, and others. Data in these databases may contain decisive information for decision making. In this chapter we will describe a data mining approach as one of the business intelligence methodologies for possible use in higher education. The importance of the model arises from the reality that it starts from a system approach to university management, looking at the university as input, processing, output, and feedback, and then applies different business intelligence tools and methods to every part of the system in order to enhance the business decision making process. The chapter also shows an application of the suggested model on a real case study at the Arab International University.

INTRODUCTION

Business intelligence (BI) is composed of several technologies, methods, and tools that may support the middle and top management in the decision making process. Almost all industries have already started to utilize BI tools, methods, and technologies to achieve competitive advantage through the utilization of data piles it has cumulated throughout its history. These huge amounts of data required special manipulation in order to enhance the decision making process. The BI approach helps in building up multiple views of the overall system of the organization comprising customers' suppliers, competitors, and human resources data (Hart, 2007).

DOI: 10.4018/978-1-61350-050-7.ch011

Data mining is considered an advanced tool in the theme of business intelligence (Folorunso, Ogunde, vincent, & Salako, 2010). Data mining helps mainly in the strategic applications of institutions. Data mining could be a very powerful tool for building, implementing higher education strategies.

The need for BI to achieve competitive advantage in higher education has gained momentum in the last decade (Dell'aquila et. al (Carlo DELL'AQUILA, 2008) (Javed et. al, 2008). The attractiveness of BI implementation in universities is due to many reasons. First, universities are facing huge competition and they need better understanding of the business forces in order to respond effectively to the already dynamic industry (Javed et. al, 2008). Second, universities always require tools to predict student performance, employment paths, course selection etc. and all these could be greatly supported by business intelligence applications (Kohavi, 2000). Third, like any other business, universities require to do cost-benefit analysis, trend analysis, value chain analysis, and so forth, which could be supported by BI applications.

In this paper we will describe a general model of university management, based on system theory, where the university is seen as input, processing, output, and feedback. Then, we will see how business intelligence in general and data mining in specific could be utilized in every part of the system, with a practical case from Arab International University.

The rest of the paper is organized as follows. First, we will start with a literature review focusing on the utilization of BI in enhancing university management, with literature focusing on every part of the university process, and then we will have a case study from Arab International University, where every part of the system is investigated with a separate case.

LITERATURE REVIEW

Data mining is a set of systems that are really embedded in a larger BI system (Apte, et. al, 2002). Data mining itself is made up of several analytical, mathematical, and statistical techniques. Before applying these methods to data, the data has to be typically organized into history repositories, known as data warehouses (Luan, 2004).

Data mining has been used in several industries such as financial, telecommunication, and education (Delavari and Beikzadeh, 2008). Education organizations have shown interest in data mining due to the potential data mining can provide in this domain. For example, (Erdoğan and Timor, 2005) used data mining in studying the effect of admission test results on students performance in higher education. (Shaeela, et al 2010). (Luan, 2002) studied the potential data mining can provide to the decision makers in higher education.

Applications of data mining in higher education can be roughly categorized into three main categories: input, output, and processing. That is, studying the use of data mining in analyzing input, processing, and output data.

In higher education input data mining we can see several studies. For example, (Superby et al, 2006) studied freshmen students to identify characteristics of students who are more likely to have successful study record. (Kovačić, 2010) tried to identify early predictors of students performance in universities, focusing on socio-demographic variables (age, gender, ethnicity, education, work status, and disability) and study environment (course program and course block), that may influence persistence or dropout of students at the Open Polytechnic of New Zealand. Using CHAID tree and CART trees he found that the most important factors that help separate successful from unsuccessful students are ethnicity, course program and course block. (Yu et al., 2007) used a data mining approach to identify predictors of retention among first year students enrolled at Arizona State University. Using the classification tree based on an entropy tree-splitting criterion they concluded that 'cumulated earned hours' was the most important factor contributing to retention. Gender and ethnic origin were not identified as significant. (Kovačić, 2010) has also investigated the students' dropout rates with the help of data mining techniques using classification trees and feature selection. (Al-Radaidehet. Al, 2006) used classification trees to predict the final grade among undergraduate students of the Information Technology & Computer Science Faculty, at Yarmouk University in Jordan. High school grade contributed the most to the separation of students in different clusters. Among background variables gender (both students and lecturers), place of residence, and funding were used to grow the classification tree.

In higher education process i.e. delivering the education process, several researchers tried to use data mining to identify factors affecting student performance, attendance habits, study habits, teaching workload, student satisfaction etc. For example, (Baepler and Murdoch, 2010) used academic analytics, which is a set of data selection methods, statistical methods, and predictive models, to create intelligence about students, instructors, and/or administrative staff behavior. They found that the use of academic analytics could be a great opportunity to assess Scholarships of Teaching and Learning SoTL strategies. They found that academic analytics, educational data mining, and Course Management System audits can begin to navigate through the noise and provide SoTL researchers with a new set of tools to understand and act on a growing stream of useful data, although they admit that these systems are still in their inception phase. (Luan, 2004), using neural newroks, CART, and CR5.0, studied the application of data mining in higher education to learn more about students' performance, and to help the top management in resource allocation and

decision making. (Shaeela, et al 2010) used data mining techniques to predict students' final grades and graduation average to help in the academic advising for students, and the overall decision making process for the top management. (Tudor, Cărbureanu,2007) used data mining techniques in order to predict number of graduates according to the characteristics and number of students admitted. (Beikzadeh, Delavari,2004) used data mining in order to enhance the higher education processes and procedures, through analyzing traditional processes in the higher education. (Merceron, and Yacef, 2007) used classification as one of data mining techniques in order to measure the effectiveness of training and internships on the overall skill development of students. ((M, 2004)) used data mining techniques to group students into different student-related characteristics, so that it enhances students' performance measures, and accordingly enhance students' performance prediction process and consequently enhance student performance.

The use of data mining in understanding higher education output was also under focus of many researches. The aim of these studies was to understand factors impacting graduates' characteristics. For example, (Bresfelean, 2007) used classification learning experiments to predict of the students' choice in continuing their education with post university studies (master degree, Ph.D. studies etc.). (Ranjan and Khalil, 2007) suggest the use of data mining in predicting the students' learning outcomes through the analysis of students', courses', and instructors' characteristics. (Ramaswami and Bhaskaran, 2010) used CHAID to predict several educational perspectives, including the post graduation profession. (Ranjan and Khalil, 2007) used data mining techniques to study the decision making process in universities based on three levels: admission, course delivery, and post graduation delivery.

We found from the literature that despite the intensive use of business intelligence in general and data mining in specific in higher education,

Figure 1. Higher education model

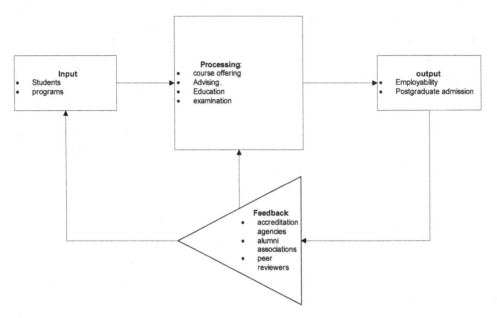

there is still less publications in using these techniques in predicting one of the most important indicators of higher education quality, which is employability. Also there is little consensus on what is the best approach for the use of data mining and business intelligence in higher education.

SUGGESTED MODEL FOR BI IN HIGHER EDUCATION

In this section we will introduce a model for BI in higher education. Our model is built upon system theory, through visualizing universities as a system with input, processing, output, and feedback.

Inputs in universities could be seen as students admitted to the universities, and study curriculum applied on these students.

Processing in universities is the process of learning and education. Here the main components are the education process including: course offering, advising, teaching and learning, and examination.

Output in universities is mainly graduates who seek job in highly ranked businesses, and/ or admission in post graduate studies for undergraduate studies.

Feedback in universities is built mainly from accreditation agencies, alumni associations, and from peer reviewers giving consultations on program and course design. Figure 1 shows the suggested model.

Our aim is to use business intelligence tools in order to maximize output through an extensive process of analysis, design, and improvement of input and processing.

In the following we describe our approach for every one of the four major components of the higher education model, providing an example from the Arab International University.

Use of Business Intelligence in Input Analysis

Admission process in universities is of sensitive importance as it decides the type of customers the university will get over the following years.

Table 1. BI suggested tool

Input data	Source of data	BI techniques	Objectives
Student- related data: age, high school marks, admission test data, gender, type of high school grade, student country of origin, financial independence, marital status, parents education, etc.	Admission computerized systems Pre-university computerized systems	Cluster analysis. Statistical techniques. Slice and dice.	Identify best admission criteria. Predict student performance in university based on admission data.
Program-related data: total number of credits, average study period, type of the program, faculty offering the program, attractiveness of the program, market information of the program (how graduates of this program are placed in the market), competitors data, syndicates and chambers data, etc.	Academic system. Syndicates, competitors, and chambers websites. Market surveys. Alumni systems.	Slice and dice, web mining, statistical methods, and artificial intelligence	Understand program attractiveness. Enhance programs to match market needs.

Proper admission criteria will help the university in picking students with high likelihood of success.

Several studies suggested the use of data mining and business intelligence tools to help either select the "right" students for programs or to predict students' performance in specific programs.

For example (Simpson, 2006) that the most important factors in predicting students' performance are the course level, followed by credit rating of a course, previous education, course program, socio-economic status, gender and age.

(Kotsiantis et. al 2004) used key demographic variables and assignment marks in the supervised machine learning algorithms (decision trees, artificial neural networks, naïve Bayes classifier, instance-based learning, logistic regression and support vector machines) to predict student's performance at the Hellenic Open University.

(Vandamme et al 2007) used decision trees, neural networks and linear discriminant analysis, to find that previous education, number of hours of mathematics, financial independence, and age are the best predictors of students' performance. However, gender, parent's education and occupation, and marital status have little impact on students' performance.

From the previous discussion we can see that use of data mining, artificial intelligence, neural networks, statistical techniques, decision trees, and classification, could be used to predict students' performance in universities.

BI tools could be used to answer one or more of the following questions:

- What are the characteristics of the students who are likely to apply for a specific program?
- What are the characteristics of programs that attract students?
- How effective is (are) admission test(s)?
- What are the admission predictors of students' performance?

Table 1 shows type of data that could be used, suggested BI tools to be used with these data, and reason.

CASE STUDY FROM AIU

For this part we will see how data mining can help us improve admission process based on the findings of IT faculty students' data analysis. The sample is composed of 999 students in the faculty of IT engineering. The aim of the study is to analyze relationship between students' performance in the university on one side, and their high school marks and English placement test on the other side.

The source of the data is the academic system where the following students' data are captured:

- University AGPA
- Number of passed credits in the university
- Gender
- Source country of high school
- High school average
- Type of high school

In the following sections we discuss the findings on the basis of the previously mentioned data.

RELATIONSHIP BETWEEN HIGH SCHOOL MARKS AND STUDENTS PERFORMANCE IN THE UNIVERSITY

Correlation between high school marks and university's AGPA in six faculties is shown in figure 2.

From the figure we can see that there is moderate relationship between students' school performance and their performance in the university,

and that IT engineering faculty has the strongest relationship amongst the six faculties. The weakest relationship is in fine arts- a faculty that depends on talent only.

Summarizing the data for only 4th year students as an example, we can see that correlation with high school marks is 0.39.

If we want to go deeper with our analysis to see the individual and collective relationship between high school marks and English, math, and physics for the 4th year students reveals that stronger correlations exist with math and physics, as seen in figure 3.

Going deeper in our analysis we can see the effect of the country of origin of the high school on the correlations, as seen in figure 4.

Slicing the data on the basis of gender reveals that female students have higher correlations than male students as shown in figure 5-a and figure 5-b.

Also, we can see the correlation on the basis of the type of high school. In Syria there are two types of high school that are allowed to be enrolled in IT engineering faculty; industrial and scientific. Figures 6 & 7 show the correlations for students from the two types.

Figure 2. Correlations between AGPA and high school grade in all faculties at AIU

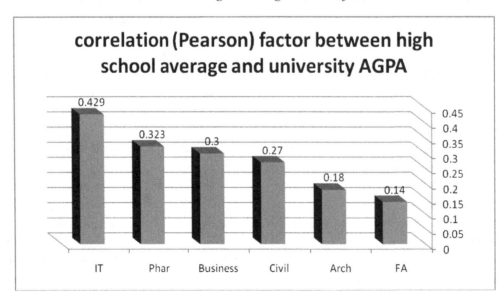

RELATION BETWEEN STUDENTS' PERFORMANCE IN ENGLISH PLACEMENT TEST AND STUDENTS' PERFORMANCE IN THE UNIVERSITY

Other peace of data that could be used, is the English admission test used by the university. The English placement test positions the students in L0, L1, L2, L3, or exempted. The later is quite rare and is ignored. Here we can use the ANOVA test on the basis of AGPA and English level. The following figure shows the results regarding this criterion.

From the figure 8 we can see that classifying students according to their English placement test reveals that the students could be roughly grouped into two groups L2 and L3 whose performance is better than the other L0, and L1 group.

From the previous discussion we can conclude that:

Figure 3. Correlations of high school marks with AGPA for all students

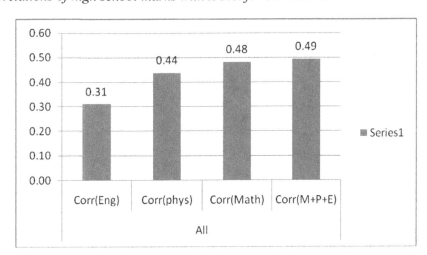

Figure 4. Correlations of high school marks with AGPA for students having high school from gulf countries

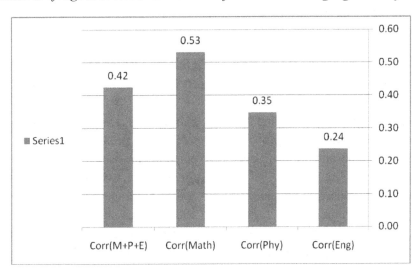

Figure 5. Correlations for female students (above) and correlations for male students(below)

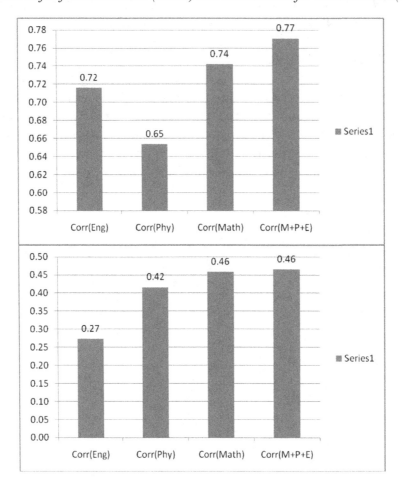

- The use of data mining tool from the BI set could be very helpful in devising the admission criteria based on the historical data.
- The use of slice and dice technique will help in devising admission criteria for every set of potential students. That is, math is the most decisive factor in deciding students performance in the university followed by physics marks and English placement test results.
- The analysis could be used in conjunction with predication algorithms to say for example that a female, who has high math and physics marks, from scientific high school, and who is placed in L2 or L3 in

the English placement test will have a high probability of satisfactory achievement in the university.

Use of Business Intelligence in the Process Analysis

Universities are becoming more and more interested in predicting students' and graduates' performance (Luan, 2004), and hence identifying for example, which students will join specific course programs i.e. course offering, (Kalathur, 2006), which students are likely to stay or drop out (Yu et al, 2010), which students are likely to face troubles in certain course or program, which

Figure 6. Correlations for 4th year students who are from scientific high school back ground

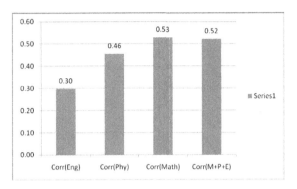

Figure 7. Correlations for 4th year students who are from industrial high school back ground

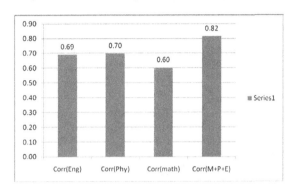

course students are likely to drop out a course (Vandamme et al., 2007), etc..

Business intelligence could be used in various issues regarding the education process. As mentioned in the overall model figure, BI could be used in various issues as shown in Table 2.

CASE STUDY FROM AIU

In the education process, AIU has experience in the use of business intelligence techniques to:

- Predict course offering.
- Estimation of instructors' student satisfaction.

Figure 8. Students grouped according to their English test results

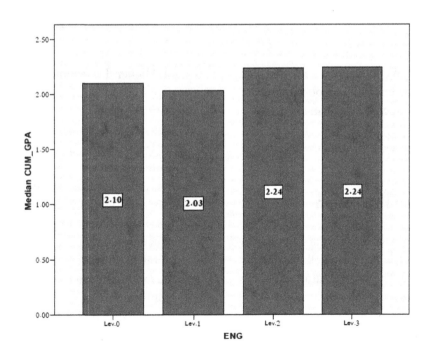

Table 2. BI usage in higher education

Input data	Source of data	BI techniques	Objectives
Students who passed the prerequisite of the course. Students who failed the course. Number of students who registered in the course in previous semesters.Number of class rooms available. Availability of tenured and non-tenured instructors. Significance of the course (how many courses for which a course is a prerequisite).	Academic system (registration and examination systems). Facilities system (infra structure database). HR system	Decision trees, Association rules. The K-Means algorithm. Genetic algorithms. Linear models Instance-based learning. Numeric prediction. Clustering. Bayesian networks	Course offering estimation
Exam results. Students' info. Instructors' info. Course info	Academic system. HR database.	Classification techniques. Prediction algorithms.	Mining examination results: What are the characteristics of students who will likely do well in certain exams? What are the characteristics of students who will likely fail the exams? What are the characteristics of instructors who will have unusual exam results (high success or failure rates).
Students' data: age, gender, faculty, specialization, type of high school, high school marks, English level, study year, AGPA, course individual marks, etc. Instructors' data: age, gender, faculty, specialization, country of graduation,			Understanding Student satisfaction factors

- Prediction of overall student performance.
- Analysis of student satisfaction parameters.
- Analysis of student performance

In the following we will see how to analyze all these.

Course Offering Prediction

Course offering plays a major role in university's effectiveness and efficiency, as well as students overall performance. The factors that affect course offering are as follows:

- Student load that goes between 12 credits and 18 credits (as per Syrian Ministry of Higher Education regulations), which could go up to 21 credits if student has a GPA above 3
- Instructors teaching load that ranges from 10 to 14 credits a week according to the professor rank
- Previous student satisfaction with the course in previous semesters
- Previous student experience with the instructor claiming the course
- Number of students failed the `course in the previous semester
- Number of the students who passed the prerequisite(s) of the course

- Number of the students expected to pass the prerequisite of the course in the current semester, on the basis of the midterm exam
- Student English level
- Previous passing rate of the course
- Course level
- Number of courses that this course is a prerequisite for

Each semester these data are fed into the data mining system of the university in an automatic way to predict how many students are likely to register for the course if it is offered in the next semester. The system is giving an accuracy rate averaging around 85%, with the following strong indicators:

If the course has previous high passing rates, and the instructor has high student satisfaction rate, then the course has high demand among students.

If the student has high GPA, and Exempted of English, and has passed average or above credits, then he/she is likely to register for all possible courses, he or she has passed their prerequisites.

Understanding Student Satisfaction Factors

Needless to say that universities' interest in student satisfaction is clearly increasing ((Jurkowitsch S., 2006), et al. 2006). This interest has increased due to many reasons. First, student satisfaction is a very important method to gain feedback in order to improve the education process through improving teaching material, teaching methodology, and assessment tools (Baek S. a., 2008); Yum, 2008). Second, student satisfaction helps in increasing students' retention rates (Baek 2008; Schreiner, 2009), which in turn improves students' loyalty (Schreiner, 2009). Third, student satisfaction affects student motivation, which helps in assuring students' achievement of required outcomes (Schreiner, 2009). Fourth, student satisfaction enhances overall university's reputation, which yields better profitability taking into consideration

that students are becoming more perceived as customers. Schreiner states that "… if they [students] have positive feelings about their experiences and would make the same decisions again, then an institution's word-of-mouth reputation remains strong and can contribute to future success in recruiting and retaining students" (Schreiner, 2009). Finally, student satisfaction is strongly emphasized in all accreditation manuals published by accreditation agencies (see for example QAA website).

All this has led to a lot of research to understand the factors that impact the student satisfaction rates. This pushed the university to continuously assess student satisfaction and measure factors that could positively or negatively impact it. The university has an online survey tool that allows the student to rate their instructors every semester. The survey is published on the website immediately after announcing the results of the midterm. The questionnaire measures three components of student satisfaction. These are: delivery of the class and teaching methodologies used, commitment of the instructor, and the instructor's fairness in grading the exams. The results of the survey are then fed to the data mining system, including the following data:

- Student personal info:, age, major, gender, nationality,
- Student academic record: passed credits, accumulative grade average point, semester grade average point, midterm exam result, quiz1 and quiz2 results, high school marks, admission test results, type of high school (vocational, scientific, literature, etc.) previous marks with the instructor, previous rating of the student to the instructor, and student course attendance habits.
- Course specifics: course credits, course level, type of the course (university requirements, faculty requirements, or major requirements), compulsory or elective), practical or theoretical, language used in the course, etc.

- Instructor info: age, gender, nationality, salary, rank, tenured or non-tenured, graduation country, university of graduation, previous experience with the course (how many times the instructor taught the course), years in the university, teaching experience, previous or current experience in the professional field, etc.
- Class specifics: class size (number of students in the course), and class timing.

As we can notice, there are tons of data about many different things that are related to a single subject, which is student satisfaction that is very important for all types of higher education institutions. Hence, dealing with all these data, using traditional statistical methods, could be time consuming, subject to human-related errors, costly, and almost impossible. This has led the university to use more sophisticated techniques such as data mining. Moreover, dealing with these data implies using multiple databases such as academic system, human resources system, and facilities system, at the same time. These databases have different platforms, which lead to the creation of a single data warehouse containing all these data. The application of C&RT algorithm on these data has led to the following findings:

- Instructors graduating from America, United Kingdom, and Germany have better student ratings.
- Younger instructors have better student ratings disregard of the salary.
- Instructors of smaller classes have better student ratings.
- There is no correlation between marks students obtain and their rank of their professors, especially for junior and senior students.
- Morning classes are more likely to have higher ratings than afternoon classes.

Dealing with University Output

Employability is considered one of the most important indicators to measure the successfulness of universities in achieving their quality goals (Mason et. al, 2006). Consequently, measuring factors that impact employability is a decisive factor for universities to enhance their study programs and equip their students with the required core or specific skills, competences, and knowledge. This was another attraction for researchers to use business intelligence and data mining in order to understand this concept in a better manner. For example, (Alboni et. al, 2008) have used clustering and causal inference methods using semi-automatic Data Mining approaches, in order to "create a system for evaluating the performance of the Provincial Job Centers, whereby the success of policies designed to guarantee equal employment opportunities can be duly monitored. Our variable target is represented by the number of people hired on full-time contracts."

Dealing with graduates databases could be one of the most difficult issues, researchers in the higher education field may face due to:

The effect of the economic state on the employability factors: for example, in economics facing troubled situations, such as those faced the world during the financial crisis in 2009, graduates may face difficulties in finding job, disregard of their skills or competences. On the other hand, booming economies may create ample opportunities for graduates, with no regard to their skills.

Some countries- such as Syria- face gender issues in employability. For example, many female graduates may not search for job although there is opportunity for them. One other factor could play role –again in Syria- is the military service which could prevent male graduates from finding jobs.

Many graduates do not search for job, and rather search for post graduate studies to continue their master of PhD. Study.

All these factors play role in employability, and data mining could create a great opportunity

Table 3. BI usage for the university

Input data	Source of data	BI techniques	Objectives
Graduates info: age, gender, major, grade point average, graduation rank, family status, financial status, and years in the university. Program specifics: number of universities offering the major, development and maturity of the program, total duration of the program, amount of practical work and internship involved, and program design. Program management: specifics of the instructors involved in the program. Economic situation: status of the economy, inflation or recession, interest rate, size of the sector the program is serving, and demand in the labor market	Academic system Government and non-government organization databases. Alumni data bases. Partnerships databases (databases of market partners) HR system	Decision trees, Association rules. The K-Means algorithm. Genetic algorithms. Linear models Instance-based learning. Numeric prediction. Clustering. Bayesian networks	Employability estimation

to analyze all these factors, leading to a better understanding of this subject. Table 3 shows how business intelligence in this regard.

Questions that could be answered by business intelligence could be:

- What are the characteristics of students who will likely find job within specific period?
- What are the characteristics of the firms that have high probability to hire our graduates?
- What are the conditions that affect the graduates' ability to find job?
- What is the expected salary of graduate carrying specific characteristics?
- What are the economic conditions that prevent or support the graduates in finding jobs?
- Which programs those are if offered will likely attract students?
- What are the characteristics of programs producing students with high salaries?

Unfortunately, the Arab International University is five years old, and has graduated only

a couple of dozens of graduates, which is not sufficient to provide statistical confidence in the results that are obtained from the system. This is however, a longitudinal study that requires no less than two to three years to accumulate data for more accurate analysis.

However, a classification study has led to some results that could be interesting. We found that a male, from finance and banking major, with a grade average point exceeding 3, and with high marks in communication skills will find job before graduation.

CONCLUSION

In this paper we examined the use of business intelligence in higher education. Our focus was on the use of data mining in understanding the three major input, processing, and output components of the high education system. The focus was on admission, education delivery, and graduation processes.

On the basis of a system that was developed at Arab International University, we demonstrated a case, in which data mining proved very powerful in estimating various issues that matter to the higher education organization.

Connecting databases that exist in almost all higher education institutions will help in utilizing the vast amount of data. The data about thousands of students, instructors, programs, regulations, job market, and economic status, stay promising for the decision making process that if utilized in an effective and efficient manner will be of great help in allocating universities resources and in the strategic planning process.

Several dishoarding and data techniques could be used. In specific, clustering, association, and statically analysis proved very powerful in predicting student performance, instructor performance, employability, and students' persistence in the university.

However, many of the findings of this research remain questionable due to the reality that they were all applied in one university. Further research should be done in different environments and contexts in order to test these findings. One more limitation of the research is the fact that amount of graduates in the university under interest is small, and more research should be carried out after the more graduates are there.

REFERENCES

Adeel Javed, M. U. (2008). *Conceptual model for decision support system based business intelligence OLAP tool for universities in context of e-learning*. World Congress on Engineering and Computer Science. San Francisco, USA.

Al-Radaideh Qasem, A., & Al-Shawakfa, E. M.-N. (2006). *Mining Student Data Using Decision Trees*. The 2006 International Arab Conference on Information Technology (ACIT'2006). Amman.

Apte, C. L., Liu, B., Pednault, E. P. D., & Smyth, P. (2002). Business applications of data mining. *Communications of the ACM –CACM, 45*(8), 49-53.

Ayesha Shaeela, M. T. (2010). Data Mining Model for Higher Education System. *European Journal of Scientific Research, 43*(1), 24–29.

Baek, S. (2006). *A review of course evaluation in colleges and universities*. Educational Development.

Baek, S. (2008). Multi-level analysis of the effects of student and course characteristics on student course evaluation: Focused on the undergraduate liberal education program. *Journal of Educational Evaluation*.

Baepler, & Murdoch (2004). *Data mining For a Web-based educational system*. Department of Computer Science and Engineering, Michigan State University.

Carlo Dell'Aquila, F. (2008). Business intelligence systems: A comparative analysis. *WSEAS transactions on Information Science & applications*.

Chong Ho Yu, & S. D.-P. (2007). A data-mining approach to differentiate predictors of retention. Educause Southwest Conference, Austin, Texas.

Delavari, N., Phon-Amnuaisuk, S., & Beikzadeh, M. R. (2008). Data mining application in higher learning institutions. *Informatics in Education, 7*(1), 31–54.

Erdogan, S. Z., & Timor, M. (2005). A data mining application in a student database. *Journal of Aeronautics and Space Technologies, 2*(2), 53–57.

Garcia, E., Romero, C., Ventura, S., & Calders, T. (2007). *Drawbacks and solutions of applying association rule mining in learning management systems* (pp. 15–25).

Hart, M., Esat, F., Rocha, M., & Khatieb, Z. (2007). Introducing Students to Business Intelligence: Acceptance and Perceptions of OLAP Software. *Issues in Informing Science and Information Technology, 4.*

Jing, L. (2004). *Data mining applications in higher education.* Retrieved June 2010, from http:// www. spss.com/ home_page/ wp2.htm: http:// www.spss. com /home_page/wp2.htm

Jurkowitsch S., Vignali, C., & Kaufmann, H.-R. (2006). A student satisfaction model for Austrian higher education providers considering aspects of marketing communications. *Innovative Marketing, 2*(3).

Kohavi, R., Rothleder, N. J., & Simoudis, E. (2002). Emerging trends in business Analytics. *Communications of the ACM, 45*(8), 45–48.

Kotsiantis, S. B., Pierrakeas, C. J., Zaharakis, I. D., & Pintelas, P. E. (2003). *Efficiency of machine learning techniques in predicting students' performance in distance learning systems. Recent advances in mechanics and related fields.* Greece: University of Patras.

Kovačić, J. (2010). Academic analytics and data mining in higher education. *International Journal for the Scholarship of Teaching and Learning.*

Kovačić, J. (2010). Early prediction of student success: Mining students enrolment data. In *Proceedings of Informing Science & IT Education Conference (InSITE) 2010.*

Ranjan, J., & Khalil, S. (2007). Application of knowledge management in management education: A conceptual framework. *Journal of Theoretical and Applied Information Technology.*

Schreiner, L. (2009). Retrieved October 2010, from https://www.noellevitz.com/.../ LinkingStudentSatis0809.pdf.

Simpson, O. (2006). Predicting student success in open and distance learning. *Open Learning, 21*(2), 125–138.

Superby, J. F., Vandamme, J.-P., & Meskens, N. (2006). Determination of Factors Influencing the Achievement of the First-year University Students using Data Mining Methods. *Workshop on Educational Data Mining.*

Vasile, B. P. (2007).mpra.ub.uni-muenchen.de/.../ Data_Mining_Applications_in_Higher_Education_and _Academic_Intelligence_Management.pdf. Retrieved october 2010, from mpra. ub.uni-muenchen.de/.../ Data_Mining_Applications_in_Higher _Education_and_Academic_ Intelligence_Management.pdf

Yum, S. (2008). Validating students' ratings of teaching scale and analyzing multilevel models. *Journal of Educational Evaluation.*

ADDITIONAL READING

Alnoukari, M., & Alhussan, W. (2008). *Using data mining techniques for predicting future car market demand.* International Conference on Information & Communication Technologies: From Theory to Applications, IEEE Conference, Syria.

Alnoukari, M., Alzoabi, Z., & Hanna, S. (2008). Using applying adaptive software development (ASD) agile modeling on predictive data mining applications: ASD-DM methodology, *International Symposium on Information Technology (ITSIM 08),* Malaysia.

Alzoabi, Z., Diko, F., & Alnoukari, M. (2008). Enhancing education quality assurance using Information Systems- QAAS System. *International Symposium on Information Technology (ITSIM 08),* Malaysia, 2008.

Blackmur, D. (2004). Issues in higher education quality assurance, *Australian Journal of Public Administration*, 105-116.

Fowler, A., & Gilfillan, M. (2003). A framework for stackholder integration in higher education Information Systems projects. *Technology Analysis and Strategic Management, 15*(4).

Gatfield, T., Barker, M., & Graham, P. (1999). Measuring student quality variables and the implications for management practices in higher education institutions: An Australian and international student perspective. *Journal of Higher Education Policy and Management, 21*(2).

Juran, J. M., & Gryna, F. M. (1988). *Juran's quality control handbook*. New York, NY: Mcgraw-Hill.

Romero, C., & Ventura, S. (2007). Educational data mining: A survey from 1995 to 2005. *Expert Systems with Applications, 33*, 135–146.

Selmoune, N., & Alimazighi, Z. (2008). *A decisional tool for quality improvement in higher education*. International Conference on Information & Communication Technologies: From theory to applications, IEEE Conference, Syria.

Shyamala, K., & Rajagopalan, S. P. (2006). Data mining for a better higher educational system. *Information Technology Journal, 5*(3), 560–564.

Smith, W. (2005). Applying data mining to scheduling courses at a university. *Communications of the Association for Information Systems, 16*, 463–474.

Spalter, A. M., & Dam, A. V. (2003). Problems with using components in educational software. *Computers & Graphics, 27*, 329–337.

Tait, A. (1997). *Quality assurance in higher education: Selected case studies*. Vancouver: The Commonwealth of Learning.

Yang, C. (2006). Problems in quality assurance under open source development mode. Retrieved from www.inf.fu-berlin.de/ inst/ ag-se/ teaching/ S-OpenSource-2006/ YangC06_Quality_Assurance_Ausarbeitung.pdf.

KEY TERMS AND DEFINITIONS

AGPA (Accumulative Grade Point Average): A numeric indicator of the student performance in universities.

Business Intelligence (BI): Composed of several technologies, methods, and tools that may support the middle and top management in the decision making process.

Classification: The task of generalizing known structure to apply to new data. For example, an email program might attempt to classify an email as legitimate or spam. Common algorithms include decision tree learning, nearest neighbor, naive Bayesian classification, neural networks and support vector machines.

Clustering: The task of discovering groups and structures in the data that are in some way or another "similar", without using known structures in the data.

Data Mining: The data processing using sophisticated data search capabilities and statistical algorithms to discover patterns and correlations in large preexisting databases. It is made up of several analytical, mathematical, and statistical techniques. Before applying these methods to data, the data has to be typically organized into history repositories, known as data warehouses.

Quality Assurance: A set of processes and techniques that are applied on the production or service offering to ensure the suitability of the final product or service to its users.

Quality Assurance in Higher Education: A set of processes and techniques that are applied in the higher education institution to ensure the suitability of the teaching material and methodology to the expectation of the students, and the suitability of the graduates features to the job market.

Regression: Attempts to find a function which models the data with the least error.

Chapter 12

Business Intelligence and Agile Methodology for Risk Management in Knowledge-Based Organizations

Muhammad Mazen Almustafa
The Arab Academy for Banking and Financial Sciences, Syria

Dania Alkhaldi
The Arab Academy for Banking and Financial Sciences, Syria

ABSTRACT

In this highly technology - dependent, knowledge- based economy, the causes for failure of most software development projects are related to rapid technology changes, in-flux business requirements, or failure to tackle risk. Accordingly, risk management plays significant and crucial role in organizations' response to this rapidly changing economy. Risk management process is illustrated in four main steps: identify the risk, analyze the risk, treat the risk and monitor the risk. This chapter discusses and explores the role of business intelligence and agile methodology to manage risk effectively and efficiently. It explores the risk management traditional tools that are commonly used, the role of business intelligence in risk management, and the role of agile methodology in risk management.

DOI: 10.4018/978-1-61350-050-7.ch012

INTRODUCTION

Project failures have been one of the most critical concerns of managers over the past decades. So many searches have conducted to investigate the different causes of these failures. In 1998, the cost of failed projects in the U.S.A only has been evaluated at $85 billion. Past projects showed that most of the encountered problems and difficulties were actually predictable. According to (Cerpa, 2009) study of 70 failed projects, risk has a noticeable role in projects failures.

As a consequence, risk management is more than a need. So many tools and techniques have been used during the past decades to manage risk but those previously used tools are no efficient anymore due to the fast pace of this century. Decisions have to be made in a matter of minutes or sometimes seconds so there is a must of getting benefits of the huge amounts of stored data in data warehouses using intelligent techniques.

This chapter investigates the role of business intelligence and agile methodology in managing risk. Firstly, the chapter gives an overall view of the concepts of risk and risk management process and why there is a need for risk management. Then the chapter lists in some details the traditional tools that are most commonly used in managing risks. It also explores the role of business intelligence in Risk Management Process and shows some tools that are effectively used in managing risk. Finally the chapter ends up with the role of agile in managing risk.

RISK MANAGEMENT (LITERATURE REVIEW)

Why Need Risk Management?

Risk can be defined as Hazard; danger; peril; obstacles; exposure to mischance or harm; venture (Canfora & Troiano, 2002). Dwaikat & Parisi-Presicce in (2005) defined risk as the probability of selfish use of software vulnerabilities. Such selfish use often causes a loss, either tangible or intangible, to the project owner. Risk according to Biswas, Debelak, & Kawamura (1989), implies a measure of some possible loss. Therefore, understanding risks and threats in any business is the first step to make a good decision. According to OXFORD dictionary risk can be defined as:

Chance or possibility of danger; the possibility that something unpleasant will happen.

Dwaikat & Parisi-Presicce (2005), classify risks into three types: project risk, like the risk of cost and time scale, technical risk, when the project doesn't meet one or more of its functional requirements, and risk to life that causes death or breakdown to project. Regardless the type of risks that have to be faced, there are so many techniques and tools to do that in this constantly changing economy.

Risk in general is a problem that could cause some loss or threaten the success of our project, but which hasn't happened until now and we work to keep it away. For the field of business, software- related risks can be defined as the multiple undesirable events that may occur.

Risk Management is a collection of methods or techniques that aim to minimize or reduce the effects of project failure (Addison, 2002) which match Crossland, Williams & McMahon(2003) definition of risk management which is a "coordinated activities to direct and control an organisation with regard to risk".

Risk management and measurement are crucial for today's organizations survival. The implementation of risk management system is one of the most crucial challenges that organizations might face in this rapid changing world in order to identify, analysis and prevent business exposure. In another words risk management benefits can be: warnings at the early stages to avoid loss, triggers or indicators for future opportunities and better decisions making process.

Figure 1. Risk management phases, adapted from As/NZS 4360:2004 standard

Risk Management Process

Due to the importance of risk management field, there are so many standards that are specified for this field like ISO 17799 and AS/NZS 4360, others deal with risk management as part of project management standard or IS development process standard as CMMI (Ewer & Mustafa, 2008). The majority of related standards approximately agree on four phases to manage risks (Crossland, Williams, & McMahon, 2003). In this context the first three phases are the essential ones while

the fourth one forms the umbrella activity of risk management process (Raza, 2009).

Risk Identification

According to the PMBOK, Risk Identification is the process of determining which risks may affect the project and documenting their characteristics. This phase is specialized to address potential risks and determine the maximum extents and the type of damage that could be caused by those risks. Therefore, this step is considered the most important phase in risk management process. Boehm

Figure 2. Risk management process, adapted from (Raza, 2009)

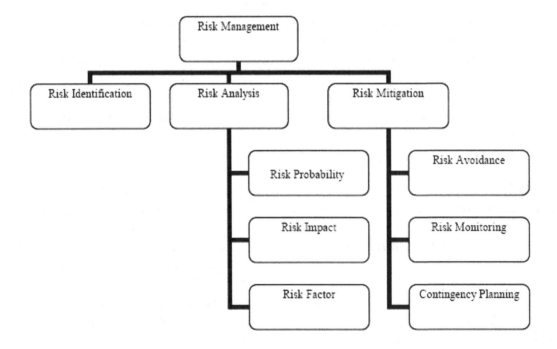

declared in (1991) that early risk identification allows avoiding many software catastrophes

In Risks identification, managers use prescriptive and creative ways to address risks. This stage usually depends on past experiences and knowledge, but at the same time risk management process must ensure that the historical information will not neglect a creative assessment of the future, where matters or events may be happened for the first time.

In this stage, we must answer two questions:

- What could be happened?
- How could it be happened?

Risk Analysis

Risk analysis is defining and analyzing the different dangers, hazards and faults that might face projects at any phase of their implementations. The outcome of this stage is an initial view of the significance of the identified risks, and scoring schemes, risks can be honestly rated very high or very low. The next stage is used to review this assignment. It is common to find large number of unimportant risks that can be removed from the process.

Risk Treatment

Treatment consists of determining what will be done and modifying the project base plans if it is needed. The best way to treat risk is adopting an alternative strategy to avoid a risk, minimize its impact or accept it. This means that risk treatment is process of selection and implementation of measures to modify risk.

Monitoring and Review

The outputs of the previous three stages must be kept under review as time moves on. Changes in the environment or discovering better information might make the original assessment out of data.

Also monitoring the risk management process and the execution must be managed to ensure that it is conducted cost-effectively.

TRADITIONAL RISK MANAGEMENT TOOLS

In practice, risk is assessed, analyzed and handled by managers using traditional tools and techniques. There are numerous amounts of tools and techniques in the risk identification process. According to Ewer & Mustafa study in (2008), the most commonly used tools:

DOCUMENTATION REVIEW

A structured review may be performed by project's documentations, including plans, assumptions, prior projects' files and other information. The quality of the plan, as well as consistency between those plans, the project requirements and assumptions can be an indicator for risk possibility in a project (PMI, 2004).

INFORMATION GATHERING TECHNIQUES

Brainstorming

Brainstorming is one of the most important tools that used by teams (a group setting) to quickly bring out the risks according to each individual point of view and present them in an orderly fashion to the rest of the team. The main aim of this tool is to provide an environment that is free of criticism for creative and unrestricted exploration of options or solutions.

DELPHI Technique

DELPHI technique was designed to elicit information and judgments from participants mainly experts without contacting them face to face (like Brainstorming technique). It facilitates risk identifying, risk solving, planning and decision-making with reducing the impact of biases and provides a systematic method to reach consensus and share opinions in a safe and effective way. One of the advantages of this technique is to permit participants to change their minds anonymously, without fear of criticism.

Nominal Group Technique (NGT)

Nominal Group Technique (NGT) is designed to encourage every group members to contribute, and prevents the more vocal group members from dominating the discussion. It allows to identifying risk, solving risk and organizational decision-making. NGT facilitates discussion, stimulates creative contributions, increases group productivity, uncovers conflicting viewpoints, and leaves group members feel satisfied that they have contributed and that their opinions have been considered.

The purpose of the NGT is to generate information in response to an issue that can then be prioritized through group discussion. Participants involved in the NGT take part in a highly structured face to-face meeting usually lasting up to two hours. The suggested size of a group is 5-9 participants, although the most effective NGT is preferred to be with larger groups (Potter, Gordon, & Hamer, 2004).

Interviewing

Interviewing experienced project participants, stakeholders and domain experts can identify risks. Interviews are one of the main sources of risk identification data gathering (PMI, 2004).

SWOT

A SWOT analysis identifies the Strengths, Weaknesses, Opportunities and Threats that face organizations (or projects). Strengths and weaknesses are an assessment of internal factors, whilst opportunities and threats are ways of defining the external environment (Cadle & Yeates, 2004).

This technique ensures examination of the project from each of the SWOT perspectives, to increase the breadth of the considered risks (PMI, 2004). A SOWT matrix would show strengths and weaknesses as in Figure 3.

PESTEL ANALYSIS

It is one of the most popular methods for examining the external factors that affect organizations (or projects) at the present or may affect them in the future within which strategy options mainly are strategy, and the possible external trends that could be significant in the future. PESTEL stands for Political, Economic, Socio-cultural, Technological, Environmental, and Legal.

- Political: political decisions affect all business
- Economic: Closely related to political influences. i.e. exchange rate
- Socio-cultural: Demography changes.
- Technological: new ways to deliver service.
- Environmental: climate change.
- Legal: monopoly laws.

This technique considers these aspects of the external world and their impact on all stakeholders. (PMI, 2004)

Root Cause Identification

Root Cause Identification is an inquiry into the essential causes of a project's risks. It sharpens the definition of the risk and allows grouping

Figure 3. SOWT matrix adapted from (Cadle & Yeates, 2004)

Strength Opportunities	**Weakness** Opportunities
Strength Threats	**Weakness** Threats

risks according to their causes. Effective risk response can be developed if the root of the risk is addressed (PMI, 2004).

Checklist Analysis

Checklists that used during risk identification are usually developed based on historical information and previous projects team experience (Heldman, 2002). Checklists are quick to use, and they provide useful guides for the organizations that deals with similar or standard projects. Sometimes these take the form of standard procedures that have a similar effect (Cooper, Grey, Raymond, & Walker, 2005).

Assumptions Analysis

Assumptions are conditions that are assumed true, certain or real for the sake of planning. Assumptions are major sources of risks. We need to document assumptions, verify them and track them. We need to check if these assumptions are stable (Sifri, 2003).

Every project is conceived and developed based on a set of hypotheses, scenarios or assumptions. Assumptions analysis is a tool that explores the validity of assumptions as they apply to the project from inaccuracy, inconsistency or incompleteness of assumptions (PMI, 2004).

Diagramming Techniques

Risk diagramming techniques include:

- *Cause-and-effect diagrams:* they are also known as fishbone or Ishikawa diagrams and useful in identifying cases of effects and risk identification process as well as quality planning process.
- *System or process flow charts:* they show how various elements of a system interrelate and mechanism of causation and help to identify cases of effects, risk identification process and quality planning process
- *Influence diagrams:* they are graphical representation of situation and typically show the causes of problems and the order of occurrence over time and other relationships among variables and outcome.

In addition to the past tools and techniques there are also many tools that are more effective in one of the risk management phases rather than the others. Monte Carlo simulation, Scenario analysis, Qualitative Risk Analysis, decision tree analysis, causal analysis, Pareto analysis, and sensitivity analysis are some of these tools and techniques. The following sections explain some of these tools and techniques in details:

Figure 4. Risk event and outcome/response probability tree adapted from (Ewer & Mustafa, 2008)

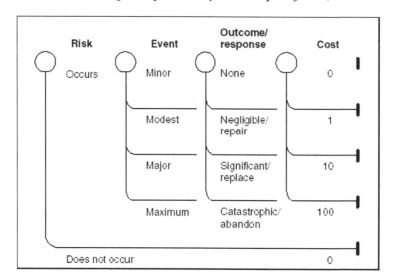

Monte Carlo Simulation

Monte Carlo Simulation looks at many possible scenarios. The calculations explain the range of potential results: the best and worst cases and hundreds of scenarios between them. It is a forecasting tool that is used to help in planning a project and its related strategies. Project or risk managers use this mathematical model to calculate and expose risk in a project future. It is a powerful simulation tool that helps in making better decisions about your project.

Scenario Analysis

This analysis of question what if the situation represented by scenario 'X' happens?

(PMI, 2004). This sort of "what if" analysis has always been a part of business decision-making.

Today, what we call scenario analysis is a formalization of the process. It is used where there are major risks that might impact on a project, or where the range of potential impacts of a risk is very wide. For example: natural disasters, large fires, industrial disputes or major changes in the economic environment. A scenario approach pro-

vides a flexible way of organizing the analysis in these circumstances.

Cooper and others in (2005) mentioned that the structure of scenario analysis is derived from probability trees. Figure 4 shows a simple probability tree structure for assessing the consequences of a risk in terms of the events that might occur, the potential outcomes associated with an individual risk event and the responses to it, and their cost implications.

Qualitative Risk Analysis

Qualitative Risk Analysis prioritizes risks for subsequent further analysis or action by assessing and combining their probability of occurrence and impact (PMI, 2004). Cooper and others suggested in (2005) three kinds of Qualitative Risk Analysis:

Qualitative analysis is based on nominal or descriptive scales for describing the likelihoods and consequences of risks. This is particularly useful for an initial review or screening or when a quick assessment is required.

Semi-quantitative analysis extends the qualitative analysis process by allocating numerical values to the descriptive scales. The numbers are then used to derive quantitative risk factors.

Quantitative analysis uses numerical ratio scales for likelihoods and consequences, rather than descriptive scales.

BUSINESS INTELLIGENCE FOR RISK MANAGEMENT

Traditional Risk Management tools, however, may consume time, cost and efforts to get approximately precise results. In traditional situations, the procedure of identifying the different risks that expected to be faced, their effects, and probabilities of occurring have been performed by a committee of experts of different backgrounds. This, in itself is a tedious and time consuming procedure (Biswas, Debelak, & Kawamura, 1989). Therefore, managers started to look for faster tools or automated tools that help them to get decisions or treat a hazard.

Nowadays there is a new trend toward using Business Intelligence Systems to manage risk more effectively and efficiently as it can help managers to get comprehensive information about enterprise probable risks when they need these pieces of information. "Business Intelligence focuses on discovering knowledge from various electronic data repositories, both internal and external, to support better decision making" (Dass, 2007).

This trend started in the seventies of last century, after the technology revolution as a consequence of presenting advanced technologies like artificial intelligence (AI) and database. Afterwards, many software applications and database file management produced numerous successful information systems in all life domains (Hoplin, 1987).

AI techniques and database technologies have a big role in replacing Risk management traditional tools with more advanced tools that helped managers in all Risk Management phases. These tools that include AI and database technologies are classified as Business Intelligence applications, according to the definition of (Dayal, Castellanos, Simitsis, & Wilkinson, 2009) "Business

Intelligence (BI) refers to technologies, tools, and practices for collecting, integrating, analyzing, and presenting large volumes of information to enable better decision making"

Business intelligence systems (BIS) are interactive computer-based systems that are developed to help decision makers using technologies, data, documents, knowledge, and analytical models in identify and solving problems.

Generally, BI systems can be classified into two main categories: model-driven and data-driven. Model driven is the one that utilizes AI techniques and Simulation While Data-driven deals with data warehouses and databases technology.

MODEL-DRIVEN BUSINESS INTELLIGENCE SYSTEM

Artificial Intelligence Tools for Risk Management

Rech and Althoff (2004) referred to new research areas, which are born between artificial Intelligence and Software engineers. Especially, Knowledge Based Systems (KBS), Agents, Computational Intelligence (CI) and Ambient Intelligence (AML) as illustrated in Figure 5.

These research areas nowadays extend to cover new areas like fuzzy logic, neural network, natural language, genetic algorithm and ontology to identify, analyze and treat any problem, uncertain risk and hazard. Today, many application areas for AI in Software Engineering have been established in fields like quality management, project management and risk management. This chapter focus will be on DSS and Expert system which are considered the essential part in any risk detection system.

Hoplin (1987) presented a model for DSS that supported by expert system, computer based system and neutral language and maximized the system by workstation. The evolution of this model started by a simple stepping stone system

Figure 5. Research areas in AI and SE and their intersections adapted from (Rech & Althoff, 2004)

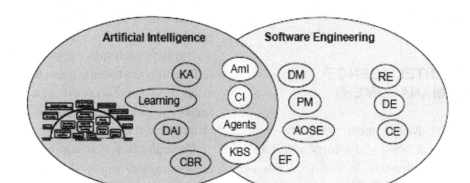

that called 'True' DSS model which consists of four layers: the two inner layers are explanatory whereas, the third level called DSS Toolkit comprises enter, transform and report information capabilities. Finally, the top level is for advanced users to insert well defined applications.

To achieve the true model, the information flow in a DSS needs to move to AI direction and use an expert system. In this context, using expert system like the use of a computer will be as an advisor to help humans in problem solving using a process called Knowledge Engineering.

Figure 6. The true DSS, adapted from (Hoplin, 1987)

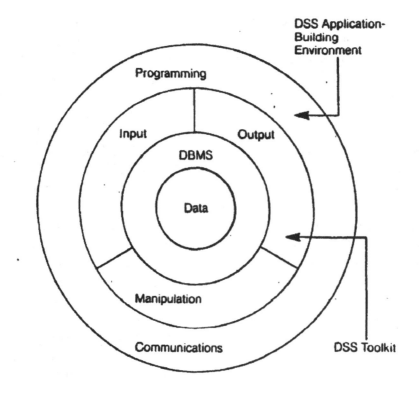

Figure 7. Information flow in a DSS adapted from (Hoplin, 1987)

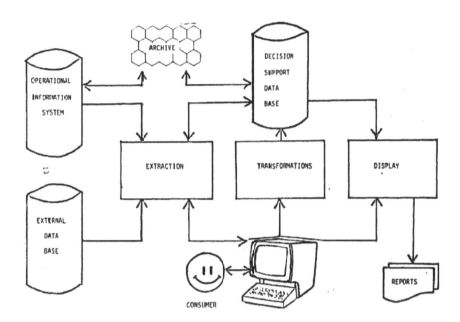

This system consists of three main components as Figure 7 show: Operational information system (OIS), external database and decision support database (DSDB). The question is how the information flows in the system? The information flow process summarized in three steps:

The Data extracted from OIS and external Database and assessed, which is data for decision making then placed in DSDB.

The user and DSS transform the data within DSDB to execute the task of DSS.

The result then can be shown and reported.

To make the model more adaptable with computerized technology Hoplin (1987) has been modified it, hence, by entering workstation concept to his model shown in Figure 8. The new model is more actual and harmonious with distributed data handling, networking, and end-user computing.

The next attempt was from (Biswas, Debelak, & Kawamura, 1989) they tried to move beyond DSS to use more efficient systems in identifying risks. The authors proposed to automate many of the modeling and defect analysis techniques in

the risk estimation and analysis process for a diversity of technological applications. The authors also depended on knowledge based system; object oriented and database technologies to get more useful in risk assessment studies. The paper suggests building structural and functional models of the system from a set of essential components and functions, and analyzing the failure model of the system in terms of these two models. This system consists of four levels:

- **User Interface Layer:** this layer uses information that got from questioners to build a suitable fault tree. The interface is supported to help user to queries and system responds. It also supports user to create, execute, and explore various risk scenarios by means of "what if" analysis.

- **RA/Domain Expert Layer:** includes the required functionality to perform various risk analysis units for assumed fault situations specified by users. Some examples of risk analysis include fault network and event tree analysis.

Figure 8. Workstation concept adapted from (Hoplin, 1987)

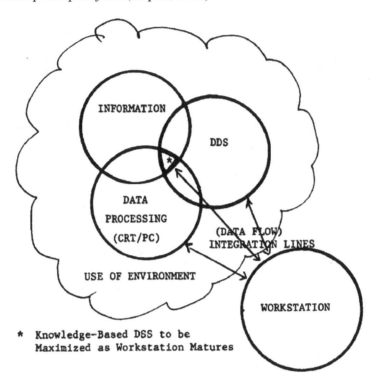

- **Network Development Layer:** includes the qualitative modeling expertise. Additional tools provide the ability for automatically generating causal network models by qualitative simulation of the process model. The system designer/domain expert basically interacts with this system through the qualitative modeling interface to build models of the domain or systems under study.

- **AI Programmer Layer:** comprises a set of programming tools and techniques that system developers can use for developing functional units for the other three layers. For example, Smalltalk contains a set of object oriented facilities, database for storing historical data.

After that, Expert system developed rapidly and became the core of any Risk Management system. That's clearly represented in Artificial Intelligence Design Framework (AIDF) which is introduced by Gurupur & Tanik in (2006).

The paper presents an imagination of a framework that can deal with risks that come up during the traditional process of software developments, where the requirements can change while the software development is still in process, or the changes may occur in the expert domain knowledge which it is the base resource of design right. This problem makes many software process ends in failure.

The main part of this framework is knowledge based engineering (KBE). It captures expert domain knowledge and automates the reasoning. AIDF supposes that the domain knowledge is available on the Internet so it connects KBE to the Internet by using search agent and ontology on the Semantic Web to elicit reliable information from the web. When the information is stored in the AIDF, the AIDF begins to rebuild the software. It verifies the correctness of the design by using

Figure 9. Design concept of generic intelligent risk assessment system adapted from (Biswas, Debelak, & Kawamura, 1989)

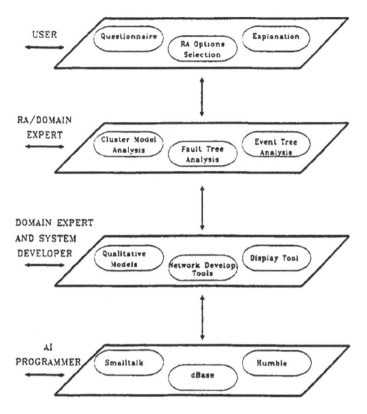

a rule-base and risk-mitigation algorithms. The verification process works as Figure 11.

Gurupur & Tanik ensured that AIDF is still in its developing stage and a conceptual phase and they are still looking at the new technologies that will help in building the AIDF.

In today's business solution there are so many tools depend on expert system to make design in identifying and assessing risks. For example Temporis Pro made in (2006) a list of commercial risk management software tools. One of these tools was RISKMAN which uses expert system as a core. It is developed by Ira A Fulton School engineering (ASU) and designed for use by software engineers with minimal software project planning experience who are involved in planning a small team software development project.

Bryant also in (2010) presented a list on risk world web sites that provides commercial Risk Management software tools, some of them uses expert systems like Vanguard Software Corporation which provides tools for forecasting, resource optimization, Web-based expert systems, and financial modeling. It presents enterprise decision analysis, collaborative web-based modeling, and knowledge capture capabilities to guarantee that the risks and opportunities throughout a company are captured and treated.

Simulation Based System for Risk Management

There are so many business intelligence tools that depend on other technologies, especially in analysis and monitoring phases. Simulation

Figure 10. Artificial intelligence design framework, adapted from (Gurupur & Tanik, 2006)

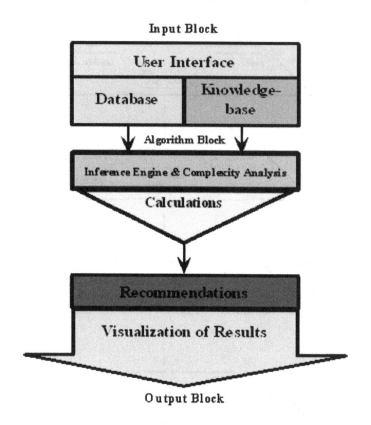

technologies are one of these tools. Most of organizations use computer simulation to tackle their problems rapidly because computer simulation is very fast in imitating a system over a period. Wang and others in (2008) described IBM General Business Simulation Environment (GBSE) and its implementation. GBSE designed for supply chain "what-if" analysis and risk analysis. GBSE uses a discrete event simulation (DES) engine and a simulation bus.

The structure of this system consists of four layers:

- Data layer: it is responsible for supervising on Data like simulation data, data in the running case and the result data
- Service layer: it includes the simulation services. These services play the role of running the inputs and producing the outputs with a controlled manner.
- Controller layer: this layer manages the order of service events and concludes messages between services. It has DES engine which considered the heart of this layer. Because it keeps an event list and schedule the events to take place at identified time when the service request.
- Presentation layer: it is the interface between the end user and GBSE system. By this interface, user can create a model, run the simulation and show the result.

This system developed by IBM China Research Lab by using a pure java programming language. The system includes many moving charts and animation to make sense that the simulation more instinctive. Figure 13 displays the running perspec-

Figure 11. The verification process, adapted from (Gurupur & Tanik, 2006)

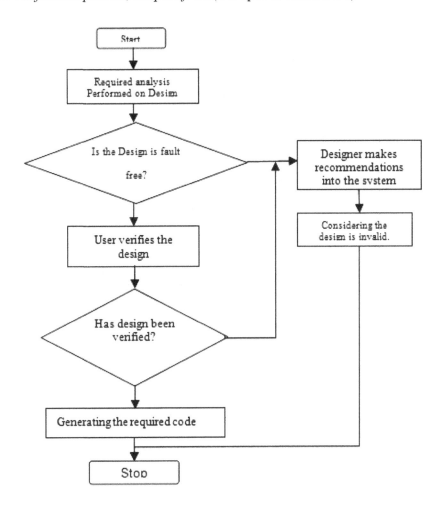

tive, which is useful for starting the simulation and observing the process through animation and moving curves.

Another example is the Monte Carlo approach; it is a simulation approach and it is one of the traditional techniques which used to analyze a risk. Many approaches and application like MCDB System depends on Monte Carlo approach to prophesy risks and uncertainty thinks (Jampani, Perez, Xu, Jermaine, Wu, & Haas, 2008).

This tool is well suited for industrial strength business-intelligence queries over uncertain warehouse data.

Excel spreadsheet also is an application that supports the Monte Carlo approach and other traditional risk management approaches that deal with project risk, like the risk to cost and time scale. It has "What If" analysis to predict the cost and benefit of a project. It also allows treating risk to time scale because it embeds PERT analysis and Gantt chart. Figure 14 shows a template for Gantt chart which is easy to use

Some powerful software tools are specialized in project management like Primavera system or MS Project. These systems assist project and risk managers to identify a schedule for the project and assign resources to each task to avoid or

Figure 12. GBSE architecture, adapted from (Wang, et al., 2008)

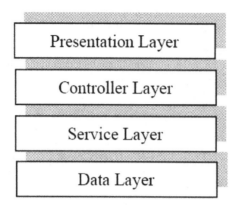

Figure 13. Running perspective, adapted from (Wang, et al., 2008)

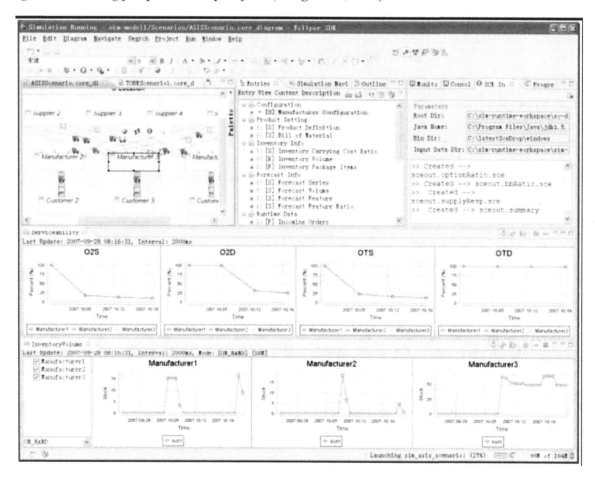

Figure 14. Gantt chart by using Excel sheet

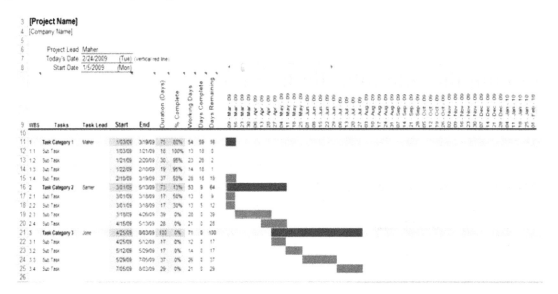

mitigate risks came up from cost and time scale risks and complete successfully the project on time. They also help to identify the critical path and project finish.

Another tools embedded fault and event tree and Qualitative Risk Analysis like RISKMAN. It deals with data analysis, system analysis, and natural hazard analysis and event tree. There are also many tools that approximately cover all traditional tools like, Checklist, SWOT and PESTEL analysis.

DATA-DRIVEN BIS FOR RISK MANAGEMENT

Data mining and knowledge discovery on databases have been the focus of so many significant researches. The importance of Data Mining and KDD has been increased recently. This is mainly due to the fact that many organizations continuously produce large amounts of machine readable data containing knowledge that is useful for strategic decisions regarding managing risks (Polese, 2002)

Due to the recent financial crisis, organizations started to give serious emphasis on various forms of potential risks and how to manage them. Therefore market risk management, credit risk management, and operational risk management are given more attention than before (Olson, 2008).

There is an urgent need for a new generation of theories of computation and tools to assist people in extracting useful information (knowledge) from the rapidly growing volumes of digital data (Fayyad, Piatetsky-Shapiro, & Smyth, 1996).

Over the years organizations have collected huge amounts of data about customers, partners, and employees in addition to the operational and financial systems. These data provide a base for analyzing and investigation for good actions to be repeated or bad once to be avoided. To get benefit of these huge databases, analyzing models for mining data are created but each organization has its own data mining model which is customized for a certain business and by an expert with certain algorithmic skills and preferences.

Data mining can be defined as a set of techniques that used to explore and uncap complex relationships in very large data sets. Han and Kamber (2001) define Data Mining as the process

Figure 15. Gantt chart and network diagram using MS Project adapted from (Hoffer, George, & Valacich, 2005)

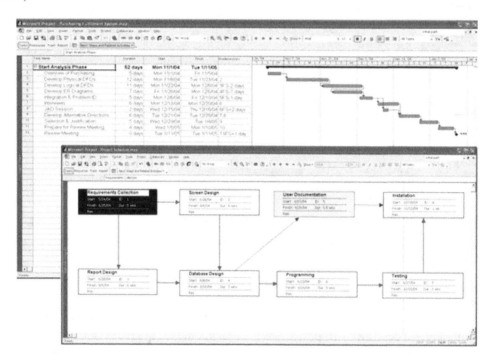

of discovering interesting knowledge from large amounts of data stored either in databases, data warehouses, or other information repositories.

Data mining process generally follows these phases to be done: Business Understanding, Data understanding, Data preparation, Modeling, Evaluation and deployment. "Data mining is branch of the applied informatics, which allows us to sift through large amounts of structured or unstructured data in attempt to find hidden patterns and/or rules" (Gramatikov, 2003). Data mining as a concept uses a mixture of explicit knowledge or codified knowledge that reside in data warehouses, advanced analytical skills, and domain knowledge or experts to interpret the hidden trends and other patterns (Tudor & Cărbureanu, 2008).

Data mining which is the extraction of hidden predictive information from data warehouses is a powerful new technology with great potential to help companies making strategic decisions.

In this chapter we adopted Daniels & Dissel (2002) definition of Data Mining. Data mining

system is to be presented as a comprehensive system that includes: the data warehouse, the mining software, the derived knowledge from data warehouse using mining software. Correctness, transparency and effectiveness are the principal attributes of knowledge derived from databases using data mining (Daniels & Dissel, 2002).

Data Mining is often used in fraud detection, risk assessment and product retailing. It involves the use of data analysis tools for pattern discovering (Pike, 2004). Many researches talked about data mining applications in different fields but little of them talked about using data mining to manage risks.

In this chapter we highlight the use of data mining to manage risk or in other words Risk Mining which is a relatively new concept that appears recently (2006) as consequence of demand and focusing of managing risk depending on data mining techniques.

Database technology is one of the most used in today's business which means there are huge

Figure 16. The use of data mining technique is a global and firm wide challenge for financial business. Adapted from (Dass, 2007).

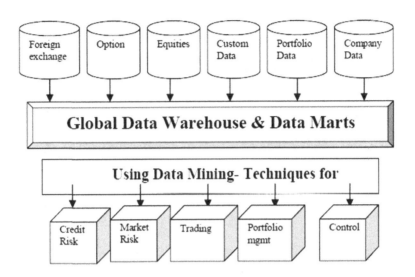

amounts of data in databases to be converted into valuable information. In other words, data mining is the process that digs the hidden and unknown valuable knowledge and principles in plenty of historical data.

Cun-bin & Jian-jun (2008) presents a new model for project risk element transmission theory based on data mining. The main idea of this theory is the relationship between the overall risk element and its partial elements. So the risk element can be seen as a sub factor that affects the overall goal of risk management.

According to this idea the risk element transmission matrix can be constructed as shown in Figure 17 as the following:

Acquiring the risk element information using WBS or other methods, keep it in data warehouse for further using.

Pre-treating the information, such as cleaning date, removing noise, and filtration and so on.

Analyzing the information using data mining technique to get the risk element transmission matrix.

Examples of BI-Based Risk Management Tool

Scorecards

A "scorecard" is a custom user interface that helps in optimizing performance of an organization by associating (internally and externally) the inputs and outputs. To be effective, the scorecard must be related to the organization's vision.

The balanced scorecard is a tool that serves several different functions including that of a measurement system, strategic management system, and communication tool (Dolins, 2006). These measures are classified using four different perspectives: financial, customer, internal process, and learning and growth.

There are lots of risks and challenges organizations face in this fast changing world. With BSC software help, organizations can manage their probable risks. Acquiring the right balance scorecard software will allow organizations to measure, interpret and understand what is happening and take the correct actions so that they

Figure 17. Data mining frame of risk element transmission matrix, adapted from (Cun-bin & Jian-jun, 2008)

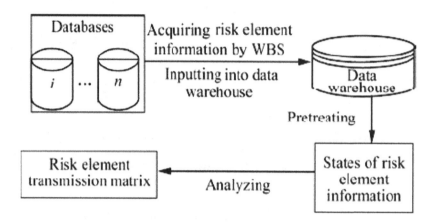

can adapt rapidly to the changing environment and therefore improve the performance of the processes and the company.

Dashboards

Dashboards are tools that "able to quickly provide a visual snapshot of the enterprise goals, metrics, benchmarks, system and workflow status as well as expected results and anomalies" (Jain, Ari, & Jun, 2008).

IT Risk Management dashboard is an example of dashboards. Figure 18 shows an example of an executive dashboard for Technology Risk. The metrics include IT Outsourcing Expenditure Tracking (Budget, Forecasts, and Actual), Server Availability, Client Outages, Current Alarms, and Transaction Failures.

Data Mining Tools Used In Risk Management

SAS, an established leader in analytics and business intelligence software with revenues of over $2.26bn, that entered the risk management filed in the late 90s. Its leadership position was fuelled by demand for Basel II solutions starting in 2003-2004.

By 2009, 400 financial institutions and non-financial corporations over the world were relying on SAS® Risk Management solutions which cover such areas as credit risk, operational risk, fraud, anti-money laundering, energy risk and Fair Banking (Chartis-research, 2009).

THE ROLE OF AGILE METHODOLOGY IN RISK MANAGEMENT

Many of researchers and developers have invented numerous methodologies like 'Waterfall', 'Spiral model' and 'RAD' methodology to overcome several challenges or problems that maybe take place during software life cycle (Jiang & Eberlein, 2008).

Agile methodology is one of these methodologies which addresses and handles many risks. Coyle &Kieran announced in (2009) that the essential purpose of applying agile methodology is to decrease risks. This one helped to increase the number of successful information systems.

Figure 18. Executive dashboard for technology risk, adapted from (Lee, 2007)

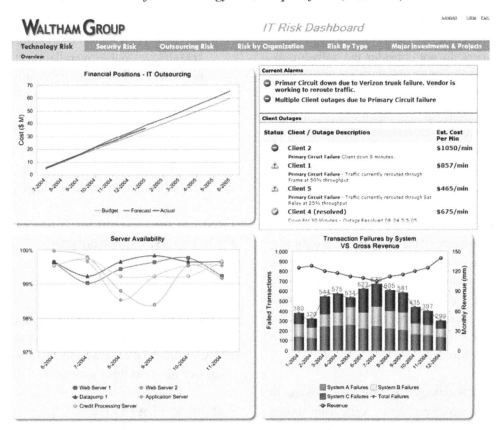

The characteristics of agile methods are precisely defined and detailed in the twelve principles behind the agile manifesto (Beedle, et al., 2001). Agile methodology involves its principles to treat and give more attention for special risks like project risks (cost and time scale) and changing requirements. According to Boehm & Turner (2003), agile methodology provide many promises like customer satisfaction increase, risk evolvement rates reduction, faster developing time, and a way of solving rapidly requirements changes.

Agile methodology also takes care of all other risk areas because the structure of agile methodology is built on iterative and incremental way of development, therefore it can dynamically adapt to changing requirements and support better risk management (Hoda, Noble, & Marshall, 2008). Garg (2009) confirmed that agile methodology

life cycle follows minimal increments with very small long-range planning which helps to reduce the overall risk, and enables the project to tune changes effectively and speedily. Leisten (2007) also mentioned that agile methodology depends on frequently repetitive releases, high integration and test so managers can manage and control risks better. Bica in (2007) explained the general risks that agile methodology can deal with:

•   Requirements risk: agile methodology can effectively treat risks that emerge from requirements. The nature of iterative development gives flexibility to the agile organization for controlling changes and completes the requirements. In addition, early feedback from users allows agile methodology to precisely describe the scope of the project.

- Architecture risk: unfortunately, many developers do not consider the software architecture as first class. As a consequence, the software will suffer from many problems including less flexibility to change. However, agile methodology with short and time iterations can verify the structure as it also relies on continuous refactoring and test driven development to make the structure more stable.
- Team risk: most of the risk comes from the team members themselves. For example, they have not worked together before, the team needs to be more collaborating to build the project quickly, the project is new and the team member need to learn and exchange many technical skills, or the team is high turnover.

Agile methodology has so many techniques to overcome pervious problems. Agile team should be small (3 to 5 member) and works in the same place. This allows the team to collaborate and exchange the experiences and knowledge easily. They work as pair programming to facilitate code review. They should also give daily status reports to maintain the sustainable pace and to reduce the turnover of the team.

- *Communication risk*: to satisfy customer and follow changes in requirements, the project needs to increase communications between team members and customers and increase communications between team itself on the other side. Hence, agile methodology assures to join customer and users to the team. The team is also responsible to give a daily report about status updates, but on other hand, making the team smaller and working in same place increase the chance of enhancing the communication of the team itself.

- *Schedule risk*: the worst risk is time and cost underestimation. Agile methodology solves this problem by estimating resources at high level for the overall project then only next iteration is accurately estimated for resources. This estimation called Rolling Wave Estimation in PMBOK.

Rajimanickam in (2005) summarized the six risks which agile methodology could identify and solve whereas other methodologies couldn't:

Cost Exceed /Extended Time Frame/ Failure to Satisfy Customer

In structured programming the analysis and design phase is doubtful to a large extent, cost and time are uncertain for this phase. Agile methodology can identify this risk by supplying a solution directly, at the smallest cost which agreed on with customer needs at this moment.

Failure to Meet Cost/ Time Frame Promises

In structured programming developers give estimated numbers for price and time to deliver the project. These are rarely very accurate. In most cases those numbers will not be met. Agile methodology can solve this problem by dividing the deliverables into small units so that exceeding the fame is less likely and the effects are not significant.

Incorporation of Untested Technology

Untested technology creates new risks because of moving the system development forward research and development project. This will produce inharmony or conflict between the cost and time estimation and cost and time of deliverables. Agile methodology tries to address this problem by breaking down the deliverables into small units, so that it can be estimated, then the remainder of

Figure 19. Agile methodology structure adapted from (Leisten, 2007)

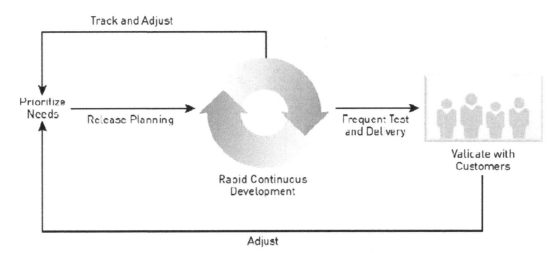

Change Requirements

Leisten illustrated in (2007) the liveliness nature of agile methodology structure which allows shorter development/feedback loops as the figure 19.

This will lead to two main advantages:

1. Delivery of a utilizable system quickly
2. Lower cost of change

The cost of change is reduced because the change curve is exponential in general, but development/feedback loops is short and frequent, which allows keeping the development project at the front side of the change curve, whereas growth is still nearly linear.

Process Focus Creates a Death-Marc

The big design in structured programming extends the process to become so complex, so that the analysis, design and documentation phases are essential and consume a lot of resources whereas customer satisfaction becomes behind that or

the project can be re-estimated regarding its scope and measured accordingly.

with less priority. Agile methodology handles this problem by reducing process constraints, instead of interesting in functionality that can be done in a brevity way.

However, there are some challenges that face agile methodology. Li, Huang, Shu, & Li found in (2006) XP specially and agile generally is suitable for small team and small project. So the most significant challenge is the size of the project and its team. Boehm & Turner had also decided in (2003) that both agile methodology and planned approaches have lack in some situations. This will lead to failure if they aren't understood. Some researchers found applying a risk-driven Method for agile as a solution for this problem (Li, Huang, Shu, & Li, 2006), whereas Boehm & Turner discovered in (2003) a method that allows to developers to make a balance between agile methodology and plan-driven approaches. This method is called a risk-based approach for structuring projects. The mentioned method is summarized in five steps and illustrated in figure (20). "Developers can use a five-step process to determine if agile methods, plan driven methods, or a combination of the two will work best for their project" (Boehm & Turner, 2003).

Figure 20. Risk-based method summary adapted from (Boehm & Turner, 2003)

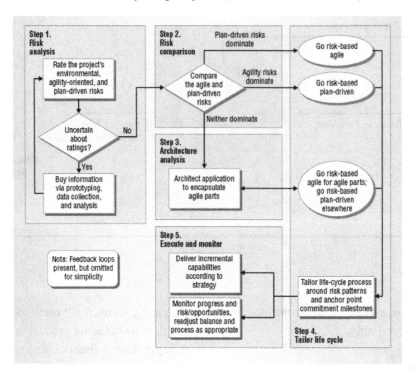

CONCLUSION

Due to the fast pace of this age and the constantly changing economy, organizations have been found themselves forced to change the way of doing business. The overall environment is not stable anymore and little things can be predicted. Risk became exist everywhere as a consequence of that, risk management techniques have been one of the most important management's concern for decades. In this chapter we tried to describe, highlight and investigate the different techniques and tools that are mostly used in Risk Management giving the focus for the Business Intelligence based ones providing examples of some of the mostly used tools. The chapter also sheds lights on the role of agile in managing risk in this knowledge based economy.

REFERENCES

Addison, V. (2002). *Controlling software project risks – An empirical study of methods used by experienced project managers. SAICSIT* (pp. 128–140). New York, NY: ACM.

Beedle, M., Bennekum, A. v., Cockburn, A., Cunningham, W., & Fowler, M. …Highsmith, J. (2001, February 13). *Principles behind the Agile Manifesto.* Retrieved on November 11, 2010, from Manifesto for Agile Software Development: http://agilemanifesto.org/ principles.html

Bica, M. (2007, November 15). *Agile inspired risk mitigation techniques for software development projects.* Retrieved on November 11, 2010, from Project Management Institute Greater Toronto Information Systems Local Interest Group: http://www.gtislig.org/ Documents/ Agile%20 Inspired%20Risk%20Management_Final.pdf

Biswas, G., Debelak, K. A., & Kawamura, K. (1989). *Applications of qualitative modeling to knowledge-based risk assessment studies*. The 2nd International Conference on Industrial and Engineering Applications of Artificial Intelligence and Expert Systems, Tullahoma, Tennessee, United States (volume 1, pp. 92-101). New York, NY: ACM.

Boehm, B. (1991). Software risk management: Principles and practices. *IEEE Software, 8*(1), 32–41.

Boehm, B., & Turner, R. (2003). Using risk to balance agile and plan-driven methods. *IEEE Computer, 36*(6), 57–66.

Bryant, M. (2010, July 07). *Risk-related software.* (Tec-Com Inc) Retrieved on August 04, 2010, from Risk World: http:// www.riskworld.com/ software/sw5sw001.htm

Cadle, J., & Yeates, D. (2004). *Management for Information Systems.* Upper Saddle River, New Jersey: Prentice Hall.

Canfora, G., & Troiano, L. (2002). *The importance of dealing with uncertainty in the evaluation of software engineering methods and tools.* The International Conference on Software Engineering and Knowledge Engineering, Ischia, Italy (pp. 691-698). New York, NY: ACM.

Cerpa, V. (2009). Why did your project fail? *Communications of the ACM*, 130–134.

Chartis-Research (2009). *RiskTech100 2009.* Chartis-research.

Cooper, D., Grey, S., Raymond, G., & Walker, P. (2005). *Managing risk in large projects and complex procurements.* Chichester, UK: John Wiley & Sons.

Coyle, S., & Kieran, C. (2009). A case study of risk management in agile systems development. Information Systems in a globalising world: Challenges, ethics and practices (pp. 1-12). Verona, Italy: *The Journal of Information Technology Teaching Cases (JITTC).*

Crossland, R., Williams, J. S., & McMahon, C. (2003). The practical application of design risk assessment models. *Proceedings of the Institution of Mechanical Engineers. Part B, Journal of Engineering Manufacture, 217*(2), 277–233.

Cun-bin, L., & Jian-jun, W. (2008). *Model of generic project risk element transmission theory based on data mining* (pp. 132–135). Berlin-Heidelberg, Germany: Springer.

Daniels, H., & Dissel, H. v. (2002). *Risk management based on expert rules and data-mining: A case study in insurance.* In Proceedings of the 10th European Conference on Information Systems (ECIS), Gdansk.

Dass, R. (2007). Data Mining In Banking And Finance: A Note For Bankers. Indian Institute of Management Ahmedabad, 1-13.

Dayal, U., Castellanos, M., Simitsis, A., & Wilkinson, K. (2009). *Data integration flows for business intelligence (EDBT '09), Saint Petersburg, Russia* (pp. 1–11). New York, NY: ACM.

Dolins, S. B. (2006). *Using the balanced scorecard process to compute the value of software applications* (pp. 881–884). New York, NY: ACM.

Dwaikat, Z., & Parisi-Presicce, F. (2005). *Risky trust: Risk-based analysis of software systems. Software engineering for secure systems-building trustworthy, St. Louis, MO, USA* (pp. 1–7). New York, NY: ACM.

Ewer, Y., & Mustafa, M. M. (2008). *The impact of risk management on IS projects success in Syria*. International Conference on Information & Communication Technologies: From theory to applications, Damascus, Syria (pp. 1 - 6). New York, NY: IEEE.

Fayyad, U., Piatetsky-Shapiro, G., & Smyth, P. (1996). From data mining to knowledge discovery in databases. *American Association for Artificial Intelligence*, 37-54.

Garg, A. (2009). *Agile software development. Defence Research & Development Organisation* (pp. 55–59). New Delhi: DESIDOC.

Gramatikov, M. (2003). *Data mining techniques and the decision making process in the Bulgarian public administration*. University of Sofia, 1-9.

Gurupur, V., & Tanik, U. J. (2006). *Software cultivationusing the arificial intelligence design framework*. ACM Southeast Conference, Melbourne, FL, USA (pp. 786-787). New York, NY: ACM.

Heldman, K. (2002). *Project management professional study guide*. Alameda, CA: Sybex Inc.

Hoda, R., Noble, J., & Marshall, S. (2008). *Agile project management*. The New Zealand Computer Science Research Student Conference, 2008 (pp. 218-221). Christchurch, New Zealand: the author/owner(s).

Hoffer, J. A., George, J. F., & Valacich, J. S. (2005). *Modern systems analysis and design*. New York, NY: Prentice Hall.

Hoplin, H. P. (1987). *Reducing managerial risk with expert systems. SIGBDP-SIGCPR, Coral Gables, FL, USA* (pp. 207–225). New York, NY: ACM.

Jain, J., Ari, I., & Jun, L. (2008). *Designing dashboards for managing model lifecycle* (pp. 14–15). New York, NY: ACM.

Jampani, R., Perez, L. L., Xu, F., Jermaine, C., Wu, M., & Haas, P. J. (2008). *MCDB: A Monte Carlo approach to managing uncertain data*. In R. Jampani, L. L. Perez, F. Xu, C. Jermaine, M. Wu, & P. J. Haas (Eds.), The International Conference on Management of Data, Vancouver, BC, Canada (pp. 687-700). New York, NY: ACM.

Jiang, L., & Eberlein, A. (2008). Towards a framework for understanding the relationships between classical software engineeringand agile methodologies. In L. Jiang, & A. Eberlein (Ed.), *Proceedings of the 2008 International Workshop on Scrutinizing Agile Practices or Shoot-Out at the Agile Corral*, Leipzig, Germany (pp. 9-14). New York, NY: ACM.

Lee, H. (2007, 01-12). Retrieved on November 11, 2010, from www.enterprise-dashboard.com: http://www.enterprise-dashboard.com/2007/01/12/ information-technology-risk-management-dashboard-screenshot/

Leisten, S. S. (2007, 03-29). *Evaluating a CM system for agile development*. Retrieved on Nov. 8, 2010, from Software Management: The IT Software Journal: http:// www.softwaremag.com/pdfs/ whitepapers/ Telelogic_wp1.pdf?CFID=30 055566&CFTOKEN=81143825

Li, M., Huang, M., Shu, F., & Li, J. (2006). *A risk-driven method for eXtreme programming release planning*. 28th International Conference on Software Engineering, Shanghai, China (pp. 423-430). New York, NY: ACM.

Olson, D. W. (2008). *Enterprise risk management: Financial and accounting perspectives* (pp. 25–38). Berlin-Heidelberg, Germany: Springer.

Pike, J. (2004, December 16). http:/ /www.fas. org/ irp/. *Retrieved August 5, 2010, from* www.fas. org:http://www.fas.org /irp/ crs/ index.html

PMI. (2004). *A guide to Project Management Body of Knowledge (PMBOK Guide)*. Pennsylvania, USA: Project Management Institute Inc.

Polese, T. T. (2002). *A data mining based system supporting tactical decisions* (pp. 681–684). New York, NY: ACM.

Potter, M., Gordon, S., & Hamer, P. (2004). The nominal group technique: A useful consensus technique: Methodology in physiotherapy research. *New Zealand Journal of Physiotherapy, 32*(3), 126–130.

Rajimanickam, D. (2005). Successful project management using agile methodology. International Quality Conference 2005, Toronto, Canada. *Journal of the Quality Assurance Institute*, 15-18.

Raza, F. N. (2009). Artificial Intelligence Techniques in Software Engineering (AITSE). []. Hong Kong: Newswood Limited. Organization: International Association of Engineers.]. *The International MultiConference of Engineers and Computer Scientists, 1*, 1–3.

Rech, J., & Althoff, K. D. (2004). Artificial intelligence and software engineering: Status and future trends. *Künstliche Intelligenz, 18*, 5–11.

Sifri, G. (2003). The identification process, Risk Management, Part 2. *Newsletter ESIHorizons, 4*(10).

Temporis-Pro. (2006, Jan. 22). *Risk management: Tools* (M. Doorenbos, Producer). Retrieved on August 4, 2010, from Pro Temporis: Consulting and Training in Risk and Project Management: http:// protemporis.com/ files/ risk_management_software_tools.pdf

Tudo, I., & Cărbureanu, M. (2008). *Data mining techniques in knowledge management in academic environment* (pp. 29–34). BULETINUL.

Wang, W., Dong, J., Ding, H., Ren, C., Qiu, M., Lee, Y. M., & Cheng, F. (2008). *An introduction to Ibm general business simulation environment.* Proceedings of the 2008 Winter Simulation Conference, Miami, Florida (pp. 2700-2707). New York, NY: IEEE.

ADDITIONAL READING

Ahmed, M., Anjomshoaa, A., Nguyen, T. M., & Tjoa, A. M. (2007). *Towards an ontology-based risk assessment in collaborative environment using the SemanticLIFE.* 2nd International Conference on Availability, Reliability and Security, Wien (pp. 1-9). New York, NY: IEEE Computer Society.

Aken, A. (2008). CHUNK: An agile approach to the software development life cycle. *Journal of Internet Commerce, 7*(3), 313–338.

Alleman, G. B. (2002). Agile project management methods for IT projects. In Carayannis, E. G., & Kwak, Y. H. (Eds.), *The story of managing projects: A global, cross– disciplinary collection of perspectives* (pp. 1–22). New York, NY: Greenwood Press / Quorum Books.

Blackmore, K. L., & Nesbitt, K. V. (2008). *Identifying risks for cross-disciplinary higher degree research students.* 10th Australasian Computing Education Conference (78, pp. 43-52). Wollongong, Australia: Australian Computer Society.

Boban, M., Pozgaj, Z., & Sertic, H. (2003). Strategies for successful software development risk management. *Management, 8*(2), 77–91.

Concha, M., Visconti, M., & Ast, H. (2007). *Agile commitments: Enhancing business risk management in agile development projects* (pp. 149–152). Berlin, Heidelberg: Springer.

Dhlamini, J., Nhamu, I., & Kachepa, A. (2009). *Intelligent risk management tools for software development. ACM special interest group on Computer science Education, Mpekweni Beach Resort, South Africa* (pp. 33–40). New York, NY: ACM.

Doernhoefer, M. (2006). Surfing the Net for software engineering notes. *ACM SIGSOFT Software Engineering Notes, 31*(2), 17–25.

Friedman, A., Wolff, R., & Schuster, A. (2008). *Providing k-anonymity in data mining* (pp. 790–804). Berlin, Heidelberg: Springer.

Fritzsche, M., & Keil, P. (2007). Agile methods and CMMI: Compatibility or conflict? *E-Informatica Software Engineering Journal, 1*(1), 9–26.

Johnston, M., Ehlen, P., Gibbon, D., & Liu, Z. (2007). The multimodal presentation dashboard. Bridging the gap: *Academic and Industrial Research in Dialog Technologies Workshop Proceedings* (pp. 17-24). Association for Computational Linguistics.

Kettunen, P., & Laanti, M. (2007). Combining agile software projects and large-scale organizational agility. *Software Process Improvement and Practice*, 183–193.

Klopper, R., Gruner, S., & Kourie, D. G. (2007). *Assessment of a framework to compare software development methodologies. South African institute for computer scientists and Information Technology, Fish River Sun, Sunshine Coast, South Africa* (pp. 56–65). New York, NY: ACM.

Leithiser, R., & Hamilton, D. (2008). *Agile versus CMMI - Process template selection and integration with Microsoft team foundation server*. The ACM Southeast Conference, Auburn, AL, USA (pp. 186-191). New York, NY: ACM.

Liu, D., Wang, Q., & Xiao, J. (2009). The role of software process simulation modeling in software risk management: A systematic review. *IEEE*, 302-311.

Lorenz, M., Gehrke, J. D., & Hammer, J. (2005). *Situation aware risk management in autonomous agents*. The ACM Conference on Information and Knowledge Management, Bremen, Germany (pp. 363-364). New York, NY: ACM.

Moyle, S. (2005). Collaborative data mining. In Maimon, O., & Rokach, L. (Eds.), *Data mining and knowledge discovery handbook* (p. 1419). Berlin-Heidelberg, Germany: Springer.

Nerur, S., Mahapatra, R., & Mangalaraj, G. (2005). Challenges of migrating to agile methodologies. *Communications of the ACM*, 73–78.

Neumann, P. G. (2005). *Risks to the Public* (pp. 19–33). New York, NY: ACM.

Odzaly, E. E., Des, G., & Sage, P. (2009). *Software risk management barriers: An empirical study* (pp. 418–421). New York, NY: IEEE.

Pino, F. J., Garcia, F., & Piattini, M. (2009). Key processes to start software process improvement in small companies. *The 24th Annual ACM Symposium on Applied Computing*, Honolulu, Hawaii, USA (pp. 509-516). New York, NY: ACM.

Theriou, N. G., Demitriades, E., & Chatzoglou, P. (2004). A proposed framework for integrating the balanced scorecard into the strategic management process. *Operations Research*, 147–165.

Walker, R., Holmes, R., & Hedgeland, I. (2006). *A lightweight approach to technical risk estimation via probabilistic impact analysis. MSR '06*, Shanghai, China (pp. 98–104). New York, NY: ACM.

Wallace, L., & Keil, M. (2004). *Software project risks and their effect on outcomes* (pp. 68–73). New York, NY: ACM.

Wu, J.-Y. (2010). *Computational intelligence-based intelligent business intelligence system: Computational intelligence-based intelligent business intelligence system: Concept and framework. Computer and network technology* (pp. 334–338). Bangkok: IEEE.

KEY TERMS AND DEFINITIONS

Agile Methodology: A group of software development methodologies based on iterative and incremental development process, where requirements and solutions are the outcome of the collaboration between self-organizing, cross-functional teams

Artificial Intelligence (AI): The area of computer science focusing on creating machines that can simulate the behaviors that humans consider intelligent.

Balanced Business Scorecard: A custom user interface that helps in optimizing performance of an organization by associating (internally and externally) the inputs and outputs

Business Intelligence: The use of analytical methods, either manually or automatically, to derive relationships from data for tactical and strategic use.

Dashboard: A tool that is able to quickly and effectively provide a visual snapshot of the enterprise goals, metrics, benchmarks, system and workflow status as well as expected results and anomalies

Data Mining: The process of finding and discovering interesting information from large amounts of data stored either in databases, data warehouses or others.

Expert System: A computer program that simulates the judgment or the behavior of a human or an organization that has expert knowledge and experience in a particular field.

Knowledge Discovery in Databases (KDD): The process of identifying valid, potentially useful, and codified understandable structure in data.

Risk: Hazard; danger; peril; obstacles; exposure to mischance or harm

Risk Management: The art and the process to identify, analyze, and respond to risk throughout the life of a project.

Chapter 13
Towards a Business Intelligence Governance Framework within E-Government System

Kamal Atieh
Arab Academy for Banking and Financial Sciences, Syria

Elias Farzali
Arab Academy for Banking and Financial Sciences, Syria

ABSTRACT

With business growth and crisis from time to time, many questions raised by so many experts, such as if the problem is the business rules or the architecture of the Information System. These questions are more important when discussing national projects like E-government projects. Therefore, we will take E-Government project in Syria as case study to explore, empirically, the main barriers of E-Government project in developing countries; how to take benefits from business intelligence (BI) to build a framework, which could be adopted by developing countries in their E-Government projects.

After reviewing the relevant literatures in Information System, E-Government and BI, we formulated a theoretical framework. This framework was applied in a real case study (E-Government project in Syria), to support data collection. This case study involved semi-structured interviews with senior officials from the public sector; E-Government project teams; a number of IT managers from government organizations; independent experts from the private sector and academics; beside documents analysis included all the key documents relating to the E-Government project published by ministry of communication and technology.

The need for such framework increase or decrease in each country depending on its status and on the relationship existed between business and IT teams.

DOI: 10.4018/978-1-61350-050-7.ch013

INTRODUCTION AND RESEARCH MOTIVATION

The main objective of BI is to have the right information, in the right format, to the right people, at the right time (Sandu, 2008). Gartner (2008) found that there are three key barriers to widespread the use of BI such as: users lack the necessary skills to use complex BI tools, the cost of ownership of deploying traditional BI tools to a large number of users is too high and existing BI tools are difficult to learn and to use.

On the other hand, many governments try to offer services to their citizens by developing E-Government projects, but they fail in their objectives especially in developing countries regardless of high spending on E-Government projects (Heeks, 2003), the problem is the lack of accepted and satisfactory services to citizens because of several factors.

Much IS literatures try to find the E-Government critical success factors (CSFs) (Prananto, 2007) and BI CSF (Yeoh et al. 2008), and some others to find the BI applications (Negash, 2004). However, despite the increasing interest in E-Government system and BI, there has been little empirical research about the factors influencing the implementation the E-Government projects in developing countries, same as the wide use of BI in public sector in general and in Government in specific. The gap in the literature reflected in low contributions to international conferences and journals, which mean that there is a need for more research in both academic and industry in BI and E-government fields. This is because the study of BI and E-Government systems is a relatively new area driven by the IT industry and vendors, and thus there is limited research into identifying the CSFs of E-Government project and the role of BI in it.

While carrying out the research, we answer the following questions:

- What is E-Government, and what are the main failure factors?
- What are the existing E-Government frameworks and what are the weaknesses in these frameworks?
- What are the existing BI frameworks, and how to deal with E-Government system?
- How to utilize BI capabilities to prevent the E-Government failures and improve its success?

RESEARCH OBJECTIVE

Given the introduction and motivation of this research, the researchers used qualitative research to:

- Investigate the key factors that affect on the success/failure of E-Government adoption in the developing countries.
- Investigate multiple BI and E-Government frameworks, in order to discuss the importance of using BI in E-Government system.
- Develop a BI framework within E-Government system, which helps in facilitating and improving E-Government services delivery.

Essentially, the researchers argue that there is a set of factors influencing the E-Government project, a multiple benefits from using BI systems and a big role of multiple factors like process, organizational and people factors using data, information and knowledge of the government to success.

Furthermore, the multiple findings of this research can be consolidated into a framework to provide a comprehensive picture of BI use in E-Government system, and hence allowing government planners and decision makers to optimize their resources and efforts on all levels (strategic, tactical and operational) to ensure E-Government project success.

In this research, the following section describes the research methodology, before elaborating on the research findings. The next section then presents a background about the research then discusses the research methodology used to have a comprehensive framework and details all the framework parts. In the last section, the researchers state the conclusion, research contribution and future study.

BACKGROUND

Information and communication technology (ICT) revolution increases day by day, this revolution offer new opportunities for organizations' planners and decision makers to take benefits from new forms of their resources. Their success or failure depends, not only on one factor of E-Government, but also on reaching to its objectives in planned time and cost.

Ndou (2004) confirms that *"recognizing the power of ICTs, many developing countries, assisted by international organizations for development, have started building and encouraging e-strategies and initiatives to address a wide range of economic, social, technological, infrastructural, legal and educational issues"*, confirming that the use of ICTs in the developing countries is at its infant stage.

UN (2008) confirms that all countries try to build their strategy toward E-Government by increasing their readiness in different domains in order to provide better public services, knowing that the majority of E-Government projects failed (Heeks, 2003). Knowing that, the E-Government project needs resources from different departments and different organizations in different forms regardless of the computerization process in each department.

A number of frameworks could be adopted to have a successful E-Government project like Kreizman and Fraga (2003) and Ndou (2004). Wagner et al (2003) state that, any E-Government

project depends on ICT in general. Furthermore most developing countries deal with E-government by spreading more computers in their organizations (Ndou, 2004); and the organizations departments must understand the benefits from ICT uses in order to provide the right information to the right people at the right time to both government organizations and citizens. Knowing that to use information to its fullest potential, the planners and decision makers need near real time access to multiple forms of data, information and knowledge resources in a properly summarized form, which is not an easy job for many governments.

To achieve the goals of e-government project, the government planners and the top-level officials/decision makers want to do detailed analysis before taking a decision, so the departments are now looking for a framework by which one can accomplish multiple goals and not for one-step or one goal.

In this research we propose the BI which helps in analyzing and selecting the right answer (means in the right form and in the right time for the right people), for E-Government applications in Government-to-Government (G2G) category of E-Government environment.

Gartner (2008), Zeng (2006), and Sherman (2003) explain how BI can offer many benefits for E-Government system like: no deal with heterogeneous and silo's systems, minimum dependence on IT staff, no need to use sophisticated tools in order to obtain needed information allowing taking the desired effect and build more strong strategies to reach government and its organizations goals. Sandu (2008) and nelson (2004) state that BI can offer many services to E-Government such as: deep understanding of government citizen's needs, operational effectiveness increase, availability of multiple resources to government planners and decision makers and providing extensive resources to support E-Government project.

Therefore, we proposed the BI technologies as a crucial component of any E-Government initiatives, and we developed a framework, which uses the BI within E-Government system.

RESEARCH METHODOLOGY

The research methodology tend to get results from effective results using procedures, ways, methods and techniques to get and analyze needed information for this research. In general, methodology could be considered as a branch of philosophy with objectives of analyzing the principles and procedures of an inquiry in particular discipline (Newman, 1997); Irny and Rose (2005) see the methodology as a guideline for solving a problem, including all needed components like phases, tasks, methods, techniques and tools in order to get the right solution.

According to Simon (1969), there are many ways to solve a problem, with unpredictable performance, but no single perfect solution; unlike problem in algebra, that has one solution. Many ways to gather information from information system such as sampling, research and site visits, observation, questionnaires, interviews, prototyping; but not all ways are goods for all problems, so it is very important to select the suitable way for a specific research depending on the environment of the research.

Upon this discussion, this research will start by setting the purpose and objectives and discover obstacles, benefits, suggestions and recommendations for building a good strategy of E-Government. Worldwide, E-Government could be considered a new phenomenon under information system umbrella where there are multiple research methodologies. This research will follow a part of them, considering the case study of Syria, and using a method for data collection and analyze the data to reach to the results of the research.

The main purpose of research methodology is to provide an E-Government framework by building a good strategy and improve it with time via an

alignment between business/IT teams in dynamic environment and discussing how to use BI for that. To get the research objectives, a systematic process is followed, after doing a literature review, a study about E-Government in Syria, information gathering and finally analyzing the information and discovering the results.

To do the research, quantitative and qualitative approaches could be used together or separately to get results (Easterby-Smith et al., 2002), the two types of research (whether quantitative or qualitative) are based on some underlying assumptions about what constitutes 'valid' research and which research methods are appropriate.

Qualitative research could be positivist, interpretive, or critical, at the other hand the quantitative research could be positivist only. Qualitative research is most important in the social sciences (Denzin & Lincoln, 2003) using qualitative data gathered by interviews, documents, and participant observations. This type of research focus on the researchers as the primary instrument for data collection and analysis (Merriam, 1998), who should be interested in flexible, evolutionary, emergent and inductive process, meaning, and understanding gained through the words, interviews, transactions, and field notes of observation in order to get qualified information (Lee et al., 1999). The output of this type is words more than numbers depending on participant's perceptions.

Unlike quantitative research, the sample in qualitative research is usually non-random in nature and small (Merriam, 1998); and generally is used to study and analyze a complex phenomenon (Yin, 2004) asking questions with a "*how*" or a "*what*". Therefore, this research followed on qualitative research techniques, and modes of analyzing and interpreting data to build a framework for E-Government using BI.

E-Government adoption success needs the efforts of all participants (public sector organizations, E-Government developers, employees, citizens, businesses etc.) in E-Government project,

Table 1. Participant's information

No	Organization Name	Classification	No of participants
A	E-Government Team	Public sector	5
B	Ministry of Communication	Public sector	2
C	Ministry of Interior	Public sector	3
D	Banking sector	Public sector	2
E	GSM provider	Private sector	2
F	Universities	Academic field	3
G	Focus Group	Multi field	3
Total			20

which is a long, broad and complex operation in a complex environment.

This research focuses on building E-Government framework with reference to strategy in general, and for all related work in E-Government project, by using BI. Using many research methods such as documents analysis and observation, interviews and focus groups as main techniques of qualitative research in case study of Syria; the case study will allow to have multiple sources and multiple methods, focus on relationship and processes, natural setting and in depth study (Denscombe, 2007). Therefore, to reach the objectives of the research, a study about E-Government in general and the project in Syria was the first step, allowing the researchers to have enough knowledge about the nature of E-Government and the barriers facing its adoption and give as a result a framework for building E-Government strategy using BI.

Table (1) lists information about the participants of this research: E-Government team (public sector such as ministry of communication, banking sector and ministry of interior), private sector (GSM providers, universities) and academic people (Damascus University) in order to get multiple points of view.

When selecting the participants, the researchers try to select the persons who have enough experience at c-level with experience of ten years at least, and the age average is 39 year. In addition,

the researchers studied many documents about E-Government strategy and related documents with 14 documents, and visited so many organizations that have good experience in information system and have successful projects on the organization level.

The researchers did a study of related documents, and interviews with individuals and focus groups of people. Documents related to E-Government project, government organizations as national documents (such as strategies, plans, newspaper clippings, schedules, presentations and reports) were gathered and studied. The documents were used to provide background information about the E-Government project in Syria and other related public organization initiatives; also, many articles and websites files were browsed in order to take a good idea about the research environment.

Documents gathering and analyzing gives good idea about the E-Government project and its barriers, but it is not enough to study all factors affecting its adoption or the enablers. At the other side, interviewing is perhaps the most significant method to getting information from people. Therefore, the researchers did many interview sessions in order to gather data and information. A set of interview questions was prepared to ask for interviews and the summarized results of the interview were studied to have the results of the research.

The interviews sessions output shows the right status from the suitable persons; the researchers did 20 interviews. Interviews of these types need a number of eight interviews to reach the results (Yin, 2003). The interviews in this research are, in general, semi structured with little number of open and structure questions, this to have more flexibility and ability to extract detailed information from the participants, which are useful in such research where discovering gaps and proposing solutions are very important. In addition, focus group interview was essential for the research, which include people from IT and business background, this will help in studying the role of relationship between business and IT people in E-Government project success, and discuss the possibility to use BI in order to reduce the gap between two teams.

Yin (2003) suggests doing data analysis that will be after gathering data, in order to discuss their results and compare them with the research questions. Data analysis is the very important step in the research, which includes data examination, categorization and tabulation. According to Hartley (1994), data collection and analysis is not for one time, in opposite, it is important to do the two steps for several times, and based on each analysis the researchers must redo a new data collection.

Since the researchers focus is on studying the effect of the business/IT alignment on E-Government success and the use of BI, so it will be better to use the strategy which relied on theoretical propositions help in focusing on certain data and ignore others. Starting by initial considerations about the framework, prior to the data collection exercise which will be a very useful tool in structuring and guiding the data collection and analysis processes.

The researchers' methodology for data analysis in this research starts by discovering the initial considerations and the interview guide which were used in identifying the primary patterns in the data. Then, the researchers started reading through all the collected data (i.e. official documents, inter-views notes, observation notes, electronic reports and other official brochures, and local newspapers articles). The data were coded according to the themes identified by the initial framework and the interview guide. Analyzing the collected data based on the themes that emerged from the literature review prior to the data collection. Separating new themes, classification and adding them to their suitable classes within specific categories or creating new classes within the same categories. Finally, coding, categorizing and classifying the identified patterns were carried out.

The researchers used many analytical techniques constitute the classifications and categorization of the data, noting regularities and patterns, deriving explanations, and reviewing and rechecking findings amongst the researchers supervisor; all these steps are related to the initial considerations and help in getting a detailed framework.

INITIAL FRAMEWORK

The research takes in consideration three points:

The Role of Business/It Alignment of E-Government Success

E-Government project is a continuous project with new objectives depending on new needs of all parts of E-Government in one framework (Irani, 2005), therefore the relationship between business and IT teams is without end. This alignment needs to start from the strategies initiatives development with continuous improvement, this development includes business and IT strategies with some integration between them (Klein, 2006).

The importance of chief information officer (CIO) role in government organizations, those people who can speak the language of business and IT terms (Earl and Feeny, 1994), to be as middleware in each organization and between government organizations, in order to achieve the E-Government objective.

Good use of government resources needs the understanding of existed resources (IT, financial and human) and not only of single organization resources (West, 2004), in order to be able to take benefits from all resources to improve an organization work, this imply the existence of such alignment. With this knowledge about all resources, it will be possible to use IT resources from business people, do staff training to manage all changes occurred in the government plan, this will help also in taking good decisions from planner and decision makers (Valentina, 2004). Beside this, the technical part will be as profit center in each organization and not as cost center by knowing its output in the whole project of the government, and with good alignment, this profit will increase and decrease the overall cost of the project.

The study of G2G side and in the same time the other E-Government categories will be in touch, since the main target of any E-Government project is to introduce better services to all citizens (Ndou, 2004).

The researchers agree on the positive role of business/IT alignment on the E-Government project success with mention to its importance increase in developing countries, which needs culture building beside the E-Government project, and this will take a lot of time.

The Role of BI Governance on the Mentioned Alignment

The planners and decision makers need to get input and take decisions on all levels: strategic, tactical and operational, those decisions depend on data, information and knowledge gathered as input of decisions process (Robinson, 2001). In addition, the human ability to take those decisions is very important; the output of this process will serve the objectives of the organization.

The researchers propose a model, which justifies the needs from any BI governance system

in order to serve in the business and IT teams' alignment, like:

1. Agility: since the E-Government services are, in general, online and 24X7 the BI governance system must not be static, in opposite must be compatible with the business and IT changes in the organization on all levels, some system like this start to be existed but with specific domain and not easy to use from all teams (Ndou, 2004).

2. Group work: to do the alignment, it is very important to work in-group, which includes business and IT members, like this, the alignment will give the desired results (Klein, 2006).

3. Avoid the traditional hierarchy in the organization, which prevent the knowledge transfer between members, and in opposite give the power to CIOs and mini CIOs on all levels of the organization (Earl and Feeny. 1994).

4. Focus on people in the decision making process who are qualified enough and have good experience in change management (Haekel, 1993).

5. The business intelligence governance (BIG) building must take multiple factor and must be designed upon the project itself and not to be imported from another project, this will need the cooperation between all parts of the project, which need to clearly define the decision domain, decision-making people, and decision process (Leonard, 2006).

6. The BIG framework must be monitored and audited by time, in order to improve its design with the change in the organization.

The Ability to Use BI Governance with E-Government System

The researchers proposes the ability to use the BIG as an enabler in E-Government system focusing on the people, process organizational and needs to data, information and knowledge at right time.

People: it is the main element in the alignment process; they take the decisions after studying the input (Whiting, 2004). People must be qualified enough to be able to success in either BIG or E-Government, since they will transform the E-Government guiding principles to BIG guiding principles, and they form the decision making bodies in E-Government project and develop the needed process and procedures needed to be existed in the E-Government project. This implies that business and IT teams work together in all phases of the project (Huang, 2007).

Process: avoid the difference between the business and IT objectives; the process must be rethinking with time and all phases of the project under the umbrella of E-Government project (Chase, 2001).

Organizational: building new cultures over all organizations, which serve the E-Government project, this culture facilitate the alignment, and on the other side consider the IT not as cost center (Shanks, 2007). This could be realized by using the BIG, besides building the convenient technology.

DEVELOPMENT OF BIG FRAMEWORK WITHIN E-GOVERNMENT

The framework in this research is a methodology that serves in building an E-Government strategy using BI and reduces the gap between business and IT. The Framework serves the business objectives by analyzing the multiple factors affecting the E-Government and BI such as people, process, and technology, with consideration to agile environment of business.

Since the alignment between the business strategy and the IT strategy is critical for E-Government, the framework shows how to use BI for that, the framework also allows BI to be defined from different perspectives in an operational sense, and the need to monitor, audit and predict. Taking all these parts into one framework

and considering its enhancement based on the findings from participants' interviews.

E-Government Characteristics

Many environmental issues must be considered like government organizations cooperation and integration in order to successfully adopt an E-Government system. The research in this study focuses on (G2G) in developing countries, taking the Syria as a case study in order to have full understanding about of E-Government adoption at an initial stage especially building strategy on all levels and help planners and decisions makers in their work. Other categories of E-Government will be affected indirectly since the G2G is considered as the backbone of E-Government. One interviewee mentions that: "*Syria transformation towards E-Government will be as need from different sides like political, social, economic, cultural and managerial sides and in same time, it will have effects on them, knowing that the Syrian E-Government project is at an initial stage*", which was confirmed by many participants.

The E-Government project is related to government so the alignment of E-Government strategy with other government initiatives is needed which not existed in general in Syria where many participants confirmed that: "*The relationship between the E-Government project and projects in other ministries start to be existed*".

Actually, the Syrian E-Government project team builds an initial strategy starting national ICT plan with related standards, prepared by a specific ministry dedicated to ICT, these strategies and standards were, initially, designed by an initial E-Government entity. The participants focus on some points to take in consideration in all E-Government phases, one E-Government team member said: "*The E-Government plan must give attention to cost efficiency, cost recovery, accountability, transparency and getting speed small good results at beginning for high important sub projects*".

The main objective of the E-Government in a country is to achieve the goal of related government; this is not easy in general. One expert mentioned to the multiple factors affected the E-Government project saying: "*Technological, organizational and human factors are very important to E-Government project especially in developing countries*". These factors must be taken in consideration at initial stage of the project. E-Government adoption is a project based on ICT, as mentioned by a senior manager who clarified: "*E-Government project must have the major components of a robust ICT infrastructure in all government organizations*".

E-Government strategy development, which includes a mission, vision and objectives, same as a detailed action plan, is very important, as explained by many participants, one of them said: "*E-Government strategy must be aligned with other government strategies, and give importance to the alignment of multiple factors affecting its adoption*". Forming E-Government entities (in the E-Government project) that are responsible for managing and operation the E-Government activities is very important. These entities will be formed from both IT and business people and the alignment between them the key success factor of the E-Government project.

One expert explained: "*The alignment will start at the first stage of developing an E-Government system when building the strategy and continue with the project lifecycle*". Some participants try to list some entities; most of them focus on the need to have a new special entity, one senior manager mention for that by saying: "*A special entity should do performance measurements, follow-up and auditing tasks during the implementation of an E-Government project*". The existence of such entity will help in dealing with changes in E-Government environment, as explained by one senior manager: "*Environment changes must be considered with all related issues in technology and people from both internal and external sides*".

A national data warehouse to provide needed information to planners and decisions makers, one E-Government team member focus on the need of such unit by saying: "*A national data warehouse must be built in order to give the right information for right people in right place and at right time*". The decisions and plans must be taken by people and with help from technical engine, which could predict some of them. One senior manager focus on the importance of the organizational structure to E-Government project saying: "*The organizational structure and culture are very important to E-Government project which needs a continuous change in organizations, existing management processes and business models*".

These points must be considered in any E-Government framework with different degrees of importance, but the alignment between IT and other teams is the critical one.

Business/ IT Alignment

The findings of this research illustrate the role of alignment between business and IT people in order to build successful E-Government strategy on all levels strategically, tactical and operational. The participants agree on a number of findings such as:

Business and IT decision makers' relationship improvement in order to achieve alignment; one senior manager explained the need for such alignment by saying: "*Alignment will lead to participation in both business and IT strategies development and their synchronization in the project lifecycle*".

Business and IT decision makers' communications improvement; one senior manager clarified the role of such communication when said: "*Business and IT people communication will allow each part speaking in another field; this will be achieved by CIOs*".

IT resources utilization improvement in order to achieve organizational goals; one expert explained that by saying: "*The good use of IT resources will enable the business people to see* the value that IT can add to the organization and justify the return on investment (ROI) and new perception of the IT function. The utilization improvement will need continuous training". All of this improvement will lead to cost reduction and better overall returns on investment: by the strategies alignment. Many participants concentrate on the role of such alignment and the factors affect on this alignment as explained by one of them, he said: "*The alignment will depend on multiple factors such as people, process and organization Factors*".

Meeting of the minds between IT and business decision makers is the most important people factor; it could be reached by performance measurement for the two groups, building one group from the two teams. On the other hand, Process factor is the most important factor and it is very important to ensure that business strategy goals are linked to IT strategy goals. Also, Organizational culture factor is very important since it facilitates alignment of IT and business decision makers; when building such culture the alignment will be improved and so the IT will be seen as value more than cost for any organization.

To do alignment, different methods could be used; the participants ensure that BI is very important in this area.

Business Intelligence

Almost all participants focus on the importance of BI in E-Government system, their opinions and remarks could be grouped to build the convenient framework.

Productivity increase of government organizations is very important; one expert explained: "*Productivity increase needs short and long-term strategies, which will be built and operated by cooperation between business and IT people*". The role of BI becomes critical in such agile environment in building, monitoring the E-Government strategies, one senior manager explained this idea when saying: "*The important use of BI includes*

information gathering, analyzing, monitoring, forecasting, resource utilization, and get feedback information into decision processes for government operation improvement*".

BI has a strategic role in governance framework that continues the flow of information from creation to its use. Almost, all participants focus on the importance of such framework, one of them said: "*The framework will ensure the full access of data using multiple types of technologies by skilled people in a standard way in any time from any place*". The advantages of building such BI governance framework are the support offered to government strategic transformation by making decisions faster and better and by reducing costs. Most participants list some parts of the framework, one of them summarized that by saying: "*This framework will adapt data gathering engine, analytical engine and decision engine*". Actually, many details could be found about the data gathering and analysis ways. The decision engine is the most important and the intelligence is needed here.

The participants list many benefits from BI use in E-Government system as the following:

- Business and analytic intelligence processes and initiatives standardization.
- Faster reaction to business changes.
- Overall cost and risk reduction in implementation and operation.
- Support end users decisions.
- Preserve and exploit the full value of technology investments.
- Independence from heterogeneous and silo's systems
- Minimized dependence on IT staff
- No need to use sophisticated tools.
- Formulation of more effective strategies and policies
- Deep understanding of citizens' needs
- More operational effectiveness
- Providing better, faster access to critical data about government services status

which is very important to planners and decisions makers on different levels of government

- Project development on national level

Therefore, BI is a critical component of any E-Government initiative, which will help planners and decisions makers in drawing key conclusions from data. It is clear that BI technologies are more oriented towards G2G than other categories; actually, all government plans and decisions can be achieved by detailed analyses of all the relevant data. Same, citizens will take benefits from those technologies like government organizations.

The necessary BI infrastructure must be built and needed teams must be trained, and the plan must go with prioritized services as a proof of concept and after that in agile way go to other sectors. The strategy of E-Government is agile in principle so the strategy will be changing over time and enhanced on all levels of E-Government project.

The design considerations initially explained in this research will be enhanced in the following with reference to the participants' explanation.

Framework Design

The initial framework is based on the main role in E-Government system with mention to people, process, technology and information to the system.

This framework needs some enhancements like the following:

1. Input/output layer (government organizations applications): Government organizations users will access the IT infrastructure via electronic channels such as web portals, web applications, point of sale (POS) terminals, self-service kiosks, mobile devices, and interactive voice response servers.

2. Presentation layer (Front end engine): E-Government system needs front end system (display engine) as the interface to users via electronic channels, Users of front office applications such as call center or customer support applications make millions and millions of decisions each day without analytical support. These decisions need some predications issues and to go far from traditional way of decisions, the decisions must be based on right information given to right people in the right time and place. To best use of analytical information derived in BI systems, the front office application users must have the BI analyst skills to work with complex BI tool sets in order to create the needed reports. On the other hand, the use of BI must bridge the gap between the operational and analytical systems, which will require the real time delivery of analytical information. Actually, these factors are not arrived in general, so, government organizations cannot optimize their front office departments since analytical insight derived in BI systems is not available to the users in these departments.

3. Technical layer (Gathering engine): Information is the most important assets to any government, it can help planners and decision makers in making informed decisions leading to positive impact on government organizations and citizens; actually, the planners and decision makers need instant access to relevant data in a properly meaningful form. Regardless of computerization projects in many countries, the government planners and decision makers are unable to obtain meaningful information in a timely manner because this information depend on IT staff for making special reports which often takes long time to generate, also without business/IT alignment most reports will be without the desired benefits. Building information warehouse will provide strategic intelligence to the planners and decision makers, which will facilitate planners and decision makers' mission in taking micro level decisions in a timely manner independent from IT staff. Knowing that the top-level

officials/ planners and decision makers need to do detailed analysis before taking a decision, the organizations departments are now looking for a framework based on multiple goals from business and IT sides on all levels of government organization.

4. Business layer (Monitor/Analysis/predict intelligence + decision engines): Monitoring Intelligence is related to know what happened in the government organizations and also what is happening in the time of monitoring; some examples such as financial statements, business alerts, operational reports, smart lists, and any in time report information.

Analytical Intelligence is related to know why something is happening; so analytical intelligence capabilities will allow planners and decision makers and end users to understand the drivers of resulted information.

Predictive Intelligence is related to predict what will happen; after having full ideas about what happened and why something happened, the next logical step in the BI process is to predict what will happen. This phase is not easy; it needs full understanding of business objectives, customer behaviors, and other influencing internal and external factors. The prediction phase needs more research on the concept of intelligence and prediction.

Decision engine: to help decision makers in their work, this engine will use mathematical models to create decisions based on a set of settings, but this engine will not take a decision without human approval; artificial intelligence will be very useful in this area and it could be as future research.

5.BIG contents: Many questions need to have answers before taking decisions and putting plans must on all government levels all the time, such as what is the information needed to make decision or plan? Is possible to access this information in the right way? Do they know all the factors affecting these decisions? Many other questions could be listed in order to take business decisions and put business plans.

Business decisions couldn't be generated only by IT people, and on the another hand business people couldn't take decisions alone without the help from IT people; regardless of the information gathering and analyzing, but the business people need to access information in their own language whereas they can understand it and in same time independent of IT people. The information must be user oriented like this divided upon its purpose. Information providing to business users will help planners and decisions makers to do their work in active way on all levels of the government. In this way, BI is a system, which will lead to have the information required to control and improve government organizations' processes, and the information needed by business users in their work in planning and decision-making. This leads to the need of BI governance.

The BI governance is not simple as many people think, its building needs having several mechanisms, which will lead to have several groups, which do their jobs in teamwork method, where the participation and collaboration of key users and mixed Business and IT teams is very important on all levels of government, as a result have the Business/IT alignment.

There are so many benefits from BI governance. Ongoing adaptability, where the environment of decisions processes is rapidly changing; Teamwork, which will lead to have IT/Business alignment on all levels of government organizations. Flexible hierarchies which will allow having changes in the government organizations hierarchies in order to have working groups facilitating information exchange and restructuring with time, and focusing on people more than technologies and processes, actually decisional processes vary all the time in such agile environment.

All these benefits will be achieved by good building of BI governance framework, which needs to have guiding principles, decision-making bodies, decisions areas and governance

Figure 1. Enhanced BIG framework with e-government system

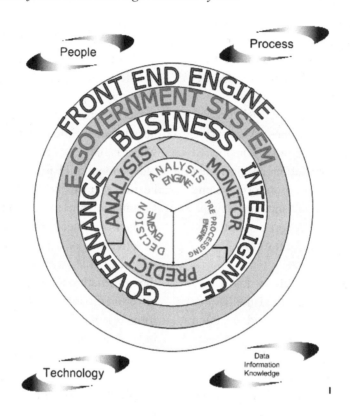

mechanisms. However, this framework will be useless if the E-Government project does not have monitoring and auditing scenarios in order to have measurement of the government performance in developing its services.

Figure 1 shows the comprehensive framework based on the results from this research and the initial framework based on literature.

The E-Government adoption is the government main challenge especially in developing countries, as the case study showed by using the example of Syria. This framework, therefore, has summarized research findings and has presented the case study findings in the shape of a framework that has been developed from a government-to-government (G2G) perspective. This framework use BI in order to minimize the gap between business and IT, this gap that was explained by many participants as the main barrier to E-Government adoption. This research discussed the multiple

framework requirements and the benefits from this framework. The framework could be considered as guide to E-Government team to draw and enhance their strategy for E-Government adoption. Empirical evidence has confirmed the framework and validates its E-Government project in Syria, and could be used in other developing countries that are similar to Syria. The framework show the importance of agility design that shows that the E-Government project is continuous and not stops after a period, and needs to be reviewed time by time.

Furthermore, the framework will be useful for E-Government planners and policy makers to enable them to understand, plan and perform their work, to face the challenges and risks that might be exist in their way, and to assess and improve the progress of E-Government.

CONCLUSION

This theory building research presents a BI governance framework within E-Government system derived from an empirical study with 20 academic and experts from public and private sector. An analysis of the findings demonstrated that the business/IT alignment is very important to E-Government success, the important role of use BI in E-Government system.

The research is likely to make both theoretical and practical contributions to the fields of BI and E-Government systems projects. The implications of the current and future research could be divided to:

Methodological issues (related to future empirical efforts): The contributions of this study that relate to methodological issues are based on the initial considerations and the use of an interpretive case study approach.

The framework developed for this study is based, initially, on ideas found in the literature concerning E-Government and BI.

Semi-structured interviews, indirect observations and documentation were used in the case study; beside local newspaper articles and workshops of E-Government in Syria where there are many researchers from different countries. The use of multiple sources of evidences and their triangulation help to have less error in the results.

The method used in this research help to open wide window on E-Government by participating E-Government team, IT manager, senior manager and independent experts, in order to have multiple point of view and good understanding related to the case study. This will reduce the bias in the results.

Practical issues: actually, the framework resulted from this research is the main contribution of this study. The framework proposed a method for E-Government adoption using BI, which will be useful researchers working in E-Government and BI researches after understanding the framework. The research in E-Government will be useful especially in developing countries and the other side BI research will be useful worldwide.

To conclude, E-Government and BI are relatively new topics where there are many areas, which still need to be studied in general and specific to special cases in some countries, so future work will be necessary to understand them. The multiple areas, which need future work with reference to this research, are:

E-Government framework validation in different countries with different context in or order to generalize the result will be necessary.

This research serves for G2G case, and the factors affect E-Government adoption in this area. The study of other different categories in relationship with this framework will be mandatory in order to do the integration of results.

It is very important to go in depth in the framework and list the details of every part in order to build it as intelligent part from all perspectives, writing a guide for the framework beneficiary.

Finally, The E-Government adoption is not trivial, it needs all government resources, and business/IT alignment between two parts, at the other hand, BI has a wide range of applications in different sectors. Many researchers tried to understand the E-Government adoption by discussing the main CSF and critical failure factors (CFFs), the researches results are not the same and differ depends on the researchers' point of view of E-Government, same for the BI system and its benefits. This research aimed to build E-Government adoption framework using BI providing both theoretical and practical insights into an E-Government system using BI in developing countries by taking Syria as a case study.

Overall, the research showed that E-Government is not a technical problem and cannot work without IT, and in countries like Syria, there is a gap between business and IT people, the use of BI help to close the gap between them, with importance role of people, process and organizational factors. This will help planners, policy makers at all levels of government operational, tactical, and strategically, in agile environment with continuous change that will increase E-Government project success rates using BI; this was the primary goal of this research.

The evidence found is that no study to date has focused on E-Government adoption using BI in order to close the gap between business and IT teams, therefore this research could be considered as one of the pioneer studies in this area. This study has made a novel contribution to the area of E-Government and BI and has expanded the body of knowledge, especially for E-Government adoption projects in developing countries.

REFERENCES

Chase, D. (2001). *Business intelligence*. e-SI Whitepaper. Retrieved on May 9th, 2009, from http:// www.dchase.com/ papers/ bi.pdf

Denscombe, M. (2007). *The good research guide: For small-scale social research projects*. Maidenhead: Open University Press.

Denzin, N. K., & Lincoln, Y. S. (2002). *The Qualitative Inquiry Reader*. Thousand Oaks, CA: Sage Publication.

Earl, M. J., & Feeny, D. F. (1994). Is your CIO adding value? *MIT Sloan Management Review, 35*(3), 11–20.

Easterby-Smith, M., Thorpe, R., & Lowe, A. (2002). *Management research* (2nd ed.). London, UK: Sage Publication.

Ebrahim, Z., Irani, Z., & Alshawi, S. (2004). A strategic framework for e-government adoption in public sector. In *Proceedings of American Conference on Information Systems*, New York, USA.

Gartlan, J., & Shanks, G. (2007). The alignment of business and Information Technology strategy in Australia. *Australasian Journal of Information Systems, 14*(2), 113–133.

Gartner (research note) (2008). *Key issues for business intelligence and performance management initiatives*. Retrieved on January 18, 2010, from www.gartner.com

Haekel, S. H., & Nolan, R. L. (1993). Managing by wire. *Harvard Business Review, 71*(5), 122–132.

Hartley, R. J. (1994). A review of Information Systems development methodologies (ISDMS). *Library Management, 15*(6), 5–19.

Heeks, R. (2003). *E-government for development: Causes of e-government success and failure: Factor model, IDPM*, University of Manchester, UK. Retrieved on April 3rd, 2009, from: http:// www. egov4dev.org/ causefactor.htm

Huang, D. C., & Hu, Q. (2007). Achieving IT-business strategy alignment via enterprise-wide implementation of balanced scorecards. *Journal of Information Systems Management, 24*(2), 173–184.

Irny, S. I., & Rose, A. A. (2005). Designing a strategic Information Systems planning methodology for Malaysian institutes of higher learning (ISP-IPTA). *Issues in Information Systems, 6*(1).

Kalakota, R., & Robinson, M. (2001). *E-business 2.0 – Roadmap for success*. New York, NY, USA: Addison-Wesley.

Klein, P. (2006). Change your thinking. *Information Week*. Retrieved on May 17th, 2010, from http:// www.informationweek.com

Kreizman, G., & Fraga, E. (2003). *Tactical guidelines best practices in country e-government, TG-19-3073*. Retrieved on November 11th, 2009, from http:// www.cira.state.tx.us/ Docs/docs/ bestpractices.

Leonard, B. (2006). *Framing BI governance*. Retrieved on March 3rd, 2010, from http:// www. bi-bestpractices.com/ view/ 4686

Merriam, S. B. (1998). *Qualitative research and case study applications in education. Revised and expanded from: Case study research in education.* San Francisco, CA: Jossey-Bass.

Ndou, V. (2004). *E-government for developing countries: Opportunities and challenges.* The Electronic Journal on Information Systems in Developing Countries.

Negash, S. (2004). Business intelligence. *Communications of the Association for Information Systems, 13,* 177–195.

Nelson, G. B., & Wright, J. (2004). *Real time decision support: Creating a flexible architecture for real time analytics.* 29th SAS User Group International Conference (SUGI29).

Newman, W. L. (1997). *Social research methods: Qualitative and quantitative approach* (3rd ed.). Boston, MA: Allyn & Bacon.

Prananto, A., & McKemmish, S. (2007). *Critical success factors for the establishment of e-government: A critical analysis of the Indonesian Cabinet Secretariat's Legal Document Retrieval System (LDRS) Project.* Australia: Swinburne University of Technology.

Sandu, S. (2008). Operational and real-time business intelligence. *Revista Informatica Economică nr, 3*(47), 33-36.

Sherman, R. (2003). *Mars, Venus and a Successful Business Intelligence Architecture, DMReview,* Available from: http:// www.dmreview.com/ article sub.cfm?articleId=6981 (Date of access 10/6/2009).

Simon, J. L. (1969). *Basic research methods in social science; The art of empirical investigation.* New York, NY: Random House.

UN. (2008). *E-government survey.* New York, NY, USA.

Valentina, N. (2004). *E-government for developing countries: Opportunities and challenges, The Electrical Journal on Information Systems in Developing Countries.* EJISDC.

Wagner, C., Cheung, K., Fion, L., & Rachael, P. (2003). Enhancing e-government in developing countries: Managing knowledge through virtual communities, *The Electronic Journal on Information Systems in Developing Countries (EJISDC), 14*(4) 1-20. Retrieved on July 2nd, 2006, from http:// www.ejisdc.org/ ojs/ include/ getdoc. php?id=89&article=100&mode=pdf

West, D. M. (2004). *E-government and the transformation of service delivery and citizen attitudes,* public administration review.

Whiting, R. (2004). *Group aims to bring structure to business-performance management, intelligent enterprise.* Retrieved on Novemeber 13th, 2009, from: http:// www.intelligententerprise.com/ 18402638

Yeoh, W., Koronios, A., & Gao, J. (2008). Managing the implementation of business Intelligence Systems: A critical success factors framework. *International Journal of Enterprise Information Systems, 4*(3), 79–94.

YIN. R. K., (2003). *A case study research: Design and methods,* 3rd edition. Thousand Oaks, CA: Sage Publications.

Zeng, L., Xu, L., Shi, Z., Wang, M., & Wu, W. (2006). *Techniques, process, and enterprise solutions of business intelligence.* 2006 IEEE Conference on Systems, Man, and Cybernetics, Taipei, Taiwan (Octover 8-11, 2006) (p. 4722, vol. 6).

KEY TERMS AND DEFINITIONS

Business Intelligence: A method that helps the organization to take the best decisions in agile environment with zero latency and predicate future decisions over time with regard to the change of all business environment conditions, inputs and desired outputs

Business/IT Alignment: A concept refers to the join between business and IT strategy and people in order to build a strategy to achieve the organization objectives.

Decision Making: A process, which has a final choice from different alternatives.

Developing Countries: The nations, which have a low level of materials.

E-Government: A project without end, use all government resources in order to deliver better services to citizens, businesses and government entities.

Governance: A method to get all data from all sources and prepare them to the decision makers (automated or human), at the right time in order to get the best decisions in the organization.

Qualitative Research: A research method of used to gather information in order to investigates the why and how of decision making.

Chapter 14
Business Intelligence in Higher Education:
An Ontological Approach

Constanta-Nicoleta Bodea
Academy of Economic Studies, Romania

ABSTRACT

The chapter presents an ontology-based knowledge management system developed for a Romanian university. The starting point for the development knowledge management system is the classic Information Management System (IMS), which is used for the education & training and research portfolio management. The knowledge management system has a general ontology, containing terms which are valid for a public institution, and specific ontology for the main two process categories, didactical and research. The ontologies were implemented using Protege. The chapter presents the usage scenario of the knowledge management system for the research area. The results are very encouraging and suggest several future developments.

INTRODUCTION

Higher education institutions are acting in a very high competitive environment. In order to become competitive, the universities should extensively use knowledge for better assessment, evaluation, planning and decision making. Knowledge

DOI: 10.4018/978-1-61350-050-7.ch014

management can lead to better decision-making capabilities, shorter development cycle for curriculum development and research, better academic and administrative services, and, finally, reduced operational costs.

The universities are deeply involved in achieving knowledge-based society following four directions: *(i) producing knowledge as a result of scientific research; (ii) communicating knowledge using education and training; (iii) dissemination of knowledge using information and communication technologies; (IV) using knowledge in technical innovation.* The universities have the key of knowledge-based society because they are at the cross of the research, education and innovation (World Bank, 2004). Although universities are deeply involved in the knowledge related processes, they have not necessarily developed and articulated a systemic approach to knowledge management. This is a critical weakness that should be corrected. In fact, it would seem that universities, research and development laboratories and public organizations funding and directing the research, should play a leading role in developing the theory, practice, and tools for knowledge management.

In (Davenport, 2001) the study of 31 knowledge management projects across 24 universities is presented. This study relived the following four broad types of objectives with different subtypes:

- Create knowledge repositories with external knowledge (competitive intelligence, market data, and surveys), internal knowledge (reports, marketing materials, techniques and methods) and informal internal knowledge (discussion databases of "know-how" or lesson learned"). In an educational setting, curriculum aids might be thought of us knowledge repositories. For example, the Milwaukee Public Schools Curriculum Design Assistant – CDA is both a source of documentation – standards, learning goals and a repository for instructional plans based on this documentation. These lesson plans are stored in the system and shared with others electronically to provide a Knowledge base for a wider audience.
- Improve knowledge access through technical expert referral, expert networks used for staffing based on individual competencies and turn-key video conferencing to foster

easy access to distributed experts. An example of this type f project is Community of Science online database, a communication recourse that functions well in education research. It links researchers, research institutions and founders together.

- Enhance the knowledge environment
- Managing knowledge as an asset.

Tables 1 through 5 illustrate how knowledge management applications could benefit a number of university processes and services: the research process, curriculum development process, student and alumni services, administrative services, and strategic planning (Serban & Luan, 2002).

ONTOLOGICAL APPROACH IN HIGHER EDUCATION

Ontology is an explicit specification of a conceptualization for a domain (Gruber, 1995). A conceptualization is a simplified view of the abstract world that we wish to represent. The ontology ccomponents are: the domain terms of vocabulary (concepts, instances, relations) specific definitions associated with each term and a set of axioms that restrict the possible interpretations of the terms defined. Basically, ontology enables knowledge sharing in a particular area, so the terms used in knowledge representation have the same meaning for both knowledge-based system and its users (humans and artificial intelligent systems). Also, the ontology allows reuse of domain knowledge.

There are a variety of ontology applications in higher education, including: academic disciplines, online resources, organizational structure. Disciplinary taxonomies, such as: NCES (National Center for Education Statistics) and NSF (national Science Foundation) classification schemes, existing already for many years are the starting point for educational ontologies development.

Higher education institutions, perceived from the organizational perspective were mapped into

Table 1. Application and benefits of knowledge management in research processes

Knowledge Management Application	Benefits, as organizational effectiveness and efficiency
• A repository of research interests within an institution or at affiliated institutions (potential subcontractors), research results (where possible) and funding organizations (federal agencies, foundations, and corporations) with easy search capabilities to facilitate interdisciplinary opportunities and commercial opportunities for research results. • A portal for research administration procedures and best practices related to: funding opportunities, pre-populated proposals, budgets, and protocols. • Proposal-routing policies and procedures. • Award notification, account setup, and negotiation policies and procedures. • Contract and grant management policies and procedures. • Technical and financial report templates and policies and procedures. • Overview of internal services, resources, and staff	• Increased competitiveness and responsiveness for research grants, contracts, and commercial opportunities. • Reduced turnaround time for research. • Minimized devotion of research resources to administrative tasks. • Facilitation of interdisciplinary research. • Improved internal and external services. • Reduced administrative costs

Table 2. Application and benefits of knowledge management in the curriculum development processes

Knowledge Management Application	Benefits, as organizational effectiveness and efficiency
• Repository of curriculum revision efforts that includes research conducted, effectiveness measures, best practices, lessons learned, and so forth. • Repository of content modularized and arranged to facilitate interdisciplinary curriculum design and development. • Portal of information related to teaching and learning with technology, including faculty development opportunities, outcomes tracking, lessons learned, best practices, technology overviews, and so forth. • Portal of information in each disciplinary area, including updated materials, recent publications, applicable research, and so forth. • Repository of pedagogy and assessment techniques, including best practices, outcomes tracking, faculty development opportunities, and research. • Repository of analyzed student evaluations updated each semester for lessons learned and best practices for all faculty. • Portal for new faculty with guides for developing curriculum, working with senior faculty, establishing effective teaching styles, advising do's and don'ts, supervising PhD students, and so forth. • Repository of corporate relationships to identify curriculum design advisory task forces, guest speakers, adjuncts, case study sites, and so forth	• Enhanced quality of curriculum and programs by identifying and leveraging best practices and monitoring outcomes.. Improved administrative services related to teaching and learning with technology. • Improved responsiveness by monitoring and incorporating lessons learned from the experiences of colleagues, student evaluations, and corporate or other constituent input. • Interdisciplinary curriculum design and development facilitated by navigating across departmental boundaries.

Table 3. Application and benefits of knowledge management in the student and alumni services

Knowledge Management Application	Benefits, as organizational effectiveness and efficiency
• Portal for student services for both students and for faculty and staff at the institution so that they are well informed to advice students. Information could include policies and procedures related to admissions, financial aid, registration, degree audit, billing, payment process, advising and tutoring, housing, dining, and other services • Portal for career placement services (potentially part of a large portal for all corporate connections) to provide a one-stop service center for students, but also for faculty and staff to ensure they are informed. • Portal for alumni and development services to minimize effort needed to realize contacts.	• Improved services for students. Improved service capability of faculty and staff. • Improved effectiveness and efficiency of advising efforts (to integrate fragmented efforts currently undertaken by faculty, academic and administrative staff.

Table 4. Application and benefits of knowledge management in the administrative services

Knowledge Management Application	Benefits, as organizational effectiveness and efficiency
• Portal for financial services that includes FAQs, best practices, procedures, templates • Portal for procurement. • Portal for human resources (that is, vacancy-to-hire, payroll, affirmative action, and so forth) that includes FAQs, best practices, procedures, templates	• Improved effectiveness and efficiency of administrative services. • Improved ability to support the trend toward decentralization of the administrative services. Improved compliance with administrative policies in the field. • Improved communication capabilities

several organizational hierarchies. For example, the CHESS taxonomy (Thomas, 2004) shows the organizational units which exists in typical education institutions. The National Association of College Auxiliary Services (NACAS) developed an organizational taxonomy, starting from the categories of the auxiliary services.

Ontologies for the online resources are mainly related to the content management systems. A learning ontology is an explicit formal specification of how to represent the learning objects, learning concepts (classes) and other entities and the relationships among them (Kanellopoulos, Kotsiantis & Pintelas, 2006). It describes the learning terms and the relationships between them and provides a clear definition of each term used. A precise and formal description of the course content will be made by explicit references to the learning ontology, using semantic annotations. The modeling of an ontology-based course can

be accomplished on two levels of knowledge organization:

• The upper level: the concepts set of the course topic selected form the ontological domain concepts
• The lower level: learning resources (books, web presentations, movies) associated with the upper level concepts; the ontology may be used as a semantic index for accessing the resources.

At the conceptual level, the learning paths can be developed based on semantic relations between the concepts, on two dimensions: the horizontal dimension and the vertical dimension. On the horizontal dimension, the learning sequence is established by moving from a given concept (the main subject), the ontology is browsed by following the decomposition relations (PO – Part Of relation). On the vertical dimension, the ontology

Table 5. Application and benefits of knowledge management in the strategic planning

Knowledge Management Application	Benefits, as organizational effectiveness and efficiency
• Office of Knowledge Management. • Portal for internal information that catalogs the strategic plans, reports developed for external audiences (for example, accreditation reports), presentations by executives, and so forth. • Portal for external information, including benchmark studies, environmental scans, competitor data, links to research groups, higher education research groups and publications, presentations, and so forth. • Monthly "market watch" developed in tandem with Admissions, Continuing Education, Alumni and Development, and others that document key trends and potential implications. • Repository of data related to accountability and outcomes, performance indicators	• Improved ability to support the trend toward decentralized strategic planning and decision (for example, block budgeting, responsibility center management). Improved sharing of internal and external information • Enhanced ability to develop up-to-date and market-focused strategic plans. • Shared knowledge in order to begin to create a "learning organization"

is browsed on the specialized connections (the IS-A relationship) with different results base on the direction: from down to up (synthesis and topic completion) and from up to down (topics development).

The followingn ontologies-based learning systems are described in (Kanellopoulos, Kotsiantis & Pintelas, 2006):

- *CIPHER*, http://www.cipherweb.org. The system supports the exploration of national and regional heritage resources.
- *Connexions*, http://cnx.rice.edu. It is an open source project that provides learning objects, a repository, a markup language and a set of tools for authoring, composing modules into courses and navigating through these courses.
- *Conzilla*, http://www.conzilla.org. It is being developed as part of the PADLR project as a means of accessing and annotating learning objects. It is a concept browser that allows the user to navigate through a space of context maps to access associated content. While the context maps are not reffered to as ontologies, they may be regarded as equivalent.
- *Edutella*, http://edutella.jxta.org. This project provides an infrastructure for Peer-to-Peer systems for exchanging educational resources. Edutella uses metadata based on standards such as IEEE LOM to decsribe resources.
- *EML: Educational Modelling Language*, http://eml.ou.nl/introduction/explanation.htm. It is a notational system developed at the Open University of the Netherlands as a means of representing the content of a study unit and the students and teachers roles, relations, interactions and activities. It now forms the basis for the IMS Learning Design Specification. As with many XML based approaches ontologies are not mentioned. However, the study

units, domain and learning theory models can be contructed as a set of ontologies.

ONTOLOGY-BASED KNOWLEDGE MANAGEMENT SYSTEMS DEVELOPMENT – A CASE STUDY FOR A ROMANIAN UNIVERSITY

The Academy of Economic Studies -AES, www.ase.ro is a national university in Romania. Its education and training programmes are delivered based on a public budget, coming from the Romanian Education and Research Ministry, and also on its own resources. It also has freedom and autonomy according the law. AES is considered a remarkable representative of superior economic studies in Romania. The university has 10 faculties, over 49.000 students and course attendants; 35500 - graduation cycle, 9400 - master programmes, 2500 - PhD enrolled, over 1600 in academic schools and post-graduation courses and 2000 didactic staff and technical and administrative personnel. In 2009-2010, AES will deliver more than 192 education & training programmes (see Table 6).

AES promotes the economic values, the administrative and judicial ones, together with the science and universal culture values. Its commitment is to achieve excellence in economic educa-

Table 6. AES Education & Training portfolio for 2009-2010

AES Education &Training Programmes	Total Number
Bachelor's degree in Economics	13
Continuing education (Trainings)	75
Scientific Master's degree	29
Professional Master's degree	46
International Master's degree	9
Online Professional Master's degree	10
Doctor's degree	10
Total	**192**

tion, and so to ensure the next generation of economists and administrative specialist is fully prepared for success on the workforce market. Based on competencies high level and responsibilities that AES has for the Romanian nation, it has the following goals in his mission:

- To educate and train qualified and high qualified personal for the economic, administrative and social domain;
- To promote free mind and critic spirit and the spirit of economic, juridical, and administrative knowledge;
- To continue develop the scientific research within economic, judicial and administrative domain, being connected with institutions of the same kind from the country and from all over the world;
- To develop programs regarding entrepreneurial activity;
- To promote the human culture and civilization;
- To defend the democratic academic framework based on fundamental liberties and human rights within a democratic state;

AES wants take a leading role in increasing the interest in economic, juridical, and administrative sciences, as few other academies and organizations can through its unique mission, workforce, facilities, research and innovations. AES is also taking a leading role to make significant impacts in engaging underserved and underrepresented communities in economy.

THE EDUCATION AND TRAINING PORTFOLIO MANAGEMENT IN AES

Higher education traditionally has evaluated itself in terms of inputs and resources rather than outcomes and amount of value added. In (Freed & Klugman, 1996) the measurement of resources determined quality, but the public is increasingly concerned about institutional performance and stakeholders' satisfaction. The success of AES's education portfolio depends upon *strategic planning* across the University. To succeed in his mission, the University tries to ensure that workforce requirements are identified and met and the education efforts are aligned and focused on building the future workforce in the specific domain. That's why it reaches the following *priorities*:

- to train specialists in economy having the specializations: business administration, cybernetic economics, accounting and management information, agro food economics, commerce economics, general economics, enterprise economics, environment economics, finances and banks, applied mathematics, management, marketing, international business, economic statistics and previsions, public administration and other according to national economy needs;
- To train specialists using programs that are using for teaching foreign languages;
- Continuing education through programs like: master programs, PhD programs and postgraduate programs;
- Developing fundamental scientific research and applied through faculties, research centers, laboratories and departments;
- Entrepreneurial activities that contain consulting programs, special assistance, business incubators;
- Recalling scientific performances of the academic community members by having organized reunions at national and international level;
- Offer education for foreign students.

The AES charter contents the coordination framework that aligns the university's total education portfolio with a strategic plan, provides a coordination structure, and creates a wide strategic planning implementation and evaluation framework for the investment in types of education of the University. The document builds on the education goals. Three of most important *goals* are:

- *Strengthen AES leading role in promoting economist profession in Romania:* University will identify and develop the critical skills and capabilities needed to achieve the vision for its specific domains. To help this demand, the University will continue to contributing to the development of the nation's economy workforce of the future through a diverse portfolio of education initiatives that target Romanian's students at all levels.
- *Attract and retain students in economy, judicial and administrative disciplines:* to compete effectively for the minds, imaginations, and career ambitions of Romania's young people, AES will focus on engaging and retaining students in its education programs to encourage their pursuit of educational disciplines critical to University's future, economic, judicial and administrative missions;
- *Engage Romanians interested people in University' missions***:** AES has already and will build more strategic partnerships and linkages between economic, judicial and administrative formal and informal providers. Through hands-on interactive, educational activities, AES will engage student, educators, teachers, specialists, families, the general public and all University external stakeholders to increase Romanian's economy, judicial and administrative literacy.

In addition to the university values and strategic management priorities, the AES education portfolio is established upon some *operating principles* to ensure programs alignment and excellence. The principles are integral to the conduct of, and apply collectively to, all AES education programs.

They form the foundation for evaluation of both new and existing education investments. The AES applies the following operating principles:

- *Relevance:* To effectively strengthen the nation's economic, judicial and administrative workforce, AES must implement activities that are useful to the education community and that strengthen their ability to engage students in the University activities and programs and in the future in the economic life of the society.
- *Content:* Education investments use University content, people or facilities to involve educators, students, and/or the public in AES activities and plans, technology, business experts, lawyer and people with a vast experience in practice.
- *Diversity:* AES strives to ensure that underrepresented and underserved students participate in University education and research programs to encourage more of these students to embrace a carrier in economic domain.
- *Evaluation:* Education investments document their intended outcomes and use metrics to demonstrate progress toward and achievement of these outcomes and annual performance goals. Evaluation methodology is based on models and techniques appropriate to the content and scale of the targeted activity, product, or program.
- *Continuity:* Projects and activities draw from the obtained results that have already demonstrated the efficiency of the programs University. Many projects and activities encourage continued young people affiliation with AES throughout their academic career.
- *Partnerships/Sustainability:* Education investments achieve sustainability through their intrinsic design and the involvement of appropriate local, regional, and/or national partners in their design, develop-

Figure 1. The AES education outcomes and operating principles

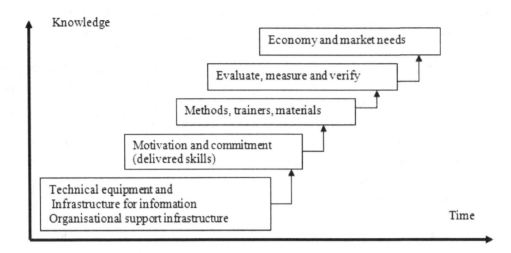

ment, or dissemination. Key aspects of projects and activities are replicable, scalable, and demonstrate potential for continuation beyond the period of direct AES funding.

The AES Education outcomes and operating principles can be mapped onto the education strategic framework scale (Figure 1). It can be found here the planning, implementation, and assessment of framework of the AES Education Portfolio.

International educational research has shown that a clear view about the education offer, a good feedback and close follow-up of students are very important determinants for their academic success (Dysthe, 2007), (Imhof & Picard 2009). The management of AES's education efforts allows through the portfolio approach a holistic view of all University education programs, projects, products, and activities as:

- Ensures that all education programs, projects, products and activities are aligned with the university strategic plan
- Coordinates programs, projects, products, and activities in a broader context so that

they work together to achieve AES's education goals
- Guides selection and assessment of new and ongoing education investments
- Facilitates performance evaluation, assessment, and accountability reporting, as well as communication of program status within AES and to external stakeholders
- Identifies programmatic gaps and/or redundancies and guides investment strategies.
- Aids in development of annual performance goals

The management also tries to offer to AES students a good feedback about their activities and information about the opportunities that they might to attempt.

Strategic management of the AES education portfolio requires the participation of the Educational Programs Department (EPD), faculties and departments of the University. This extensive participation provides broad education engagement with the economic content, people, and facilities. Close and effective consultation, coordination, and cognizance among all entities are critical to the optimal fulfillment of AES's objectives relative to its education investment. A coordinated and effective

Figure 2. The main processes of the education & training portfolio management

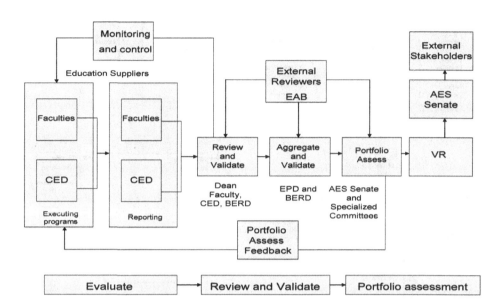

university education portfolio requires clear roles, responsibilities and a very well-defined management processes. Different authors addressed the education & training portfolio management issue, most of them proposing multi-criteria decision-making processes. In (Mustafa & Goh, 1996) we can find a comprehensive analysis of literature recommendations. (Politis & Siskos, 2004) proposed an educational portfolio evaluation model for enhancing the educational quality and internal organization of an engineering department inside of a Greek university.

In carrying out its role of assessing and guiding the total portfolio, the AES Senate and its committees have the ability to:

- Measure performance, including key performance indicators and metrics.
- Monitor ongoing status of operations, events, and resources.
- Set overall performance goals for the University.
- Establish measures and criteria for monitoring progress.

- Ask input from external reviewers on the status of the overall portfolio and future trends/needs in economic education related to AES's workforce needs.

Figure 2 presents the main processes of the education & training portfolio management.

AES success in implementing its education portfolio is determined by the university management ability to accomplish the proposed goals. It uses performance metrics, regular review processes, and defined tools to assess its performance at all level—portfolio, goals, and the individual program. It will be a direct connection between "Review and Validate" position, represented by the Faculty leader (Dean, Pro-Dean) and Educational Suppliers that handle the "Executing programs". "Review and Validate" sends information based on information received from External Reviewers. This fact optimized the results send to Educational Suppliers. Effectual consultation, coordination, and cognizance among all entities are critical to the optimal fulfillment of AES's education investment.

Figure 3. The structure of the operational database

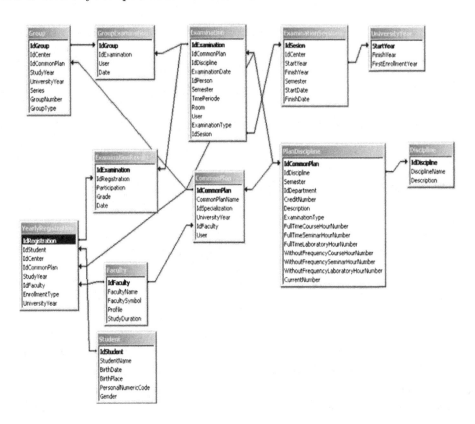

AES's education portfolio is evaluated in some steps from the beginning of the process. First, an external reviewer evaluates the results of internal reviewer and valuator, then the activity of ADP, then the Senate and specialized commissions. After that, the last one sends a feedback to Educational Suppliers. The management of education programs/projects complies with current AES directives on program and project management, processes, and requirements. The evaluation plans will measure intended impact and be scaled appropriately to the size of the investment "one size does not fit all." The Programmes Directors regularly monitor and evaluate the programs, and report the results of those evaluations to their funding organizations. The main tool for the education programmes evaluation is the student opinion survey. New modes of evaluation in contrast to traditional formats of evaluation indicate to students that their success depends not on *how much* (quantity) but rather on *how well* (quality) they have learned (Struyven & Dochy, 2006) and (Van der Schaaf & Stokking, 2008).

The review and validation are made by the Educational Programmes Department. The tools used are:

A common database and format used with very detailed information about the content of the education & training programmes and required resources (academic staff and software). This database is used for the results interpretations and for further decisions.

The ability to trace budget and actual costs from a single project up through the university education. It is very important to know how much the University can spend with a program/project/activity.

Figure 4. The structure of the database used by Educational Programmes Department

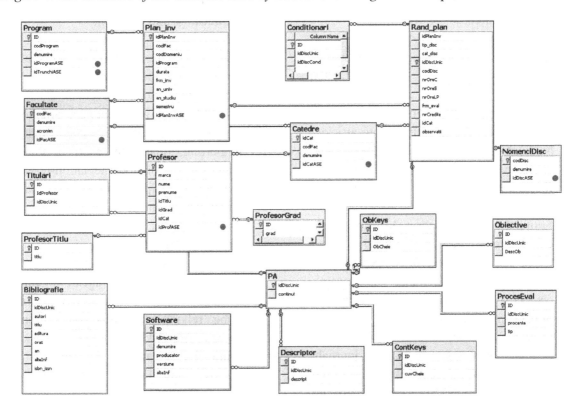

The operational database, administered at the university level (figure 3) is developed and updated by the IT Department, using the secretariat network. The data reflect the academic curricula and the students' grades.

The education & training programmes content and required resources (academic staff and software) are organized in a data base, administered by the Educational Programmes Department, with a high level of granularity (figure 4).

THE RESEARCH PROJECT PORTFOLIO MANAGEMENT IN AES

The main difference between universities, collectives and teaching staff consist in the capacity to do scientific research at a national and especially international level. Scientific research can bring substantial revenue to the people and institutions. Scientific research enhances quality improvement in the educational process, it motivates work adequately and it brings recognition.

Specific objectives of the AES regarding the research are the following:

- To promote excellence in the scientific research process, to promote the areas with a high potential in processing, transmitting and using knowledge.
- To stimulate competition in order to attract financial resources.
- To encourage diversity and access to resources and diverse opportunities.
- To encourage the accomplishment of some strategic programs for research development and efficient capitalization on the research results.

- To develop international excellence in scientific research.

The main means to accomplish the objectives are:

- Encouraging and recognizing fundamental scientific research, turned into articles, books, treaties, monographs, reports, scientific events, etc.
- Increasing the share of the scientific research activity in academic assessment.
- Stimulating participation to the grants competitions,
- Consolidating the accredited research centers and setting up others. The research centers will be reassessed periodically.
- Supporting, financially as well, the organization of scientific events, the issuing of their volumes and that of the journals edited by different teams. We will start the procedures for CNCSIS recognition of the new journals, and for some of them, international recognition.
- Setting up some agreements among different teaching departments in the AES and departments of other universities in order to elaborate reference works, such as treaties, encyclopedias, dictionaries.
- Stimulating article publication in national and foreign journals; in 2007 we intend to have 10% of the articles written by the teaching staff of the Academy of Economic Studies published in ISI journals.
- Further implementing ASE's project regarding quality assessment of scientific research, in different domains, in order to facilitate access to complimentary funds and to obtain an as good as possible position for the AES in a hierarchy of Romanian universities.
- Consolidating the national thematic networks, with international participation, with excellence in research, which would

entice access to the funds of the Ministry of Education and research.
- Starting up new joint ventures, under the framework of research consortiums at regional and European level.
- Encouraging students to obtain PhD and post–PhD grants and creating accommodation for the post – PhD grant beneficiaries.
- Supporting, financially as well, the accomplishment of documentation-research trainings, participation in national and international scientific events, by creating a special annual fund, in RON and other currencies, obtained from accumulated research overhead costs.
- Setting up an internal financial system for the research that the institution finds interesting, relying on similar competition to the one sustained by CNCSIS.
- Continuing research in domains such as pedagogy and didactic teaching of economic subjects.
- Improving the organization of student's scientific events.
- Supporting the inter- and pluri-disciplinary doctoral schools. We will prepare in due time the transition to the PhD included in the last educational cycle. The efforts will aim especially at developing research through PhDs and a better usage of the PhD theses.

The Department of Economic Research (DCE) offers logistics and consultancy in order to get involved in research programs and to cooperate with specialists from different domains. It also ensures support for cooperation with different institutions and departments of national and foreign universities; it organizes and takes part in national and international workshops and conferences. The scientific research activity is organized and carried out through projects and themes from the institutional programs of the departments, faculties and research centers.

Figure 5. The conceptual structure of the research project database

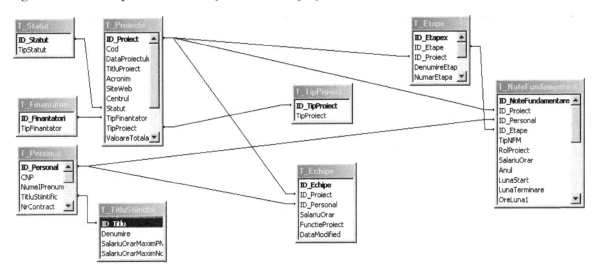

The Department of Economic Research coordinates and guides the executive activity of the authorized research centers. The results of the scientific research activity take shape in: the number and value of the research grants obtained in the national and international contests and the research contracts carried out; the research reports and final analyses given to the research beneficiaries; the products with intellectual property rights, program products, solutions to modernize and increase the economic efficiency accompanied by appropriate documentation given to the research beneficiaries, to the libraries of the AES and DCE archive; the books, handbooks and monographs with original scientific content published by editorial houses known at national and international level; volumes of scientific papers at national and international level; articles published in specialized journals in the country or abroad (ISI journals); PhD theses; membership in academies and international organizations; national and international awards. Together with the teaching departments, deans and rector, DCE takes part in organizing the annual students' scientific session and professional contests.

One of the major concerns of a higher education institution is to assess scientific and technical

implementation of projects and scientific research programs nationally and internationally funded. The research projects and programs are multidimensional entities, so to characterize it is necessary to use a system of indicators, having a large number of indicators as components, which allow qualitative and quantitative characterization the performance of research programs and projects. The large number of indicators makes difficult an evaluation process based on traditional methods.

The Research Projects Database

The research project database is owed by DCE. The database conceptual structure is shown in Figure 5. The database contains information about more than 1000 research projects funded by public or business organization and implemented by the university in the last 10 years, meaning 2007-2009.

All these data bases were integrated into a Management Information System (MIS) at the university level, developed in-house by a large team of teachers and researchers, starting with 2008. The conceptual structure of the integrated institutional database is shown in figure 6.

Figure 6. The conceptual structure of the integrated AES database

THE METHODOLOGY FOR KNOWLEDGE MANAGEMENT SYSTEM DEVELOPMENT

Developing knowledge management systems involves modeling knowledge, which is the application of languages, techniques, methods, tools and methodologies for developing abstract models of knowledge related to the specific domain. For university knowledge management system, knowledge will address both institutional management process and teaching and research processes as well. For example, the teaching knowledge management will include identifying and shaping personal and collective knowledge existing in the university (at departments' level) and share it to the people directly concerned (e.g., students).

There are a number of requirements to be met by the knowledge models. The knowledge model must be close to the human intuition, to be easily made operational, to be reused (for system modularity), to capture epistemological aspects (knowledge of the domain, general knowledge and specific knowledge). Knowledge models can be task-oriented (procedural knowledge), field-oriented (declarative knowledge that is included in the ontology), focused on the knowledge application (knowledge about tasks and domain, which explains the behavior of resolving problems in the field).

According to (Makhfi, 2007), the main models types are the following:

- Diagnostic models (used to diagnose a problem or to identify the possible causes from symptoms)
- Connotative models (to generate options for a specific case or to identify alternatives from a problem description)
- Selective models (for decision-making problems with multiple options or the identification of the best solution)
- Analytical models (to analyze pre-selected options or to identify if a good and appropriate solution was selected for a given target)
- Instructional models (a guide to problem solving or solution paths identification)
- Design models (to design and develop solutions or to identify the specifications)
- Hybrid models (for complex problems requiring a combination of several models)

The knowledge modeling flow may involve developing the following models: Diagnostic model >> Connotative model >> Selective model >> analytical model >> design model. Currently there are a variety of methods and technologies that can be used to implement abstract models associated to knowledge. These include: decision trees, Bayesian networks, genetic algorithms and evolutionary artificial neural networks, expert systems, statistical models, inference engines, agent technology etc. In general, the solutions offered by technologies fall into three categories: case-based systems, knowledge-based systems and intelligent agent-based systems (multi-agent systems).

Knowledge-based systems are intelligent systems that incorporate knowledge from one area of expertise and solve problems in that area by the application of reasoning strategies. As problems solved using knowledge-based systems we can consider: analysis, monitoring, diagnosis, planning, monitoring, prediction, and classification. The main components of knowledge-based systems are knowledge base, inference engine, knowledge acquisition module, user interface and, optionally, an explanatory mode and learning mode. Knowledge database includes explicit knowledge and tacit knowledge (e.g., knowledge relating to ways of solving problems related application). Typically, explicit knowledge is included in the knowledge database, while tacit knowledge is included either in the reasoning mechanisms, or is transformed to the extent possible, the explicit knowledge.

Internal representation of knowledge is done based on different methods of representation: frames and scripts, symbolic logic (predicate-order logic, modal logic, temporal logic, for example), semantic networks, production rules, procedural methods, scenarios, dependency graphs and conceptual knowledge representation methods uncertain (probabilistic methods, Bayesian networks, Dempster Shafer theory, fuzzy model, confidence rating method). Knowledge-based systems are developed applying different knowledge engineering techniques. Modeling knowledge is important for understanding the system functionality, such as for example, generating new knowledge through inference, knowledge acquisition for

Figure 7. CommonKADS methodology models

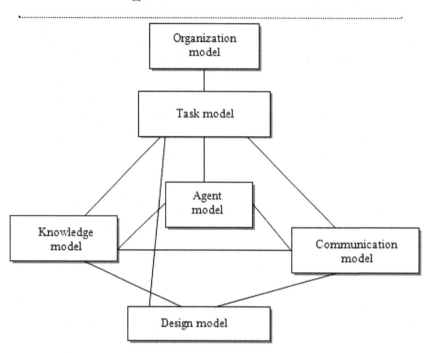

domain-specific expertise and associated patterns of explanation and learning. Modeling is a process of knowledge transfer of knowledge from human experts and other sources of knowledge by knowledge-based systems. This allows more rapid development of knowledge-based systems and increases their efficiency by reusing existing models for different areas of domain knowledge expertise. Main knowledge modeling techniques are techniques of knowledge engineering, ontologies, language modeling, and multi-perspective modeling techniques.

Traditional knowledge engineering techniques were widely used for building knowledge-based systems. Knowledge engineering includes methods and techniques for acquisition, modeling, representation and use of knowledge (Schreiber, 2000). The most common methodology applied in knowledge engineering are Cognitech (based on the notion of prototype) and KADS, a variant of CommonKADS. CommonKADS has become a European standard for modeling knowledge in knowledge-based systems. This methodology

was extended to include modeling knowledge in multi-agent systems. CommonKADS includes structured techniques of knowledge engineering, providing tools for knowledge management and includes methods to conduct a detailed analysis of tasks and processes knowledge. Also CommonKADS methodology is a powerful library of generic models which include operational models, logical models and physical models.

CommonKADS was developed and validated by several companies and universities within the European ESPRIT IT Programme. CommonKADS methodology is an object-oriented methodology using specific modeling language UML notation for class diagrams, activity diagrams, state diagrams, etc... CommonKADS methodology also comprises specific graphical notations for task decomposition sites for generating schemes for domain specific application. Modeling knowledge in a knowledge-based system includes organization modeling, specifying which roles performed the task, specifying entities (e.g. agents) that perform tasks, specifying the actual

Table 7. Description of the CommonKADS models

CommonKADS model	General description	University implementation
Organization model	It describes the organization. Actions: analysis of the major characteristics of the organization in order to establish the feasibility and the impact of the KBS; Role: It is a tool for analyzing the organization;	University model structure human resources
Task model	It describes associated tasks, as relevant components of business processes; Actions: identification of tasks to be performed in an organizational environment, analysis of the organization. Role: It provides a framework to distribute tasks to agents sites.	Teaching (including assessment) activity Research activity
Agent model	It is a high-level description of the agents. Agent can be human, a computer system or an entity capable of executing a task. Actions: analysis of the agents responsible for task execution as they were defined in task model, including the description of the agents' characteristics, in terms of skills and limitations; Role: It provide the description of the entities that perform tasks.	Teacher Student Researcher Educational software package
Communication model	It describes the interaction between the agents during task performance. Action: modeling communication between agents involved in problems solving Role: It is a tool for agents' interaction.	Teacher - student Student - Educational software package
Knowledge model	Agents describe the knowledge used to solve various tasks, using a generic library component modeling (e.g., methods for solving specific tasks and the domain ontology); Knowledge are described at the following levels: domain (declarative knowledge which includes properties, concepts, relations, instances), inference (a library of generic inference structures), and task (ordering inference); Actions: explain the knowledge types and structures used to execute a task, provides an independent implementation description of the role that different components of the knowledge have in the solving process; Role: It provides an interface for communication between human experts and users.	Organization ontology Educational ontology Research Ontology
Design model	It describes the architecture and detailed functionality of the system to be implemented; Action: provide KBS's technical specification in terms of architecture, implementation platform, software modules, interfaces for communication; Role: it is a link between conceptual models (tasks, knowledge, communication) and the actual implementation of the KBS	

knowledge of the mechanisms of communication and knowledge and design knowledge management system. In terms of practical application, CommonKADS methodology involves developing a number of models that provide different perspectives on knowledge infrastructure. These models are: the organization model, task model, model agent, model knowledge (expertise), communication model and design model. Top five models cover the analysis of the knowledge-based system and the latest model refers to its design.

Figure 7 schematically shows developed models when applying CommonKADS methodology.

In table 7 is the general description of the CommonKADS models and the characteristics of these models for knowledge management system in a university.

Figure 8 schematically describes the relationship between agents (teachers, students), knowledge assets (educational software, books, course support, laboratory work, etc.) and processes. It should be noted that software packages can be modeled both as agents (active agents interacting,

Figure 8. CommonKADS methodology models

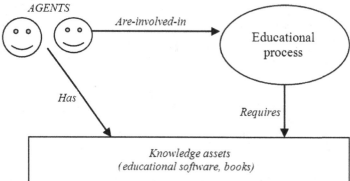

such as teacher, student) as well as knowledge assets.

Developing a knowledge-based system involves the development of an ontology specific area of expertise. One of the usual ontology development methodologies (Uschold, 1995) includes the following steps: identifying the purpose (domain application), construction of the ontology (knowledge acquisition, coding, and integration), evaluation and documentation. In general, ontology can be composed of two parts: a general ontology (with customary terms, generally valid, that does not depend on the domain application) and a specific ontology (with specific terms of the application). Currently there are a number of ontology development environments (Protégé, Ontolingua and Chimaera). Some of these tools use object-oriented methodology for defining hierarchies of classes and objects. In such systems, the classes are also called concepts, properties and attributes are called slots, building concepts and roles or properties and restrictions on slots which are called facets and restrictions on roles.

Object-oriented approach to ontologies development requires the following steps:

• Definition of ontology classes
• Arranging classes in a taxonomic hierarchy (class-subclass)

• Defining slots and describing allowed values
• Setting the values for slots courts

The taxonomic relations is a and a kind of that appear in the hierarchy of classes allow inferences. Knowledge base development is done by defining classe instances with the specific values filling the slot and additional restrictions.

Ontology implementation in knowledge-based systems can be done using dedicated tools. Protege, an ontology editor based on Java, uses frameworks (frames) as a method for knowledge representation. The ontology includes classes, slots, facets and axioms. Classes are abstract representations of concepts in the field. They form a taxonomic hierarchy and provide templates for individual frames of the courts. Multiple inheritances are allowed in Protege. Developing a knowledge base involves following steps:

• Defining ontology (defining concepts and relations between them);
• Acquisition of knowledge (domain experts introduce specific knowledge through knowledge acquisition tool);
• Consulting the knowledge base (problem solving techniques are used to answer questions and concerns related application with the knowledge base).

Figure 9. The university ontology

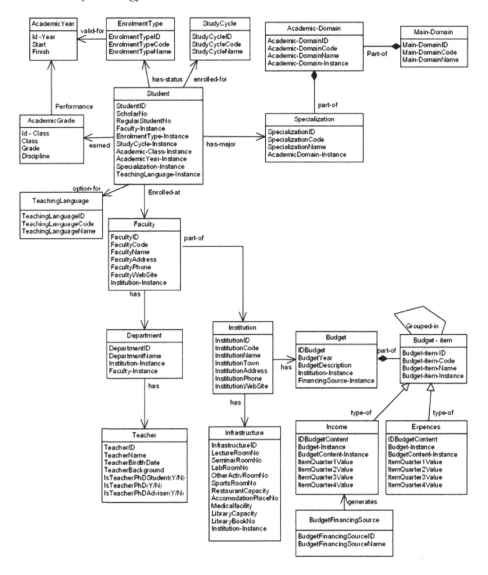

The following options exist regarding the definition and validation of ontology:

- Classes: definition and visualization of classes
- Slots: definition and visualization of slots
- Forms: definition and visualization of forms
- Instances: definition and visualization of instances
- Queries: definition of queries for ontology validation

AES KNOWLEDGE MANAGEMENT SYSTEM

The figure 9 presents the general ontology hierarchy and figure 10 presents a part of the ontology hierarchy, with specific terms of university academic processes. The figure specifies also some of the relationships between terms. The figure 11 presents the research hierarchy of the knowledge system with specific terms of a research university.

Figure 10. The didactic area ontology

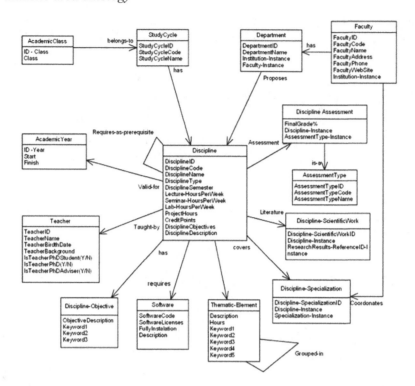

APPLICATION OF THE KNOWLEDGE MANAGEMENT SYSTEM IN RESEARCH

The purpose of this paragraph is to illustrate how the knowledge management system could be used in order to determine the research projects' complexity and the competences level needed by a project manager to successfully conduct the research projects' implementation and to check if the project managers assigned to the existing projects are competent enough. If competence mismatches were discovered, another query for determining the compatible staff ls made. A set of project manager instances and research project instances were defined in the research area ontology.

The *PMCatalog* ontology structure resembles with a tree with nodes and hyper-connections. It has one metaclass, *MyMetaClass* and 15 classes, four abstract classes and 11 concrete classes. The

abstract classes are set in a taxonomic hierarchy: the class *Catalog* is the super-class for the other three classes – *Technical_Competence_Range*, *Behavioural_Competence_Range* and *Contextual_Competence_Range*. The sub-classes correspond to the three groups of competences from ICB (International Project Management Association 2006): 20 technical competences for project management, 15 behavioural competences for project personnel and 11 contextual competences of projects, programmes and portofolios. The *Catalog* class has only one slot, named *description*. All 4 abstract classes, among them is the *Catalog* class, have the class *MyMetaclass* as a metaclass. This metaclass was created to modify the characteristics of those 4 classes so that the class editor could display a supplementary property called *Explanation*. Through this slot in the *Catalog* class it is explained the motivation for ICB usage: "The IPMA Competence Baseline is

Figure 11. The research area ontology

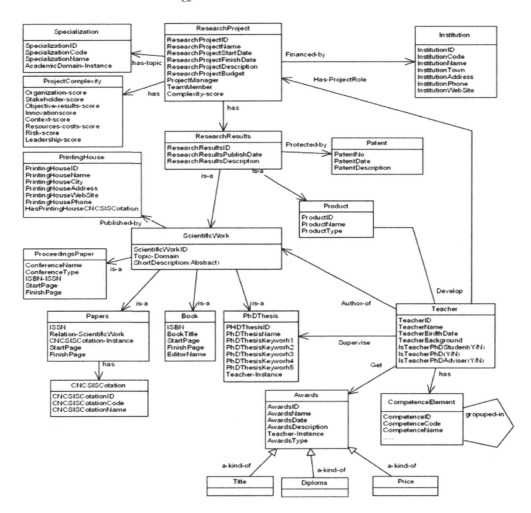

the common framework document that all IPMA Member Associations and Certification Bodies abide by to ensure that consistent and harmonised standards are applied" (International Project Management Association, 2006).

The *slot* named *description* is an extrinsic property, which can contain a primitive value (a string). Slots are defined at the top level in Protégé, meaning that there is only one slot named *description* in the knowledge base. It is attached to several classes: besides the *Catalog* class, another important class which has a description is the *Competence_Element* class. This class is a concrete sub-class of *Technical_Competence_*

Range, *Behavioural_Competence_Range* and *Contextual_Competence_Range* classes. It has 46 instances, corresponding to the 46 elements of competence of the ICB (International Project Management Association, 2006). This class has the following 16 attributes (see Figure 12):

- Code, description, key_competence_element_A, key_competence_element_B, key_competence_element_C, key_competence_element_D *and* name *(as string attributes);*

- Behavioural_pattern, knowledge_component, personal_attitude_component,

305

Figure 12. The competence_element class

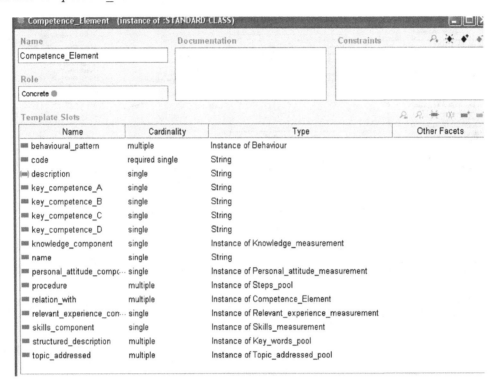

Name	Cardinality	Type	Other Facets
behavioural_pattern	multiple	Instance of Behaviour	
code	required single	String	
description	single	String	
key_competence_A	single	String	
key_competence_B	single	String	
key_competence_C	single	String	
key_competence_D	single	String	
knowledge_component	single	Instance of Knowledge_measurement	
name	single	String	
personal_attitude_compc···	single	Instance of Personal_attitude_measurement	
procedure	multiple	Instance of Steps_pool	
relation_with	multiple	Instance of Competence_Element	
relevant_experience_con···	single	Instance of Relevant_experience_measurement	
skills_component	single	Instance of Skills_measurement	
structured_description	multiple	Instance of Key_words_pool	
topic_addressed	multiple	Instance of Topic_addressed_pool	

procedure, relation_with, relevant_experience_component, skills_component, structured_description *and* topic_addressed *(as instance attributes).*

The big number of attributes proves that *Competence_Element* class is the core of the proposed ontology. Each competence element has a title (*name* in our ontology), a general description (*description* slot), list of possible process steps (*procedure* slot), a list of addressed topics (*topic_adressed* slot), key competence for each of the four levels (*key_competence_element_A, key_competence_element_B, key_competence_ element_C, key_competence_element_D*) and main relations to other competences from the ICB standard (*structured_description* slot). The procedures have guidance value: they have the role to make the candidates and the assessors understand how the competence elements can be applied. In ontological language, procedures are instances of the *Steps_pool* class. Topics addressed indicate further reading and internet searching and are instances of *Topic_addressed_pool* class. The logic behind the ontology classes resembles to the one standing behind relational databases. The *structured_description* slot is an instance of *Key_words_pool* class. The key words are indicated at the end of ICB and are meant for comprehensive reading. They should also be reflected in *relation_with* slot, which links competences and helps the candidates to build a cognitive map of ICB elements.

Behaviour class includes the set of behavioral patterns related to the behavioural elements of competence. The class attributes are the following: *adequate_behaviour* and *improved_behaviour*. An example of project manager instance can be seen in Figure 13 and an example of project instance can be seen in Figure 14. The Jess procedure developed for query interrogation

Figure 13. Instance of a project manager: Ionescu Ion

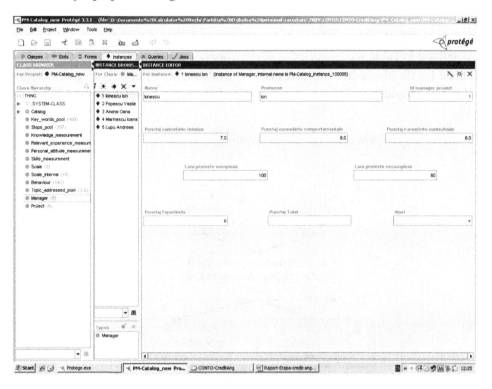

Figure 14. Instance of a research project: A

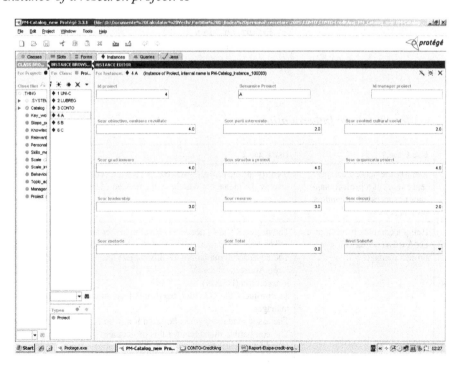

contains several modules, depicted in Figure 15. Jess is a facts-based language.

In order to exemplify the query process two use cases are defined in Table 8.

The Jess code for the above two use cases is available in Figures 16 and 17.

CONCLUSION

The ontology–based competency modeling improves the functionality of competence-based systems, because ontology gives a better definition of the types of relations and hierarchies among

Figure 15. Modules in Jess procedure for ontology interrogation

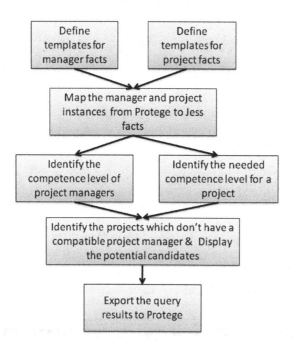

Table 8. Use Cases for Ontology Interrogation

	Use Case 1	Use Case 2
Query	Identify the needed competence level of a project manager to successfully conduct project A.	Identify all the projects which don't have a compatible project manager and display the managers who have the needed competence level.
Results	Being a complex project, project A (id 4) needs a B-level project manager.	The project C (id 6) needs a B-level manager and has no such compatible manager. The associated manager is Popescu Valise, who is a D-level certified manager. The compatible managers for this project are: Lupu Andreea (B level) Ionescu Ion (B level) The project CONTO (id 3) needs a B-level manager and has no such compatible manager. The associated manager is Popescu Ion, who is a C-level certified manager. The compatible managers for this project are: Lupu Andreea (B level) Ionescu Ion (B level)

Figure 16. Jess code for ontology interrogation, the use case 1

```
 (defmodule evalproiect)
;definire reguli pentru evaluarea nivelului de competenta solicitat pentru un proiect
(defrule evalproiect::calculscortotal
?p<-(MAIN::proiect(id_proiect ?idp)(denumire_proiect ?denproiect)
     (scor_ob_evrez ?s1)(scor_partint ?s2)(scor_contcs ?s3)
     (scor_grinovare ?s4)(scor_strproiect ?s5)(scor_orgproiect ?s6)
     (scor_leadership ?s7)(scor_resurse ?s8)(scor_riscuri ?s9)
     (scor_metode ?s10)(nivel_solicitat nil))
=>
  (bind ?stotal (+ ?s1 ?s2 ?s3 ?s4 ?s5 ?s6 ?s7 ?s8 ?s9 ?s10))
  (if (>= ?stotal 25) then
      (bind ?nivelsolicitat B)
      (modify ?p (scor_total ?stotal)(nivel_solicitat ?nivelsolicitat))
      (printout t "Proiectul " ?denproiect " cu numarul " ?idp " solicita nivelul de competenta " ?nivelsolicitat crlf)
    else
      (bind ?nivelsolicitat C)
      (modify ?p (scor_total ?stotal)(nivel_solicitat ?nivelsolicitat))
      (printout t "Proiectul " ?denproiect " cu numarul " ?idp " solicita nivelul de competenta " ?nivelsolicitat
crlf)))
```

Figure 17. Jess code for ontology interrogation, the use case 2

```
(defrule evalproiect::linienoua
=>
(printout t crlf crlf "PROIECTELE CARE NU AU ASOCIAT UN MANAGER COMPATIBIL SUNT
URMATOARELE:"))
 (defmodule verifcompatib)
;definirea regulii care cauta proiectele la care managerii nu sunt compatibili
(defrule verifcompatib::manageriincompat
(MAIN::proiect(id_proiect ?idp)(denumire_proiect ?denproiect)(id_manager_proiect ?idm)(nivel_solicitat ?n1))
(MAIN::manager(id_manager_proiect ?idm)(nume ?n)(prenume ?p)(nivel ?n2&:(< (str-compare ?n1 ?n2) 0)))
=>
(printout t crlf "Proiectul " ?denproiect " cu id-ul " ?idp " nu are un manager compatibil cu nivelul solicitat, si
anume " ?n1 "." crlf)
(printout t "Managerul asociat acestui proiect este " ?n " " ?p " care este certificat(a) cu nivelul de competenta "
?n2 "." crlf)
(printout t "Acestui proiect i se pot atribui urmatorii manageri:" crlf)
(assert (MAIN::incompat ?idp ?denproiect ?n1)))
 (defrule verifcompatib::manageripotential
?i<-(MAIN::incompat ?idp ?denproiect ?n1)
    (MAIN::manager(nume ?n)(prenume ?p)(nivel ?n2&:(<= (str-compare ?n2 ?n1) 0)))
=>
  (printout t ?n " " ?p " care are nivelul " ?n2 crlf))
 (defrule verifcompatib::linienoua
=>
  (printout t crlf crlf "PROIECTELE CARE NU AU ASOCIAT UN MANAGER SUNT URMATOARELE:"))
```

competencies. It extends the measure scales to be used by the competence assessment process. Ontology provides an extended set of modeling elements for defining in competency schemas

different kinds of competency, different relationships, several measurement scales.

The chapter presents the ontology usage, for the competency gap analysis at individual, project and organizational level for project-oriented organizations. Future work will be done in order to integrate the ontology into the knowledge management system and to extend the inferential part of the ontology.

REFERENCES

Chimaera, la http:// www.ksl.stanford.edu/ software/ chimaera

Common K. A. D. S. http:// www.commonkads. uva.nl

Davenport, T. (2001). Successful knowledge management projects. *Sloan Management Review*, *39*(2).

Freed, J., & Klugman, M. (1996). *A culture for academic excellence: Implementing the quality principles in higher education*. San Francisco, CA: Jossey-Bass Publisher.

Gruber, T. (1995). Towards principles for the design of ontologies used for knowledge sharing. *International Journal of Human-Computer Studies*, *43*, 5–6. doi:10.1006/ijhc.1995.1081

http:// nces.ed.gov/

http:// www.nacas.org/

International Project Management Association. (2006). *IPMA: Competence Baseline*. Nijkerk, Netherlands: IPMA.

Kanellopoulos, D., Kotsiantis, S., & Pintelas, P. (2006). Ontology-based learning applications: A development methodology. In the *Proceedings of the 24th IASTED International Multi-Conference Software Engineering*, February 14-16, Innsbruck, Austria.

Makhfi, P. (2007). Introduction to knowledge modeling. Retrieved from www.makhfi.com.

Mustafa, A., & Goh, M. (1996). Multi-criterion models for higher education administration, Omega. In . *International Journal of Management Science*, *24*, 167–178.

OMG - UML. la http:// www.omg.org/ uml

Ontolingua, la http:// www.ontolingua.org

Politis, Y., & Siskos, Y. (2004). Multicriteria methodology for the evaluation of a Greek engineering deparment. *European Journal of Operational Research*, *156*, 223–240. doi:10.1016/S0377-2217(02)00902-5

Protégé-2000, la http://protégé.stanford.edu

Schreiber, G., Akkermans, H., Anjewierden, A., de Hoog, R., Shadbolt, N., de Velde, W. V., & Wielinga, B. (2000). *Knowledge engineering and management: The CommonKADS Methodology*. Cambridge, MA: MIT Press.

Serban, A., & Luan, J. (2002). *Knowledge management – Building a competitive advantage in higher education. New Directions for Institutional Research, no. 113*. NY, USA: Jossey-Bass, Wiley Periodicals, Inc.

Struyven, K., Dochy, F., Janssens, S., Schelfhout, W., & Gielen, S. (2006). The overall effects of end-of-course assessment on student performance: A comparison between multiple choice testing, peer assessment, case-based assessment and portfolio assessment. [Amsterdam, Netherlands: Publisher Elsevier.]. *Studies in Educational Evaluation*, *32*, 202–222. doi:10.1016/j.stueduc.2006.08.002

Thomas, C. R. (2004). *CHESS data definitions* (2nd ed.). Boulder, CO: National Center for Higher Education Management System.

Uschold, M., & King, M. (1995). Towards a methodology for building ontologies. *Proceedings of IJCAI-95 Workshop on Basic Ontological Issues in Knowledge Sharing*, University of Edinburgh, UK.

Van der Schaaf, M., & Stokking, K. (2008). Teacher beliefs and teacher behavior in portfolio assessment [Amsterdam, Netherlands: Publisher Elsevier.]. *Teaching and Teacher Education, 24,* 1691–1704. doi:10.1016/j.tate.2008.02.021

World Bank (2004). *Tertiary Education and Innovation Systems Analysis* (TEIS). Country Policy Report.

ADDITIONAL READING

Anjewierden, A., Kollöffel, B., & Hulshof, C. (2007). *Towards educational data mining: Using data mining methods for automated chat analysis to understand and support inquiry learning processes. ADML 2007* (pp. 27–36). Greece: Crete.

Bodea, C. (2007). An innovative system for learning services in project management. In *Proceedings of 2007 IEEE/INFORMS International Conference on Service Operations and Logistics. And Informatics,* Philadelphia, USA, 2007. IEEE.

Castells, M., & Pekka, H. (2002). *The information society and the welfare state. The Finnish model.* Oxford, UK: Oxford University Press.

Demirel, M., (2009). Lifelong learning and schools in the 21st century. *Procedia social and behavioral sciences, 1,* 1709–1716.

Garcia, A. C. B., Kunz, J., Ekstrom, M., & Kiviniemi, A. (2003). *Building a project ontology with extreme collaboration and VD & C (CIFE Technical Report #152).* CA, USA: Stanford University.

Gareis, R. (2007). *Happy Projects! Romanian version.* Bucharest, Romania: ASE Printing House.

Guardado, M., & Shi, L. (2007). ESL students' experiences of online peer feedback. *Computers and Composition, 24,* 443–461. doi:10.1016/j.compcom.2007.03.002

Kalathur, S. (2006). An object-oriented framework for predicting student competency level in an incoming class. *Proceedings of SERP '06,* Las Vegas, NV (pp. 179-183).

Kanellopoulos, D., Kotsiantis, S., & Pintelas, P. (2006). Ontology-based learning applications: A development methodology. In *Proceedings of the 24th IASTED International Multi-Conference Software Engineering,* Innsbruck, Austria, 2006.

Lytras, M. D., Carroll, J. M., Damiani, E., & Tennyson, R. D. (2008). *Emerging technologies and Information Systems for the knowledge society. In 1ˢᵗ World Summit on the Knowledge Society.* Athens, Greece: WSKS. doi:10.1007/978-3-540-87781-3

Markkula, M. (2006). *Creating favourable conditions for knowledge society through knowledge management, e-governance and e-learning,* Budapest, Hungary, 2006. FIG Workshop on e-governance, knowledge management and e-learning.

Teekaput, P., & Waiwanijchakij, P. (2006). E-learning and knowledge management, symptoms of a reality. In *3ʳᵈ International Conference on eLearning for Knowledge-Based Society,* Bangkok, Thailand, 2006.

Turner, R. J., & Simister, S. J. (2004). *Gower handbook of project management* (Romanian version ed.). Bucharest, Romania: Codecs Printing House.

Young, A., & Norgard, C. (2006). Assessing the quality of online courses from the students' perspective. *The Internet and Higher Education, 9,* 107–115. doi:10.1016/j.iheduc.2006.03.001

KEY TERMS AND DEFINITIONS

Competence: A combination between knowledge, skills, attitudes and strategic thinking.

Educational Technology: The study and practice of facilitating learning and improving performance by creating, using and managing appropriate technological processes and resources.

Knowledge-Based Systems: Intelligent systems that incorporate knowledge from one area of expertise and solve problems in that area by the application of reasoning strategies. The main components of knowledge-based systems are: the knowledge base, inference engine, knowledge acquisition module, user interface and, optionally, an explanatory mode and learning mode. Knowledge database includes explicit knowledge and tacit knowledge (e.g., knowledge relating to ways of solving problems related application). Typically, explicit knowledge is included in the knowledge database, while tacit knowledge is included either in the reasoning mechanisms, or is transformed to the extent possible, the explicit knowledge.

Learning Ontology: An explicit formal specification of how to represent the learning objects, learning concepts (classes) and other entities and the relationships among them.

Ontology: A formal representation of the knowledge by a set of concepts within a domain and the relationships between those concepts.

Chapter 15
Web Engineering and Business Intelligence:
Agile Web Engineering Development and Practice

Haroon Altarawneh
Arab International University, Syria

Sattam Alamaro
Arab International University, Syria

Asim El Sheikh
Arab Academy for Banking and Financial Sciences, Jordan

ABSTRACT

The objectives of this chapter are to highlight the main issues related to Web engineering practices and how they support business intelligence projects, the need for Web engineering, and the development methods used in web engineering. "Web Engineering is the application of systematic, disciplined and quantifiable approaches to development, operation, and maintenance of Web-based applications". It is a response to the early, chaotic development of Web sites and applications as well as recognition of a divide between Web developers and conventional software developers. Viewed broadly, Web engineering is both a conscious and pro-active approach and a growing collection of theoretical and empirical research.

Web engineering is the process used to create high-quality Web-based systems and applications that deliver a complex array of content and functionality to a broad population of end-users. Web engineering is concerned with the establishment and use of sound scientific, engineering and management principles and disciplined and systematic approaches to the successful development, deployment and maintenance of high quality Web-based systems and applications.

In this chapter, a short description of some agile software development methods is reviewed and a detailed description of XP is provided.

DOI: 10.4018/978-1-61350-050-7.ch015

XP will be introduced and reviewed by using a defined structure where process, roles and responsibilities, practices, adoption and experiences, and scope of use regarding to XP is identified. Process refers to the description of phases in the product life-cycle through which the software is being produced. Roles and responsibilities refer to the allocation of specific roles through which the software production in a development team is carried out.

Agile BI is as much about how BI applications are used and what they enable businesses to do, as it is about how the applications themselves are built.

INTRODUCTION

There has been much research and many efforts made in recent years in the area of web development using a variety of different technologies. With the emergence and mass availability of communication channels, this is no surprise. Many authors have written books and articles identifying good practices in the realm of web design. Some have sought out metrics and measures to quantify web application design to give some level of evaluation of the quality of web application. This book seeks to add value to the understanding of web applications design by investigating the current agile development methods and web engineering best practices.

If there is no disciplined approach to Web-based Applications development, we will find sooner or later that Web-based applications are not delivering desired performance and quality, and the development process becomes increasingly complex and difficult to manage and refine and also expensive and grossly behind schedule. Web Engineering, an emerging new discipline, advocates a process and a systematic approach to development of high quality Internet- and Web-based systems.

The history of web development is relatively short. Initially, many web applications were small and simple with little thought given to planning or design before constructing the application, and few have been tested properly. Today, many web applications are large-scale and involve sophisticated interaction with visitors and databases;

such applications are often regarded as mission critical. In parallel with this evolution, a need for web engineering has become apparent. Yet, within education, the plethora of web courses primarily addresses the implementation of web applications with very little about the analysis and design of web applications. An early consideration of a web engineering process suited for inexperienced users is important.

The objectives of this chapter are to highlight the main issues related to agile web engineering practices, the need for web engineering, and the agile development methodologies used in web engineering. The chapter also covers important topics of Web Engineering, including requirements analysis, design, architectures, technologies, test, operation and maintenance; this is complemented by in-depth knowledge about Web project management and process issues as well as important quality aspects of Web applications like usability, performance and security.

History

The World Wide Web (WWW) originated at the European Particle Physics Laboratory known as 'CERN' in 1990. Mr. Tim Berners-Lee with a background in text processing and real-time communications, wanted to create an information system in which researchers could exchange information during the course of a project. He came up with a method of linking documents together using hypertext technology. Since then

Figure 1. The major milestone of Web Engineering

1990 - 1995	• World Wide Web originates-1990 • Hypertext Markup Language written-1991 • Text-based browser opens WWW for use-1992 • New Web terms: HTTP and URL-1992 • Graphical user interface, Mosaic, developed-1993 • HTML introduced as code for web design-1993 • World Wide Web Consortium, W3C founded-1994
1996 - 2001	• First Paper about Web Engineering related problems appear at the 5th WWW Conference in France-1996 • Microsoft releases Explorer 3.0 Web browse-1996 • Web Engineering Homepage published WebEngineering.org -1997 • First workshop on Web Engineering organized at the 7th WWW Conference in Australia-1998 • First International Conference on Web Engineering (ICWE)-2001
2002 - 2005	• For the first time Web Engineering became part of the main program-2002 • First international Journal on Web Engineering published by Rinton Press, USA-2002 • Web Engineering became an area of the refereed paper track at the WWW conference, demonstrating the emerging need for a discipline on development, operation, and evolution of Web applications-2003 • W3C describes principles of Web architecture-2004 • W3C actively busy in standardizing protocols and web technologies-2005

this emerging discipline went through many mile stones. Figure 1 mentions some of the major mile stones (Rashid Ahmad, et al 2005).

Need for Web Engineering

If there is no disciplined approach to Web-based Applications development, we will find sooner or later that Web-based applications are not delivering desired performance and quality, and the that development process becomes increasingly complex and difficult to manage and refine and also expensive and grossly behind schedule(Lowe, D and W. Hall 1999). Web Engineering, an emerging new discipline, advocates a process and a systematic approach to development of high quality Internet- and Web-based systems (Emilia Mendes, et al 2006).

How Web Engineering Differs from Software Engineering

Where web engineering involves some programming and software development, and adopts some of the principles of software engineering, Web-based system development is different from software development, and also there is a difference between web engineering and software engineering(Ginige, A 1998).

Most Web-based systems, at least as of now, are document-oriented containing static or dynamic Web pages.

Web-based systems will continue to be focused on look and feel, favoring visual creativity and incorporation of multimedia (in varying degrees) in presentation and interface. More emphasis will be placed on visual creativity and presentation

Figure 2. Web Engineering: A multidisciplinary field

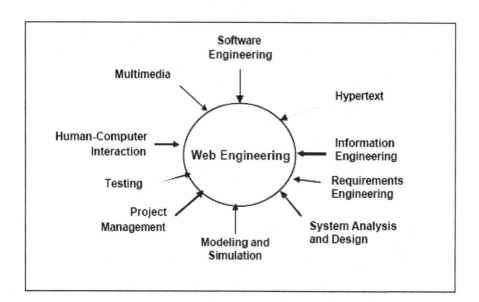

as regards to the front-end interface with which a user interacts.

Most Web-based systems will continue to be content-driven – often Web-based systems development include development of the content presented.

Multiplicity of user profiles – Most Web-based systems need to cater to users with diverse skills and capability, complicating human-computer interaction, user interface and information presentation.

The nature and characteristics of the medium of Web is not well understood as the software medium.

The Web exemplifies a greater bond between art and science than generally encountered in software development.

Most Web-based systems need to be developed within a short time, making it difficult to apply the same level of formal planning and testing as used in software development.

Also Web is different from software as related to the delivery medium.

Further, the type of individuals who build/develop Web-based systems are vastly varied in their background, skills, knowledge and system understanding, and as well as their perception of Web and quality Web-based system.

Web Engineering Disciplinarians

Web-based systems "involve a mixture between print publishing and software development, between marketing and computing, between internal communications and external relations, and between art and technology." (Powell, T.A 1998). In view of the nature of the Web and Web-based applications, Web engineering is bound to be a multidisciplinary field, with encompassing inputs from diverse areas such as human-computer interaction, user interface, systems analysis and design, software engineering, requirements engineering, hypermedia engineering, information structures, testing, modeling and simulation and project management, as well as social sciences, arts and graphic design (Figure 2).

Web Engineering Activities

Web Engineering is composed of a set of activities and tasks. It deals with all aspects of Web-based system development, starting from conception and development to implementation, performance evaluation, and continual maintenance (Powell, T.A 1998).

Major Web engineering tasks include:

- Requirements specification and analysis
- Web-based system development methodologies and techniques
- Integration with legacy systems
- Migration of legacy system to Web environments
- Web-based real-time applications development
- Testing, verification and validation
- Quality assessment, control and assurance
- Configuration and project management
- "Web metrics" - metrics for estimation of development efforts
- Performance specification and evaluation
- Update and maintenance
- Development models, teams, staffing
- Human and cultural aspects
- User-centric development, user modeling and user involvement and feedback
- End-user application development
- Education and training

Web Engineering Process?

Traditional software engineering projects are primarily concerned with the creation of software components with supporting systems, which are often generic. These software components and supporting systems are often developed independently of the data upon which they will operate. Web engineering on the other hand results in deliverables, comprising software components and supporting systems that are developed in parallel with the creation of the data that they will

operate upon or in conjunction with. In essence, each Web engineering project results in a bespoke solution comprising data and software. In addition, the importance of understanding End-User usage has never been so critical to the success of a class of software applications as it is with Web engineering projects (Constantine L. L. & Lockwood L. A. D. 2000) Consider the number of different ways information in a Web application can be displayed to End-Users, and the ease with which End-Users can find and change to alternative Web-based solutions should they lack satisfaction with their current usage experience. Nielsen and Ginige believe (Constantine L. L. & Lockwood L. A. D. 2000) that if one is to build successful Web applications then great focus has to be placed on understanding End-User usage of the proposed system.

Consider the models involved in any traditional software engineering process. We would argue that there are only three models of any great significance reflected by traditional software engineering processes: the software model, the business model and the domain model. The software model reflects a view of the issues associated with developing a software solution that achieves the business objectives reflected by the views of the business model. The domain model reflects views of the domain to which the business objectives and the proposed software solution are to be applied. The primary impact reflected by the traditional software engineering process used to develop the legacy system was in the software model, driven by views from the business and domain models (Ginige, 2002).Rarely do traditional software engineering processes explicitly give feedback into the business and domain models.

Figure 3 shows the impact business, domain and software models have upon each other in such traditional software engineering process. The software model is impacted only by a partial section of business and domain models. This impact is exerted usually only once or twice during the development life-cycle and the information that

Figure 3. The impact the software, business and domain models exert upon each other in traditional software engineering processes

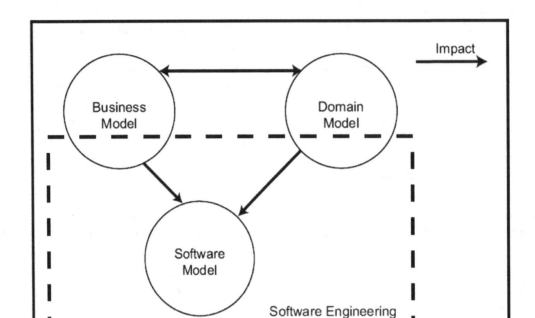

the software model holds regarding the business and domain models is primarily seen to be static. Rarely does the software model have a radical impact on the business and domain models. As a result, many of the software solutions resulting from these traditional software engineering processes are largely implementations of existing business practice.

Web Engineering on the other hand is complicated by the addition of a creative design model, that reflects the issues associated with the aesthetic aspects of the user interface. In addition, Web engineering requires the business and domain models to design and develop data, influence Web site structure and therefore requires them to not only impact and affect change in the software and creative design models, but requires the software model to impact and affect change in the business and domain models. The business and domain models also have to address impact and affect

change between them in Web engineering (Murugesan, et al 1999).See Figure 3 for the impact business, domain, creative design and software models have upon one another in Web engineering.

We believe that the development of Web-based applications often requires a degree of re-engineering in the business, domain and software models. Such is the impact exerted between the four models in Web-application development, that if an organization wishes to harness this impact to their benefit, then a re-engineering initiative is required to adapt the models in order to ensure the success of the proposed system. It is crucial that those organizations and individuals involved in Web-based endeavors understand the impact exerted amongst the models in Web engineering. Indeed many of the e-words, such as e-Revolution and e-Transformation, associated with Web-based developments indicate the importance of such

Figure 4. The impact the software, business, domain and creative design models have on each other in Web Engineering

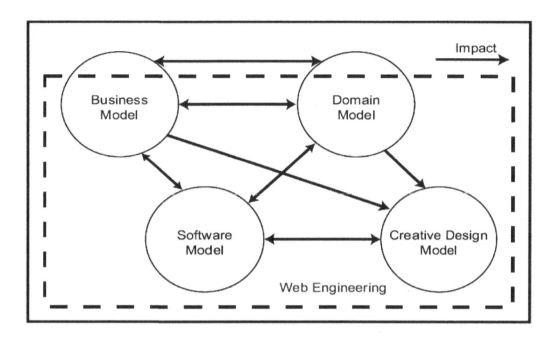

re-engineering activities. Ultimately, Murugesan (Murugesan, et al 1999) believe that organizations and individuals that do not understand the significance of re-engineering during Web application development risk the success of their projects and long term survival of their organization.

Web-Based Application Development

Web engineering activities span the entire Web life cycle from conception of an application to development and deployment, and continual refinement and update/upgrade systems.

Web Development Process Models

To help to reduce the difficulty in building Web-based systems we need a process model that describe the phases of Web-based system development - some of the aspects that make Web-system difficult include complexity, changeability, invisibility and unrealistic schedule (Ginige, 2002). A

process model should help developers "to address the complexities of Web-based systems, minimize risks of development, deal with likelihood of change, and deliver the site quickly, while providing feedback for management as the project goes along(Ginige, 2002). Further, the progress of Web-based development should be monitorable and trackable. The process besides being easy to apply should facilitate continual update/refinement and evolution, based on feedback from users/clients(Gellersen, H., and Gaedke 1999).

Web Analysis and Design

Requirement analysis and Web-based system design is a very important activity and calls for a systematic and disciplined approach (Bala subramanian, V., et al., 1995).

Object Orientation in Web-Based Systems:

Integration of Web and object technologies offer foundation for expanding the Web to a new generation of applications. (According to Frank Manolo 1999). Web must improve its data structuring capabilities, and integrate aspects of object technology with the basis infrastructure of the Web. He also argues that if the Web is to support complex enterprise applications, it must support generic capabilities similar to those provided by the OMA (Object management Architecture), but adapted to the more open, flexible nature of the Web and to the specific requirements of Web applications.

Usability and User-Centered Designs:

Effective Web site design requires attention to usability. Web-based systems need to be designed for easy navigation, and also they need to be attractive and useful (Siegel D. 1997) User-centered design methods for Web sites is presented in(Detroyer, O.M.F., and C.J. Leune 1998) while (Scharl, A 1999) presents a User-Centric Approach to Modeling Web Information Systems.

Testing of Web-Based Systems

Testing, verification and validation (V & V) of web-based systems is an important and challenging task in the Web engineering process. And, yet very little attention is given by Web developers to testing and evaluation. Web-based system testing differs from conventional software testing and poses new challenges. Web-based systems need to be tested not only to check and verify whether it does what it is designed to do but also to evaluate how well it appears on (different) Web browsers. Importantly, they need to be tested for security and also for usability, from the ultimate user's perspective. However, the unpredictability of the Internet and Web medium makes testing Web based systems difficulty. Currently, not much attention is given to Web–based system testing by developers. Also we need to develop new approaches and techniques for testing and evaluation of complex Web-based systems.

Web Development Management

Web development Management is a difficult task, especially in the midst of change which is a fact of life in the web environment. Requirements for management of Web- based application and the tools and a mechanism for organizing and manipulating web based development is needed.

Web Configuration Management

Web-based systems undergo changes, perhaps more often and quite extensively, in their development and operational period. The changes called for may include trivial to large-scale change of information/data and major modification to requirements, and also may vary in their significance. These changes need to be handled in a rational, controlled manner. Web configuration management (WCM) encompasses a set of activities for controlling and facilitating change: identification, version control, change control, auditing and reporting. It also provides a framework for handling change in a rational, controlled manner. It could adopt commonly practiced software configuration management (SCM) concepts, principles and approaches to the Web environment. In (Dart, S., 1999) Susan Dart discusses how software configuration management techniques and practices could be used for WCM and to contain the web crisis.

Tools for Web Engineering

There are many tools available to support the building of web applications, but few that support their planning or design. Some, allow the drawing of artifacts like navigation charts, but these tools are still essentially designed to support implementation.

To help understand the state of the practice, Dart has grouped existing tools into six categories, which exhibit homogeneous features.

The individual categories are:

1. Visual editors and site managers: contain productivity tools that evolved directly from the HTML editor, which do not really support the development of large-scale Web-database applications.
2. Web-enabled hypermedia authoring tools: originates from a different application domain, offline hypermedia publishing, but recently added facilities for Web and database integration.
3. Web-DBPL integrators: is the first one that explicitly addresses the integration of Web and databases to achieve a higher level of scalability, and includes very powerful, yet basic, products.
4. Web form editors, report writers: a database-centric, approach to Web development by addressing the migration of client/ server, form-based applications and database publishing wizards;
5. Multiparadigm tools: the integration of different development approaches and technologies, drawn from the previous four tool families.
6. Model-driven application generators: a complete coverage of all the development activities, from conceptualization to implementation, by leveraging state-of-the-art software engineering techniques.

For example, the CAWE tool provides an operational environment that supports all the methodological aspects of OO-H(Object-Oriented Hypermedia) Method. It simplifies the design and implementation of web-based Information Systems from an object-oriented perspective, providing a comfortable and friendly interface for elaborating the OO-H Method models. The most interesting contribution of this CAWE environment is its ability to generate the web application front-end for well-known industrial software development environments. This CAWE Tool is being used at this moment for the resolution of real web applications.

Current Practice and Research

The growing importance of Web-based applications to organizations has become increasingly evident within the last 5 years. The rapid and successful deployment of these Applications is often critical to the business strategy of many organizations - particularly with respect to the way in which they interact with customers, clients, and/or business partners. Despite this importance, these applications and the role that they can play within an organization are often poorly understood, particularly during the early stages of their development (David B. Lowe 2005) In particular, there is significant anecdotal evidence that Web projects have particular characteristics that differentiate them from more conventional software systems (Lowe, D. 2001) For example, these projects typically have tighter timeframes, increased visibility to customers, business partners and other third-parties, much finer-grained ongoing evolutionary maintenance, and generally serve a less specific user group. They are often developed very quickly from templated solutions, using coarse-grained authoring tools, and by the efforts of a multi-disciplinary team. One of the more significant differences is related to the identification of requirements (David B. Lowe 2005).

Web projects can be viewed as exemplars of an emerging class of applications where the client has difficulty in *a priori* articulating their specific needs as they relate to the system to be developed. Rather, the clients' understanding of their specific needs (indeed, the needs themselves) evolve as a system emerges and is utilized (Lowe, D. 2001) We believe that this is, at least in part, a conse-

Figure 5. An iterative design model

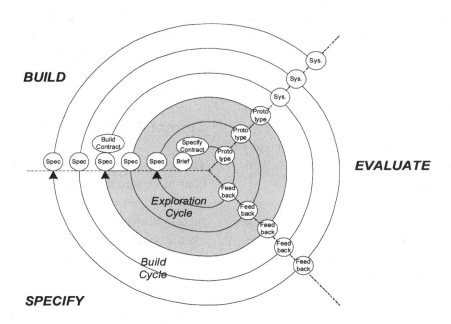

quence of the fact that the systems extend beyond the organizational boundaries, to be utilized in a broader context. (For example, whereas a conventional software application will be utilized within an organization to support its business processes, most Web applications actually form the channel between the organization and its business partners or customers). This complicates the ability to clearly determine the system requirements.

In traditional software development the project moves more clearly from a requirements/specification phase, through successive designs that are evaluated and refined, until the system is built. In Web development, there is far less clarity in these phases, with significant overlap. Designs are part of the build process, and lead through evaluation to a modification of specifications. Designs become successively deeper, moving from flat screens to functional prototypes, and there is an unclear distinction between the design process and the specification process, as in Figure 5.

Web Development Research

There is a small but growing body of research literature regarding the differences between Web systems and more conventional software systems. In general, this literature identifies unique characteristics of these systems that reflect technical, usability and organizational issues (Lowe, D. 2001).

These include aspects such as: a tighter linkage between the business architecture (which are usually coupled to significant changes to the business model of the client) with both a complex information architecture and a highly component-based technical architecture (Burdman, J. 1999) increased importance of quality attributes (since applications are typically more visible externally); open modularized architectures; and rapidly changing technologies. Usability considerations reflect an increased emphasis on user interfaces and the requirement of the system to meet the needs of end users, who are more often broader and more general demographic than for larger software systems. These considerations include both user acceptance of the system as well as making them usable - developed according to interface standards and matching user preferences and workflow. More fundamental than the technical or usability aspects are some of the developmental, or organizational, characteristics that are either unique or heightened in Web systems (England, E. and Finney 1999)These include: uncertainty in the project domain, volatility of the client needs, a highly uninformed competitiveness, short delivery timeframes, and fine-grained evolution and maintenance.

Web Development Methods

There is, as yet, little assistance from the research literature to be gained in addressing these issues. The design methods that have been emerging (for example, OOHDM and more recently WebML, and various adaptations of UML) have yet to become widely adopted, and focus on design approaches rather than understanding requirements. One exception is the work by IBM on patterns for e-Business (Henderson-Sellers, et al 2001) which identifies common business patterns that can form the basis of client discussions, but even this fails to address specific processes for resolving client and user requirements. Existing software processes for eliciting, analyzing and understanding requirements (Lord, J. 2000) assume that clients either understand their requirements, or at the very least understand the problem that is being addressed. Even when the client is not able to articulate their requirements precisely, they are at least able to understand whether a given design will address their needs.

Many practitioners and researchers recommend that this problem can be addressed by the adoption of lightweight iterative and/or incremental approaches, such as eXtreme Programming (XP) (Lowe, D. 2001) These approaches allow a system to be built incrementally, thereby facilitating feedback from the client as the system develops. They do not, however, consider how

the emerging designs can be used to explicitly improve clients understanding of their problem domain, and hence don't directly assist in the client's formulation of their needs.

Agile Development Methods Overview

The field of software development is not shy of introducing new methodologies. Indeed, in the last 25 years, a large number of different approaches to software development have been introduced, of which only few have survived to be used today.

The term agile has recently been used to categorize a number of lightweight approaches to building software. These include: Extreme Programming (XP), Adaptive Software Development and Dynamic Systems Development Methodology (DSDM). Among other seventeen advocates and methodologists of the aforementioned and other agile processes convened in February 2001. The result of this meeting was the formation of the Agile Alliance (Beck, K 1999)and the production of The Manifesto for Agile Software Development (Beck K. et al., 2001)

The following quote from The Manifesto for Agile Software Development1 gives a summary of it's purpose (Fowler M. & Highsmith J 2001)"We are uncovering better ways of developing software by doing it and helping others do it. Through this work we have come to value:

- Individuals and interactions over processes and tools.
- Working software over comprehensive documentation.
- Customer collaboration over contract negotiation.
- Responding to change over following a plan.

That is, while we value the items on the right, we value the items on the left more."

AWE is an iterative and incremental process, researchers believe this will allow for: early and continuous delivery of valuable software ; the ability to harness changing requirements, even late in development ; and the delivery of working software frequently. The AWE Process supports multidisciplinary development treating business experts, domain experts, and creative designers as developers alongside software engineers(Fowler M. & Highsmith J 2001).

Beck[81] believes that the developers and organizations involved in web engineering projects are the primary factor in the success or failure of web application development. Given the diversity of disciplines required to develop Web-based applications.

Fowler (Fowler M. & Highsmith J 2001) believes that people are the most important factor in project success is the fundamental reason why we have not tried to develop a monumental process to tackle the problems associated with web application development. Many monumental processes attempt to codify good practice and experience in too much detail and for developers who do not understand the importance of what they are doing! This often results in development projects using monumental processes as cookbook recipes, where developers are lulled into a false sense of security by following the recipe in detail rather than using the ingredients selectively to help them build software deliverables that solve their problem space.

The following are the characteristics of agile software processes from the fast delivery point of view, which allow shortening the life-cycle of projects (Constantine L 2001):

- Modularity on development process level
- Iterative with short cycles enabling fast verifications and corrections
- Time-bound with iteration cycles from one to six weeks
- Parsimony in development process removes all unnecessary activities

- Adaptive with possible emergent new risks
- Incremental process approach that allows functioning application building in small steps
- Convergent (and incremental) approach minimizes the risks
- People-oriented, i.e. agile processes favor people over processes and technology
- Collaborative and communicative working style.

Existing Agile Methods

In this section, a short description of some agile software development methods is reviewed and a detailed description of XP is provided.

XP will be introduced and reviewed by using a defined structure where process, roles and responsibilities, practices, adoption and experiences, and scope of use regarding to XP is identified. Process refers to the description of phases in the product life-cycle through which the software is being produced. Roles and responsibilities refer to the allocation of specific roles through which the software production in a development team is carried out.

Scrum

The Scrum approach has been developed for managing the systems development process. It is an empirical approach applying the ideas of industrial process control theory to systems development resulting in an approach that reintroduces the ideas of flexibility, adaptability and productivity (Miller, G. 2001) It does not define any specific software development techniques for the implementation phase. Scrum concentrates on how the team members should function in order to produce the system flexibly in a constantly changing environment. The main idea of Scrum is that systems development involves several environmental and technical variables (e.g. requirements, time frame, resources, and technology) that are likely to change

Figure 6. Scrum process

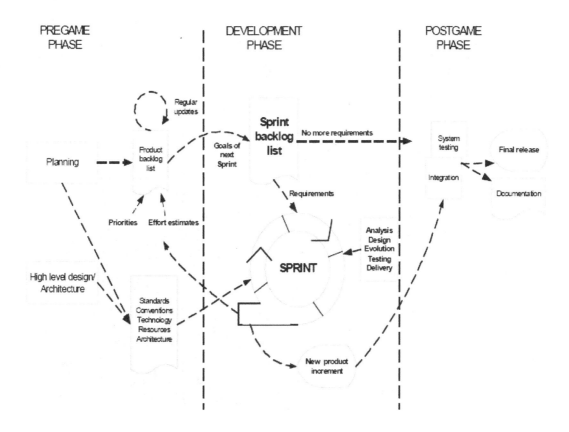

during the process. This makes the development process unpredictable and complex, requiring flexibility of the systems development process for it to be able to respond to the changes.

As a result of the development process, a system is produced which is useful when delivered. Scrum process includes three phases: pre-game, development and post-game (see Figure 6).

Crystal Family of Methodologies

The Crystal family of methodologies includes a number of different methodologies for selecting the most suitable methodology for each individual project. Besides the methodologies, the Crystal approach also includes principles for tailoring the

methodologies to fit the varying circumstances of different projects.

Each member of the Crystal family is marked with a color indicating the 'heaviness' of the methodology, i.e. the darker the color the heavier the methodology. Crystal suggests choosing the appropriate color of methodology for a project based on its size and criticality (Figure 7). Larger projects are likely to ask for more coordination and heavier methodologies than smaller ones. The more critical the system being developed the more rigor is needed. The character symbols in Figure 7.6 indicate a potential loss caused by a system failure (i.e. the criticality level): Comfort (C), Discretionary money (D), Essential money (E) and Life (L) (Cockburn, A. 2002) In other words, criticality level C indicates that a system

Figure 7. Dimensions of Crystal methodologies

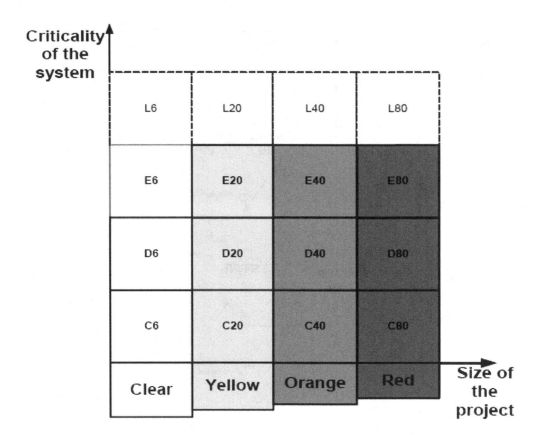

crash due to defects causes a loss of comfort for the user whereas defects in a life critical system may literally cause loss of life.

All of the methodologies of the Crystal family provide guidelines of policy standards, work products, "local matters", tools, standards and roles to be followed in the development process. Crystal Clear and Crystal Orange are the two Crystal family members that have been constructed and used Crystal Clear is designed for very small projects (D6 project category projects), comprising up to six developers. Crystal Orange is designed for medium-sized projects, with a total of 10 to 40 project members (D40 category), and with a project duration of one to two years.

Feature Driven Development

Feature Driven Development (FDD) is an agile and adaptive approach for developing systems. The FDD approach does not cover the entire software development process, but rather focuses on the design and building phases(Cockburn, A. 2002).

However, it has been designed to work with the other activities of a software development project and does not require any specific process model to be used.

The FDD approach embodies iterative development with the best practices found to be effective in industry. It emphasizes quality aspects throughout the process and includes frequent and tangible deliveries, along with accurate monitoring of the progress of the project. FDD consists

Figure 8. Processes of FDD

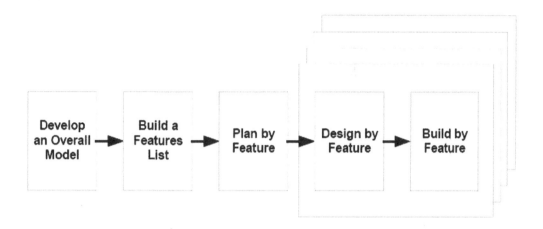

of five sequential processes and provides the methods, techniques and guidelines needed by the project stakeholders to deliver the system. Furthermore, FDD includes the roles, artifacts, goals, and timelines needed in a project. Unlike some other agile methodologies, FDD claims to be suitable for the development of critical systems (Cockburn, A. 2002).

FDD consists of five sequential processes during which the designing and building of the system is carried out (Figure 8). The iterative part of the FDD processes (Design and Build) supports agile development with quick adaptations to late changes in requirements and business needs (Palmer, S. R. and Felsing 2002).

Adaptive Software Development

Adaptive Software Development, or ASD for short, was developed by (Highsmith, J. A. 2000). Many of ASD's principles stem from Highsmith's earlier research on iterative development methods. ASD focuses mainly on the problems in developing complex, large systems. The method strongly encourages incremental, iterative development, with constant prototyping. Fundamentally, ASD

is about "balancing on the edge of chaos". Its aim is to provide a framework with enough guidance to prevent projects from falling into chaos, but not too much, which could suppress emergence and creativity. An Adaptive Software Development project is carried out in three-phase cycles. The phases of the cycles are Speculate, Collaborate, and Learn (see Figure 9).

Dynamic Systems Development Method

Since its origin in 1994, DSDM, the Dynamic Systems Development Method, has gradually become the number one framework for rapid application development (RAD) in the UK (Highsmith, J. A. 2000). DSDM is a non-profit and nonproprietary framework for RAD development, maintained by the DSDM Consortium. The developers of the method maintain that in addition to serving as a method in the generally accepted sense DSDM also provides a framework of controls for RAD, supplemented with guidance on how to efficiently use those controls (Highsmith, J. A. 2000).

The fundamental idea behind DSDM is that instead of fixing the amount of functionality in

Figure 9. The ASD cycle

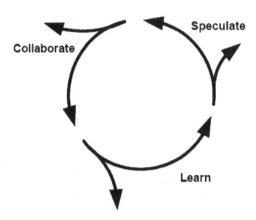

a product, and then adjusting time and resources to reach that functionality, it is preferred to fix time and resources, and then adjust the amount of functionality accordingly.

DSDM consists of five phases: feasibility study, business study, functional model iteration, design and build iteration, and implementation (Figure 10).

Extreme Programming

Extreme Programming (XP) has evolved from the problems caused by the long development cycles of traditional development models. It first started as "simply an opportunity to get the job done" (Beck, K. 1999), with practices that had been found effective in software development processes during the preceding decades (Staple-

Figure 10. DSDM process diagram

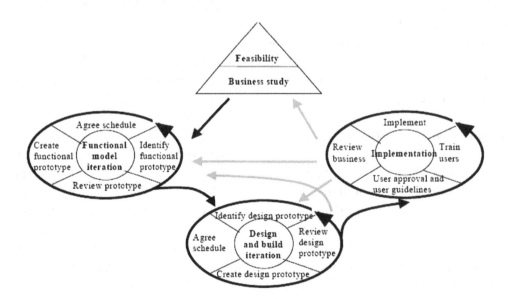

Figure 11. Life cycle of the XP process

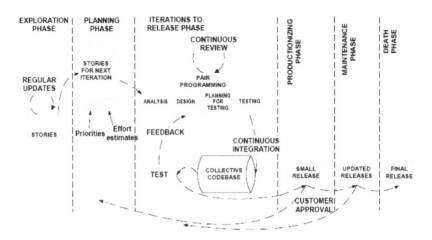

ton, J. 1997). After a number of successful trials in practice, the XP methodology was "theorized" on the key principles and practices used. Even though the individual practices of XP are not new as such, in XP they have been collected and lined up to function with each other in a novel way thus forming a new methodology for software development. The term 'extreme' comes from taking these commonsense principles and practices to extreme levels.

XP Process

XP consists of five phases: Exploration, Planning, Iterations to Release, Productionizing, Maintenance and Death (see Figure 11).

According to Beck's [90] these phases are introduced as follow:

In the *exploration phase,* the customers write out the story cards that they wish to be included in the first release. Each story card describes a feature to be added into the program. At the same time the project team familiarize themselves with the tools, technology and practices they will be using in the project. The technology to be used will be tested and the architecture possibilities for the system are explored by building a prototype of the system.

The *planning phase* sets the priority order for the stories and an agreement of the contents of the first small release is made. The programmers first estimate how much effort each story requires and the schedule is then agreed upon.

The *iterations to release* phase includes several iterations of the systems before the first release. The schedule set in the planning stage is broken down to a number of iterations that will each take one to four weeks to implement. The first iteration creates a system with the architecture of the whole system.

The *productionizing phase* requires extra testing and checking of the performance of the system before the system can be released to the customer. At this phase, new changes may still be found and the decision has to be made if they are included in the current release.

After the first release is productionized for customer use, the XP project must both keep the system in the production running while also producing new iterations.

The *death phase* is near when the customer does no longer have any stories to be implemented. This requires that the system satisfies customer needs also in other respects.

Figure 12. Roots of extreme programming

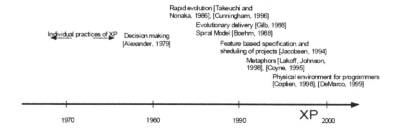

XP Roles and Responsibilities

According to (Beck, K. 1999) there are different roles in XP for different tasks and purposes during the process and its practices:

- **Programmer**: Programmers write tests and keep the program code as simple and definite as possible.
- **Customer:** The customer writes the stories and functional tests, and decides when each requirement is satisfied.
- **Tester**: Testers help the customer write functional tests. They run functional tests regularly, broadcast test results and maintain testing tools.
- **Tracker**: Tracker gives feedback in XP. Tracker traces the estimates made by the team (e.g. effort estimates) and gives feedback on how accurate they are in order to improve future estimations.
- **Coach**: Coach is the person responsible for the process as a whole.
- **Consultant**: Consultant is an external member possessing the specific technical knowledge needed.
- **Manager (Big Boss)**: Manager makes the decisions. In order to be able to do this, he communicates with the project team to determine the current situation, and to distinguish any difficulties or deficiencies in the process.

XP Practices

XP is a collection of ideas and practices drawn from already existing methodologies (Stapleton, J. 1997) (see Figure 12).

XP consists of 12 related practices and works best for small teams of 5 to 15 developers. Rather than focus on paper-based requirements and design documentation, XP concentrates on producing executable code and automated test drivers (Beck, K. 1999). This focus on source code makes XP controversial, leading some to compare it to hacking. (Beck, K. 1999) believes this comparison is unjustified because XP highly values simple design, and counters hacking claims by emphasizing refactoring, strong regression testing, and continuous code inspections through pair programming.

XP's focus on small teams lets it replace paper-based documentation with face-to-face communication. Hence, it's a good fit for many Web based software projects, which often postpone documentation efforts because of time-to-market constraints. In XP, all developers work closely together so they can communicate informally rather than spending time documenting designs and decisions. As long as teams remain small, this approach pays off: It's faster to talk directly than to write down development knowledge. In addition, direct communication is typically limited to existing issues.

To produce documentation, writers often have to make assumptions about what information will be useful for readers. If these assumptions are wrong or if the software design changes drastically, the documentation effort is wasted. As the development organization grows, however, time spent exchanging product knowledge and training new people increases and often renders XP unsuitable. XP's focus on reduced documentation should obviously improve productivity—at least in the short run (J. Zettel et al., 2001).

Building a high-quality software system is irrelevant if it does not solve the customer's problem. To increase customer satisfaction, XP uses two practices: on-site customer and small releases.

On-Site Customer

Determining and prioritizing requirements is essential for any successful software project. However, trying to "get the requirements right" before the software is designed and implemented is problematic in Web-based systems, where requirements frequently change. In XP, developers initially document requirements through *user stories*, which are basically textual use-case descriptions. To clarify these requirements and set priorities, XP uses an on-site customer representative who works with the team. This practice improves the software's business value: When issues arise, programmers can get customer input immediately rather than speculate on customer preferences. This also lets customers change requirements on very short notice—thereby helping the team flexibly refocus development efforts on the most pressing needs.

Small Releases

Given that requirements change often, XP keeps release cycles short and ensures that each release produces a useful software system that generates business value for the customer. Short cycles reduce customer risk, letting the customer quickly terminate projects that fail to deliver business value. A short release cycle also helps developers deal with changing requirements and reduces the impact of planning errors. XP proposes a set of software development practices to increase productivity while maintaining quality.

XP employs various practices to keep software quality high. Although some might appear unusual, their combined effects ensure that the team maintains high quality without slowing down the development process (Beck, K. 1999).

Software Testing

Specifically, automated regression testing is a key part of XP. The customer defines functional (acceptance) tests, which the development team implements. From a business perspective, these tests verify that the program does what it is supposed to do. According to the XP philosophy, a feature lacking automated tests does not exist.

To ease the project-management burden, XP includes practices aimed at reducing management overhead, while keeping the customer's interest at close range.

XP Adoption and Experiences

One of the fundamental ideas of XP is that there is no process that fits every project as such, but rather practices should be tailored to suit the needs of individual projects (Beck, K. 1999). Practical viewpoints for adopting XP have been documented in Extreme Programming Installed. The book describes a collection of techniques, covering most XP practices, mostly elaborated during an extensive industrial software project, where XP was used.

XP is the most documented one of the different agile methods and it has triggered new research, articles and experience reports on the individual XP practices, such as pair programming, as well as on applying the method itself.

A study by (Maurer, F. and Martel, S. 2002) showed some concrete numbers regarding the productivity gains from using XP in a web development project. They report an average increase of 66.3% in the new lines of code produced, 302.1% increase in the number of new methods developed and 282.6% increase in the number of new classes implemented in a development effort.

Scope of Use

The XP methodology is by no means suitable everywhere, nor have all its limits yet been identified. This calls for more empirical and experimental research on the subject from different perspectives. However, some limits have been identified.

XP is aimed for small and medium sized teams. The physical environment is also important in XP. Communication and coordination between project members should be enabled at all times.

The business culture affecting the development unit is another focal issue in XP. Any resistance against XP practices and principles on behalf of project members, management or customer may be enough to fail the process. Also technology might provide insuperable obstacles for the success of an XP project.

The Agile Web Engineering Process Life-Cycle

The agile web engineering process identifies all the major activities we feel need to be addressed during Web application development. Anyone who has experience of software processes, particularly variants on the Waterfall Model, may initially shudder at the diagram in Figure 12. While many of the names for each stage: Business Analysis, Requirements, Design, Implementation, Testing and Evaluation, should look familiar from other processes and methodologies, the similarity should end there. The only deliverable that is required to be produced from the AWE Process is the web application itself. That is not to say that you will

not benefit from the production of intermediate documents, diagrams and other notations. The onus is on the organization and the developers to find, integrate, evaluate and create techniques, if necessary, to support the activities outlined in (Figure 13) (Andrew McDonald and Ray Welland 2001).

Web Application Characteristics

There are many characteristics to Web applications, but the most important one that researchers have found is usability of a Web application.

The definition of usability, in general, suggests that there are four common factors that impact the usability of the interactive system (Bruno, V., & Al-Qaimari, G. 2004): users, tasks, technology and context. The characteristics reviewed will be grouped into these four factors.

Users

The stakeholders of a web application can be categorized by the users affected by the web interface (Hackos, J. T., & Redish, J. C. 1998): primary users, secondary users, user communities, users as buyers, and surrogate users. Primary users of a web application can be examined based on their competence, which will change over time: novice, advance beginners, competent performers, and experts. This competence can be examined from three perspectives: subject matter knowledge, computer skill, and experience with the web application.

If novice users are important to the web application, then ease of use (learnability) is an important usability attributes, whereas an expert user may require greater focus on efficient use.

The *loyalty* of users to a web application is an important characteristic, especially to e-commerce web applications. The basic spectrum of loyalty to a web application is discretionary or compulsory (Tomiuk, D. 2005).

Figure 13. The Agile Web Engineering (AWE) process life-cycle

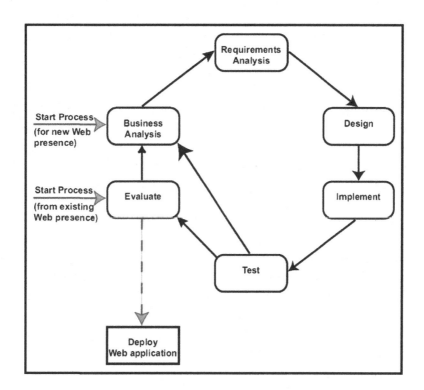

Accessibility is an important characteristic of a web application. Accessibility focuses on people with disabilities. A web application needs to consider assistive technologies, and compliance to the Web Content Accessibility Guidelines 1.0 (Chisholm, et al 1999) This characteristic can impact on many of the other characteristics of a web application, like the impact of interaction styles and support for different input and display devices (system variables). For example, a visually impaired user may use a screen magnifier or Braille display device, which requires support for alternative devices.

Task

A taxonomy of web applications categories is proposed by Deshpande et al (Deshpande, Yas et al 2002) follow: informational, interactive, transaction, workflow, collaborative work environments, online communities (market places),

web portals, web services. Transactional type web applications are commonly found in e-commerce applications and can be further broken down into: transaction type, domain/site type, vendor type and product type.

The interaction style(s) that can be implemented on a web application is constrained by the technological aspects. The interaction styles provide various levels of usability, and support different types of users, these could include: Batch, Question-answer, Command language, Function keys, Form fill-in, Menus, Direct manipulation, Non-command, Natural language.

The interface design characteristic of a web application can be represented by its: structure describes the organization of the information space presented by a web application; navigation enables moving through the information space presented by the web application; presentation describes the interaction styles used to present the information and behavior of the web application (Bruno & Tam, 2005).

Technology

The tools used to implement a web application can dictate the degree of usability possible, through the architecture developed with the tool. (Fraternali, P. 1999) describes these various web development tools as: visual editors and site managers; hyper-media web generators; web database gateways; web-based form editors and database web publishing wizards; model-driven application generators.

(Karlsbjerg, J., et al 2003) describes implementation strategies for intranet web applications from two perspectives. First, the architecture of the web application is tailor-made or ready-made. Second, it is implemented or configured in-house or outsourced. This ownership characteristic of the web application, impacts on the ease by which the web application can dynamically meet the needs of the website owner and its visitors in web time.

Context

An industry classification provides the context of the environment where the users perform the interaction. An industry classification is a characteristic of a web application that highlights special needs of an industry in relation to usability. For example, finance industry requires greater focus on security, while government web applications need greater focus on accessibility. The contextual properties (Finkelstein, A et al 2002) of a user that is interacting with a web application can vary with each web application. User context allows identification and enables personalization.

Network provides network and bandwidth context. Location captures information about the location that can enhance context of web application.

Time context represented at a web server may dictate opening and closing times or relate to a timetable or schedule. (Finkelstein, A et al 2002)

states that because "web application suffering from the anytime/anywhere/any media syndrome", that the focus on customization can tackle these contextual issues.

Contextual properties, customization and industry classification provide the characteristics of web application that enable the environment to be tailored to the stakeholders, their tasks and the technology to support the interaction. These contextual characteristics will enable a better focus on usability attributes.

Modeling Web-Based Application

The internet, and in particular the World Wide Web, have introduced a new era of computing, providing the basis for promising application areas like e-applications.

At the beginning, the web has been employed merely for simple read-only information systems, i.e., systems realized by some web server offering static web pages for browsing, only. Nowadays, the web is more and more used as a platform for full-fledged, increasingly complex information systems, where a huge amount of change-intensive data is (partly) managed by underlying database systems. The data can be navigated through, queried, and updated by means of web browsers, whereby web pages may either be generated in advance or dynamically in response to the requests of users whose number and type is not necessarily predictable.

This emerging kind of information systems is further on called Web applications (B. Pröll et al 1999) Considering these applications from a software engineering point of view, as their complexity increases, so does the importance of modeling techniques.

Models of a web application prior to its construction are essential for comprehension in its entirety, for communication among project teams, and to assure architectural soundness and maintainability. There are already a couple of methods especially dedicated to the modeling of Web applications. These methods focus on unique characteristics of web applications comprising among others the usage of the hypermedia paradigm in terms of hypertext and multimedia in combination with traditional application logic. One major requirement posed on today's web applications, however, is not considered by the majority of modeling methods, namely the issue of customization.

A key aspect, and perhaps the hardest part, of analyzing web applications is handling the dynamic nature of the software. The dynamic aspects are caused by uncertainty in the program behavior, changes in application requirements, rapidly evolving web technology itself, and other factors. The dynamic nature of web software not only brings challenges to analysis, testing, and maintenance, it also raises another important problem.

When one part of the application changes, is it necessary to change every related component(Ye Wu and Jeff Offutt 2006).There are dimensions to be considered when modeling Web applications, comprising levels, aspects and phases (see Figure 14).

The first dimension of Web application modeling comprises, similar to the Model/View/Controller (MVC) paradigm in object-oriented software development (R.E. Johnson, B. Foote 1988), three different levels namely, the content level, the hypertext level, and the presentation level. The content level refers to domain-dependent data used by the DataWeb application and is often managed by means of a database system. The hypertext level denotes the logical composition of web pages and the navigation structure. The presentation level, finally, is concerned with the representation of the hypertext level, e.g., the layout of each page and user interaction.

The second dimension comprises the aspects of structure and behavior, which are orthogonal to the three levels of the first dimension. Concerning the content level, besides structuring the domain by means of standard abstraction mechanisms such as classification, aggregation and generalization, the behavioral aspect in terms of domain-dependent application logic has to be considered too. Similarly, at the hypertext level, structure in terms of page compositions and navigational relationships in between as well as behavior like computing the endpoint of a certain link at runtime have to

Figure 14. Modeling dimensions

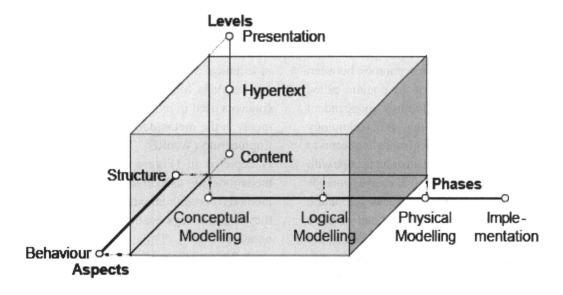

be modeled. At the presentation level, finally, user interface elements and their hierarchical composition have to be modeled concerning the structural aspect.

The third dimension of modeling web applications comprises the different phases of a software life cycle, ranging from analysis to implementation. This dimension is orthogonal to the two previously presented ones, meaning that structure and behavior of content, navigation and presentation has to be addressed in each phase of the development process. At this time, there is no consensus on a general model for the lifecycle of web application development.

Phases: Analysis, Logical Modeling, Physical Modeling and Implementation

This dimension is orthogonal to the two previously presented ones, meaning that structure and behavior of content, navigation and presentation has to be addressed in each phase of the development process. At this time, there is no consensus on a general model for the lifecycle of web application development (D. Lowe, R. Webby 1998). However, the influence of technological aspects tailoring the model towards the implementation environment, such as distribution, heterogeneity and database aspects, should certainly increase within the later phases of the modeling process.

(D. Lowe, R. Webby 1998) believe that, similar to database design, a separation between an abstract representation of the domain called conceptual modeling, technology independent design, i.e., logical modeling, and technology dependent design, i.e., physical modeling seems to be appropriate. Furthermore, in order to cope with the characteristics of aggressive release demands and rapid technology changes, web development should be much more incremental and iterative than development in other domains. That is, the need for prototyping and intensive testing with users is essential because user tolerance to errors

in Web applications is very low. A development process, which is part of an appropriate modeling method, has to take these requirements into account.

Analysis Model

The major complexity of analyzing web software comes from the dynamic aspects, including dynamically generated client components, dynamic interaction among clients and servers, and the continual changes in the system context and web technologies.

The stereotypical methods for specifying requirements from the technical rationality perspective is the unified modeling language, UML (Booch, G., Rumbaugh, J. & Jacobson, I. 1999).

UML use cases were developed to describe the major functionality of the proposed system, including registration and purchase, research queries, and maintenance. Given that this is a data-intensive application that would be implemented around a relational database, it is not surprising that the heaviest use of UML was in the development of class diagrams.

Limited use was made of OO principles, such as encapsulation and inheritance, because it was known that the implementation environment had no explicit support for OO mechanisms. Although the analysis was approached from a logical stance, i.e. independent of the implementation platform, the methods used were influenced by the choice of technical platform for implementation.

(Escalona, M.J., Koch, N 2006) summarize the concepts used in modeling Web system requirements in the metamodel for Web Requirements Engineering (WebRE). The WebRE metamodel is depicted in (Figure 14). Instances of this metamodel are used in several Web Engineering methods for requirements specification, although they do not always use the same terminology and notation.

A WebUser is any user who interacts with a Web System and may be either registered or not.

The basic use case type is Navigation, which comprises a set of browse actions that the Web user performs to reach a target node. Browse is the action of following a link and is represented by an instance of the metaclass browse.

The special browse action Search models a query that the Web user makes to the Web system. A special kind of the Navigation use case is webprocess, which includes user transactions like checkout or providing credit card data.

Design Model

After the requirements of a Web application are laid down with requirements models, its design is performed in platform independent models, where the content, the navigation structure, the business processes and the presentation are defined on an abstract level without considering technical details of implementations. The

concepts required for modeling are defined in the UWE metamodel(Koch, N., Kraus 2002). This metamodel includes a package for each of these concerns and is defined as a conservative extension of the UML metamodel.

See (Figure 15) for the package navigation. The metamodel is complemented with well formedness rules formulated in the Object Constraint Language (OCL). The content of a Web system is modeled in a content model built with UML class diagrams and "pure" UML modeling elements. In the navigation model, navigable nodes are represented by instances of subclasses of Node, which is derived from the UML metaclass Class. Direct links between navigation nodes are modeled by instances of NavigationLink, a subclass of the UML metaclass Association. There are several kinds of nodes defined: navigation classes represents the navigable information units of the Web application; menus model the common

Figure 15. Model-driven approach for web systems

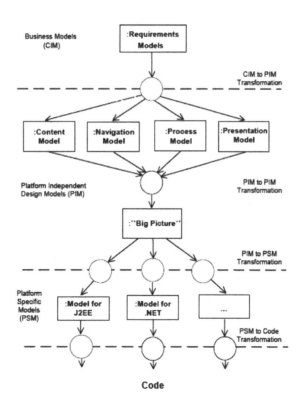

Code

337

Figure 16. UWE metamodel: navigation package

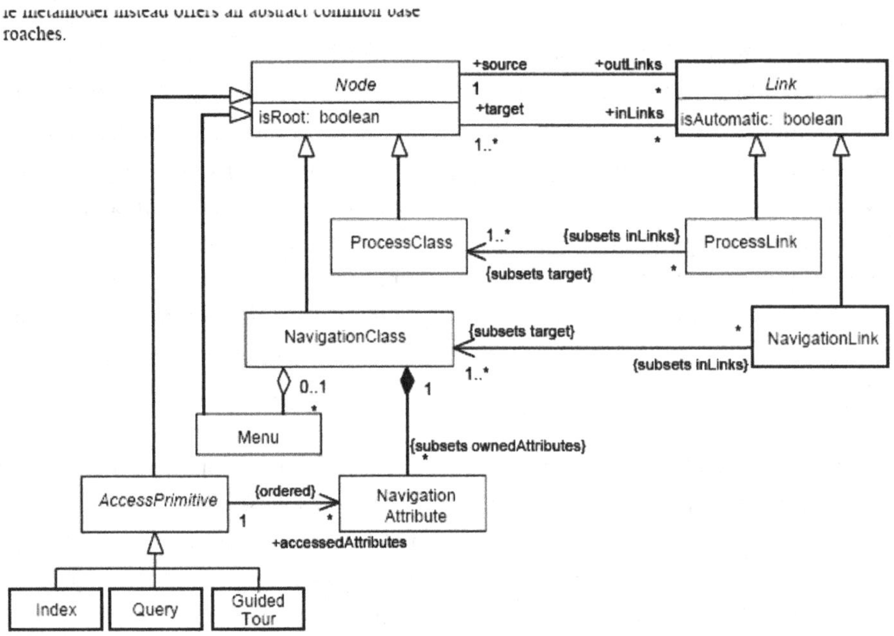

starting point of alternative links leaving a node; access primitives are used to represent special constructs in Web navigation: indexes, queries and guided tours.

Business Intelligence and Agile Methods

In order to help an organization to review its business, its competition and its external environment from time to time and take smarter and faster decisions not only for survival and sustenance but also to stay one step ahead of its competition, we need the Business Intelligence (BI) initiatives. Or in other words, BI serves to keep an organization agile and vigilant at the same time (www. analyticbridge.com).

There is a fundamental difference between a typical application development project that we routinely come across in a software industry and a BI project. The difference is that the requirements in an application development exercise are well-defined and static by nature; whereas the requirements in a BI project are more amorphous and dynamic since these BI projects are closely aligned with the business goals. As the goals and objectives change in response to the demand-supply economics at a given point in time, the expectations from BI are also bound to change. For instance business consolidation arising out of mergers and acquisitions could lead to a total revamp of an organization's goals and objectives.

Given the difficulty that many organizations have faced in delivering the BI applications their managers and executives need to understand performance and make critical business decisions, it's not surprising that an alternative development approach is being embraced. Indeed, there is a broad and growing consensus that Agile BI's time has come. Significant momentum has been building, and Agile BI is on its way to becoming the industry standard for BI project delivery.

For more than 20 years, custom software development teams have used a mature toolset of agile delivery methods like Scrum and Extreme Programming (XP) to deliver a broad range of software in critical business functions. Agile BI refers to the application of the agile software development methodology to the project delivery and development of business intelligence applications. Specifically, that means an iterative process noted for rapid prototype development through a series of "Sprints" to produce specific functionality that is shared with users, who are given full and repeated opportunities to provide feedback. But the principles of Agile BI extend beyond the realm of software development to enable operational and organizational agility – the ability to execute nimbly and efficiently, and respond rapidly to new markets and opportunities. The point is, Agile BI is as much about how BI applications are used and what they enable businesses to do, as it is about how the applications themselves are built (www-test.balancedinsight.com).

Defining Our Terms:

Agile Methods Benefits to Business Intelligence

At the simplest level, Agile BI refers to the use of the agile software development methodology for BI projects. BI delivery teams have discovered they can realize significant benefits from these methods because the agile approach solves several fundamental and longstanding challenges to effective BI delivery:

- **Rising Demand:** Demand for information about business performance has risen dramatically. (The Information Age could just as well be called the BI Age.) BI delivery teams have a large backlog of projects from business users looking for more information to support their decisions. But it's not just more information users want; it's more information faster. Agile BI helps IT meet the imperatives for quantity and speed in unlocking the full value of data assets.

- **Flexibility:** The agile methodology is designed to adjust to changing requirements – and BI requirements change more frequently and profoundly than those for nearly all other types of software projects.

- **User Engagement**: The great strength of the agile methodology is that it fosters collaboration between IT and the business. While traditional approaches have struggled to place user needs at the core of the process. Agile BI is all about giving users faster access to functionality and more opportunities to provide feedback. Ultimately, user engagement equates to higher user satisfaction and adoption rates.

- **Manageable Scope**: Budget overruns and blown schedules can damage IT's credibility, besides costing the company real money. Because Agile BI focuses on the delivery of smaller sets of functionality in shorter time periods, projects are driven by business defined scope and value. Project timelines and budgets can be tracked in smaller units, and users pay for the value defined. Avoiding scope creep is good news, but it's better news that these budgets are significantly smaller and the project timelines much shorter.

- **Lower Costs, Higher Value**: Agile methods in BI have a strong track record in reducing project costs and shortening timelines. Further, because project budgets are aligned to high-priority deliverables and outcomes – that is, high-powered, easy-to-consume applications that users like and that material and urgent business needs – overall technology ROI also increases (www-test.balancedinsight.com).

CONCLUSION

In this chapter we reviewed web engineering from different perspectives, firstly we defined it from many perspectives and we reached that

Web Engineering is concerned with the establishment and use of sound scientific, engineering and management principles and disciplined and systematic approaches to the successful development, deployment and maintenance of high quality Web-based systems and applications.

Web engineering is an emerging new discipline, advocates a process and a systematic approach to development of high quality Internet- and Web-based applications. Also it differs from conventional software in the way of development, where it needs a rapid development, short time to market.

The characteristics of web based applications are also different from conventional software applications; where web based applications have special features like usability, loyalty, accessibility, and context.

There is a great need for web engineering, where in the case of no standards approach to Web-based applications development, we will find sooner or later that web-based applications are not delivering desired performance and quality.

Web-engineering is a multi disciplinarians science, where it involves a mixture between print publishing and software development, between marketing and computing, between internal communications and external relations, and between art and technology.

Secondly we discussed the web engineering process and development methods, traditional software engineering projects are primarily concerned with the creation of software components with supporting systems, which are often generic.

Web engineering on the other hand results in deliverables, comprising software components and supporting systems that are developed in parallel with the creation of the data that they will operate upon or in conjunction with. Web Engineering is complicated by the addition of a creative design model that reflects the issues associated with the aesthetic aspects of the user interface. To help to reduce the difficulty in building Web-based systems we need a process model that describe the phases of Web-based system development - some

of the aspects that make Web-system difficult include complexity, changeability, invisibility and unrealistic schedule.

Requirement analysis and web-based system design is a very important activity and calls for a systematic and disciplined approach and testing, and verification and validation (V & V) of Web-based systems is an important and challenging task in the Web engineering process. Also Web development management and Web configuration management are difficult tasks, especially in the midst of change which is a fact of life in the Web environment.

There is a need for using tools in web engineering process, where there are many tools available to support the building of web sites, but few that support their planning or design, some, allow the drawing of artifacts like navigation charts, but these tools are still essentially designed to support implementation.

Web development research and practice are a small but growing body of research literature regarding the differences between Web systems and more conventional software systems. In general, this literature identifies unique characteristics of these systems that reflect technical, usability and organizational issues.

Thirdly we discussed Agile development methods and showed many agile methods aspects and properties.

The field of software development is not shy of introducing new methodologies. Indeed, in the last 25 years, a large number of different approaches to software development have been introduced, of which only few have survived to be used today. A short description of some agile software development methods is reviewed and a detailed description of XP is provided.

The Scrum approach has been developed for managing the systems development process. It is an empirical approach applying the ideas of industrial process control theory to systems development resulting in an approach that reintroduces the ideas of flexibility, adaptability and productivity.

The Crystal family of methodologies includes a number of different methodologies for selecting the most suitable methodology for each individual project. Besides the methodologies, the Crystal approach also includes principles for tailoring the methodologies to fit the varying circumstances of different projects.

Feature Driven Development (FDD) is an agile and adaptive approach for developing systems. The FDD approach does not cover the entire software development process, but rather focuses on the design and building phases.

An Adaptive Software Development project is carried out in three-phase cycles. The phases of the cycles are Speculate, Collaborate, and Learn.

The Dynamic Systems Development Method, has gradually become the number one framework for rapid application development (RAD) in the UK.

In this chapter we have discussed Extreme Programming (XP) in detailed manner, because we will use it in our proposed frame work. Extreme Programming (XP) has evolved from the problems caused by the long development cycles of traditional development models. It first started as "simply an opportunity to get the job done". XP consists of five phases: Exploration, Planning, Iterations to Release, Productionizing, Maintenance and Death. There are different roles in XP for different tasks and purposes during the process and its practices: Programmer, Customer, Tester, Tracker, Coach, Consultant, and Manager. XP is a collection of ideas and practices drawn from already existing methodologies.

XP consists of 12 related practices and works best for small teams of 5 to 15 developers. The XP methodology is by no means suitable everywhere, nor have all its limits yet been identified. This calls for more empirical and experimental research on the subject from different perspectives. However, some limits have been identified.

XP is aimed for small and medium sized teams. The physical environment is also important in XP. Communication and coordination between project members should be enabled at all times. Models of a web application prior to its construction are essential for comprehension in its entirety, for communication among project teams, and to assure architectural soundness and maintainability.

Finally, the principles of Agile BI extend beyond the realm of software development to enable operational and organizational agility – the ability to execute nimbly and efficiently, and respond rapidly to new markets and opportunities. The point is, Agile BI is as much about how BI applications are used and what they enable businesses to do, as it is about how the applications themselves are built.

REFERENCES

Ahmad, R., Li, Z., & Azam, F. (2005). *Web engineering: A new emerging discipline*. International Conference on Emerging Technologies, September 17-18, Islamabad, Pakistan. IEEE.

Balasubramanian, V., Ma, B., & You, J. (1995). A systematic approach to designing a WWW application [New York, NY: ACM.]. *Communications of the ACM, 38*(8), 47–48.

Beck, K. (1999). Embracing change with extreme programming. *IEEE Computer, 32*(10), 70–77.

Beck, K. (1999). *Extreme programming explained: Embrace change*. Reading, MA: Addison-Wesley.

Beck, K., Beedle, M., van Bennekum, A., Cockburn, A., Cunningham, W., & Fowler, M. … Thomas, D. (2001). *Manifesto for Agile Software Development, The Agile Alliance*. Retrieved on February, 2001, from http://www.agilealliance. org/

Booch, G., Rumbaugh, J., & Jacobson, I. (1999). *The unified modelling language*. Reading, MA: Addison-Wesley.

Bruno, V., & Al-Qaimari, G. (2004). *Usability attributes: An initial step toward effective user-centred development*. Wollongong, Australia: OZCHI.

Burdman, J. (1999). Collaborative Web Development. In Carmichael, A. (Ed.), *Strategies and best practices for Web teams*. Reading, MA: Addison-Wesley.

Chisholm, W., Vanderheiden, G., & Jacobs, I. (1999). *Web content accessibility guidelines 1.0.*

Cockburn, A. (2002). *Agile software development*. Boston, MA: Addison-Wesley.

Constantine, L. L. (2001). *Lightweights, heavyweights and usable processes for usable software*, Keynote at software development 2001, San Jose, CA.

Constantine, L. L., & Lockwood, L. A. D. (2000). *Software for use*. Boston, MA: Addison Wesley.

Dart, S. (1999). Containing the Web crisis using configuration management, In *Proceedings of the 1st ICSE Workshop on Web Engineering*. New York, NY: ACM. Retrieved from http:// fistserv. macarthur.uws.edu.au/ san/ icse99-webe/.

De Troyer, O. M. F., & Leune, C. J. (1998). WSDM: A user-centered design methods for Web sites. *Proceedings of the 7th International World Wide Web Conference*, Brisbane, Australia.

Deshpande, Y., Murugesan, S., Ginige, A., Hansen, S., Schwabe, D., & Gaedke, M. (2002). Web engineering. *Journal of Web Engineering*, *1*(1), 3–017.

England, E., & Finney, A. (1999). *Managing Multimedia: Project Management for Interactive Media*. Reading, MA: Addison-Wesley.

Escalona, M. J., & Koch, N. (2006). Metamodeling requirements of Web systems. In *Proceedings of the International Conference on Web Information System and Technologies (WEBIST 2006)*, INSTICC (pp. 310-317), Setúbal, Portugal.

Finkelstein, A. C. W., Savigni, A., Kappel, G., Retschitzegger, W., & Kimmerstorfer, E. (2002). *Ubiquitous Web application development - A framework for understanding. 6th World Multiconference on Systemics, Cybernetics and Informatics, Orlando, Florida, US*. W.: Schwinger.

Fowler, M., & Highsmith, J. (2001). *The agile manifesto, Software Development Magazine*. Retrieved on August, 2001, from http:// www. sdmagazine.com/ documents/s=844/ sdm0108a/ 0108a.htm

Fraternali, P. (1999). Tools and approaches for developing data-intensive Web applications: A survey. *ACM Computing Surveys, 31*, 227–263.

Gellersen, H., & Gaedke, M. (1999). An object-oriented model for the Web application development process, *IEEE Internet Computing*, January - Feb 1999.

Ginige, A. (1998). Web engineering: Methodologies for developing large and maintainable. *Proceedings IEEE International Conference on Networking the India and the World (CNIW'98)*, Ahmedabad, India.

Ginige, A. (2002). *Web engineering: Managing the complexity of Web systems development (SEKE 2002)* (pp. 721-729). Italy: ACM press.

Hackos, J. T., & Redish, J. C. (1998). *User and task analysis for interface design*. Canada: John Wiley & Sons Inc.

Henderson-Sellers, B., Haire, B., & Lowe, D. (2001). Adding Web support to OPEN. *Journal of Object Oriented Programming*, *14*(3), 34–38.

Highsmith, J. A. (2000). *Adaptive software development: A collaborative approach to managing complex systems*. New York, NY: Dorset House Publishing.

Johnson, R. E., & Foote, B. (1988). Designing reusable classes. [JOOP]. *Journal of Object-Oriented Programming, 1*(2).

Karlsbjerg, J., Damsgaard, J., & Scheepers, R. (2003). A taxonomy of intranet implementation strategies: To make or to buy? *Journal of Global Information Management, 11*(3), 39–62.

Koch, N., & Kraus, A. (2002). The expressive power of UML-based Web engineering. In *Proceedings 2nd International Workshop on Web-oriented Software Technology (IWWOST '02)* (pp. 105-119), Málaga, Spain.

Lord, J. (2000). Patterns for e-business: Lessons learned from building successful e-business applications. *IBM, 4*.

Lowe, D. (2001). A framework for defining acceptance criteria for Web development projects. In Murugesan, S., & Deshpande, Y. (Eds.), *Web engineering: Managing diversity and complexity of Web application development* (pp. 279–294). Berlin, Heidelberg: Springer-Verlag.

Lowe, D., & Hall, W. (1999). *Hypermedia and the Web: An engineering approach*. Hoboken, New Jersey: Wiley.

Lowe, D., & Henderson-Sellers, B. (2001). *Web development: Addressing process differences*. Cutter IT Journal.

Lowe, D., & Henderson-Sellers, B. (2001). Impacts on the development process of differences between Web systems and conventional software systems (SSGRR 2001), In *Proceedings of the International Conference on Advances in Infrastructure for Electronic Business, Science, and Education on the Internet* (L'Aquila, Italy, 2001), Scuola Superiore Guglielmo Reiss Romoli, 21.

Lowe, D., & Webby, R. (1998). Web development process modelling and project scoping: Work in progress, In *Proceedings of the Workshop on Web Engineering held in conjunction with The 7th International World Wide Web Conference (WWW7)*, Brisbane, Australia.

Lowe, D. B. (2005). Client needs and the design process in Web projects. *Journal of Mobile Multimedia, 1*(1).

Manola, F. (1999). Technologies for a Web object model. *IEEE Internet Computing, 3*(1), 38–47.

Maurer, F., & Martel, S. (2002). Extreme programming: Rapid development for Web-based applications. *IEEE Internet Computing, 6*(1), 86–90.

McDonald, A., & Welland, R. (2001). *Agile Web engineering (AWE) process*. Retrieved from www.dcs.gla.ac.uk/ publications/ PAPERS/ 7087/ TR-2001-98%5B1%5D.pdf.

Mendes, E., Mosley, N., & Counsell, S. (2006). *Web engineering*. Berlin–Heidelberg, Germany: Springer.

Miller, G. G. (2001). The characteristics of agile software processes. *The 39th International Conference of Object-Oriented Languages and Systems (TOOLS 39)*, Santa Barbara, CA.

Murugesan, S., Deshpande, Y., Hansen, S., & Ginige, A. (1999). Web engineering: A new discipline for development of Web-based systems, In *Proceedings of the 1st International Conference of Software Engineering (ICSE) Workshop on Web Engineering*, Los Angeles, CA.

Palmer, S. R., & Felsing, J. M. (2002). *A practical guide to feature-driven development*. Upper Saddle River, NJ: Prentice-Hall.

Powell, T. A. (1998). *Web site engineering: Beyond Web page design*. Upper Saddle River, NJ: Prentice Hall.

Pröll, B., Retschitzegger, W., Sighart, H., & Starck, H. (1999). Ready for prime time – Pre- generation of Web-pages in TIScover, *Proceedings of the ACM Conference on Information and Knowledge Management (CIKM'99)*, Kansas City, Missouri.

Scharl, A. (1999). A conceptual, user-centric approach to modeling Web Information Systems, *Proceedings of the Australian Web Conference (Ausweb99)*, Ballina, Australia.

Siegel, D. (1997). *Secrets of Successful Web Sites*. Hayden Books.

Stapleton, J. (1997). *Dynamic systems development method – The method in practice*. Reading, MA: Addison-Wesley.

Tomiuk, D. (2005). Companies' ability to foster loyalty in traditional versus Web-based service environments: A relational perspective. *International Journal on WWW/Internet*, 582-586.

Vince Bruno, V., & Tam, A. (2005). Characteristics of Web applications that affect usability: A review, In *Proceedings of the 19th Conference of the Computer-Human Interaction Special Interest Group (CHISIG) of Australia on Computer-Human Interaction: Citizens Online: Considerations for Today and the Future.*

Wu, Y., & Offutt, J. (2006). *Modeling and testing Web-based applications*. Retrieved on December 10th, 2006, from http:// citeseer.ist.psu.edu/551504.html

Zettel, J., Maurer, F., Münch, J., & Wong, L. (2001). LIPE: A lightweight process for e-business startup companies based on extreme programming, In *Proceedings of the 3rd International Conference of Product-Focused Software Process Improvement (PROFES 2001)*. Berline-Heidelberg, Germany: Springer-Verlag.

KEY TERMS AND DEFINITIONS

Agile Business Intelligence: The use of the agile software development methodology for BI projects.

Agile Development: A group of software development methodologies based on iterative development, where requirements and solutions evolve through collaboration between self-organizing cross-functional teams

Extreme Programming: A software development methodology which is intended to improve software quality and responsiveness to changing customer requirements

Process Models: An explicit description of the tasks of a project with their precedence and information and rework dependencies.

Web-Based Applications: An application that is accessed over a network such as the Internet or an intranet

Web Development: A broad term for the work involved in developing a web site for the Internet (World Wide Web) or an intranet (a private network

Web Engineering: The application of systematic and quantifiable approaches (concepts, methods, techniques, tools) to cost-effective requirements analysis, design, implementation, testing, operation, and maintenance of high-quality Web applications.

About the Contributors

Asim Abdel Rahman El Sheikh is Dean of Information Technology in the Arab Academy for Banking and Financial Sciences (AABFS). He supervised a number of theses in simulation and software engineering. He earned his PhD and MSc from London School of Economics & Political Science, and his BSc from University of Khartoum. He was a researcher in the Computer-Aided Simulation Modeling (CASM) Research Group. He worked as programmer, system analyst & designer in many organizations. He has authored two books and many articles. His research interest areas include SW piracy, software outsourcing, simulation modeling, and SW engineering.

Mouhib Alnoukari received his PhD degree from the Arab Academy for Banking and financial Sciences (Damascus, Syria). He already received three master degrees: MS in Computer Sciences from Montpellier University (France), MS in Mathematics from Damascus University (Syria), and MBA from the Higher Institute for Administration Development, Damascus University (Syria). He is currently working as a Faculty member at the Arab International University, Damascus (Syria). His research interests are in the areas of: Business Intelligence, Data Mining, Data Warehousing, Agile methodology, Software Engineering, and Databases in which he published many journal and conferences papers. He published more than 20 books both in Arabic and English languages. He has been appointed many times as track chair, reviewer in many international conferences: ICCAIE, ICOS, ISCI, and Co-Chaired BISY2010. He is an editorial board member at the *Journal of Computing Applications* (JCA).

* * *

Hatem Abd Alnafea has graduated from of faculty of Information Technology in Damascus University (specialized in networking and operating systems). He has graduated in 2004 and is now studying "management information system" for a Master degree at the Arab Academy for Banking and Financial Sciences. He is currently working in a Syrian Internet service provider (SCS-Net) in the Network Operation Center as a Networking and System Engineer, and he is working also as an "ICT Consultant" in the exchange and money transfer in Syria.

Sattam Alamaro, born in Jordan 1972, earned a PhD in Management Information System at Arab Academy for Banking and financial Sciences, Amman, Jordan. He is Assistant Professor in Management Information System. He is an instructor in Management Information System in Albalqa Applied University, Karak University College, Jordan. His principal research interests include e-commerce, knowledge management, e-learning development and software process improvement. He is currently investigating how to implement e-commerce standards in Jordanian firms. He has published conference and journal papers in e-commerce and e-banking.

Humam Alhammami Alhawasli studied IT Engineering in the faculty of Information Technology in Damascus University and specialized in networking and operating systems field. He has graduated in 2006. He is currently studying MIS for a Master degree in the Arab Academy for Banking and Financial Sciences. He is currently working in a Syrian Internet service provider (SCS-Net) in the Network Operation Center as a system operation supervisor.

Dania Abdulwahab Alkhaldi is a computer engineer and performance measurement and evaluation leader in the IT department of the Commercial Bank of Syria. She earned her MSc degree in Computer Information System (CIS) from Arabic Academy of Banking and Financial Sciences (AABFS) in 2007 and her BA degree in Computer Engineering from Aleppo University in 2004. She is a candidate to get a PhD degree in Management Information System (MIS) from Arabic Academy of Banking and Financial Sciences (AABFS). She has worked at the Commercial Bank of Syria since 2006 as a system analyst and system administrator. She also worked as a free lancer translator of many IT specialized articles with Ray for Publishing and Science. Her main research interest areas include Knowledge Management, Software Engineering, Risk management and IT Business alignment.

Firas M. Alkhaldi is an associate professor of knowledge management and enterprise systems, He holds a BA in economics from Yarmouk University, Jordan; MA in Applied Economics from WMU, USA; and a PhD in Business Information Systems/Knowledge Management from Huddersfield University, UK. He is a Leading International KM Expert, a certified knowledge and enterprise systems professional and a certified e-business and ecommerce consultant. He was the Dean of Scientific Research and Graduate Studies (2006-2009) at the Arab Academy for Banking and Financial Science-Jordan and a lecturer at the faculty of Information Systems and Technology, A Chairman of the MIS department (2005-2009), AABFS- Jordan, Chairman of the MIS department (2004-2005), University of Petra-Jordan. He is currently the head of Quality and Academic Accreditation Unit at the Faculty of Business Administration, and also he is filling an associate professor position at the department of MIS, King Saud University. He is affiliated with a number of international professional societies on KM and e-business. He had a leadership role in the design and implementation of many professional and academic programs. He supervised 16 successful PhD thesis and great number of MS graduation research projects. His research interest is in Knowledge management; knowledge conversion and transfer, organizational knowledge theory, knowledge culture; Innovative work environment; human and social implications of enterprise systems (ERP, CRM, and SCM), electronic business and Net entrepreneurship. His work appears in number international Journals and conferences.

Mohammad Mazen Almustafa is a lecturer at the International University for Sciences & Technology (IUST). He graduated from Damascus University as electronic engineer in 1999. He received a High Studies Diploma in Programming and Operating system from Damascus University, Electronics department in 2004. Then he got MSc Degree from Arabic Academy for Banking Sciences, Computer Information System division in 2007. He is a PhD Candidate from Arabic Academy for Banking Sciences Computer Information System division. The first publishing of him was in International Conference on

Information & Communication Technologies: From Theory to Applications, IEEE Conference, Syria, 2008, "the Impact of Risk Management on IS Projects Success in Syria".

Haroon Al-tarawneh, born in Jordan 1970, received a PhD in computer Information System from Arab Academy for Banking and financial Sciences, Amman, Jordan. He is assistant professor in computer Information System. He is an instructor in computer Information System in Albalqa Applied University, Karak University College, Jordan. His principal research interests include software engineering, Web Engineering (Agile Development, Extreme programming), E-learning development and software process improvement. He is currently investigating how to implement software process improvements standards in small software development firms. He has published conference and journal papers in Web development and software process improvement.

Zaidoun Alzoabi holds a PhD degree in management information system with specialty in knowledge management in the software process in general and agile methods in specific. His main interests are knowledge management in software process models and in Agile methods in specific. Also he is interested in quality assurance in higher education, and the application of data mining and business intelligence to obtain maximum quality. He is currently the director of quality assurance at the Arab International University, and a member of the Syrian Business Intelligence National Team.

Kamal Atieh graduated as an Electronic System Engineer from the Higher Institute for Science and Technology in Syria (1995). In 2006, he earned a Masters Degree in Computer Information System from the Arab Academy for Banking and Financial Sciences, and he has a PhD in Computer Information Systems from the Arab Academy for Banking and Financial Sciences (2010). Beside his preparation for his PhD, he worked as an IT manager and Business development manager in commercial bank of Syria. In addition, he worked as a consultant for many IT and financial companies. He worked at Damascus Computer Science Faculty as an instructor for many courses.

Constanta-Nicoleta Bodea is a professor at the Academy of Economic Study Bucharest (ASE), Faculty of Cybernetics, Statistics and Economic Informatics, and Economic Informatics Department. Currently, she teaches Artificial Intelligence, Data Mining and Project Management. She coordinates numerous research projects at a national level and achieved a high expertise in managing projects with multiple consortia. She is an author of 11 books and more than 50 papers on Project Management, Information Systems, and Artificial Intelligence, being honored by IPMA with the Outstanding Research Contributions in 2007.

Jagdish Chand is a proven leader with over 13 years of experience in delivering leading edge analytic products to create business value from the world's largest data collections. Over the last 10 years at Yahoo! as Director of Engineering, he developed and deployed innovative and highly scalable solutions such as recommendation engines, audience analytics, and advertising and campaign analytics that resulted in better user experience and increased monetization for Yahoo!. Jagdish is an innovative leader who converts data into business weapons by building solutions that provide actionable insights. Jagdish's recommendations engine was adopted by over 10 Yahoo properties leading to increased audience engagement and as much as triple the increase in conversion rates. He was the architect and team leader for the Yahoo's advertiser analytics offering and has led the development of audience analytic solutions for user value and audience segmentation. Jagdish led the architecture and development of the Path Analyses Platform to analyze frequently used paths, funnels drop off and inflow/outflow for over 500 million users across over 10 million pages with billions of page views per day. Multiple products such as Full Business Insight, providing deep insight into user engagement and monetization, use this platform. Jagdish has also built multiple versions of Marketing Analytics product to attribute conversions across multiple campaigns and marketing channels resulting in optimized campaigns. In 10 years at Yahoo!, Jagdish grew from a developer to Director of Engineering, delivering high quality projects on time using architectures that have scaled and run smoothly for years in production. In addition to leading the development of new products, Jagdish has also taken over existing analytics products, which were not scaling with huge data, and converted them into linearly scalable and operable systems. He builds high performing teams that are proud of their work, leads by example and ensures that work gets done and gets done right. Jagdish has filed over 10 patents in the field of recommendations and advanced analytics and has one approved patent in the area of efficient computation of affinity for recommendation on large dataset. Jagdish received his BS in Computer Science and Engineering from N.I.T. in Hamirpur, India. He was awarded the Gold Medal for the best graduating student across all disciplines as well as the Gold Medal for Computer Science.

Faek Diko has a PhD in Mechanical Engineering from Dublin City University. He is currently working at the Arab International University as the Vice President for Administrative Affairs since 2005. He has worked as the Academic Manager at the Syrian Computer Society, and the Administration Manager in Virtual University, Damascus, Syria. He has worked before in the Academic staff in Higher Institute of Science and Technology, Damascus, Syria. He has had many papers published in different conferences and journals: Conference on Advanced Manufacturing Technology, DCU, Dublin, Aug. 1989, Conference on Manufacturing Technology, Hong Kong, 1991,National conference on production Res., Hatfield, U.K., 1991, Conference on Computer Integrated Manufacturing, Singapore, 1991, The NUMIFORM92 Conference, Sep. 1992, Sophia Antipolis, France, The Asia Pacific Conference on materials Processing, February 23rd, 1993, Singapore & the *Journal of Materials Processing Technology*, February 1993, Vol. 38, The IMF8, Irish Material Forum No. 8, Sept. 1992, UCD, Dublin, The 30th International MATADOR Conference. 31th March 1993, Umist, U. K., The International Conference on Advances in Materials and Processing Technologies, 2-5 November 2008, Bahrain, International Symposium on Information Technology, ITSIM 08, Malaysia, 2008.

Elias Farzali is currently a PhD student at the Arab Academy for Banking and financial Science (AABFS), Damascus, Syria. He has a Master degree in CIS (Computer Information Systems) from Arab Academy for Banking and financial Science (AABFS), Damascus, Syria. He has more than 12 years of experience in Banking Sector. He is working as a System analysis and design for many solutions. He has more than 3 years working in developing banking application software.

Jorge Fernández-González is an Informatics Engineer from the Informatics School of Barcelona (FIB) at the Technical University of Catalonia (Barcelona Tech) (UPC) and is currently pursuing his doctorate in the Software program, specializing in Information Systems. He is the Chief of Business Intelligence Consulting Department at Abast Solutions in Barcelona. He has worked as consultant in several different areas like ERP, CRM, BPR, and R&D accumulating more than 15 years of expertise. At the same time, he is currently assistant lecturer in the Services and Information Systems Engineering Department (ESSI) at the UPC on the subject Information Systems for Organizations. He has also been a collaborating lecturer at UOC (Universitat Oberta de Catalunya), Academic Director of a master and postgraduate studies at the UPC School, and he also participates in several business schools as invited lecturer. His research interests are in Business Intelligence, Agile Methodologies, Software Engineering, Business Process Management and Enterprise Information Systems.

Samir Hammami is a lecturer at the International University for Science & Technology (IUST). He graduated from Damascus University as an electronic engineer in 1997. He got his MSc Degree from Arabic Academy for Banking and Financial Sciences, Computer Information System division in 2005. He got his PhD from the Arab Academy for Banking and Financial Sciences, the Faculty of Information System in 2010. He worked at the Arab Academy for Banking and Financial Sciences as an expert and researcher until 2010, and he has several activities in the Syrian community. In addition, he is an E-Business consultant. His research interests are in Management Information Systems, Knowledge Management, e-Business, supply chain management, business process reengineering, Enterprise systems and organizational behavioral.

Saiid Hanna studied IT Engineering in the faculty of Information Technology in Damascus University and specialized in software engineering's field. He has graduated in 2003. He is currently studying MBA for a Masters degree in the Syrian Virtual University. He is currently working in the Arab International University as the Database Administrator.

Deanne Larson is an active practitioner and academic focusing on Business Intelligence and Data Warehousing with over 20 years of experience. Dr. Larson's doctoral degree is a Doctorate of Management in Information Technology Leadership. Her doctoral dissertation research focuses on a grounded theory qualitative study on establishing enterprise data strategy. She holds Project Management Professional (PMP) and Certified Business Intelligence Profession (CBIP) certifications. Larson attended AT&T Executive Training at the Harvard Business School in 2001, focusing on IT leadership. She is a regular contributor to The Data Warehouse Institute (TDWI) publications and presents several times at year at conferences. Dr. Larson is a member of the Associate Faculty at American Public University and University of Phoenix in the United States.

Enric Mayol Sarroca is currently a lecturer at the Services and Information Systems Engineering Department (ESSI) of the Universitat Politècnica de Catalunya (BarcelonaTech) (UPC) in Barcelona. He received his PhD at the same university in 2000. He has worked on deductive database, database updates, integrity constraints maintenance, conceptual modeling and Information Systems. His teaching activities rely at the Barcelona School of Informatics about Software Engineering, Information Systems and Databases. Current research interests are involved with Conceptual Modeling, Business Information Systems, Business Process Modeling, Genealogy and Service Science (SSME). He participates in several funded Research Projects at the university with collaboration of enterprises.

Vojtěch Merunka has MSc degree in Computer Engineering (Czech Technical University in Prague) in 1991, PhD in data processing and mathematical modeling in 1998 (Czech University of Life Sciences). Since 2006 he is a permanent associate professor of information management. He lectures on object-oriented programming, object databases and methodologies of system development to undergraduates and postgraduates on a number of degree programs at both universities. Currently his main research is in theoretical foundations of OOP and in business system modeling used for requirement specification of software systems. He was a member of an international research project sponsored by the British Council on software development methods. As a result of this research he is a co-author of the BORM (Business and Object Relation Modeling) method that has been developed to support the design of complex object oriented systems in business environment.

Martin Molhanec earned an MSc degree in Electrical Engineering (Czech Technical University in Prague, Faculty of Electrical Engineering) in 1979 and a PhD in e-Technology in 1995. Since 1980, he has been a lecturer, since 1982 he has been a researcher and since 1989 he has been an Aassistant Professor at Czech Technical University in Prague. He lectures on software engineering, databases, software architecture, Web methodologies, project management and software process to undergraduates and postgraduates on a number of degree programs at Faculty of Electrical Engineering and Faculty of Nuclear Sciences and Physical Engineering at Czech Technical University in Prague. Currently his main research is in ontology and theoretical foundations of conceptual and business process modeling. He has a special interest in theoretical methods for analyses and design of complex Web sites. Also, he is a member of standardisation committee for data standards of Czech Normalisation Institute.

Joan A. Pastor holds a BSc and a MSc in Informatics and a PhD in Informatics Engineering from the Technical University of Catalonia (UPC-BarcelonaTech). He also has the Global Senior Management Program from the University of Chicago GoB and the IE Business School, and a Masters in Leadership and Management in Science and Innovation from the Catalan Universities UAB, UB and UPF. Since 2007, he has been an assistant professor and researcher at the Open University of Catalonia (UOC) and part-time lecturer at UPC. He has held university management posts, and is now leading a new research group on Services and IS at UOC, in sync with the GMC research group at UPC. His teaching and research topics are focused around services and Information Systems, currently on IS/IT services management, enterprise IS/IT acquisition and implementation, Services Science and curriculum innovation in university computing degrees. He is now the Academic Director of the UOC <aster on IS/IT management.

Amjad Jalal Zamreek is a computer engineer graduated From MUST (Cairo, Egypt). Preparing MS in MIS in the Arab Academy for Banking and financial Sciences (Damascus, Syria). Amjad Jalal Zamreek's research interests are in the areas of: Knowledge Management and Business Intelligence.

Index

C

campaign exposure collection system 216-217

campaign exposure counter system 220

campaign exposure merger system 217-218

candidate conversion attribution system 218, 220

candidate generation system 215

candidate merger system 216-218

CART trees 224

CASE analysis 120-121

CHAID tree 224

change oriented 136, 142

checklist analysis 245

Class (Code) Ownership 27

classification 6, 75, 191, 194, 197-198, 225, 227, 235, 238, 273, 286, 299, 334-335

clustering 75, 191, 194, 197-198, 200, 234, 236, 238

coach 21, 330, 341

collaboration 16-17, 25, 28, 32-33, 89-90, 101-105, 108-109, 111, 113-114, 116, 129, 136, 142-143, 154, 156, 160, 184, 186, 191, 196, 198, 266, 279, 311, 323, 339, 344

combination 4, 6, 8, 36, 71, 139, 141, 161-162, 164, 169, 176-177, 184, 191, 210, 261, 299, 311, 335

configuration generation system 215-216

configuration management 27, 32, 320, 340, 342

content and document management systems 2, 5

continuous integration 19-20, 34, 41, 193

Control Objectives for Information and Related Technology (COBIT) 161, 167, 169-170, 176, 178, 180-182

conversion 28, 210-222

conversion attribution 218-220, 222

conversion collection system 216, 218

conversion window 212, 222

Craft. CASE 120

CRISP-DM 6, 11, 73, 79, 82-87, 96-97, 99, 185-188, 190-191, 204

cross-functional 136, 139-140, 142, 153-154, 160, 266, 344

Crystal 15, 23-25, 184, 325-326, 341

D

dashboard 160, 201, 258-259, 266-267

data analyst 76-77, 86, 192-193, 195-196

data destination 74, 187-188

data-driven DSS 2-3

data layer 2, 5, 252

data mart 5-6, 11, 75, 85, 96, 111, 188, 197

data miner 74, 78, 86, 185, 192-193, 195

data mining applications 11, 79, 89, 96, 183, 186, 194, 203, 237, 256

data mining approaches 234

Data Mining (DM) 2, 5, 10-11, 13, 79, 83-84, 95, 100, 118, 158, 205, 207

data preparation 3, 7, 74, 78, 80-81, 83, 85, 87, 92, 185, 188-190, 192, 197, 256

data understanding 7, 73-74, 83-86, 88-89, 113, 186, 188, 190, 192, 195-196, 256

Data Warehouse (DW) 2-3, 5, 13, 100, 159, 207

decision making 3-5, 8-9, 11, 36, 90, 102, 118-119, 121, 133, 135, 138, 141, 155, 163, 181, 186-187, 194-195, 206-207, 223, 225, 236, 238, 247, 249, 264, 274-275, 284-285

Decision Support System (DSS) 2-5, 8, 13, 117-118, 247-249

DELPHI technique 244

developing countries 162, 268-270, 274-276, 280-284

dexterity in motion 18

diagramming techniques 245

direct marketers 209

documentation review 243

domain expert 74, 86, 192-193, 195, 249-250

Domain Object Modeling 26-27

E

e-government 268-278, 280-284

e-government characteristics 275

e-government framework 271-272, 276, 281

equation modeling 37, 172

ETL tools 2, 5, 188

Executive Information System (EIS) 2

expert system 206, 247-248, 250-251, 267

explicit knowledge 7-8, 35-36, 38-40, 42-43, 45-46, 48-51, 53-54, 56, 58-59, 61, 63, 71, 187-188, 256, 299, 312

explicit knowledge sharing 35, 38-40, 43, 45-46, 48-51, 53-54, 56, 58-59, 61, 63, 71

external data sources 2, 5, 194

externalization 36, 71, 193

Extract, Transformation and Load (ETL) 2, 5, 74, 89, 103, 108, 111-113, 119, 136, 188, 190, 197

Extreme Programming (XP) 15, 19-21, 31, 37, 45, 104, 116, 118, 142, 184, 193, 261, 313-314, 323-324, 328-332, 338, 340-341

F

face-to-face (F2F) 42-43